Rainbow Reiki
Advanced Energy Healing for the Multidimensional Soul

Chelsey Sarah Prusha, B.Msc.
Art by Camille Marie Rauscher

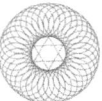

Copyright © 2025 by Chelsey Sarah Prusha
All rights reserved.

Reading this book does not constitute formal training or certification in Rainbow Reiki. The information provided is for educational and personal development purposes only. To become a certified practitioner of Rainbow Reiki, formal training through an authorized instructor is required.

Art by Camille Marie Rauscher

ISBN-13: 979-8-9990769-3-9 (paperback)
ISBN-13: 979-8-9990769-0-8 (hardcover)
ISBN-13: 979-8-9990769-2-2 (eBook)

www.SynergyWellnessCollective.com

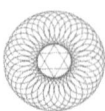

Dedication

To Donna Aldridge —

At a time when I was unraveling and rediscovering who I truly was, you saw me.
Your words, *"I'm proud of you,"* spoken without condition or ego, cracked open a space in my heart that had long been closed. It was the first time someone expressed pride in me that wasn't about them — it was about me.

You saw who I was becoming long before I ever could.
That vision, that unwavering belief, planted the seed for everything that has bloomed since — including Rainbow Reiki.

This work, this journey, this healing — I dedicate it to you.
Thank you for helping me remember my light.

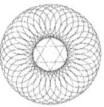

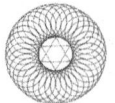

Acknowledgments

With hands pressed to my heart, I offer my deepest gratitude to the mentors, teachers, guides, colleagues, and friends who have lit the path before me: Joy Anderson, Michelle Carbone, Carrie Roberts, Mirantha O'Rouke, Dr. Anemona Peres, Noreen Young, Izabella Vega, Laura Klock, and Erika Bier. Each of you has been a steady star in my sky, illuminating the road when I felt lost. Your wisdom, encouragement, and unwavering belief in me have been the gentle hands that kept me aligned with my soul's purpose.

My heart overflows with gratitude for the hundreds of clients and students who entrusted me with their healing journeys. Each of you opened your heart to me and, in turn, opened mine a little more. To those who have walked beside me from the very beginning — you know who you are — thank you for growing alongside me. Your trust has been a sacred gift, and your courage to heal has inspired my own journey.

To my children Kadalyn, Everleigh, and Brooks, who have been my most sacred teachers and soul guides in this life: thank you for teaching me more about love and truth than any book or doctrine ever could. Kadalyn, my eldest, you braved pain and struggle by my side and embraced every version of "mom" I have been, standing with me even in the fire with a warrior spirit as mighty as a dragon's army. Everleigh, my savage daughter and dark goddess aficionado, you have never hesitated to speak your truth, and in doing so you helped me reclaim my own voice. Brooks, my beloved youngest, the gentle miracle of your birth reopened a heartspace in me I hadn't known was closed, reminding me that love is love is love and love is all there is.

To my angel baby in Heaven, you bridged the space between Earth and the divine — teaching me how to feel what cannot be touched and to love what cannot be held. I didn't know how I would survive another day without you, but your presence became the thread

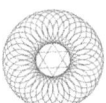

that wove me back into life. Thank you for teaching me that love transcends form, and that no goodbye is ever truly final.

Camille Marie Rauscher, my middle school best friend turned life and business partner, you are a living blessing in my world. Thank you for loving me unwaveringly, even when our path was convoluted and things didn't make sense. When others stepped away, you stepped forward — co-parenting my children as if they were your own, shining your light when all other lights had dimmed. You have been my rock and my safe harbor, a guiding star on the darkest nights. I am endlessly grateful for your steadfast presence, your faith in me, and the unconditional love that has carried me through every storm.

I honor all the past versions of myself that led me here, each a necessary thread in the tapestry of my becoming. I see the innocent little girl, wide-eyed and hopeful; the rebellious, addicted teen, lost yet learning; the young mother finding her way; the military wife standing strong through long separations; the stepmother opening her heart to children of another; the divorced woman rising from heartbreak; the lesbian embracing her truth; and the healer-therapist-mystic-seer-sage who now stands whole. Each self has been a teacher and a guide, carrying me through darkness and into dawn. I hold them all with compassion and deep gratitude.

To my beloved departed — the ones whose blood runs through my veins and whose wisdom whispers on the wind — thank you. Especially to my mother, whose spirit has walked beside me since her physical form faded. You have never truly left me. You speak through dreams, through song, through the stillness. Your presence has been a quiet strength, a soul-deep knowing that I am always loved. To all my ancestors who came before me, thank you for your sacrifices, your prayers, your pain, and your power. I am the living continuation of your stories.

My gratitude extends beyond what the eyes can see. I thank the angels and archangels who shield and guide me, the ancestors

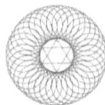

whose whispers and blood-born wisdom light my way, and the ascended masters, elementals, and animal spirits that softly impart ancient truths to my soul. To the luminaries and Galactics who remind me that we are all connected among the stars, and to the sacred Blue Rose Order who has quietly woven its protection and knowledge into my journey — I offer my humble thanks. In the embrace of seen and unseen forces, I have never walked alone.

And to those who doubted me, dismissed me, or placed obstacles in my way, I offer my gratitude as well. To the doctors, therapists, teachers, and anyone who insisted my path was misguided or impossible: thank you. In your skepticism, I found my resolve. Your resistance became the friction that ignited my transformation, the fuel that propelled me to grow and heal beyond anyone's expectations. You taught me how to alchemize and transmute energy — turning fear into strength, pain into power. In the end, even your opposition was a gift, and I am grateful for every spark it provided to light my fire.

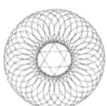

Foreword

When I met Chelsey in 2022, we were both keeping it very professional and formal ... The academic in me was fascinated with the research thesis of the fresh graduate of Metaphysical Studies, and we had some good conversations about the neuroscience underpinnings of the clinical hypnotherapy method we were both practicing at the time. We were part of the same professional community of hypnotherapists—where anything remotely 'woo-woo' was frowned upon, seen as bringing reputational damage to the profession.

Myself a partially undercover mystic at the time, not having fully embraced my spiritual identity as a psychologist and psychotherapist, I was, however, very much attuned to the Magdalene's energies ...

While talking to Chelsey, I was feeling a very distinct and powerful energy that I could not have mistaken. And so, I broke the ice: "Why do I feel such a strong Magdalene energy about you?!" The rest is history, as we both like to joke about ...

Chelsey Sarah Prusha is probably one of the most complete healers I know, with a wealth of knowledge in anatomy and physiology, neuroscience, nutrition, hypnotherapy, and a relentless passion for neurodivergence. She possesses an incredible ability to bridge and bring together two worlds: modern science and esoteric ancient wisdom. Her extensive studies in alternative, holistic, and energy healing modalities—as well as her deep scientific and medical knowledge—are only exceeded by her personal healing journey. A powerful story of self-led transformation that makes her an authentic, credible, and highly effective healer. A *Wounded Healer Journey*, as C.G. Jung would describe it.

Chelsey's personal healing and transformation is a true *Heroine's Journey*—to paraphrase a Joseph Campbell masterpiece. From being a mislabeled, misjudged, misunderstood neurodivergent

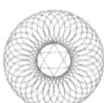

teenager and young woman—forced and squeezed into a procrustean bed of medical, educational, and religious systems that consistently failed (and still fail) to understand multi-gifted and advanced brains like hers—to becoming a teacher, healer, and mentor of those who represent the very systems that pathologized her experience in the first place.

These outdated societal systems brought significant trauma into her life. But paradoxically, they also presented the choiceless opportunity for Chelsey to attempt the impossible—the unthinkable, the counterintuitive, the unprecedented: to heal herself when nothing else worked. Through years of trial and error, she tested protocols on her own body, mind, and soul. Her painful path toward becoming who she is today not only raises critical questions about how neurodivergence is understood and addressed in mainstream psychiatry and education—it also reveals profound gaps in spiritual and energy healing modalities, like traditional Reiki.

Reiki has long been seen as a last resort—where people turn when nothing else works. But as Chelsey's experience shows, many of those old energy systems are no longer calibrated to today's energetic needs. The planetary frequency has risen. The old ways—though sacred in their time—can no longer meet the demands of the *Children of the New Earth*, who are here to midwife a new way of being. These souls are the Future Human—and the old systems simply cannot cater to them. They are here to *bring* the future into being.

Have you noticed how traditional Reiki no longer brings the same results? Or how any temporary relief it offers often fades, returning the client to their original state? I say this as someone initiated in Reiki over 30 years ago. I never resonated with it. It felt obsolete, incomplete—like it belonged to another age. I couldn't articulate why. But when I heard Chelsey speak about it, it clicked deeply: many older modalities are not attuned to the new frequency ranges. They are built to heal the problems of the past. And much

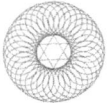

like mainstream medicine and education, they are losing their relevance for the energetically evolved human.

Rainbow Reiki is a different story.

Rainbow Reiki uncovers and revitalizes a wealth of ancient mystical teachings and esoteric practices from the Egyptians, Essenes, Tibetans, Gnostics, and Indigenous Earthkeepers, and integrates the sacred teachings of the Mystery Schools. It draws upon the wisdom handed down through the Atlantean and Lemurian lineages, forming an energetic bridge back through our Pleiadian, Venusian, and even Andromedan origins—tracing all the way to the Source of All That Is. It is a complete circle back to the Advanced Human, not through regression or bypass, but through evolution and deep remembrance.

Chelsey's unique ability to ground this high-frequency healing system in neuroscience, physiology, and somatic integration is rare and profoundly needed. Rainbow Reiki is not just for energy healers. It is a modality that speaks to skeptical physicians, psychologists, trauma therapists, and researchers—offering them a language that unites left-brain logic with right-brain knowing. In this way, she affirms what many of us intuitively understand: science is a language we use to demystify the mystical, as Dr. Joe Dispenza so beautifully says.

As a professional, I have had the privilege to witness Chelsey's evolution—personally and professionally. The alchemy she has performed—transmuting her deepest wounds into medicine for the world—has given birth to one of the most advanced, multidimensional healing systems I have ever encountered.

In my personal capacity, I feel deeply honored to have crossed paths with her. Chelsey Sarah Prusha is a transformational leader, a Creator Soul, and a consciousness teacher who is here to fast-track humanity's ascension process through her presence, her teachings, and her miraculous healing modality.

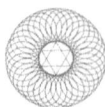

To the readers and students of this sacred book: Fasten your seatbelts.

The path ahead will stretch your consciousness to cosmic horizons and bring you back into your precious body. You will befriend your nervous system, remember your energetic blueprint, and awaken to a deep and enduring self-liberation.

Rainbow Reiki is not just a healing modality. It is a living transmission—a call to wholeness, a blueprint for humanity's evolution, and an invitation to rise.

And as we rise for ourselves, we rise for the collective.

Ascension is an inner job—and Chelsey is the embodiment of that sacred truth.

Now, through Rainbow Reiki, this level of profound transformation is possible—and accessible—to all who have hearts to hear and minds to open.

Dr. Anemona Peres
Psychologist, Therapist, Supervisor

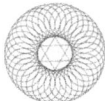

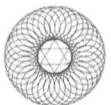

Prologue

It has been a profound honor to serve as editor for *Rainbow Reiki: Advanced Energy Healing for the Multidimensional Soul*, a work that is not only a testament to Chelsey Prusha's brilliance but also a sacred transmission of wisdom that the world so deeply needs.

Chelsey is a passionate and dedicated healer. Watching her grow, evolve, and embody her calling has been a great pleasure of my professional and personal life. One of Chelsey's gifts is her sheer excitement for learning. When something piques her interest, she does not just skim the surface. She dives deep, fully immersing herself until she embodies the subject with mastery. This quality, paired with her innate intuition and her deep sensitivity to energy, has led her to develop remarkable expertise in the areas of metaphysics, energy healing, and neurodiversity.

I have been particularly moved by the ways in which Chelsey's path has illuminated my own. It was through her insight and support that I came to a new understanding of my neurodivergence. Her intuitive way of seeing people, naming truths, and holding space without judgment allowed me to accept all parts of myself. This kind of compassionate clarity is one of Chelsey's many gifts, and it permeates her work.

Rainbow Reiki is not simply another method—it is a multidimensional, heart-led modality born of Chelsey's lived experience, deep study, and divine communion. Her willingness to transmute her own trauma into tools for collective healing is inspirational. She has synthesized vast and esoteric concepts into something tangible, grounded, and useful to everyone.

With care, clarity, and attunement to spirit, she offers a system that honors both ancient energetic wisdom and the unique needs of modern humans. Whether you are brand new to Reiki or a seasoned practitioner, her clear, down-to-earth communication

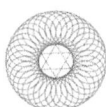

provides both guidance and depth. You will find yourself learning, remembering, and deepening all at once.

Chelsey's years in Western medicine give her practical grounding, while her spiritual gifts and metaphysical studies provide the expansive vision this healing system is built upon. She has crafted something truly integrative, revolutionary, and accessible for those ready to heal at the root.

This book is both a companion and a reference, designed to be read straight through or opened again and again as a reference guide. However you choose to engage with it, trust that the pages will meet you where you are and guide you forward.

May this work open hearts, deepen awareness, and continue to ripple light across the planet.

With profound admiration and love,

Joy S. Anderson, MA, LPC-MH, ACHT
Founder, Joy of Healing & Joy of Ascending
Counselor, Hypnotherapist, Spiritual Counselor & Guide

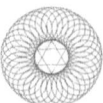

Opening Reflection

As a long-time Healing Touch provider, I approached the Rainbow Reiki training with a grounded understanding of energy work and a deep commitment to client healing. What I did not anticipate, however, was the profound impact this modality—particularly through Chelsey's teaching—would have on my personal and professional evolution.

Chelsey's curriculum offered something I had been unconsciously seeking: a visual, structured framework that I previously couldn't fully articulate. Her guidance provided clarity and confirmation for many of the intuitive insights and energetic phenomena I had encountered in my own sessions. The training didn't replace what I knew—it elevated and expanded it.

Through Chelsey's skillful instruction and the intentional design of her Rainbow Reiki curriculum, I experienced energetic work in a new dimension. The meditative practices allowed me to feel the work on a deeper level within myself, which in turn has strengthened my ability to hold space and facilitate transformation for others. It has refined my awareness, enhanced my energetic precision, and expanded the depth of healing I offer in my practice.

Working directly with Chelsey—both through her teachings and the Rainbow Reiki community—has been an invaluable part of this journey. Her integrity, insight, and devotion to this work are evident in every aspect of the training. I encourage anyone who feels called to explore further.

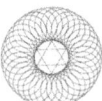

For those considering this path: Rainbow Reiki is more than a modality—it is a transformational lens. Whether you are an experienced practitioner or just beginning your journey in energy healing, this work will meet you with resonance and depth. It is both mystical and practical, intuitive and structured. It is a gift.

With deep respect,

Laura Klock
Founder of Elevate | Rainbow Reiki Practitioner | Healing Touch Provider

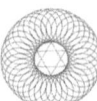

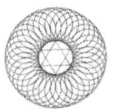

Table of Contents

Dedication iii
Acknowledgments v
Foreword viii
Prologue xiii
Opening Reflection xv
Rainbow Reiki 1
Spiritual Gifts 3
Grounding 85
Chakras 114
Aura 134
Rainbow Reiki History 203
Basic Anatomy 225
Rainbow Reiki Chakra Symbols 329
Elementals 551
Sacred Spiritual Space 566
Self-Care 576
Spiritual Support Teams 579
Best Practices, Ethics, and Professional Guidelines for Advanced Rainbow Reiki Practitioners 587
The Return to Rainbow Light 592

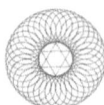

Rainbow Reiki

Rainbow Reiki is a unique and advanced healing modality created as a combination of Usui/Tibetan Reiki levels 1 through 20, Egyptian Reiki, Magdalene Reiki, and Shadow Reiki. It stands apart from traditional Reiki by integrating these diverse practices to align with the evolving consciousness of humanity. While traditional Reiki focuses on channeling universal life force energy for healing and balance, Rainbow Reiki offers a more multidimensional and amplified approach.

The process, amplified energy, and methods to effectively blend the various Reiki modalities and energy healing techniques were channeled to Chelsey in May of 2024 from the Galactic Order of Divinity and the Counsel of Nine, a collective of ascended masters, galactic beings, and planet keepers who serve as overseers of the Galactic Federation. This profound connection brought forth insights and practices designed to meet the energetic and spiritual needs of humanity as they continue to evolve.

Egyptian Reiki and Magdalene Energy Initiations bring ancient wisdom and feminine energies of unconditional love, empowerment, and deep transformation, connecting practitioners to powerful archetypes and frequencies. Shadow Reiki addresses hidden or suppressed aspects of the self, supporting profound emotional healing and the integration of the shadow, leading to greater wholeness.

Rainbow Reiki also emphasizes the activation of enhanced chakras and DNA crystalline structures, allowing individuals to align with the planet's ascension process and their own soul's evolution. Additionally, it incorporates the multidimensional frequencies of Pleiadian and Arcturian Reiki, tapping into galactic energies that

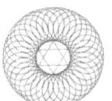

support awakening, higher consciousness, and expanded healing capabilities.

The energy flow within Rainbow Reiki is amplified far beyond traditional Reiki, providing the heightened energetic inputs necessary for this stage of human evolution. This comprehensive system blends traditional Reiki practices with multidimensional tools and teachings, empowering practitioners and recipients to achieve profound transformation, balance, and spiritual growth.

Spiritual Gifts

Spiritual gifts and the *Clairs* represent intuitive or metaphysical abilities that allow people to perceive and connect with energy, consciousness, or spiritual dimensions beyond the physical senses. Each gift or Clair has unique characteristics but often overlaps with others, forming an interconnected web of intuitive abilities.

Spiritual gifts and the "clairs"—clairvoyance (clear seeing), clairaudience (clear hearing), clairsentience (clear feeling), claircognizance (clear knowing), clairalience (clear smelling), and clairgustance (clear tasting)—represent intuitive abilities believed to bridge the physical and spiritual worlds. These gifts are not new; they have been recognized and revered throughout human history, though interpretations have varied across cultures and eras. Ancient civilizations such as the Egyptians, Greeks, and Hindus recorded practices and philosophies that align with these gifts, associating them with divine communication, prophecy, and heightened states of consciousness. In Hinduism, for instance, the chakras—energetic centers within the body—are believed to be channels for these abilities, with the third eye chakra specifically linked to clairvoyance.

The term "clairvoyance" first gained prominence in the 17th century, derived from the French words "clair" (clear) and "voyance" (vision), used to describe the ability to perceive things beyond ordinary sight. The broader concept of the "clairs" became more structured in the 19th and 20th centuries, particularly through the rise of Spiritualism, a movement that emphasized communication with the spirit world. Pioneers of Spiritualism, such as Emanuel Swedenborg and Franz Mesmer, explored altered states of consciousness and psychic phenomena, laying the groundwork for modern understandings of spiritual gifts. Later, figures like Helena Blavatsky, founder of Theosophy, and Edgar Cayce, the "Sleeping Prophet," expanded

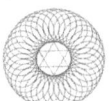

public awareness of these abilities through their teachings and practices.

Education and training in spiritual gifts have evolved, from ancient mystery schools to contemporary metaphysical practices. Ancient shamans and priests often served as intermediaries between the spiritual and physical realms, honing their abilities through ritual and apprenticeship. Today, spiritual gifts are often explored through meditation, energy work, and intuitive development programs. Tools like tarot cards, pendulums, and crystals are frequently used to enhance the clairs, while mindfulness practices help individuals tune into their inner awareness.

The scientific community remains divided on the nature of these gifts, with skeptics attributing them to psychological phenomena or chance. However, studies in parapsychology and quantum physics suggest that human consciousness might extend beyond known physical limitations, offering intriguing possibilities for understanding the clairs. Regardless of interpretation, the enduring presence of spiritual gifts in human history highlights a universal desire to connect with realms beyond the visible, seeking meaning and guidance in the mysteries of existence.

In the Westernized world, spiritual gifts and the "clairs" have taken on a diverse identity, blending traditional mystical practices with modern interpretations of intuition and personal empowerment. These gifts often manifest as heightened perceptions or "gut feelings" that individuals use for guidance, healing, or understanding life's deeper mysteries. Practices like meditation, energy healing (e.g., Reiki), and the use of tools such as tarot, pendulums, and crystals are common among those who embrace these gifts. Western culture tends to categorize the clairs—clairvoyance (clear seeing), clairaudience (clear hearing), clairsentience (clear feeling), and more—as psychic abilities or intuitive skills that anyone can develop through intentional practice. This approach often aligns these abilities with self-help and personal growth movements, reflecting a broader societal shift toward individuality and spiritual exploration outside of traditional religious frameworks.

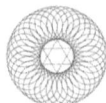

In Christianity, spiritual gifts have a long-standing theological foundation rooted in biblical scripture, particularly in passages like 1 Corinthians 12, where Paul describes the "gifts of the Spirit." These gifts include prophecy, discernment, healing, and speaking in tongues, which parallel some of the clairs in their function. For instance, prophecy can be likened to claircognizance (clear knowing), while discernment shares similarities with clairsentience (clear feeling). However, Christianity tends to frame these abilities as divinely granted and used to serve God's will rather than as personal abilities to be cultivated independently. In more charismatic and Pentecostal denominations, spiritual gifts are celebrated as signs of the Holy Spirit's presence, often demonstrated through experiences like prophetic visions, words of knowledge, or miraculous healings.

Despite these parallels, there is tension between mainstream Christianity and practices associated with the clairs in broader spiritual or metaphysical contexts. Many Christian teachings caution against psychic phenomena or divination, labeling them as occult or unaligned with God's teachings. Still, a growing number of Christians embrace a more integrative approach, viewing spiritual gifts and intuitive abilities as interconnected, universal expressions of divine connection. This blending of traditions reflects a broader Western trend of exploring spirituality in ways that transcend rigid dogma, allowing for a richer and more inclusive understanding of intuitive gifts in both religious and secular contexts.

Christianity, a religion centered on the teachings of Jesus Christ, is often perceived as rooted solely in Jewish tradition. However, a deeper exploration of Jesus' life and education suggests that His wisdom extended beyond Judaic teachings, incorporating elements of Egyptian mysticism and Buddhist philosophy. Historical and esoteric studies propose that Jesus may have traveled and studied in Egypt, where the mysteries of the ancient world, including spiritual alchemy, sacred geometry, and advanced healing practices, were preserved. Additionally, parallels between Jesus' teachings and Buddhist principles, such as compassion, meditation, and the pursuit

of enlightenment, indicate an understanding of universal spiritual truths that transcended cultural boundaries. These influences likely informed His profound ability to perform miracles, heal the sick, and exhibit advanced spiritual gifts like clairvoyance, clairaudience, and energy healing.

Many practices that modern Christianity labels as "occult" or forbidden, such as divination, meditation, and energy work, were integral to Jesus' teachings and methods. For example, Jesus' ability to heal through touch and intention aligns with principles found in energy healing modalities. His instructions to His disciples to "Heal the sick, raise the dead, cleanse those who have leprosy, and drive out demons ..." (Matthew 10:8, *New International Version*) demonstrate an encouragement to develop advanced spiritual abilities. These teachings align more closely with esoteric practices than with strict religious orthodoxy. The rejection of these methods by institutional Christianity may stem from a desire to maintain control and a misunderstanding of their origins and purposes, rather than their alignment with Jesus' life and mission.

Understanding Jesus' broader educational influences allows for a more nuanced perspective on Christianity and its teachings. It reveals that many practices deemed "occult" by the Church are, in fact, rooted in the very traditions and knowledge that enabled Jesus to perform miracles and teach His disciples profound spiritual truths. This awareness invites a deeper integration of ancient wisdom into modern Christian practice, honoring the universal spirituality that Jesus embodied.

Egyptian Teachings on Spiritual Gifts
Spiritual gifts, often described as divine abilities or powers granted to individuals to fulfill their higher purpose, are a concept that can be found in both biblical teachings and ancient Egyptian spiritual practices. While the Bible speaks of spiritual gifts as gifts from God through the Holy Spirit (e.g., prophecy, healing, wisdom), ancient Egyptian teachings offer a parallel framework where spiritual abilities were seen as divine endowments connected to the energy and consciousness of the gods, the cosmos, and the self. In ancient

Egypt, spiritual gifts were believed to be cultivated through the connection to divine principles embodied by the Neteru (deities), alignment with Ma'at (truth, balance, and order), and the awakening of the "Ba" (spiritual essence) and "Ka" (life force energy). These teachings emphasized that humans were co-creators with the divine, and unlocking spiritual gifts required self-mastery, ritual, and alignment with cosmic energies.

For instance, the gift of healing, akin to modern energy healing or the biblical "gift of healing" (1 Corinthians 12:9), was a sacred art in ancient Egypt practiced by priests and priestesses who invoked the divine energies of deities like Sekhmet, the goddess of healing and transformation, or Thoth, the god of wisdom and knowledge. These healers used prayers, sound vibrations, and sacred symbols (such as the ankh) to channel divine energy into the physical and spiritual bodies of individuals. Similarly, prophecy, as described in the Bible, was mirrored in ancient Egyptian practices through the oracular traditions of temples where priests, often in trance-like states, would receive visions and messages from the gods to guide their communities.

The ancient Egyptians also understood spiritual gifts as part of the human journey toward enlightenment and unity with the divine. They believed that through initiation into the mysteries of life, death, and rebirth, symbolized by the myth of Osiris and Isis, individuals could awaken latent abilities such as clairvoyance, telepathy, or heightened intuition. These abilities were cultivated through meditative practices, purification rituals, and the awakening of energy centers, similar to the concept of chakras, which they visualized as linked to the spine and associated with the serpent energy of the "Uraeus."

Both the Bible and ancient Egyptian teachings highlight that spiritual gifts are not self-serving but are intended for service to others and alignment with divine will. In ancient Egypt, spiritual gifts were seen as tools to maintain harmony (Ma'at) within oneself and the community, just as the Bible teaches that gifts are given "for the common good" (1 Corinthians 12:7). These parallels reveal that

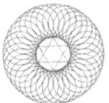

spiritual gifts, whether understood through a biblical lens or ancient Egyptian teachings, are deeply rooted in the idea of aligning human potential with divine purpose and cosmic order.

Tibetan Teaching on Spiritual Gifts
The Usui Tibetan teachings, rooted in Reiki practices, and ancient wisdom traditions provide a profound perspective on the cultivation and use of spiritual gifts. These teachings emphasize that spiritual gifts are innate abilities, dormant within every individual, waiting to be awakened through self-discipline, energy work, and alignment with universal life force energy. In both Usui Tibetan Reiki and ancient wisdom traditions, spiritual gifts are viewed as divine blessings meant for healing, transformation, and the greater good.

In the Usui Tibetan lineage of Reiki, spiritual gifts are awakened through the practice of attunements, meditations, and energy channeling. The core principle is that every individual is a vessel of universal life force energy (ki or chi), which flows through the chakras and subtle energy systems. Reiki practitioners are taught that spiritual gifts such as healing, intuition, and spiritual sensitivity are unlocked when energy channels are cleared and aligned. This process is initiated through attunements, sacred rituals performed by a Reiki Master to open the student's connection to universal energy. Spiritual gifts in this tradition include the ability to intuitively sense energy imbalances in others, channel healing energy, and connect with higher dimensions of consciousness. The Tibetan component of this lineage, with its use of powerful symbols like the Tibetan Master Symbol (Dai Ko Myo), reinforces the idea that spiritual gifts can be enhanced through the use of sacred geometry and sound vibrations.

Ancient wisdom traditions, including those of Tibetan Buddhism and other mystical systems, similarly view spiritual gifts as a natural result of spiritual awakening and alignment with universal truth. In Tibetan teachings, spiritual gifts, or siddhis, are considered extraordinary abilities that arise from deep meditation, mindfulness, and self-realization. Siddhis, such as clairvoyance, telepathy, and the ability to heal, are described in texts like the Buddhist Yoga Sutras

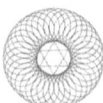

and are seen as by-products of enlightenment rather than ends in themselves. Tibetan monks often engage in extensive meditative practices, mantra recitation, and energy work to awaken these abilities. These gifts are rooted in compassion and service, and practitioners are taught to use them for the benefit of others rather than personal gain.

Both Usui Tibetan Reiki and ancient wisdom teachings emphasize the importance of humility, purity of intent, and alignment with universal energies in the development of spiritual gifts. They teach that these gifts are tools for service, helping others release suffering, balance energy, and achieve spiritual growth. Spiritual gifts are not seen as something external or granted to a select few, but as inherent potentials within all beings. The key to unlocking these gifts lies in a commitment to personal healing, spiritual discipline, and the cultivation of unconditional love and compassion. This perspective reminds us that spiritual gifts are both a responsibility and a blessing, meant to align individuals with their divine purpose and contribute to the collective harmony of humanity.

Galactic Teaching on Spiritual Gifts
The Arcturian and Pleiadian teachings on spiritual gifts emphasize the innate potential within all beings to access higher-dimensional abilities that serve both personal evolution and the collective good. According to Arcturian wisdom, spiritual gifts are encoded in the soul's energy field and activated through the process of raising one's vibrational frequency. They teach that these gifts, such as telepathy, healing, and interdimensional awareness, are awakened by aligning with universal life force energy and integrating light codes into the body. The Arcturians emphasize mastery of energy systems, including the chakras and auric fields, as well as the use of sacred geometry like the Merkaba to stabilize and enhance spiritual abilities. Their teachings often highlight the importance of grounding these higher frequencies through connection to Earth's crystalline grid, ensuring that spiritual gifts remain balanced and practical tools for healing and service.

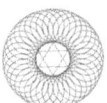

The Pleiadians, on the other hand, approach spiritual gifts from a heart-centered perspective, emphasizing the power of love and emotional healing in activating these abilities. They teach that the heart chakra is the gateway to higher consciousness, and through cultivating unconditional love and joy, individuals can awaken gifts such as heightened intuition, empathy, and energetic sensitivity. The Pleiadians also stress the importance of reconnecting with nature as a grounding practice to support the flow of spiritual energy. They believe that spending time outdoors, honoring Gaia's nurturing energy, and engaging in creative expression, such as art, music, and dance, enhance spiritual gifts by fostering alignment with one's true essence. For the Pleiadians, joy and play are essential components of spiritual growth, as they help individuals integrate higher vibrational frequencies with ease.

Both Arcturian and Pleiadian teachings share the belief that spiritual gifts are divine tools meant for unity and service. They stress that these abilities are not for self-glorification but for contributing to the greater good, uplifting others, and supporting Earth's ascension process. They teach that spiritual gifts unfold gradually, in alignment with one's spiritual readiness, and emphasize the importance of grounding and balance to avoid feelings of overwhelm. By raising one's vibrational frequency and remaining rooted in love and connection to Earth, individuals can refine and expand their spiritual abilities. Together, the Arcturian and Pleiadian teachings provide a multidimensional framework for understanding and developing spiritual gifts as pathways to higher consciousness and tools for creating harmony in the world.

Biblical Scripture Backing Spiritual Gifts
- There are different kinds of gifts, but the same Spirit distributes them. There are different kinds of service, but the same Lord. There are different kinds of working, but in all of them and in everyone it is the same God at work. Now to each one the manifestation of the Spirit is given for the common good. To one there is given through the Spirit a message of wisdom, to another a message of knowledge by means of the same Spirit, to another faith by the same Spirit,

to another gifts of healing by that one Spirit, to another miraculous powers, to another prophecy, to another distinguishing between spirits, to another speaking in different kinds of tongues, and to still another the interpretation of tongues. All these are the work of one and the same Spirit, and he distributes them to each one, just as he determines. (1 Corinthians 12:4-11)
- We have different gifts, according to the grace given to each of us. If your gift is prophesying, then prophesy in accordance with your faith; if it is serving, then serve; if it is teaching, then teach; if it is to encourage, then give encouragement; if it is giving, then give generously; if it is to lead, do it diligently; if it is to show mercy, do it cheerfully. (Romans 12:6-8)
- So Christ himself gave the apostles, the prophets, the evangelists, the pastors and teachers, to equip his people for works of service, so that the body of Christ may be built up until we all reach unity in the faith and in the knowledge of the Son of God and become mature, attaining to the whole measure of the fullness of Christ. (Ephesians 4:11-13)
- Each of you should use whatever gift you have received to serve others, as faithful stewards of God's grace in its various forms. If anyone speaks, they should do so as one who speaks the very words of God. If anyone serves, they should do so with the strength God provides, so that in all things God may be praised through Jesus Christ. To him be the glory and the power for ever and ever. Amen. (1 Peter 4:10-11)
- For this reason I remind you to fan into flame the gift of God, which is in you through the laying on of my hands. For the Spirit God gave us does not make us timid, but gives us power, love, and self-discipline. (2 Timothy 1:6-7)
- "Follow the way of love and eagerly desire gifts of the Spirit, especially prophecy" (1 Corinthians 14:1)

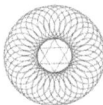

Advanced Grounding and Spiritual Gift Reclamation Meditation
Begin by finding a quiet and comfortable space where you can be undisturbed for the next 30+ minutes. Sit or lie down with your spine straight and your body relaxed. Close your eyes and take a deep breath in through your nose, holding it for a moment before releasing it through your mouth. Repeat this three times, feeling your body relax deeper with each exhale. Allow yourself to become fully present in this moment.

Imagine roots extending from the base of your spine and the soles of your feet deep into the Earth, anchoring you securely. Feel the Earth's nurturing energy rise up through these roots, filling your body with a sense of stability, grounding, and safety.

Connecting with Spirit Guide and Higher Self
Now, in your mind's eye, invite your spirit guide to join you. This guide may be someone you are familiar with, or they may appear for the first time. Trust whoever comes forward. Feel their calming and supportive presence. Next, call upon your higher self, the divine aspect of you that holds infinite wisdom and unconditional love. Together, your spirit guide and higher self will escort you on this journey.

Regression to the Time of Disconnection
With their guidance, allow yourself to gently regress to a time in your life when a part of your inner child or soul felt the need to shut down their spiritual gifts. This may be a moment in your current life, a past life, or an ancestral memory. Let your spirit guide lead you to this specific moment.

As the scene unfolds, notice everything around you—the timeframe, the environment, the clothing you or others are wearing, and the consciousness level of the space you are in. Tune into the thoughts, feelings, emotions, and beliefs that were present at this time.

What was happening in the situation? What was the child or soul part intuitively aware of regarding the people, the environment, and the energy surrounding them? What belief was formed about their

spiritual gifts and their ability to ground fully into the human experience?

Understanding the Needs of the Inner Child or Soul Part
Ask this child or soul part what they needed to hear from those around them but did not. What words or reassurances would have comforted and supported them in that moment? Now, ask what this part of you needed to say to others that they could not express at the time. Listen to their response without judgment. Allow them to share freely and fully.

Healing and Reintegrating the Soul Part
Now, envision a beautiful rainbow ray of light extending from your heart. This ray reaches out to this part of you that has been disconnected, wrapping them in love, compassion, and safety. As you hold this rainbow ray, remind this aspect of yourself that they are safe now. Assure them that the situation from the past is over and cannot be repeated. It is done.

Guide this part of yourself to step onto the rainbow bridge created by this ray of light. Watch as they walk along the bridge, moving toward your heart. As they merge with your heart center, feel their wisdom, knowledge, and spiritual gifts reintegrating with your present self. Breathe deeply and allow this healing energy to flow through every cell of your being.

Projecting Forward into Full Integration
With your spirit guide and higher self still present, now project yourself forward in time to a moment when your spiritual gifts are fully reintegrated into your life experience. Observe everything about this future moment—where you are, who you are with, and what you are doing. What do you see, feel, hear, and know in this reality? Notice the sense of empowerment, alignment, and joy that comes with living fully grounded in your spiritual gifts.

Anchor this awareness and these felt sensations into your cellular memory. With each breath, let this new reality solidify within you.

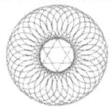

When you feel ready, bring your awareness back to the present moment, holding onto the wisdom and integration you have achieved. Thank your spirit guide and higher self for their support and guidance on this journey.

Take three deep breaths to anchor the experience fully into your body. On your final exhale, say aloud or in your mind: *"By the power of three, a holy trinity: it is done, it is done, it is done. I let it be so, and so it is."*

When you feel ready, gently open your eyes and take a moment to reorient yourself, carrying this sense of wholeness and integration with you into your life.

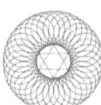

Clairvoyance (Clear Seeing)
Clairvoyance, or "clear seeing," is the ability to perceive intuitive or spiritual information through visual images, symbols, or visions. This information is typically received as mental images or symbolic visions in the mind's eye, often associated with the third eye chakra. It may occur spontaneously, during meditation, or through dreams.

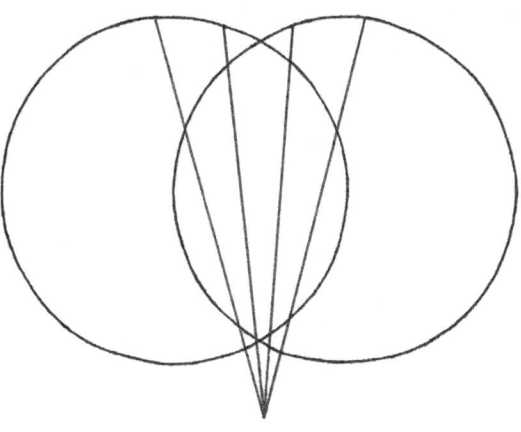
Rainbow Reiki Clairvoyance Symbol

This gift can manifest in various ways, such as seeing colors, shapes, or auras around people or objects; visualizing detailed events, people, or places without prior knowledge; or experiencing vivid dreams or flashes of insight that feel symbolic or prophetic. These experiences are often subtle, resembling a "movie" playing in the mind, but can become more pronounced with visualization practices.

Clairvoyance frequently works in harmony with other intuitive abilities, such as claircognizance (to intuitively "know" the meaning behind the vision) and clairaudience (to "hear" additional context or messages), creating a richer, multidimensional understanding of the information received.

Clairvoyance Across Traditions
Clairvoyance, or the ability to see beyond the physical realm, has been a sacred skill revered in Egyptian, Tibetan, and galactic teachings. In ancient Egypt, clairvoyance was closely tied to the wisdom of the gods and the activation of the "Eye of Horus," symbolizing heightened perception and divine insight. Egyptian

initiates, particularly in the Mystery Schools, underwent rigorous spiritual training to unlock their clairvoyant abilities, often meditating within the resonant chambers of pyramids or utilizing sacred symbols and oils to awaken the third eye. These teachings emphasized that clairvoyance was not merely a gift but a responsibility to serve as a channel for Ma'at—the principle of truth, harmony, and cosmic order.

In Tibetan traditions, clairvoyance is seen as one of the *siddhis* (spiritual powers) attained through deep meditation, yogic practices, and unwavering dedication to the path of enlightenment. Tibetan monks and practitioners often focused on achieving clarity of vision through the cultivation of *samadhi* (profound concentration) and the use of sacred mantras, mandalas, and visualization techniques. The Tibetan perspective views clairvoyance as a tool for perceiving karma, understanding past lives, and guiding others on the path to liberation. These teachings underline the importance of purity of intent and the alignment of one's vision with compassion and universal truth.

Galactic teachings, shared through channeling and multidimensional awareness, often describe clairvoyance as an inherent ability tied to humanity's higher DNA potential and energetic alignment. Galactic beings, such as the Pleiadians and Arcturians, teach that clairvoyance stems from activating the pineal gland and raising one's vibrational frequency to access higher-dimensional realities. Through practices like light code activations, sacred geometry, and energetic recalibrations, these teachings aim to help individuals expand their consciousness and tap into the universal field of information. In these traditions, clairvoyance is seen as a bridge connecting individuals with their galactic heritage and empowering them to co-create with the universe.

Across these diverse traditions, clairvoyance is revered as a divine gift and a powerful tool for spiritual evolution, emphasizing discipline, integrity, and the pursuit of higher wisdom.

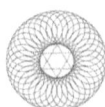

Biblical References

While the Bible does not directly use the term "clairvoyance," there are scriptures that refer to spiritual gifts such as prophecy, visions, dreams, and discerning spirits, which could align with the concept of clairvoyance as a divinely inspired ability to see beyond the physical realm. Here are some scriptures that may support this idea:

- "In the last days, God says, I will pour out my Spirit on all people. Your sons and daughters will prophesy, your young men will see visions, your old men will dream dreams" (Acts 2:17) This passage speaks about the gift of visions and dreams, which align with a divinely inspired ability to see beyond the physical.
- "To another miraculous powers, to another prophecy, to another distinguishing between spirits, to another speaking in different kinds of tongues, and to still another the interpretation of tongues" (1 Corinthians 12:10) This verse highlights spiritual gifts, including prophecy and the discernment of spirits, which may include supernatural insight akin to clairvoyance.
- "During the night the mystery was revealed to Daniel in a vision. Then Daniel praised the God of heaven" (Daniel 2:19) Daniel often received divine visions and interpretations of dreams, showing a clear example of spiritual insight.
- "And Elisha prayed, 'Open his eyes, LORD, so that he may see.' Then the LORD opened the servant's eyes, and he looked and saw the hills full of horses and chariots of fire all around Elisha" (2 Kings 6:17) Elisha's prayer enabled his servant to see into the spiritual realm, which closely resembles the concept of clairvoyance as the ability to perceive beyond the physical world.
- "In my thirtieth year, in the fourth month on the fifth day, while I was among the exiles by the Kebar River, the heavens were opened and I saw visions of God" (Ezekiel 1:1) Ezekiel describes a vision where he is granted insight into the divine, another example of spiritual sight.
- "Then Joseph said to Pharaoh, 'The dreams of Pharaoh are one and the same. God has revealed to Pharaoh what he is about to do'" (Genesis 41:25) Joseph's ability to interpret

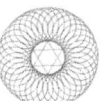

dreams is an example of God-given insight into future events.
- "On the Lord's Day I was in the Spirit, and I heard behind me a loud voice like a trumpet, which said: 'Write on a scroll what you see and send it to the seven churches ...'" (Revelation 1:10-11) John's visions in the Book of Revelation involve spiritual sight, as he is shown heavenly and prophetic images.
- "He said, 'Listen to my words: 'When there is a prophet among you, I, the LORD, reveal myself to them in visions, I speak to them in dreams'" (Numbers 12:6) This verse emphasizes that God uses visions and dreams to communicate with His prophets.
- "Surely the Sovereign LORD does nothing without revealing his plan to his servants the prophets" (Amos 3:7) This passage suggests that God reveals His plans through spiritual insight given to His prophets.

These scriptures demonstrate that spiritual sight, dreams, visions, and prophetic abilities are recognized and celebrated as gifts from God throughout the Bible. However, these abilities are consistently attributed to divine inspiration and used for God's purposes, distinguishing them from secular or non-spiritual interpretations of clairvoyance.

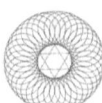

Clairaudience (Clear Hearing)

Clairaudience, or "clear hearing," is the ability to perceive messages, sounds, or voices from the spiritual realm or higher consciousness. This gift can manifest as internal messages that feel like thoughts or external sounds that resemble actual voices, tones, or music. Often, clairaudience is linked to guidance from spiritual beings, ancestors, or one's higher self.

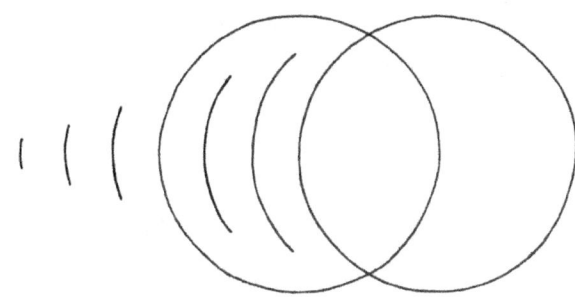

Rainbow Reiki Clairaudience Symbol

This ability may show up as hearing a distinct voice offering guidance or insight, perceiving high-frequency sounds or tones that others cannot hear, or experiencing an internal dialogue that feels separate from one's own thoughts. The messages received are typically clear and concise, leaving a strong sense of certainty and emotional resonance. External sounds might appear faint or distant yet evoke a profound connection.

Clairaudience often works in harmony with other intuitive abilities, such as clairvoyance (to visually "see" what is being described) and claircognizance (to intuitively "know" the truth of the message), creating a multidimensional understanding of the information received.

Clairaudience Across Traditions

Clairaudience, the ability to hear beyond the physical plane, holds a sacred role in Egyptian, Tibetan, and galactic teachings as a pathway to divine communication and spiritual understanding. In ancient Egypt, clairaudience was linked to the resonance of divine sound and the sacred power of spoken words. The ancient Egyptians believed that sound was a creative force, capable of shaping reality, as reflected in their use of sacred chants and invocations. Priests and initiates were trained to attune their inner hearing to the frequency of the gods, often within the acoustic precision of temple chambers or while engaging with hieroglyphs encoded with vibrational knowledge. Clairaudience was considered a connection to the voices of deities, ancestors, and the harmonic principles of Ma'at, the cosmic order.

Tibetan teachings regard clairaudience as one of the siddhis (spiritual powers) attained through advanced meditation and yogic mastery. Tibetan monks often used specific mantras, bells, and gongs to create soundscapes that guided them into deeper states of consciousness, where they could access messages from higher realms. Clairaudience was seen as an extension of the practitioner's ability to cultivate inner stillness and presence, allowing them to hear the wisdom of enlightened beings, the whispers of karma, and guidance from compassionate bodhisattvas. Tibetan traditions emphasize that the development of clairaudience requires a pure mind and heart, ensuring that the messages received are in alignment with universal truth and compassion.

Galactic teachings describe clairaudience as a multidimensional sense, connected to the vibrational fields of higher frequencies and the activation of humanity's dormant energetic potential. Galactic beings, such as the Arcturians and Pleiadians, teach that clairaudience is amplified when one attunes to the harmonics of the universe and clears their energetic channels, particularly through practices like sound healing, light language activations, and pineal gland recalibration. According to these teachings, clairaudience allows individuals to hear transmissions from galactic guides, spirit teams, and even the song of the cosmos itself, fostering a deep sense of connection to universal consciousness. Galactic perspectives often remind practitioners that the quality of their vibrational state determines the clarity and purity of the messages received.

In all three traditions, clairaudience is seen as both a gift and a skill to be cultivated with respect, integrity, and alignment to higher wisdom. It serves as a bridge between realms, a tool for spiritual

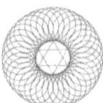

guidance, and a means to access the divine symphony that underlies all existence.

Biblical References

The Bible does not explicitly use the term "clairaudience," which is commonly understood as the ability to hear messages from the spiritual realm. However, there are several scriptures that describe individuals hearing the voice of God, angels, or other divine messages. These instances align closely with the concept of clairaudience as the spiritual gift of receiving auditory messages from the divine:

- The following passage describes young Samuel audibly hearing God calling him:

    Then the LORD called Samuel. Samuel answered, "Here I am." And he ran to Eli and said, "Here I am; you called me." But Eli said, "I did not call; go back and lie down." So he went and lay down. Again the LORD called, "Samuel!" And Samuel got up and went to Eli and said, "Here I am; you called me." "My son," Eli said, "I did not call; go back and lie down." "Now Samuel did not yet know the LORD: The word of the LORD had not yet been revealed to him. A third time the LORD called, "Samuel!" And Samuel got up and went to Eli and said, "Here I am; you called me." Then Eli realized that the Lord was calling the boy. So Eli told Samuel, "Go and lie down, and if he calls you, say, 'Speak, LORD, for your servant is listening.'" So Samuel went and lay down in his pace. The LORD came and stood there, calling as at the other times, "Samuel! Samuel!" Then Samuel said, "Speak, for your servant is listening" (1 Samuel 3:4-10)

- "My sheep listen to my voice; I know them, and they follow me" (John 10:27) This verse highlights the ability of believers to hear and recognize the voice of Jesus spiritually.
- "When the LORD saw that he had gone over to look, God called to him from within the bush, 'Moses! Moses!' And Moses said, 'Here I am'" (Exodus 3:4) Moses audibly heard the voice of God calling to him from the burning bush.

- "While he was still speaking, a bright cloud covered them, and a voice from the cloud said, 'This is my Son, whom I love; with him I am well pleased. Listen to him!'" (Matthew 17:5) This passage describes God's voice being audibly heard during the Transfiguration of Jesus.
- "He fell to the ground and heard a voice say to him, 'Saul, Saul, why do you persecute me?' 'Who are you, Lord?' Saul asked. 'I am Jesus, whom you are persecuting,' he replied" (Acts 9:4-5) Saul (later Paul) audibly hears the voice of Jesus during his transformative encounter on the road to Damascus.
- "Then the LORD spoke to you out of the fire. You heard the sound of words but saw no form; there was only a voice" (Deuteronomy 4:12) This emphasizes God's ability to communicate audibly without physical manifestation.
- "Whether you turn to the right or to the left, your ears will hear a voice behind you, saying, 'This is the way; walk in it'" (Isaiah 30:21) This scripture supports the idea of divine auditory guidance, which resonates with the concept of clairaudience.
- "On the Lord's Day I was in the Spirit, and I heard behind me a loud voice like a trumpet, which said: 'Write on a scroll what you see and send it to the seven churches …'" (Revelation 1:10-11) John receives auditory messages from the Spirit that guide his writings in the Book of Revelation.
- In the following passage, Elijah experiences God speaking to him in a "gentle whisper," illustrating divine communication through sound:

    > After the earthquake came a fire, but the LORD was not in the fire. And after the fire came a gentle whisper. When Elijah heard it, he pulled his cloak over his face and went out and stood at the mouth of the cave. Then a voice said to him, "What are you doing here, Elijah?" (1 Kings 19:12-13)

- "The voice of the LORD is powerful; the voice of the LORD is majestic" (Psalm 29:4) This verse celebrates the power and majesty of God's voice, often heard by prophets and believers.

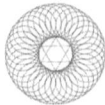

These scriptures demonstrate that hearing divine messages or communication is a spiritual experience described in the Bible. Such experiences, always attributed to God or His messengers, align with the idea of "clairaudience" as a spiritual gift used for divine purposes.

Clairsentience (Clear Feeling)

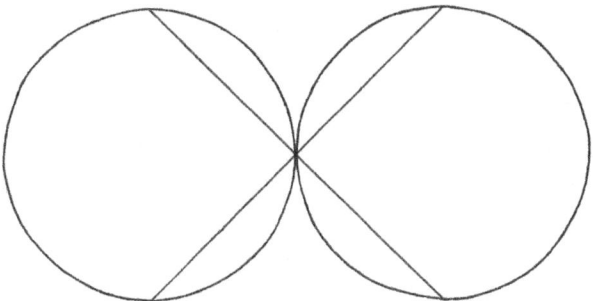

Rainbow Reiki Clairsentience Symbol

Clairsentience, or "clear feeling," is the ability to intuitively sense emotions, energies, or physical sensations. This gift allows individuals to feel these impressions as if they are their own, fostering an empathic connection to people, animals, or spaces. It often manifests as sudden emotions that do not belong to the individual, physical sensations like headaches or tingling that correspond to someone else's energy, or a strong "gut feeling" about situations or decisions.

For untrained empaths, clairsentience can sometimes feel overwhelming due to the intensity of the emotions and sensations experienced. However, it also creates a profound sense of connection and understanding of others, offering insights that go beyond verbal communication. Clairsentience often complements claircognizance by providing emotional or physical validation for intuitive knowledge, enhancing the accuracy and depth of intuitive perceptions.

Clairsentience Across Traditions

Clairsentience, or the ability to sense beyond the physical realm, is a revered spiritual skill in Egyptian, Tibetan, and galactic teachings, offering profound insight into the energy and emotions of people, places, and situations. In ancient Egypt, clairsentience was considered an intrinsic part of the soul's intuitive wisdom, often linked to the *ka* (spiritual essence) and the heart as a center of knowing. Egyptians believed that the heart was the seat of truth and intuition, and clairsentience was developed through rituals, sacred oils, and ceremonial practices to heighten sensitivity to energetic vibrations. Priests and initiates in the Mystery Schools honed this ability to read the subtle energies within temples, the natural world, and even the afterlife, using it as a guide for decision-making and spiritual alignment.

In Tibetan teachings, clairsentience is cultivated as a natural extension of mindfulness and heightened awareness. Tibetan monks emphasize the importance of tuning into the *prana* (life force) flowing through the body and surrounding environment. Through practices like body scanning meditations, energy balancing, and the use of sacred symbols, practitioners develop the ability to sense energetic imbalances and subtle emotional undercurrents. Tibetan Buddhism views clairsentience as a reflection of deep compassion, allowing practitioners to intuitively perceive the suffering of others and respond with wisdom and care. It is considered a vital tool on the path to enlightenment, as it fosters connection and unity with all living beings.

Galactic teachings view clairsentience as a multidimensional ability rooted in the activation of the heart chakra and the energetic body. Pleiadian and Arcturian guides teach that clairsentience is a key aspect of humanity's evolutionary potential, allowing individuals to feel the vibrational signatures of higher dimensions and connect with galactic frequencies. Practices such as heart coherence meditations, light activations, and energy clearing are recommended to strengthen this ability, helping practitioners sense messages, emotions, and even energetic shifts within the collective consciousness. Galactic teachings emphasize that clairsentience

connects individuals to the universal energy grid, enhancing their ability to co-create and navigate their spiritual journey.

In all three traditions, clairsentience is regarded as a sacred gift that deepens one's connection to the unseen and fosters greater understanding of the energetic interplay between all things. It requires practice, emotional awareness, and alignment with higher vibrations to ensure that the sensations and impressions received are clear and beneficial. Clairsentience is ultimately a tool for deep empathy, intuitive knowing, and spiritual growth.

Biblical References
Clairsentience, or "clear feeling," refers to the ability to sense or feel spiritual or emotional energies. While the Bible does not use the term "clairsentience," it does reference spiritual discernment, emotional sensitivity, and the ability to perceive God's will or presence through the heart and spirit.
- "But solid food is for the mature, who by constant use have trained themselves to distinguish good from evil" (Hebrews 5:14) This passage reflects the gift of spiritual discernment, which involves sensing or feeling what is good or evil through spiritual maturity.
- "The Spirit himself testifies with our spirit that we are God's children" (Romans 8:16) This verse highlights the deep spiritual connection and inner knowing, a form of spiritual "feeling" or sensing guided by the Holy Spirit.
- "The person without the Spirit does not accept the things that come from the Spirit of God but considers them foolishness, and cannot understand them because they are discerned only through the Spirit" (1 Corinthians 2:14) This speaks to the spiritual sensitivity required to discern or "feel" the things of God.
- The following passage reveals Jesus' profound empathy and the ability to feel others' emotions deeply—a hallmark of clairsentience:

    > When Jesus saw her weeping, and the Jews who had come along with her also weeping, he was deeply moved in spirit and troubled. "Where have you laid

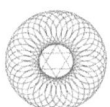

him?" he asked. "Come and see, Lord," they replied. Jesus wept. (John 11:33-35)

- "Dear friends, do not believe every spirit, but test the spirits to see whether they are from God, because many false prophets have gone out into the world" (1 John 4:1) This emphasizes the importance of discerning or "sensing" the nature of spirits and energies.
- "But Jesus said, 'Someone touched me; I know that power has gone out from me'" (Luke 8:46) This verse shows Jesus' awareness of spiritual energy, as He senses power leaving Him when the woman with the issue of blood touches His garment.
- "But the fruit of the Spirit is love, joy, peace, forbearance, kindness, goodness, faithfulness, gentleness and self-control ..." (Galatians 5:22-23) These fruits of the Spirit often manifest as an inner "feeling" or sensitivity to God's presence and will.
- "The LORD is close to the brokenhearted and saves those who are crushed in spirit" (Psalm 34:18) This verse speaks to God's sensitivity to human emotions and His closeness to those who are suffering.
- "Immediately Jesus knew in his spirit that this was what they were thinking in their hearts, and he said to them, 'Why are you thinking these things?'" (Mark 2:8) This demonstrates Jesus' ability to sense what others were feeling or thinking within their hearts.
- The following verses speak to the transformation of the heart and an increased sensitivity to spiritual guidance:
  > I will give you a new heart and put a new spirit in you; I will remove from you your heart of stone and give you a heart of flesh. And I will put my Spirit in you and move you to follow my decrees and be careful to keep my laws. (Ezekiel 36:26-27)
- "The human spirit is the lamp of the LORD that sheds light on one's inmost being" (Proverbs 20:27) This suggests that our spirit acts as a vessel of discernment and spiritual awareness, aligning with the idea of clairsentience.

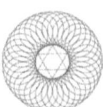

- The following passage emphasizes spiritual discernment that goes beyond physical senses—feeling and knowing through the Spirit:
    > The Spirit of the LORD will rest on him—the Spirit of wisdom and of understanding, the Spirit of counsel and of might, the Spirit of the knowledge and fear of the LORD—and he will delight in the fear of the LORD. He will not judge by what he sees with his eyes, or decide by what he hears with his ears. (Isaiah 11:2-3)

These scriptures highlight the biblical foundation for spiritual sensitivity, discernment, and the ability to feel divine guidance or emotional/spiritual energies, all of which align with the concept of clairsentience.

Claircognizance (Clear Knowing)

Claircognizance, or "clear knowing," is the ability to know information suddenly and intuitively without prior learning or logical reasoning. This gift often manifests as insights that arrive instantaneously, frequently as a complete concept or understanding. It is closely connected to the crown chakra and higher states of consciousness, allowing for a direct link to universal knowledge or spiritual guidance.

Rainbow Reiki
Claircognizance Symbol

Claircognizance often appears as sudden "aha" moments or revelations about people, situations, or concepts, accompanied by a strong sense of certainty about decisions or future outcomes. These moments may also involve downloading complex ideas during meditation or focused thought. The experience feels as though information is "dropped" directly into the mind, leaving a deep sense of clarity and trust in the knowledge received.

This ability serves as a bridge between other intuitive gifts, integrating visual (clairvoyance), auditory (clairaudience), and emotional (clairsentience) information into a cohesive understanding. Its unifying nature enhances the depth and reliability of intuitive perceptions.

Claircognizance Across Traditions

Claircognizance, or the ability to know information spontaneously without logical explanation, is regarded as a profound spiritual gift across Egyptian, Tibetan, and galactic teachings. In ancient Egypt, claircognizance was seen as a divine spark of wisdom bestowed by the gods, often linked to Thoth, the deity of knowledge and divine intelligence. Egyptian initiates in the Mystery Schools honed this

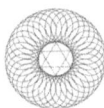

ability through sacred study, meditation, and ritual practices designed to access the universal mind. Claircognizance was believed to arise when one's consciousness aligned with Ma'at, the principle of cosmic truth and order, allowing divine insights and intuitive understanding to flow effortlessly. This ability was particularly valued in leadership, prophecy, and spiritual teachings, where clear and immediate knowing was essential for guidance.

In Tibetan traditions, claircognizance is understood as a byproduct of profound mental clarity and spiritual awakening. Through meditative disciplines and advanced yogic practices, practitioners silence the conscious mind, allowing pure knowledge to arise from the depths of the alaya-vijnana (the storehouse consciousness). Tibetan monks often attribute claircognizance to the awakening of wisdom through samadhi (deep meditative absorption) and the dissolution of mental barriers. This knowing is seen as an expression of the interconnectedness of all things, where the practitioner taps into universal truth without interference from ego or analytical thinking. Tibetan teachings emphasize humility and mindfulness, ensuring that this knowledge is used for the benefit of all sentient beings.

Galactic teachings, particularly those shared by the Pleiadians and Arcturians, describe claircognizance as an innate aspect of higher-dimensional consciousness that becomes accessible as individuals raise their vibration and activate dormant aspects of their DNA. Galactic guides often refer to claircognizance as a connection to the Akashic Records, the universal library of all knowledge and experience. They teach that this ability is strengthened through practices like light code activations, heart-brain coherence, and energetic alignment. Claircognizance is seen as a direct download of information from higher-dimensional sources, bypassing the need for logic or sensory input. It is a key tool for navigating multidimensional realities and aligning with one's soul purpose.

In all three traditions, claircognizance is revered as a sacred ability that reflects alignment with higher wisdom and universal truth. It requires mental discipline, spiritual integrity, and a deep trust in

one's intuitive knowing. Whether accessed through ritual, meditation, or energetic practices, claircognizance is seen as a profound gift that empowers individuals to serve their higher purpose and the collective good with clarity and insight.

Biblical References

Claircognizance, or "clear knowing," refers to the ability to intuitively know something without prior knowledge or reasoning. In the Bible, this aligns with the concept of divine wisdom, revelation, or knowledge imparted by the Holy Spirit. While the term "claircognizance" is not explicitly biblical, many scriptures describe instances of supernatural knowing, divine insight, and revelation.

- "To one there is given through the Spirit a message of wisdom, to another a message of knowledge by means of the same Spirit" (1 Corinthians 12:8) This describes the spiritual gift of knowledge, which is often revealed directly by God.
- "But when he, the Spirit of truth, comes, he will guide you into all the truth. He will not speak on his own; he will speak only what he hears, and he will tell you what is yet to come" (John 16:13) The Holy Spirit provides divine knowledge and insight, guiding believers into truth beyond human understanding.
- "Call to me and I will answer you and tell you great and unsearchable things you do not know" (Jeremiah 33:3) This verse demonstrates God's ability to reveal hidden knowledge to those who seek Him.
- God is the source of wisdom and knowledge, revealing hidden truths to those He chooses, as shown here:
    > He changes times and seasons; he deposes kings and raises up others. He gives wisdom to the wise and knowledge to the discerning. He reveals deep and hidden things; he knows what lies in darkness, and light dwells with him. (Daniel 2:21-22)
- "For the Lord gives wisdom; from his mouth come knowledge and understanding" (Proverbs 2:6) This verse speaks to God as the ultimate source of knowledge and understanding, often imparted supernaturally.

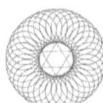

- "But you have an anointing from the Holy One, and all of you know the truth" (1 John 2:20) This describes the spiritual anointing that provides believers with a sense of divine knowing.
- "Simon Peter answered, 'You are the Messiah, the Son of the living God.' Jesus replied, 'Blessed are you, Simon son of Jonah, for this was not revealed to you by flesh and blood, but by my Father in heaven'" (Matthew 16:16-17) Peter's recognition of Jesus as the Messiah was an example of divine revelation and knowing.
- "Then Peter said, 'Ananias, how is it that Satan has so filled your heart that you have lied to the Holy Spirit and have kept for yourself some of the money you received for the land?'" (Acts 5:3) Peter demonstrated supernatural knowledge about Ananias' deceit, given by the Holy Spirit.
- "The Spirit of the LORD will rest on him—the Spirit of wisdom and of understanding, the Spirit of counsel and of might, the Spirit of the knowledge and fear of the Lord" (Isaiah 11:2) This highlights the gift of divine knowledge and wisdom as part of the Holy Spirit's work.
- "Surely the Sovereign LORD does nothing without revealing his plan to his servants the prophets" (Amos 3:7) Prophets often receive direct insight from God about His plans, an example of divinely imparted knowledge.
- The following passage shows Solomon's wisdom and discernment were gifts from God, enabling him to know and judge rightly:

    > So give your servant a discerning heart to govern your people and to distinguish between right and wrong. For who is able to govern this great people of yours?' The LORD was pleased that Solomon had asked for this. So God said to him, 'Since you have asked for this and not for long life or wealth for yourself, nor have asked for the death of your enemies but for discernment in administering justice, I will do what you have asked. I will give you a wise and discerning heart ...' (1 Kings 3:9-12)

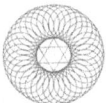

- This verse describes divine knowledge and understanding provided by the Holy Spirit:
    > For this reason, since the day we heard about you, we have not stopped praying for you. We continually ask God to fill you with the knowledge of his will through all the wisdom and understanding that the Spirit gives. (Colossians 1:9)

These scriptures reflect the biblical foundation for the idea of supernatural knowing, often granted by God through the Holy Spirit to accomplish His purposes. Claircognizance, in a biblical sense, could be seen as a manifestation of this divine gift of wisdom, discernment, or knowledge.

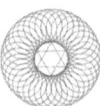

Clairalience (Clear Smelling)

Clairalience, or "clear smelling," is the ability to perceive intuitive or spiritual information through scents. This gift allows individuals to detect specific smells that are often associated with memories, spiritual guidance, or connections to loved ones, even when there is no physical source for the scent.

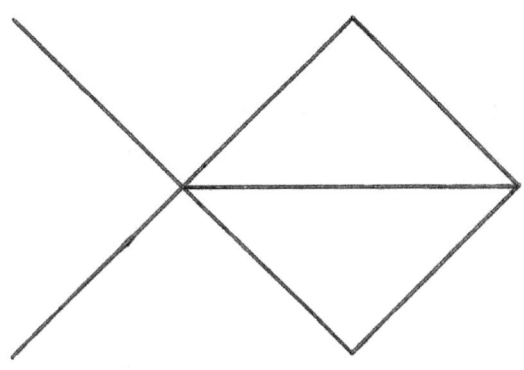
Rainbow Reiki Clairalience Symbol

Clairalience frequently manifests as the sudden smell of perfume, flowers, or incense tied to a loved one who has passed, or as spiritual symbols that arise during meditation or moments of reflection. These experiences are often brief and subtle but carry profound emotional significance, offering comfort and a sense of connection to the spiritual realm.

This ability is closely linked to clairsentience, as the scents perceived often evoke strong emotional resonance and help validate intuitive impressions. The subtlety and power of clairalience make it a unique yet deeply meaningful way to experience spiritual communication.

Clairalience Across Traditions

Clairalience, or the ability to perceive psychic information through the sense of smell, is a lesser known but deeply significant spiritual ability explored in Egyptian, Tibetan, and galactic teachings. In ancient Egypt, scents were considered sacred tools for spiritual connection and divine communication. Clairalience was often associated with the use of sacred oils, resins, and perfumes such as frankincense, myrrh, and blue lotus, believed to carry the essence of the gods. Egyptian priests and priestesses used their heightened sense of smell to interpret divine messages, often receiving intuitive guidance through specific fragrances during rituals and ceremonies.

This ability was regarded as a form of communion with the divine, where scents served as a bridge between the physical and spiritual realms.

In Tibetan traditions, clairalience is closely tied to the practice of mindfulness and heightened sensory awareness. The Tibetan use of incense, herbs, and aromatic offerings like *sang* (ritual smoke offerings) was designed not only to purify the environment but also to awaken subtle psychic senses. Tibetan monks often reported intuitive insights triggered by certain scents during meditation or rituals, interpreting them as messages from enlightened beings or signs of karmic conditions. Clairalience was seen as a tool for understanding energetic imbalances, as certain smells could reveal subtle energies, emotional states, or spiritual presences.

Galactic teachings explain clairalience as an energetic sensitivity to vibrational frequencies encoded within scents. Pleiadian and Arcturian guides describe this ability as a natural extension of humanity's multidimensional awareness, allowing individuals to perceive energetic signatures through olfactory senses. Galactic teachings often reference the connection between smell and memory, explaining that certain cosmic or otherworldly scents can trigger deep soul memories, activating latent wisdom or past-life awareness. Practices such as working with high-vibrational essential oils or engaging in breathwork with aromatic elements are recommended to refine this ability. Clairalience is also linked to perceiving energetic shifts in one's environment, offering a subtle yet powerful tool for navigating higher-dimensional energies.

In all three traditions, clairalience is seen as a sacred gift that fosters connection to the divine, enhances intuitive understanding, and deepens sensory perception. It requires mindfulness, energetic attunement, and an openness to interpreting subtle signs. Whether experienced through sacred rituals, meditative practices, or multidimensional guidance, clairalience offers a unique and profound way to access spiritual wisdom and connect with unseen realms.

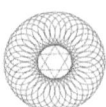

Biblical References

Clairalience, or "clear smelling," refers to the ability to sense smells that are not physically present but may hold spiritual significance. While the Bible does not explicitly use the term "clairalience," there are several scriptures that refer to the sense of smell in a spiritual context, particularly in relation to offerings, the presence of God, and divine revelations. Here are some examples that align with the concept of spiritual smelling:

- The following passage uses the metaphor of aroma to describe spiritual influence and the presence of God:
    > But thanks be to God, who always leads us as captives in Christ's triumphal procession and uses us to spread the aroma of the knowledge of him everywhere. For we are to God the pleasing aroma of Christ among those who are being saved and those who are perishing. To the one we are an aroma that brings death; to the other, an aroma that brings life ... (2 Corinthians 2:14-16)
- This verse describes God being pleased by the aroma of Noah's offering, indicating that spiritual meaning can be conveyed through scent:
    > The LORD smelled the pleasing aroma and said in his heart: 'Never again will I curse the ground because of humans, even though every inclination of the human heart is evil from childhood. And never again will I destroy all living creatures, as I have done.' (Genesis 8:21)
- The sacred use of incense represents a spiritual connection through fragrance, as indicated here:
    > Then the LORD said to Moses, 'Take fragrant spices—gum resin, onycha, and galbanum—and pure frankincense, all in equal amounts, and make a fragrant blend of incense, the work of a perfumer. It is to be salted and pure and sacred. Grind some of it to powder and place it in front of the ark of the covenant law in the tent of meeting, where I will meet with you. It shall be most holy to you.' (Exodus 30:34-37)

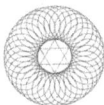

- The following verse shows that offerings and their aromas held deep spiritual significance:
  > And take it to Aaron's sons the priests. The priest shall take a handful of the flour and oil, together with all the incense, and burn this as a memorial portion on the altar, a food offering, an aroma pleasing to the LORD. (Leviticus 2:2)
- "Pleasing is the fragrance of your perfumes; your name is like perfume poured out. No wonder the young women love you!" (Song of Solomon 1:3) This poetic verse uses fragrance to symbolize spiritual attraction and connection.
- "May my prayer be set before you like incense; may the lifting up of my hands be like the evening sacrifice" (Psalm 141:2) The comparison of prayer to incense connects spiritual devotion to the sense of smell.
- "Instead of fragrance there will be a stench; instead of a sash, a rope; instead of well-dressed hair, baldness; instead of fine clothing, sackcloth; instead of beauty, branding" (Isaiah 3:24) This contrasts pleasant fragrances with stench as a metaphor for spiritual or moral decay.
- God uses the metaphor of fragrance to signify His acceptance and holiness here:
  > I will accept you as a fragrant incense when I bring you out from the nations and gather you from the countries where you have been scattered, and I will be proved holy through you in the sight of the nations. (Ezekiel 20:41)
- "Then Mary took about a pint of pure nard, an expensive perfume; she poured it on Jesus' feet and wiped his feet with her hair. And the house was filled with the fragrance of the perfume" (John 12:3) The physical fragrance of the perfume signifies deep spiritual devotion and reverence.
- Incense and its fragrance are directly tied to prayers and spiritual offerings, shown here:
  > Another angel, who had a golden censer, came and stood at the altar. He was given much incense to offer, with the prayers of all God's people, on the golden altar in front of the throne. The smoke of the

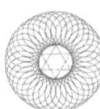

> incense, together with the prayers of God's people, went up before God from the angel's hand. (Revelation 8:3-4)
- The following verse emphasizes the spiritual significance of a "fragrant offering" as a metaphor for acceptable and pleasing sacrifices to God:
  > I have received full payment and have more than enough. I am amply supplied, now that I have received from Epaphroditus the gifts you sent. They are a fragrant offering, an acceptable sacrifice, pleasing to God. (Philippians 4:18)

These scriptures show that scents, both physical and spiritual, carry symbolic and divine significance in the Bible. While clairalience as a term is not used, the spiritual awareness or connection through scent is referenced multiple times, often symbolizing God's presence, prayers, and offerings.

Clairgustance (Clear Tasting)

Clairgustance, or "clear tasting," is the ability to perceive tastes that have no physical source, often tied to spiritual or energetic messages. This ability connects specific flavors to memories, spirits, or symbolic meanings, providing a unique form of intuitive insight.

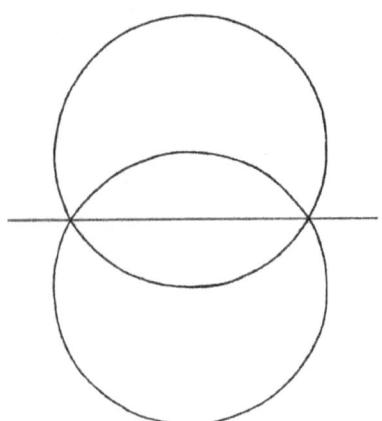

Rainbow Reiki
Clairgustance Symbol

Clairgustance may manifest as tasting food or drinks associated with a loved one who has passed, evoking a strong sense of connection. It can also involve experiencing symbolic tastes, such as bitterness to signal a warning or sweetness to convey joy or celebration. These experiences are typically subtle and brief but carry profound significance, often validating other intuitive impressions.

This gift is closely connected to other intuitive abilities, adding depth to messages received through clairvoyance, clairaudience, or clairsentience. By engaging an additional sensory layer, clairgustance enriches the overall understanding of spiritual or energetic communication.

Clairgustance Across Traditions

Clairgustance, the ability to perceive psychic information through the sense of taste, is a rare but powerful spiritual gift recognized in Egyptian, Tibetan, and galactic teachings as a unique channel for divine communication and energetic understanding. In ancient Egypt, clairgustance was often associated with the sacred practice of consuming ritual offerings, elixirs, and herbal infusions designed to connect the individual with higher realms. Egyptian initiates believed that the flavors of certain substances, such as honey, lotus wine, or sacred herbs, could convey spiritual insights or messages

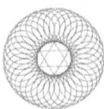

from the gods. This ability was particularly valued in temple ceremonies, where priests and priestesses would intuitively interpret the energetic essence of offerings through taste to determine the favor of the divine or the presence of specific energies.

In Tibetan traditions, clairgustance is less explicitly named but is understood as part of the broader development of heightened sensory awareness through spiritual practice. Tibetan monks and practitioners often engage in rituals involving sacred offerings, such as *tsok* (food offerings), where the taste of the offerings is believed to carry energetic and karmic significance. Practitioners in deep meditative states sometimes report tasting the essence of spiritual teachings or karmic imprints, using this sensory input to guide their understanding of energetic conditions or spiritual truths. The Tibetan perspective emphasizes that such experiences arise when the mind and subtle senses are purified, allowing the practitioner to connect deeply with the spiritual essence of all things.

Galactic teachings from beings such as the Pleiadians and Arcturians describe clairgustance as a multidimensional ability tied to energy perception and vibrational alignment. According to these teachings, the taste sensations experienced during meditation, energy work, or interaction with higher realms are often encoded messages from spirit guides or reflections of energetic frequencies. For example, a sweet taste might symbolize divine love, while a metallic or bitter taste might indicate energetic cleansing or karmic processing. Galactic guides encourage the use of mindfulness and breathwork to attune to these subtle experiences, teaching that clairgustance is a tool for understanding energetic shifts and accessing spiritual insights through the body's sensory pathways.

In all three traditions, clairgustance is seen as a sacred ability that bridges the physical and spiritual realms. It requires openness, sensitivity, and attunement to subtle energies to fully develop. Whether experienced through rituals, meditative states, or interactions with higher-dimensional frequencies, clairgustance

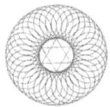

offers a unique and profound way to access spiritual wisdom and understand the energetic nature of existence.

Biblical References

Clairgustance, or "clear tasting," is the ability to taste substances without physically consuming them, often associated with spiritual or divine messages. While the Bible does not explicitly refer to clairgustance, it does include instances where taste is used symbolically or spiritually to convey a deeper message or divine experience.

- "Taste and see that the Lord is good; blessed is the one who takes refuge in him" (Psalm 34:8) This verse uses "taste" metaphorically to encourage believers to experience the goodness of God, symbolizing a deep spiritual connection.
- In the following passage, Ezekiel's act of tasting the scroll represents receiving and internalizing God's word, which tasted sweet as a sign of its divine origin:
  > And he said to me, 'Son of man, eat what is before you, eat this scroll; then go and speak to the people of Israel.' So I opened my mouth, and he gave me the scroll to eat. Then he said to me, 'Son of man, eat this scroll I am giving you and fill your stomach with it.' So I ate it, and it tasted as sweet as honey in my mouth. (Ezekiel 3:1-3)
- In the following verses, the vision given to John demonstrates tasting as part of a spiritual experience, symbolizing the bittersweet nature of prophecy:
  > So I went to the angel and asked him to give me the little scroll. He said to me, 'Take it and eat it. It will turn your stomach sour, but in your mouth it will be as sweet as honey.' I took the little scroll from the angel's hand and ate it. It tasted as sweet as honey in my mouth, but when I had eaten it, my stomach turned sour. (Revelation 10:9-10)
- The following passage compares the sweetness of honey to the sweetness of wisdom, using taste as a spiritual metaphor for receiving divine knowledge:

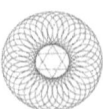

> Eat honey, my son, for it is good; honey from the comb is sweet to your taste. Know also that wisdom is like honey for you: If you find it, there is a future hope for you, and your hope will not be cut off. (Proverbs 24:13-14)

- "Tasting" is used metaphorically to describe experiencing the spiritual gifts of God and the blessings of the Holy Spirit here:
  > It is impossible for those who have once been enlightened, who have tasted the heavenly gift, who have shared in the Holy Spirit, who have tasted the goodness of the word of God and the powers of the coming age. (Hebrews 6:4-5)
- "Does not the ear test words as the tongue tastes food?" (Job 12:11) This verse draws a parallel between the physical sense of taste and the ability to discern or test spiritual truths.
- "How sweet are your words to my taste, sweeter than honey to my mouth!" (Psalm 119:103) The psalmist describes the experience of God's words as sweet, symbolizing their nourishing and fulfilling spiritual impact.
- "Like newborn babies, crave pure spiritual milk, so that by it you may grow up in your salvation, now that you have tasted that the Lord is good" (1 Peter 2:2-3) This passage uses taste as a metaphor for experiencing and desiring spiritual growth and God's goodness.
- "The people of Israel called the bread manna. It was white like coriander seed and tasted like wafers made with honey" (Exodus 16:31) The description of manna's taste connects the physical and spiritual provision of God, emphasizing its divine nature.
- "You are the salt of the earth. But if the salt loses its saltiness, how can it be made salty again? It is no longer good for anything, except to be thrown out and trampled underfoot" (Matthew 5:13) This verse highlights the symbolic importance of taste, using salt as a metaphor for spiritual influence and preservation.

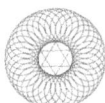

These scriptures illustrate that the Bible often uses taste as a spiritual metaphor, connecting it to the experience of God's goodness, wisdom, and divine revelation. While clairgustance as a concept is not directly mentioned, the symbolic use of taste in the Bible aligns with its spiritual significance.

Psychometry (Energy Reading of Objects)

Psychometry is the ability to perceive information about a person, place, or event by touching or holding an object associated with it. This ability relies on the understanding that objects absorb and retain energy from their surroundings and from the people who interact with them. By holding or focusing on an object, someone with psychometric abilities can "tune in" to its energetic imprint.

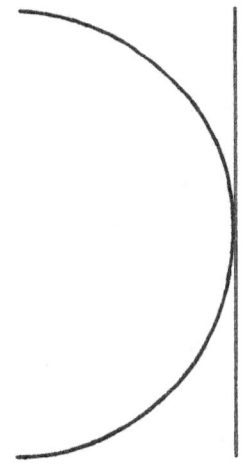
Rainbow Reiki Psychometry Symbol

Psychometry often manifests as receiving images, emotions, or sensations tied to the object's history. These impressions may include flashes of past events or insights about the object's owner. The experience can feel like a stream of impressions flowing into the mind, accompanied by physical sensations like warmth or tingling or emotional responses such as sadness or joy.

This ability is closely linked with clairsentience, as it involves feeling the energy associated with the object, and clairvoyance, which provides visual insights related to its history. Psychometry is often used in combination with intuitive or mediumistic abilities to gain deeper understanding and connect with the stories or energies tied to the object.

Psychometry Across Traditions

Psychometry, the ability to perceive information or energy from physical objects through touch, is a highly respected skill in Egyptian, Tibetan, and galactic teachings. Across these traditions, psychometry is regarded as a form of energetic reading that bridges the material and spiritual realms, allowing individuals to access the history, emotions, or vibrations associated with an object or its owner.

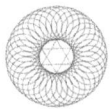

In ancient Egypt, psychometry was closely tied to the sacred practice of connecting with artifacts, relics, and ceremonial tools. Priests and priestesses trained in the Mystery Schools were believed to use psychometric abilities to access the energetic imprints left on objects by their creators, users, or environments. For instance, sacred amulets, statues, and tools used in rituals were thought to hold the vibrations of the gods or the intentions of those who made them. Psychometry was often used to discern the purity of these objects, ensuring their alignment with Ma'at, the principle of cosmic truth and order.

In Tibetan teachings, psychometry aligns with the Buddhist understanding of interconnection and the subtle imprints left by karma. Tibetan monks and practitioners often used sacred tools, such as prayer wheels, malas, or ritual implements, as conduits for energy and memory. Through heightened awareness developed in meditation, practitioners could sense the energetic resonance of objects, discerning their history or spiritual significance. Psychometry, in this sense, was not only a way to connect with objects but also a practice of mindfulness and compassion, recognizing the interconnected web of energy and intention behind all things.

In galactic teachings, psychometry is explained as an ability to access the energetic records of an object, much like tapping into the Akashic Records. Galactic guides, such as the Pleiadians and Arcturians, teach that all objects hold energetic imprints, which can be read by those attuned to higher vibrations. This ability is linked to the activation of the palm chakras and the expansion of one's subtle energy field. Galactic beings encourage the use of psychometry as a tool for understanding multidimensional connections, retrieving past-life insights, and accessing information encoded in objects from other timelines or dimensions. Practices such as energy clearing, grounding, and pineal gland activation are often recommended to refine this skill.

Across these traditions, psychometry is viewed as a sacred gift that requires mindfulness, energetic sensitivity, and a pure heart to

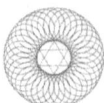

ensure that the information received is accurate and beneficial. Whether accessing the history of an artifact, tuning into the emotions tied to a personal item, or connecting with higher-dimensional knowledge, psychometry serves as a profound bridge between the seen and unseen, deepening one's spiritual awareness and understanding of the energetic nature of reality.

Biblical References

Psychometry, or the ability to receive information about a person, place, or event by touching an object, is not explicitly mentioned in the Bible. However, there are scriptures and examples that indirectly align with the concept of receiving spiritual insight, discernment, or revelation through physical interaction or divine connection. These instances demonstrate that touch can be a conduit for spiritual power, revelation, or knowledge. Here are some examples:

- "God did extraordinary miracles through Paul, so that even handkerchiefs and aprons that had touched him were taken to the sick, and their illnesses were cured, and the evil spirits left them" (Acts 19:11-12) This passage highlights the transfer of divine power through objects that were touched by Paul. While it does not describe psychometry, it supports the idea that objects can carry spiritual significance or energy.
- The following passage demonstrates the flow of divine power through touch, with both the woman and Jesus being aware of the spiritual exchange:

    > When she heard about Jesus, she came up behind him in the crowd and touched his cloak, because she thought, "If I just touch his clothes, I will be healed." Immediately her bleeding stopped, and she felt in her body that she was freed from her suffering. At once Jesus realized that power had gone out from him. He turned around in the crowd and asked, "Who touched my clothes?" (Mark 5:27-30)

- "'Who touched me?' Jesus asked. When they all denied it, Peter said, 'Master, the people are crowding and pressing against you.' But Jesus said, 'Someone touched me; I know

that power has gone out from me'" (Luke 8:45-46) This further emphasizes the transfer of spiritual energy and the awareness of touch being connected to divine power.
- "For seven days make atonement for the altar and consecrate it. Then the altar will be most holy, and whatever touches it will be holy" (Exodus 29:37) This verse implies that objects and their physical interactions can hold and transfer sacredness, hinting at a deeper spiritual connection.
- The following is a striking example of divine power associated with a physical object (Elisha's bones), resulting in a miraculous event:

    > Once while some Israelites were burying a man, suddenly they saw a band of raiders; so they threw the man's body into Elisha's tomb. When the body touched Elisha's bones, the man came to life and stood up on his feet. (2 Kings 13:21)

- While not directly about touch, the following passage highlights the spiritual connection between objects (bones) and divine revelation or power:

    > The hand of the LORD was on me, and he brought me out by the Spirit of the Lord and set me in the middle of a valley; it was full of bones. ... He asked me, "Son of man, can these bones live?" I said, "Sovereign LORD, you alone know." Then he said to me, "Prophesy to these bones and say to them, 'Dry bones, hear the word of the Lord!'" (Ezekiel 37:1, 3-4)

- The following verses again demonstrate the spiritual significance of touch and the ability for physical objects to convey divine power:

    > And when the men of that place recognized Jesus, they sent word to all the surrounding country. People brought all their sick to him and begged him to let the sick just touch the edge of his cloak, and all who touched it were healed. (Matthew 14:35-36)

- Although not psychometry per se, the following passage shows a belief in the transfer of spiritual power through

physical proximity, further emphasizing the idea of spiritual connection through physical means:

> As a result, people brought the sick into the streets and laid them on beds and mats so that at least Peter's shadow might fall on some of them as he passed by. Crowds gathered also from the towns around Jerusalem, bringing their sick and those tormented by impure spirits, and all of them were healed. (Acts 5:15-16)

- While not directly related to objects, the following passage highlights divine revelation and knowledge given by the Spirit, which could conceptually align with receiving insight or information spiritually:

  > These are the things God has revealed to us by his Spirit. The Spirit searches all things, even the deep things of God. For who knows a person's thoughts except their own spirit within them? In the same way, no one knows the thoughts of God except the Spirit of God. (1 Corinthians 2:10-11)

- Here, Jacob consecrates a stone after a divine encounter, showing that physical objects can hold spiritual significance:

  > Early the next morning Jacob took the stone he had placed under his head and set it up as a pillar and poured oil on top of it. He called that place Bethel, though the city used to be called Luz. (Genesis 28:18-19)

These passages suggest that, while psychometry as a term is not explicitly biblical, the idea of objects holding or conveying spiritual power or knowledge is present. This aligns with the broader biblical themes of divine revelation, spiritual discernment, and the sanctity of physical touch.

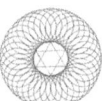

Telepathy (Mind-to-Mind Communication)
Telepathy is the ability to transmit or receive thoughts, feelings, or information directly from one mind to another without the use of physical communication. This form of connection operates through the energy fields (auras) and frequencies shared between individuals, requiring a strong energetic or emotional bond between the sender and receiver.

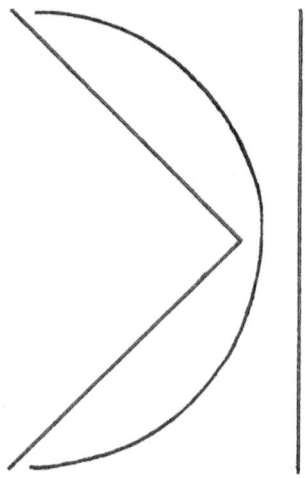
Rainbow Reiki Telepathy Symbol

Telepathy often manifests as an intuitive knowing of what someone is thinking or feeling without them expressing it verbally. It may also involve receiving mental images, words, or sensations during meditation or daily interactions. Synchronicities, such as saying what another person is thinking, are common examples of telepathic exchanges. These experiences typically feel like an unspoken understanding or a sudden awareness, and strong telepathic connections are often found in close relationships, such as between twins, partners, or parents and children.

Telepathy works closely with claircognizance (clear knowing) and clairsentience (clear feeling) to interpret the thoughts and emotions perceived. It also enhances energy healing by allowing the healer to intuitively sense and respond to the recipient's emotional or energetic needs, deepening the connection and the effectiveness of the healing process.

Telepathy Across Traditions
Telepathy, the ability to exchange thoughts, emotions, or energy directly between minds without the use of words or physical senses, is a revered and universal skill recognized in Egyptian, Tibetan, and galactic teachings. Across these traditions, telepathy is seen as a

profound connection between beings, allowing for the transmission of truth, unity, and divine understanding.

In ancient Egypt, telepathy was believed to be a natural ability of the soul, especially among those who had activated their higher consciousness. The priests and priestesses of the Mystery Schools trained in telepathic communication, which they considered a sacred skill tied to the divine principle of Ma'at, representing harmony and interconnectedness. Telepathic exchanges were often used during rituals, particularly when communicating with the gods, ancestors, or other initiates within temple spaces. Hieroglyphic symbolism itself is thought to have been designed to evoke telepathic understanding, conveying layers of meaning beyond the written word. Telepathy was also associated with the pineal gland, often symbolized by the "Eye of Horus," which represented intuitive perception and the ability to connect with the unseen.

In Tibetan teachings, telepathy is understood as one of the *siddhis* (spiritual powers) attainable through deep meditation, focused intention, and the purification of the mind. Tibetan monks and yogis practicing advanced levels of *samadhi* (deep meditative absorption) are said to develop telepathic abilities, allowing them to receive teachings, guidance, or insights directly from enlightened beings or fellow practitioners. Telepathy is seen as a natural expression of *shunyata* (emptiness), where the boundaries of individual ego dissolve, allowing for direct energetic communication between sentient beings. In Tibetan Buddhism, telepathy is used as a tool for compassion, enabling the practitioner to understand the needs and suffering of others on a deeper level and offer appropriate guidance or healing.

Galactic teachings from Pleiadians, Arcturians, and other higher-dimensional beings view telepathy as a foundational mode of communication in advanced civilizations. These beings often emphasize that telepathy is humanity's birthright, accessible as individuals raise their vibration and align their energy with higher frequencies. Telepathic communication in galactic traditions is described as multidimensional, encompassing not only thoughts but

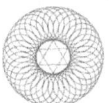

also emotions, images, and energetic imprints. Practices such as light code activations, heart-brain coherence meditations, and DNA recalibration are recommended to awaken telepathic abilities. Telepathy is seen as a tool for unity consciousness, fostering a deeper sense of connection between individuals, collective groups, and universal consciousness itself.

Across these traditions, telepathy is regarded as a sacred and natural ability that transcends physical limitations and reflects the interconnectedness of all life. Its cultivation requires mindfulness, energetic attunement, and alignment with higher principles of truth and compassion. Whether used to communicate with the divine, bridge understanding between beings, or navigate multidimensional realities, telepathy serves as a powerful reminder of humanity's potential for unity and spiritual evolution.

Biblical References
Telepathy, or the ability to communicate thoughts or feelings directly without speaking, is not explicitly named in the Bible. However, there are examples of spiritual communication, divine insight, and instances where knowledge or understanding is conveyed without words. These examples align with the concept of telepathic communication, particularly through the Holy Spirit or divine revelation.
- The following passage describes the Holy Spirit enabling believers to understand divine truths and communicate spiritually, which resonates with the concept of telepathic understanding:
  > For who knows a person's thoughts except their own spirit within them? In the same way, no one knows the thoughts of God except the Spirit of God. What we have received is not the spirit of the world, but the Spirit who is from God, so that we may understand what God has freely given us. This is what we speak, not in words taught us by human wisdom but in words taught by the Spirit, explaining spiritual realities with Spirit-taught words (1 Corinthians 2:11-13)

- "Surely the Sovereign Lord does nothing without revealing his plan to his servants the prophets" (Amos 3:7) God often communicates with prophets directly, bypassing spoken words, through visions, dreams, and divine impressions.
- "Immediately Jesus knew in his spirit that this was what they were thinking in their hearts, and he said to them, 'Why are you thinking these things?'" (Mark 2:8) Jesus demonstrates an ability to perceive the unspoken thoughts of others, aligning closely with the concept of telepathy.
- "But Jesus knew what they were thinking and said to the man with the shriveled hand, 'Get up and stand in front of everyone.' So he got up and stood there" (Luke 6:8) Again, Jesus displays the ability to know the thoughts of those around Him without verbal communication.
- "Knowing their thoughts, Jesus said, 'Why do you entertain evil thoughts in your hearts?'" (Matthew 9:4) This highlights Jesus' capacity to perceive inner thoughts, emphasizing divine awareness of the mind and heart.
- "After the earthquake came a fire, but the LORD was not in the fire. And after the fire came a gentle whisper" (1 Kings 19:12) While not direct telepathy, this illustrates the subtlety of God's communication, often bypassing physical senses.
- "While Peter was still thinking about the vision, the Spirit said to him, 'Simon, three men are looking for you. So get up and go downstairs. Do not hesitate to go with them, for I have sent them'" (Acts 10:19-20) Peter receives direct communication from the Spirit, guiding him in what to do.
- "But when he, the Spirit of truth, comes, he will guide you into all the truth. He will not speak on his own; he will speak only what he hears, and he will tell you what is yet to come." (John 16:13) The Holy Spirit enables communication and understanding that transcends verbal language.
- Here, Daniel demonstrates an ability to know and interpret what was in King Nebuchadnezzar's mind, through divine revelation:

    > But there is a God in heaven who reveals mysteries. He has shown King Nebuchadnezzar what will happen in days to come. Your dream and the visions

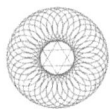

that passed through your mind as you were lying in bed are these: "As Your Majesty was lying there, your mind turned to things to come, and the revealer of mysteries showed you what is going to happen. As for me, this mystery has been revealed to me, not because I have greater wisdom than anyone else alive, but so that Your Majesty may know the interpretation and that you may understand what went through your mind. (Daniel 2:28-30)

- "'None of us, my lord the king,' said one of his officers, 'but Elisha, the prophet who is in Israel, tells the king of Israel the very words you speak in your bedroom'" (2 Kings 6:12) Elisha, through divine insight, is aware of private conversations, which parallels telepathic-like knowledge.
- "Before they call I will answer; while they are still speaking I will hear" (Isaiah 65:24) God demonstrates His ability to know and respond to thoughts and needs before they are verbally expressed.
- The following verse shows God's direct understanding of internal thoughts and feelings, a concept closely tied to telepathy:

    > But the LORD said to Samuel, "Do not consider his appearance or his height, for I have rejected him. The LORD does not look at the things people look at. People look at the outward appearance, but the LORD looks at the heart." (1 Samuel 16:7)

- "In your relationships with one another, have the same mindset as Christ Jesus" (Philippians 2:5) The idea of sharing the "mindset of Christ" suggests a spiritual connection and alignment of thoughts.

These passages emphasize that the Bible contains numerous examples of divine or spiritual communication that transcends spoken words. While "telepathy" as a term is not directly mentioned, the concept of knowing or sharing thoughts through divine means is a recurring theme, especially in the context of prophecy, revelation, and spiritual connection.

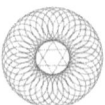

Mediumship

Mediumship is the ability to connect with spirits or entities from other dimensions, facilitating communication between the physical and spiritual realms. This connection often occurs through visions, sounds, feelings, or direct communication and requires the medium to create a safe and clear energetic space for the interaction.

Mediumship may manifest as receiving messages from deceased loved ones, spirit guides, or other spiritual entities. It can also involve physical sensations that indicate a spirit's presence, such as chills, warmth, or a tingling sensation. These experiences are often deeply emotional, profound, and healing for both the medium and those receiving the messages.

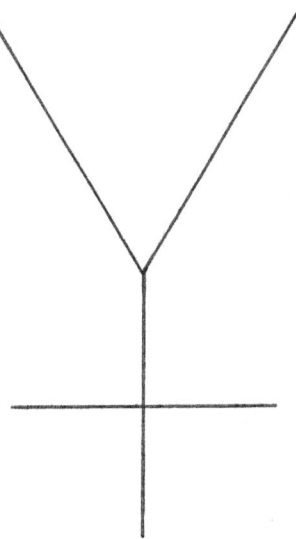

Rainbow Reiki Mediumship Symbol

This ability frequently utilizes multiple *clairs*—such as clairvoyance, clairaudience, and clairsentience—to interpret the messages clearly and provide a comprehensive understanding of the spiritual communication. Mediumship serves as a bridge to offer comfort, closure, and insight from the spiritual realm.

Mediumship Across Traditions

Mediumship, the ability to communicate with spirits, ancestors, or beings from other realms, is a deeply respected and spiritually significant skill across Egyptian, Tibetan, and galactic teachings. This gift is viewed as a bridge between the physical and non-physical realms, allowing for profound guidance, healing, and understanding of the soul's journey.

In ancient Egypt, mediumship was practiced as a sacred art by priests, priestesses, and temple initiates. It was believed that the veil between the living and the afterlife was thin, and skilled mediums

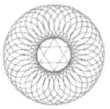

could communicate with the spirits of the departed, ancestors, and gods. The Egyptians saw mediumship as essential for maintaining Ma'at (cosmic order), as messages from the spirit world were often sought to ensure balance and harmony in the physical realm. Mediumship often took place in temple spaces designed to amplify spiritual connection, such as the Hall of Osiris, where rituals involving sacred oils, incense, and invocations helped facilitate contact with the divine. Mediums served as conduits for the wisdom of the gods, interpreting messages to guide rulers and communities.

In Tibetan teachings, mediumship is considered a natural expression of deep spiritual practice and the interconnectedness of all beings. Tibetan Buddhist practitioners, particularly those trained in advanced meditation and *phowa* (the practice of transferring consciousness), often report receiving messages from enlightened beings, bodhisattvas, or the spirits of the deceased. Mediumship is used to help souls transition peacefully, offer guidance to the living, and provide karmic insight. In Tibetan rituals, mediums (or *oracle-like practitioners*) often enter trance states, allowing compassionate energies or deities to communicate through them. The emphasis in Tibetan mediumship is on compassion and ethical responsibility, ensuring that the connection serves the highest good of all beings.

Galactic teachings from beings such as the Arcturians and Pleiadians describe mediumship as a multidimensional communication skill that aligns with humanity's innate spiritual potential. According to these teachings, mediumship is not limited to connecting with departed human souls but extends to communicating with higher-dimensional beings, collective consciousnesses, and galactic guides. Galactic perspectives often explain mediumship as a result of raising one's vibrational frequency and expanding one's energetic field to access realms beyond the third dimension. Practices such as pineal gland activation, energy clearing, and meditation are recommended to strengthen one's ability to serve as a clear channel. In these traditions, mediumship is viewed as a way to access universal wisdom, foster spiritual evolution, and assist humanity in remembering its multidimensional nature.

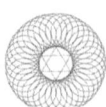

Across these traditions, mediumship is revered as a sacred gift that requires dedication, humility, and alignment with higher principles of truth and compassion. Whether used to communicate with ancestors, spirits, or cosmic guides, mediumship is seen as a powerful tool for healing, connection, and spiritual growth. The medium serves as a vessel for divine messages, helping to bridge the gap between realms and facilitate deeper understanding and harmony within the soul's journey.

Biblical References

The historical and cultural context surrounding the Bible, particularly its warnings against mediums and spirit communication, reveals a complex interplay of theology, politics, and societal control. During the periods when the Bible was compiled and translated, various religious and political institutions, such as the Roman Catholic Church, sought to centralize spiritual authority. This centralization often led to the suppression of practices that allowed individuals direct access to spiritual realms, such as mediumship or personal communion with spirit.

In the ancient world, spiritual practices, including communicating with ancestors and spirits, were common in many cultures. Practices of divination, prophecy, and spirit consultation were integrated into daily life in Mesopotamia, Egypt, and Canaan. These practices were seen as natural and accessible ways to interact with the divine or gain guidance.

However, as monotheistic religions like Judaism and later Christianity grew, these practices were reframed as dangerous or heretical. Biblical prohibitions against mediums (e.g., Leviticus 19:31, Deuteronomy 18:10-12) were partly aimed at differentiating the worship of Yahweh from the polytheistic practices of neighboring cultures. The intent may not have been to suppress spirit communication outright but to ensure it was done under God's authority rather than through foreign rituals.

By the time Christianity became institutionalized under the Roman Empire, particularly after Constantine's conversion in the 4th

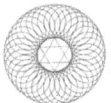

century CE, the church sought to centralize spiritual authority under its leadership. Practices that allowed individuals direct access to divine realms, such as mediumship, divination, or ecstatic experiences, were often deemed threatening to the church's control.

The church labeled such practices as "witchcraft," "sorcery," or "paganism" and often associated them with demonic activity to create fear. This ensured that people relied on clergy as intermediaries between themselves and God, effectively blocking their direct connection to spirit. The church emphasized the idea that only ordained clergy could commune with God or interpret spiritual matters, stripping the average person of their spiritual autonomy.

From a spiritual perspective, all humans possess the ability to connect with spirit, whether through intuition, dreams, prayer, or other means. This connection is natural and rooted in the divine essence present within all people. Practices like mediumship, prophecy, and visions were originally seen as gifts available to all, as referenced in Joel 2:28, "... I will pour out my Spirit on all people. Your sons and daughters will prophesy, your old men will dream dreams, your young men will see visions."

By labeling spirit communication as evil or dangerous, institutions created fear and mistrust around these practices. Spirit communication was often associated with demonic forces, even though many cultures had long understood it as a sacred act of connecting with ancestors or the divine. Fear-based doctrines alienated people from their innate spiritual abilities, fostering dependence on religious institutions for guidance and validation.

Spirit, from a broader perspective, represents the divine energy that permeates all creation. It is the essence of God, the universal consciousness, or the Source that connects all living beings. When individuals commune with spirit, they are accessing this universal energy to receive guidance, healing, and insight.

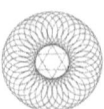

The Bible itself provides numerous examples of spirit communication, such as the transfiguration of Jesus (Matthew 17:1-3), the visions of the prophets (Ezekiel, Isaiah, Daniel), and the Pentecost event where the Holy Spirit descended upon the apostles (Acts 2:1-4). These instances demonstrate that spirit communication is not inherently evil but rather a divine gift.

The fear-based narrative propagated by institutions like the Roman Catholic Church can be seen as an attempt to maintain control rather than encourage individual empowerment. Reclaiming spiritual autonomy involves recognizing that every individual has the ability to connect with spirit and that this connection is a divine birthright.

While certain scriptures warn against mediums and necromancy, others affirm that God desires direct communication with His people, such as in these verses: "Call to me and I will answer you and tell you great and unsearchable things you do not know" (Jeremiah 33:3) and "My sheep listen to my voice; I know them, and they follow me" (John 10:27)

By understanding the historical context of how fear was used to suppress spiritual practices, individuals can reclaim their connection to spirit as a natural and divine process. Spirit communication, when done with love, respect, and intention, aligns with the universal teachings of seeking truth, guidance, and healing.

The Bible reflects a complex relationship with spirit communication, blending divine revelations with cultural and institutional biases. While fear was instilled to discourage practices like mediumship, the deeper truth is that everyone has the ability to commune with spirit. This connection, when rooted in love and divine alignment, empowers humanity to access higher wisdom and live in harmony with the divine essence that connects all. Reclaiming this understanding is part of rediscovering humanity's true spiritual potential.

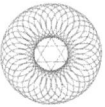

The Bible includes several examples and references to communication with spirits or the divine realm, which are often associated with prophecy, visions, and supernatural insight. However, the topic of mediumship, specifically communicating with the spirits of the deceased, is a more complex subject in biblical theology. The Bible generally discourages seeking mediums or necromancers, but there are instances where individuals communicate with spirits under divine circumstances. Below is a breakdown of examples and perspectives, both supportive and cautionary, that might align with mediumship:

- Saul and the Witch of Endor
  King Saul seeks out a medium (the Witch of Endor) to summon the spirit of the prophet Samuel. Samuel appears and delivers a prophecy to Saul about his impending death. (1 Samuel 28:7-19) While this account involves a medium, it also shows that God allowed Samuel's spirit to appear, suggesting that such communication can occur but should not be sought through forbidden practices.
- The Transfiguration of Jesus
  "There he was transfigured before them. His face shone like the sun, and his clothes became as white as the light. Just then there appeared before them Moses and Elijah, talking with Jesus" (Matthew 17:2-3) This event involves Jesus communicating with the spirits of Moses and Elijah. It demonstrates communication with the deceased in a divine and holy context, sanctioned by God.
- The Rich Man and Lazarus
  In this parable, the rich man speaks to Abraham after death, asking for help for his brothers on Earth. (Luke 16:19-31) While this interaction occurs in the afterlife, it implies the possibility of communication between realms.
- Souls under the Altar
  The following verse shows that the spirits of the deceased can communicate and petition in the heavenly realm.
  > When he opened the fifth seal, I saw under the altar the souls of those who had been slain because of the word of God and the testimony they had maintained. They called out in a loud voice, "How long, Sovereign

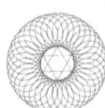

Lord, holy and true, until you judge the inhabitants of the earth and avenge our blood?" (Revelation 6:9-10)
- <u>The Great Cloud of Witnesses</u>
  "Therefore, since we are surrounded by such a great cloud of witnesses, let us throw off everything that hinders and the sin that so easily entangles ..." (Hebrews 12:1) This verse speaks of the saints who have passed on and are witnesses to the actions of those on Earth, suggesting a spiritual connection.

While there are instances of divine communication with the deceased, the Bible often warns against seeking mediums or engaging in necromancy, emphasizing reliance on God for guidance:
- "Do not turn to mediums or seek out spiritists, for you will be defiled by them. I am the LORD your God" (Leviticus 19:31)
- Let no one be found among you who ... practices divination or sorcery, interprets omens, engages in witchcraft, or casts spells, or who is a medium or spiritist or who consults the dead. Anyone who does these things is detestable to the LORD ... (Deuteronomy 18:10-12)
- "When someone tells you to consult mediums and spiritists, who whisper and mutter, should not a people inquire of their God? Why consult the dead on behalf of the living?" (Isaiah 8:19)

The Bible acknowledges spiritual gifts that involve communication with the divine, which can align with aspects of mediumship when done in accordance with God's will:
- "To another miraculous powers, to another prophecy, to another distinguishing between spirits, to another speaking in different kinds of tongues, and to still another the interpretation of tongues" (1 Corinthians 12:10) The gift of "distinguishing between spirits" may involve spiritual insight into the presence or nature of spirits.
- "And afterward, I will pour out my Spirit on all people. Your sons and daughters will prophesy, your old men will dream

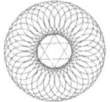

dreams, your young men will see visions" (Joel 2:28) Prophecy and visions often involve divine communication.
- "But the Advocate, the Holy Spirit, whom the Father will send in my name, will teach you all things and will remind you of everything I have said to you" (John 14:26) The Holy Spirit serves as the ultimate guide for spiritual communication and revelation.

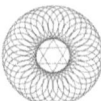

Energy Healing (Manipulating and Balancing Energies for Healing)

Energy healing is the ability to sense, channel, and manipulate energy to promote physical, emotional, and spiritual well-being. Practitioners connect with universal life force energy—such as Reiki, prana, or chi—to clear blockages, balance chakras, and restore harmony in the energy field. This process can involve hands-on techniques or be performed remotely through distance healing.

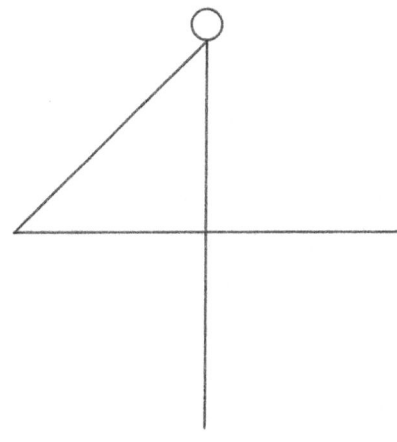

Rainbow Reiki
Energy Healing Symbol

Energy healing often manifests as sensations in the practitioner's hands, such as warmth, tingling, or a magnetic pull when channeling energy. Practitioners may intuitively sense areas of imbalance within the client's body or energy field, while clients frequently report feelings of warmth, deep relaxation, or emotional release during sessions. These experiences can range from subtle shifts to profound transformations, depending on the individual's needs and receptivity.

This modality heavily relies on clairsentience, allowing practitioners to feel energy imbalances, and claircognizance, offering intuitive guidance on how to direct the healing process. Telepathic abilities can also enhance energy healing by providing insight into the client's emotional or mental state, further deepening the connection and effectiveness of the healing session.

Energy Healing Across Traditions

Energy healing, the practice of channeling and balancing life force energy to promote physical, emotional, mental, and spiritual well-being, is a cornerstone of spiritual traditions in Egyptian, Tibetan, and galactic teachings. Across these systems, energy healing is

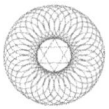

understood as a sacred art that restores harmony to the body, mind, and spirit by addressing imbalances in the energetic field.

In ancient Egypt, energy healing was deeply integrated into temple practices and closely linked to the principles of *heka* (divine magic) and Ma'at (cosmic balance). Egyptian healers believed that life force energy, often referred to as *ka*, flowed through the body and could be influenced through rituals, sacred oils, sound, and symbols. Healing ceremonies often utilized the power of sacred geometry, such as the ankh, and sound resonance within the acoustically tuned spaces of temples like Dendera. Energy healers, including priests and priestesses, acted as conduits for divine energy, channeling the wisdom and power of deities such as Sekhmet, Isis, and Thoth to realign the energetic body, clear blockages, and restore vitality.

Tibetan teachings emphasize energy healing as a natural extension of spiritual practice, rooted in the understanding of *prana* (life force energy) and the subtle body. Tibetan healers focus on balancing the energy centers, or chakras, and clearing pathways such as the *nadis* (energy channels) to ensure the free flow of prana. Techniques like Reiki (which has Tibetan influences), *Tsa Lung* (breathwork), and *mantra healing* are used to harmonize the energetic body. Tibetan medicine also incorporates natural remedies and visualization practices to clear energetic imbalances that manifest as physical or emotional ailments. Tibetan Buddhism views energy healing as an act of compassion and mindfulness, allowing the healer to serve as a channel for universal wisdom and love.

In galactic teachings, energy healing is described as an advanced multidimensional practice that taps into higher frequencies and cosmic energies. Galactic guides, such as the Arcturians and Pleiadians, often teach that energy healing involves the activation and recalibration of the human energetic system, including the DNA, auric field, and light body. Practices such as light code activations, crystal healing, and sound frequencies are used to raise the vibrational frequency of the body, clear karmic imprints, and align the individual with their divine blueprint. Galactic teachings emphasize that energy healing is a co-creative process between the

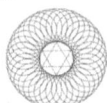

healer, the recipient, and higher-dimensional energies, fostering both individual and collective evolution.

Across these traditions, energy healing is seen as a sacred and powerful modality that restores balance and promotes holistic well-being. It requires alignment, integrity, and a deep connection to divine energy, ensuring that the healing serves the highest good of all. Whether performed through ritual, meditation, or multidimensional practices, energy healing reflects the universal truth that we are energetic beings, interconnected with the greater flow of life and capable of profound transformation and self-healing.

<u>Biblical References</u>
Energy healing, as a concept, aligns with various biblical principles and examples of divine healing, the laying on of hands, and the transfer of spiritual power. While the Bible does not use the modern term "energy healing," it frequently describes spiritual or divine forces flowing through individuals to heal, restore, and bring balance. These examples affirm that healing can occur through faith, touch, and spiritual alignment.
- The following passage supports the idea that believers have the power to channel healing energy through their hands, acting as vessels of divine power:
  > And these signs will accompany those who believe: In my name they will drive out demons; they will speak in new tongues; they will pick up snakes with their hands; and when they drink deadly poison, it will not hurt them at all; they will place their hands on sick people, and they will get well. (Mark 16:17-18)
- "At sunset, the people brought to Jesus all who had various kinds of sickness, and laying his hands on each one, he healed them" (Luke 4:40) Jesus consistently used touch to heal, indicating that physical contact could transfer divine or spiritual energy.
- The following passage illustrates the flow of divine energy from Jesus to the woman through touch, supporting the concept of energy transfer for healing:

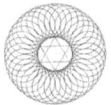

> When she heard about Jesus, she came up behind him in the crowd and touched his cloak, because she thought, "If I just touch his clothes, I will be healed." Immediately her bleeding stopped, and she felt in her body that she was freed from her suffering. At once Jesus realized that power had gone out from him. He turned around in the crowd and asked, "Who touched my clothes?" (Mark 5:27-30)

- "But Jesus said, 'Someone touched me; I know that power has gone out from me'" (Luke 8:46) Jesus directly acknowledges the movement of power or energy, affirming the spiritual principle of energy healing.
- The following example highlights that healing does not always require physical touch but can occur through faith and intention, which are fundamental principles of energy healing:

    > The centurion replied, "Lord, I do not deserve to have you come under my roof. But just say the word, and my servant will be healed." ... When Jesus heard this, me was amazed and said to those following him, "Truly I tell you, I have not found anyone in Israel with such great faith." (Matthew 8:8, 10)

- Here, Peter channels divine energy to heal, demonstrating that believers can act as conduits for God's healing power:

    > Then Peter said, "Silver or gold I do not have, but what I do have I give you. In the name of Jesus Christ of Nazareth, walk." Taking him by the right hand, he helped him up, and instantly the man's feet and ankles became strong. (Acts 3:6-7)

- The following passage suggests that spiritual energy can emanate from individuals to bring healing, even without direct touch:

    > As a result, people brought the sick into the streets and laid them on beds and mats so that at least Peter's shadow might fall on some of them as he passed by. Crowds gathered also from the towns around Jerusalem, bringing their sick and those

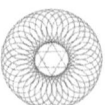

- tormented by impure spirits, and all of them were healed. (Acts 5:15-16)
- God is described as the ultimate source of healing, which believers can channel, as shown here:
    > He said, "If you listen carefully to the LORD your God and do what is right in his eyes, if you pay attention to his commands and keep all his decrees, I will not bring on you any of the diseases I brought on the Egyptians, for I am the LORD, who heals you." (Exodus 15:26)
- If the body is a temple of the Holy Spirit, then it naturally contains divine energy that can be used for healing and restoration:
    > Do you not know that your bodies are temples of the Holy Spirit, who is in you, whom you have received from God? You are not your own; you were bought at a price. Therefore honor God with your bodies. (1 Corinthians 6:19-20)
- The following passage shows that healing energy can be directed through prayer and faith:
    > Is anyone among you sick? Let them call the elders of the church to pray over them and anoint them with oil in the name of the Lord. And the prayer offered in faith will make the sick person well; the Lord will raise them up ... (James 5:14-15)
- "He heals the brokenhearted and binds up their wounds" (Psalm 147:3) Healing in the Bible often refers to both physical and emotional restoration, which aligns with energy healing principles that address mind, body, and spirit.

The biblical examples of Jesus and the apostles show that energy healing is a divine gift accessible to those who act in faith and alignment with God's will. Over time, institutionalized religion (such as during the Roman Catholic Church's centralization) created fear around spiritual practices like energy healing, labeling them as "pagan" or "demonic" to maintain control. However, these practices are deeply rooted in the Bible as divine expressions of faith and love.

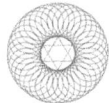

Spirit in the Bible is often described as the breath of life or divine essence (e.g., Genesis 2:7), which resonates with the idea of life force energy. The Holy Spirit, described as a source of power and guidance, aligns with the understanding of spiritual energy that can flow through believers to heal and restore.

The Bible provides numerous examples of energy healing through the laying on of hands, faith, prayer, and the flow of divine power. These principles affirm that energy healing is a natural and divinely inspired practice, accessible to those who align with God's will. Far from being something to fear or dismiss, energy healing reflects the biblical truth that God works through individuals to bring healing and restoration to the world.

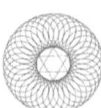

Bilocating (Perceiving or Traveling to Distant Locations)

Bilocation is the ability to perceive or energetically project awareness to a location, person, or event that is physically distant. This ability involves shifting consciousness to connect with the energy of a specific place or individual and can manifest through remote viewing, where one observes without being physically present, or astral projection, where the energy body is projected to another location.

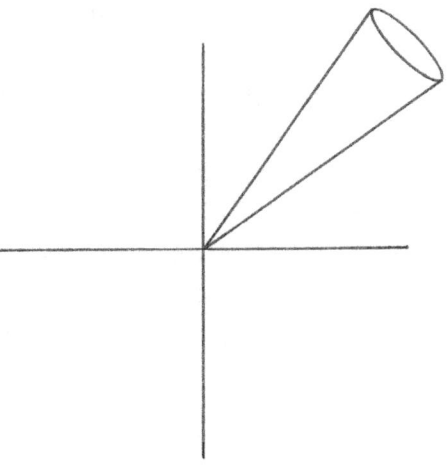

Rainbow Reiki Bilocating Symbol

Bilocation often appears as the visualization or sensing of details about a distant place or event. Practitioners may feel physically present in a location despite not being there or experiencing impressions about people or environments before arriving. These experiences typically occur in a deep meditative state, accompanied by vivid imagery or sensations, and can arise spontaneously or intentionally, particularly during meditation or dream states.

This gift works closely with clairvoyance, which allows for the visual perception of distant locations, and clairsentience, which helps sense the energy of the place or person. It can also complement telepathy, facilitating a deeper connection with individuals in the perceived location, making bilocation a powerful and multidimensional intuitive ability.

Bilocation Across Traditions

Bilocating, the ability to be present in two places simultaneously, is a phenomenon deeply rooted in Egyptian, Tibetan, and galactic teachings, where it is regarded as a sacred practice that transcends physical limitations and expands consciousness. Across these traditions, bilocation is seen not only as a mystical ability but also as a profound spiritual tool for exploring multidimensional realities, offering guidance, and engaging in higher service.

In ancient Egypt, bilocation was considered a manifestation of the soul's divine nature, particularly through the *ba* (spiritual aspect of the soul capable of movement and freedom). Egyptian priests and initiates in the Mystery Schools were trained to separate their spiritual essence from the physical body during deep meditative states, often in the resonant chambers of pyramids or temples. Through this practice, they could access other locations, sacred spaces, or even realms of the gods while maintaining awareness of their physical presence. This was used for guidance, healing, and receiving divine knowledge. Bilocation was believed to reflect the interconnected nature of existence, where the barriers of time and space dissolved, allowing the soul to serve the cosmic order of Ma'at.

In Tibetan teachings, bilocation is viewed as one of the *siddhis* (spiritual powers) attainable through advanced yogic and meditative practice. Known as *pratibhā* or a form of astral projection, Tibetan practitioners achieve bilocation by cultivating deep states of concentration and awareness. The subtle body, liberated from physical constraints, can travel to distant locations or other realms while the practitioner remains conscious of both realities. This ability is often used by advanced monks and yogis to assist others, deliver teachings, or connect with distant energies or beings. Tibetan Buddhism emphasizes that bilocation arises as a natural result of profound spiritual attainment, humility, and a compassionate intent to serve the collective good.

In galactic teachings, bilocation is described as a multidimensional skill that aligns with humanity's evolving spiritual potential. Galactic beings such as the Pleiadians and Arcturians explain that bilocation involves expanding one's consciousness beyond the third dimension, allowing the soul or energetic body to exist simultaneously in multiple locations or timelines. This is often achieved through practices like light body activation, raising one's vibrational frequency, and connecting to the universal energy grid.

Bilocation is used for a variety of purposes, including assisting others energetically, gathering information from other dimensions, and facilitating spiritual ascension. Galactic guides emphasize that bilocation is a co-creative process involving one's intention, alignment, and collaboration with higher-dimensional energies.

Across these traditions, bilocation is revered as a sacred gift that reflects the interconnectedness of all existence. It requires discipline, spiritual alignment, and a pure intent to ensure that this ability serves the highest good. Whether used to communicate with distant beings, explore higher realms, or provide energetic assistance, bilocation demonstrates the limitless potential of the human soul and its ability to transcend physical boundaries, offering a deeper understanding of the unity of all things.

Biblical References

Bilocation, the ability to be in two places simultaneously, is not explicitly named in the Bible. However, there are several instances in scripture that describe miraculous events or experiences where individuals are seen or present in two places or are transported supernaturally. These examples suggest a biblical basis for bilocation as a spiritual or divine phenomenon.

- The following account describes Philip being transported supernaturally by the Spirit of the Lord, appearing in another location instantly. While not traditional bilocation, it demonstrates supernatural movement that aligns with the concept:

    > When they came up out of the water, the Spirit of the Lord suddenly took Philip away, and the eunuch did not see him again, but went on his way rejoicing. Philip, however, appeared at Azotus and traveled about, preaching the gospel in all the towns until he reached Caesarea. (Acts 8:39-40)

- "Then their eyes were opened, and they recognized him, and he disappeared from their sight ... While they were still talking about this, Jesus himself stood among them and said to them, 'Peace be with you'" (Luke 24:31, 36) After His resurrection, Jesus appeared and disappeared in multiple

places, showing a supernatural ability to be present beyond physical limitations.
- "On the evening of that first day of the week, when the disciples were together, with the doors locked for fear of the Jewish leaders, Jesus came and stood among them and said, 'Peace be with you!'" (John 20:19) Jesus appeared in a locked room, indicating a spiritual presence that transcends physical barriers.
- Elisha describes his spirit witnessing an event that occurred elsewhere, suggesting a form of spiritual bilocation or remote presence:
   > But Elisha said to him, "Was not my spirit with you when the man got down from his chariot to meet you? Is this the time to take money or to accept clothes—or olive groves and vineyards, or flocks and herds, or male and female slaves?" (2 Kings 5:26)
- In the following passage, Paul's description of his experience suggests that he was simultaneously in a physical state and present in a spiritual realm, which aligns with the concept of bilocation:
   > I know a man in Christ who fourteen years ago was caught up to the third heaven. Whether it was in the body or out of the body I do not know—God knows. And I know that this man—whether in the body or apart from the body I do not know, but God knows—was caught up to paradise and heard inexpressible things, things that no one is permitted to tell. (2 Corinthians 12:2-4)
- "He had a dream in which he saw a stairway resting on the earth, with its top reaching to heaven, and the angels of God were ascending and descending on it" (Genesis 28:12) Angels often appear in multiple locations or transcend physical realms, which reflects the ability to exist in more than one place at once.
- "Are not all angels ministering spirits sent to serve those who will inherit salvation?" (Hebrews 1:14) This verse suggests that angels, as spiritual beings, have the ability to be present in multiple locations to fulfill their divine missions.

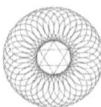

- "'Who can hide in secret places so that I cannot see them?' declares the LORD. 'Do not I fill heaven and earth?' declares the LORD" (Jeremiah 23:24) God's omnipresence is a foundational principle, and while humans are not omnipresent, being created in God's image may allow for extraordinary spiritual experiences like bilocation through divine empowerment.
- "Very truly I tell you, whoever believes in me will do the works I have been doing, and they will do even greater things than these, because I am going to the Father" (John 14:12) This suggests that believers, empowered by the Holy Spirit, may experience extraordinary spiritual phenomena, possibly including bilocation.
- "But whoever is united with the Lord is one with him in spirit" (1 Corinthians 6:17) Spiritual unity with God may grant believers access to supernatural abilities beyond the physical realm.

The concept of bilocation is not foreign to Christian mysticism. Numerous saints are reported to have experienced bilocation, including St. Padre Pio, known for reportedly appearing in two places at once to help those in need; and St. Alphonsus Liguori. Witnesses claimed he appeared at a dying person's bedside while also remaining in his monastery.

Bilocation in the Bible and historical accounts often serves a divine purpose: healing, revelation, protection, or spiritual teaching. It is never self-serving but aligns with God's will to accomplish His plans.

While bilocation is not explicitly named in the Bible, various accounts demonstrate a precedent for supernatural presence or spiritual transport. Jesus, prophets, and apostles exhibited abilities that transcend physical limitations, which align with the concept of bilocation. These occurrences often highlight divine power working through individuals for a higher purpose. Additionally, historical Christian mysticism supports the idea of bilocation as a spiritual gift granted by God for service and ministry.

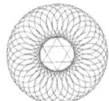

Channeling (Connecting with Higher Consciousness)

Channeling is the ability to connect with and receive guidance, information, or energy from higher consciousness, spiritual beings, or universal wisdom. This transformative gift enables individuals to act as a bridge or vessel for messages from realms beyond the physical, offering healing, wisdom, and inspiration for both the channeler and those they serve. Channeling can involve connecting with various sources, such as spirit guides, ascended masters, angels, universal consciousness, the higher self, or even deceased loved ones or ancestors. Its purpose is to provide insight, healing, and understanding that transcend the limitations of the ego and physical world.

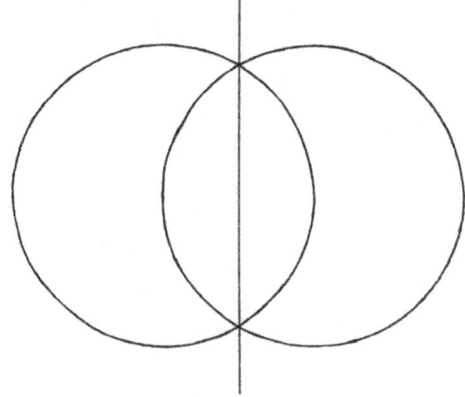

Rainbow Reiki Channeling Symbol

This process involves raising one's vibration to align with the frequency of the spiritual source, while the source lowers its vibration to facilitate the connection. Channeling can occur in different modes, such as conscious channeling, where the channeler remains fully aware and actively translates messages; trance channeling, where the channeler enters a deep meditative state, allowing the source to speak or act directly through them; and intuitive channeling, where messages are perceived as thoughts, feelings, or impressions. As a conduit, the channeler allows energy and information to flow through them while maintaining personal boundaries.

Channeling often manifests in various ways, including receiving words, ideas, or spontaneous downloads of complex knowledge. Physical sensations such as warmth, tingling, or pressure in the head, throat, or heart can accompany the experience, along with feelings

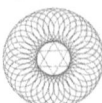

of peace, connection, or lightness. Messages may also come through behavioral changes, such as speaking in a tone or style different from the channeler's norm, or through automatic writing. Visual impressions like symbols, images, or visions may further enhance the messages received. For the channeler, it may feel like stepping aside to let information flow, often accompanied by a sense of trust and clarity. For the receiver, the messages resonate deeply, offering validation, guidance, or healing.

Channeling can take many forms, including spiritual guidance from spirit guides or ancestors, energy channeling for healing, creative channeling for artistic inspiration, or transdimensional channeling, where connection is made with beings or consciousness from other dimensions. This ability is deeply interconnected with other intuitive gifts, such as claircognizance (clear knowing), clairaudience (clear hearing), and clairvoyance (clear seeing), which help interpret and complement the messages. Channeling may also overlap with mediumship and can enhance energy healing and telepathic communication.

To enhance channeling abilities, practices like meditation, journaling, grounding, and energy work are vital. Trusting intuition and creating a safe, clear energetic space are essential to fostering strong, reliable connections. Channeling can be applied in personal growth, offering clarity and spiritual understanding; in healing, by providing emotional or spiritual support; in guiding others through spiritual wisdom; and in creative inspiration, channeling ideas that resonate with universal truths.

The ethics of channeling are critical, requiring pure intentions, strong boundaries, and discernment to ensure that messages align with love and truth. By maintaining humility and self-awareness, channelers can avoid ego interference and serve as effective vessels for higher consciousness. With practice and intention, channeling evolves into a powerful tool for transformation, integrating divine wisdom into everyday life and fostering profound spiritual connection.

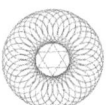

Channeling Across Traditions

Channeling, the ability to receive and convey messages, energy, or knowledge from higher realms, spirits, ancestors, or cosmic beings, is a profound spiritual practice honored in Egyptian, Tibetan, and galactic teachings. This ability is seen as a bridge between dimensions, enabling the channeler to access divine wisdom and serve as a conduit for spiritual guidance and healing.

In ancient Egypt, channeling was an integral part of temple practices and spiritual leadership. Priests and priestesses, especially those devoted to deities such as Isis, Thoth, and Sekhmet, were highly trained to act as intermediaries between the divine and humanity. Through rituals, meditation, and sacred ceremonies, they would align their energy to receive messages and energies from the gods, ancestors, or cosmic forces. Egyptian channeling often took place within sacred spaces, such as temples and pyramids, designed to amplify spiritual connection through their geometry and resonance. Symbols like the ankh and the Eye of Horus were used to enhance the flow of divine energy, allowing channelers to deliver messages of guidance, healing, or prophecy with clarity and integrity.

In Tibetan teachings, channeling aligns with the practice of connecting with enlightened beings, bodhisattvas, and spiritual energies for the benefit of others. Tibetan oracles, for instance, enter altered states of consciousness to receive messages or guidance from deities or protectors. Advanced monks and practitioners develop this ability through years of meditation, breathwork, and visualization, which purify the mind and attune the practitioner to higher vibrations. Tibetan Buddhism emphasizes the ethical responsibility of channeling, ensuring that the messages received are rooted in compassion, wisdom, and the intention to alleviate suffering. Channeling is also used to connect with ancestral wisdom and to guide souls in their transition or karmic journey.

Galactic teachings view channeling as a multidimensional ability that allows individuals to connect with higher-dimensional beings, collectives, or universal consciousness. Galactic guides, such as the Pleiadians, Arcturians, and other star beings, teach that channeling

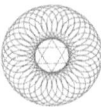

is a natural ability of the human soul, often dormant until activated through vibrational alignment, DNA recalibration, or energetic practices. Channeling in this context involves receiving messages encoded in light, sound, or intuitive impressions, which are then translated through the channeler's consciousness. Practices such as meditation, grounding, and heart-brain coherence are essential for developing this skill. Galactic teachings stress that channeling is not limited to verbal messages—it can manifest as creative expressions, energetic transmissions, or healing frequencies meant to assist in humanity's spiritual evolution.

Across these traditions, channeling is seen as a sacred gift requiring dedication, integrity, and alignment with higher spiritual principles. The channeler must cultivate humility, emotional clarity, and a strong connection to their own higher self to ensure that the messages or energies received are accurate and for the highest good. Whether delivering divine wisdom, facilitating healing, or connecting others to universal truth, channeling is a powerful practice that embodies the unity of all life and the limitless potential of the human spirit to connect with the greater cosmos.

Biblical References
The concept of channeling or receiving messages or insights from spiritual realms or divine sources, has parallels in the Bible, particularly in the experiences of prophets, apostles, and other biblical figures. While the term "channeling" is not explicitly used in scripture, there are numerous examples of individuals serving as vessels through which God, the Holy Spirit, or divine beings communicate. Below, we explore biblical support and context for channeling, along with its alignment with scripture.
- "Then the LORD reached out his hand and touched my mouth and said to me, 'I have put my words in your mouth'" (Jeremiah 1:9) Jeremiah served as a direct channel for God's words, receiving and speaking divine messages.
- "As he spoke, the Spirit came into me and raised me to my feet, and I heard him speaking to me" (Ezekiel 2:2) Ezekiel's experience demonstrates the Spirit entering him and using him as a vessel for communication.

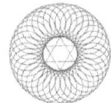

- Here, Jesus explicitly states that His words are not His own but come directly from the Father, exemplifying the ultimate channeling of divine will:
    > For I did not speak on my own, but the Father who sent me commanded me to say all that I have spoken. I know that his command leads to eternal life. So whatever I say is just what the Father has told me to say. (John 12:49-50)
- "But when he, the Spirit of truth, comes, he will guide you into all the truth. He will not speak on his own; he will speak only what he hears, and he will tell you what is yet to come" (John 16:13) The Holy Spirit serves as a divine communicator, channeling God's truth and revelations to believers.
- "All of them were filled with the Holy Spirit and began to speak in other tongues as the Spirit enabled them" (Acts 2:4) The apostles channeled the Holy Spirit, speaking languages they did not know, demonstrating divine communication flowing through them.
- "On the Lord's Day I was in the Spirit, and I heard behind me a loud voice like a trumpet, which said: 'Write on a scroll what you see and send it to the seven churches ...'" (Revelation 1:10-11) John receives visions and messages directly from the spiritual realm, acting as a channel for the Book of Revelation.
- "During the night the mystery was revealed to Daniel in a vision. Then Daniel praised the God of heaven" (Daniel 2:19) Daniel channels divine wisdom to interpret King Nebuchadnezzar's dream, a process that involves receiving insight from God.
- "To another miraculous powers, to another prophecy, to another distinguishing between spirits, to another speaking in different kinds of tongues, and to still another the interpretation of tongues" (1 Corinthians 12:10) Prophecy involves channeling divine messages, often through inspiration from the Holy Spirit.
- "All Scripture is God-breathed and is useful for teaching, rebuking, correcting and training in righteousness" (2

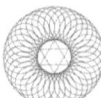

Timothy 3:16) This affirms that the Bible itself was written by individuals who acted as channels for divine inspiration.

- "And afterward, I will pour out my Spirit on all people. Your sons and daughters will prophesy, your old men will dream dreams, your young men will see visions" (Joel 2:28) This prophecy speaks of widespread spiritual channeling, where people receive divine messages through dreams, visions, and prophecy.
- The Bible is clear that channeling should be done in alignment with God and under the guidance of the Holy Spirit. Communication with divine sources (e.g., God, the Holy Spirit, angels) is encouraged. "For those who are led by the Spirit of God are the children of God" (Romans 8:14) Spiritual communication is valid when aligned with the Holy Spirit and God's will.
- "Dear friends, do not believe every spirit, but test the spirits to see whether they are from God, because many false prophets have gone out into the world" (1 John 4:1) This passage emphasizes discernment in spiritual communication, ensuring that the source is divinely aligned.
- While divinely inspired communication is supported, practices that involve unauthorized or harmful spirits are discouraged.

> Let no one be found among you who sacrifices their son or daughter in the fire, who practices divination or sorcery, interprets omens, engages in witchcraft, or casts spells, or who is a medium or spiritist or who consults the dead. Anyone who does these things is detestable to the LORD ... (Deuteronomy 18:10-12)

In the early church, the institutionalization of Christianity (e.g., through the Roman Catholic Church) often discouraged or suppressed personal spiritual practices that allowed individuals to commune directly with spirit. This was partly to centralize spiritual authority within the clergy. However, scripture consistently supports the idea that all believers have access to divine communication when guided by the Holy Spirit.

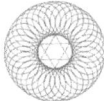

- Scripture affirms that all believers can channel divine messages when aligned with God. "But you have an anointing from the Holy One, and all of you know the truth" (1 John 2:20)
- "For you can all prophesy in turn so that everyone may be instructed and encouraged" (1 Corinthians 14:31) This demonstrates that prophecy, a form of channeling, is accessible to all believers for the purpose of teaching and encouragement.
- The Bible describes spirit as the "breath of life" (Genesis 2:7), connecting all living beings to God. Channeling divine energy, guidance, or wisdom is a natural expression of this connection.

The Bible provides strong support for the concept of channeling as a form of divine communication. Prophecy, visions, dreams, and spiritual insight are all examples of individuals serving as vessels for God's messages. While scripture warns against unauthorized spiritual practices, it emphasizes that channeling through the Holy Spirit is a sacred and accessible gift for all believers. This ability connects humanity to the divine, empowering individuals to act as conduits of love, truth, and healing.

Discover Your Dominant Spiritual Gift
Developing and strengthening intuitive and metaphysical abilities requires dedication, practice, and openness to higher frequencies of awareness. To enhance clairvoyance (clear seeing), practice visualization exercises, meditate regularly to quiet your mind, and work with your third eye chakra. Paying attention to dreams and symbolic imagery in everyday life can also deepen your intuitive vision. For clairaudience (clear hearing), create a practice of deep listening in silence, activate your throat and ear chakras through chanting or singing, and trust any subtle auditory messages or phrases that arise intuitively.

Strengthening clairsentience (clear feeling) involves cultivating body awareness through practices like yoga, breathwork, and mindfulness. Pay attention to the sensations in your body and

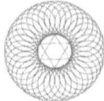

emotions when entering new spaces or meeting people, as these can be subtle indicators of energy. Developing claircognizance (clear knowing) requires trust in spontaneous insights or thoughts that seem to arise without logical reasoning. Journaling and reflecting on these moments can help distinguish genuine intuitive knowledge from random ideas.

To enhance clairalience (clear smelling) and clairgustance (clear tasting), heighten your sensory awareness by practicing mindful eating and paying attention to subtle scents and tastes that may carry intuitive meaning. These abilities are often linked to strong memories or emotional connections, so being receptive to such associations is key.

Psychometry, the ability to read energy from objects, can be developed by holding personal items and noting the impressions, images, or feelings they evoke. Practice with items from friends or loved ones to validate your insights.

Building telepathic abilities involves honing your empathy and mental focus. Practice sending and receiving thoughts with trusted individuals or pets to develop this connection. For mediumship, meditation and grounding are essential to connect with spirits in a safe, protected space. Working with experienced mentors or attending workshops can also provide guidance. Energy healing can be strengthened by studying energy systems like Reiki or Qigong and practicing grounding, cleansing, and focusing your energy flow.

Advanced practices like bilocating, the ability to project your awareness to another location, and channeling, receiving messages from higher realms, require disciplined meditation and a deep trust in your inner guidance. For bilocating, visualization exercises and remote viewing techniques can help; for channeling, creating a sacred space, setting intentions, and entering a receptive state are vital. Across all these practices, self-care, grounding, and protection are crucial to maintaining balance and well-being as you expand your spiritual abilities.

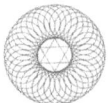

Dominant Spiritual Gift Self-Assessment

Instructions: For each question, choose the option that resonates most with you. At the end, tally your answers to determine your dominant spiritual gift.

1. How do you most often receive intuitive insights?
    a) I see vivid images, symbols, or dreams.
    b) I hear voices, sounds, or words internally.
    c) I feel emotions or sensations in my body.
    d) I just know things without understanding how.
    e) I notice distinct smells connected to memories or meanings.
    f) I sometimes taste flavors that are not physically present.

2. In new environments, what stands out most to you?
    a) The visual details or atmosphere.
    b) The sounds, tones, or conversations.
    c) The energy or emotional vibes of the space.
    d) A sudden realization about the space or people in it.
    e) Subtle scents that others might not notice.
    f) An unusual taste or impression in your mouth.

3. When holding an object, do you:
    a) See flashes of imagery or events associated with it?
    b) Hear a message or name connected to its history?
    c) Feel an emotional connection or physical sensation?
    d) Instantly know something about its past or owner?

4. How do you most naturally connect with others?
    a) Through interpreting visual cues or body language.
    b) Through deeply understanding their words or tone.
    c) Through sensing their emotions or energy.
    d) Through understanding their needs without them explaining.

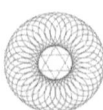

5. Do you often:
   a) Have detailed and meaningful dreams or visions?
   b) Hear guidance in the form of inner or external voices?
   c) Feel physical sensations that align with others' experiences?
   d) Receive random, clear insights that later prove true?
   e) Smell fragrances that evoke emotions or memories without a source?
   f) Taste something unusual when certain events occur?

6. Do you find it easy to:
   a) Imagine or visualize scenes in great detail?
   b) Hear subtle changes in sound, tone, or music?
   c) Sense shifts in emotional or energetic states?
   d) Solve problems or offer advice without needing much information?
   e) Pick up on scents that others do not notice?
   f) Experience phantom tastes that carry meaning?

7. In moments of heightened intuition, do you:
   a) See visions or flashes of insight?
   b) Hear messages, music, or phrases?
   c) Feel chills, warmth, or emotional waves?
   d) Know the answer without knowing why?
   e) Smell something significant to the situation?
   f) Taste something unique or symbolic?

Scoring:
- Mostly As: You are dominant in Clairvoyance (Clear Seeing).
- Mostly Bs: You are dominant in Clairaudience (Clear Hearing).
- Mostly Cs: You are dominant in Clairsentience (Clear Feeling).
- Mostly Ds: You are dominant in Claircognizance (Clear Knowing).
- Mostly Es: You are dominant in Clairalience (Clear Smelling).
- Mostly Fs: You are dominant in Clairgustance (Clear Tasting).

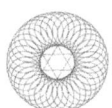

Advanced Abilities:

If none of these feel dominant, consider exploring these gifts:

- Psychometry: Focus on the questions related to holding objects.
- Telepathy: Reflect on your ability to understand others mentally.
- Mediumship: Pay attention to questions about receiving messages or connecting with energies.
- Energy Healing: Notice how you respond to emotional or physical sensations.
- Bilocating: Consider your ease with visualizing yourself in other places.
- Channeling: Reflect on whether you often feel like a vessel for higher wisdom.

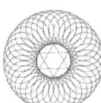

Guided Meditation: Discover Your Dominant Spiritual Gift

Find a quiet, comfortable space where you will not be disturbed. Sit or lie down in a relaxed position. Close your eyes, take a deep breath, and let go of any tension in your body. Feel grounded and present. Take a deep breath in through your nose, and exhale slowly. Feel yourself relaxing deeper with each breath. Imagine a warm, golden light surrounding you, protecting and calming your energy. This light creates a safe and sacred space for exploration. Visualize roots growing from the base of your spine or your feet, anchoring you deeply into the earth. Feel the earth's nurturing energy rising through these roots, grounding you. Now, see a beam of light descending from above, entering the crown of your head, connecting you to divine wisdom.

Exploration of the Senses
Clairvoyance (Clear Seeing)
In your mind's eye, imagine yourself walking through a peaceful forest. Notice the colors, shapes, and details of your surroundings. As you move forward, ask, "What images or visions can guide me to my spiritual gift?" Allow any scenes, symbols, or flashes of insight to appear. Observe without judgment.

Clairaudience (Clear Hearing)
Pause and listen. Hear the sounds of the forest: rustling leaves, singing birds, a gentle breeze. Gradually, notice if any words, music, or voices come through. Ask, "What messages do I need to hear about my spiritual gift?" Trust the sounds that come to you.

Clairsentience (Clear Feeling)
Focus on your body. Feel the energy of the forest around you—perhaps the warmth of sunlight, the coolness of shade, or the gentle brush of the wind. Ask yourself, "What sensations or emotions point me to my spiritual gift?" Allow any feelings to surface.

Claircognizance (Clear Knowing)
Take a moment to simply be. Let go of effort and allow insights to arise. You might feel a sudden, clear thought or understanding about

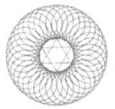

your gift. Ask, "What do I need to know about my spiritual gift?" Trust the clarity that comes.

Clairalience and Clairgustance (Clear Smelling and Tasting)
Breathe deeply and notice if any unique scents appear, perhaps the smell of flowers, spices, or something meaningful to you. Then, pay attention to your mouth. Do you sense a flavor or taste? Ask, "How do these sensations connect to my spiritual gift?"

Psychometry, Telepathy, Mediumship, Energy Healing, Bilocating, and Channeling
Imagine picking up an object in the forest. Feel its energy. Ask, "What can this object teach me about my abilities?" Visualize yourself connecting to another being or presence. Ask, "How can I use my gift to connect, heal, or guide?" Allow any impressions, thoughts, or feelings to come naturally.

Now, see yourself sitting in a clearing, surrounded by the gifts you have uncovered—images, words, feelings, or sensations. Thank the forest, your guides, and your higher self for this experience. Know that you can return here anytime to deepen your understanding. Bring your awareness back to your breath. Slowly wiggle your fingers and toes, and when you are ready, open your eyes. Take a moment to journal any impressions or messages you received during the meditation.

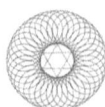

Grounding

Grounding is a therapeutic technique that involves connecting with the present moment to calm the mind and body. Its primary purpose is to help individuals manage intense emotions, anxiety, or dissociation, especially during stress, trauma responses, or overwhelming thoughts. Grounding can benefit anyone, but it is particularly useful for people experiencing chronic pain, anxiety, trauma-related conditions, or neurodivergent challenges.

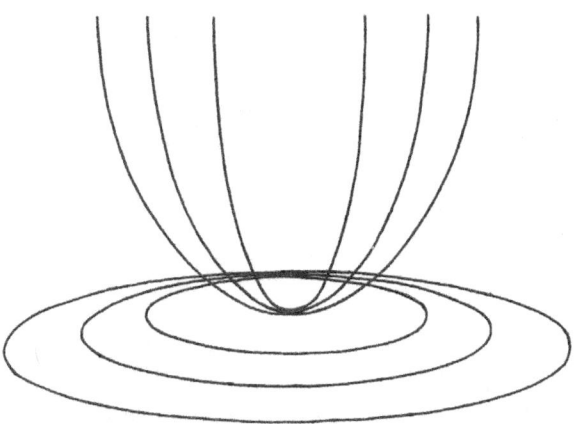

Rainbow Reiki Grounding Symbol

Grounding helps manage overwhelming feelings, allowing individuals to stay present and avoid emotional spirals. Techniques like deep breathing, body scans, or connecting with nature reinforce the mind-body connection. Grounding techniques encourage a sense of presence, which is particularly helpful for individuals with complex post-traumatic stress disorder (C-PTSD) or those who experience dissociation. Grounding provides stability and a sense of safety, which can be calming for those dealing with anxiety, post-traumatic stress disorder, or neurodivergent issues. By staying in the present, grounding practices can help individuals reconnect with their authentic selves, fostering self-acceptance and self-awareness. For those experiencing chronic pain or fatigue, grounding may help alleviate symptoms by directing focus away from the pain or discomfort and helping to release tension.

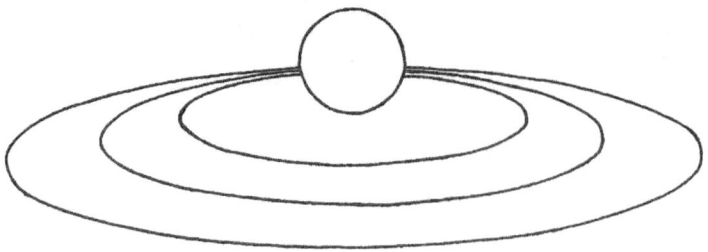

Rainbow Reiki Grounded Symbol

On a spiritual level, grounding is often seen as a way to connect deeply with the earth's energy and the present moment, fostering a sense of unity with nature and the universe. Grounding can help clear mental clutter and open up intuitive channels, allowing for clearer insights and a deeper connection to one's inner guidance. Spiritually, grounding creates a foundation, helping you feel rooted and supported. This sense of stability can promote inner peace, which is vital for navigating life's ups and downs. Many believe grounding helps the energy flow more freely through the body by releasing stagnant energy into the earth. This can lead to feeling more vibrant, open, and energetically balanced. Grounding can enhance your connection to both the Earth and the divine or universal consciousness. This connection can bring a sense of belonging, wholeness, and purpose. Grounding brings you back to your true essence, helping one to feel more authentic and aligned with who they truly are. Grounding is often seen as a protective practice, shielding oneself from external negative influences and strengthening their energy field. These benefits can be particularly meaningful on a healing journey, helping one feel more centered and aligned as they work through life's challenges. Grounding practices can involve direct physical contact with the Earth's surface, often through walking barefoot, sitting, or lying on natural surfaces like soil, grass, or sand. The practice is rooted in the belief that the earth's natural electric charge has health benefits. Modern research has begun to explore its implications in Western medicine, particularly in areas like inflammation, chronic pain, sleep disorders, and stress.

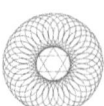

The earth's surface carries a mild negative charge of free electrons, which proponents suggest may balance the body's electrical systems, mitigate free radicals, and reduce inflammation. Grounding focuses on reconnecting the body to the earth's negative electrical potential.

Grounding Across Traditions
In ancient Egyptian teachings, grounding was deeply intertwined with the principles of balance, harmony, and connection to both the physical and spiritual realms. The Egyptians understood grounding as not only a physical practice but also a metaphysical process that aligned an individual with the earth's energy (Geb, the Earth deity) while maintaining harmony with cosmic forces (Nut, the Sky deity). Grounding was seen as essential for maintaining Ma'at—the principle of truth, balance, and divine order—which governed all aspects of life, from the cosmos to personal well-being.

In Egyptian spirituality, Geb, the god of the earth, was considered the source of physical stability and nourishment. The Egyptians viewed the earth as a living, sacred entity that provided humans with sustenance and a foundation for life. Being grounded meant maintaining a strong connection to Geb, ensuring that one's energy was rooted in the physical world while remaining in harmony with the spiritual realms. This connection was cultivated through rituals, prayers, and offerings to Geb, particularly during agricultural ceremonies, as the cycles of the earth were seen as reflections of divine rhythms.

The physical act of walking barefoot on the earth, especially near the Nile River, was seen as a way to draw energy from the life-giving soil and align oneself with the vitality of Geb. This practice mirrored modern grounding techniques, which emphasize connecting with the earth's natural energy for physical and emotional balance.

Ma'at, the goddess and concept of truth, balance, and cosmic order, was central to grounding in ancient Egypt. Grounding was not just a physical process but also a spiritual alignment with Ma'at. To be grounded in Ma'at meant to live in alignment with truth and

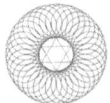

harmony, maintaining balance between the spiritual and material aspects of existence. This required mindfulness, ethical behavior, and a commitment to living a life of integrity.

The heart, considered the seat of the soul in Egyptian belief, was weighed against the feather of Ma'at in the afterlife. This act symbolized the importance of remaining grounded in righteousness during life. Practices such as meditation, prayer, and rituals to honor Ma'at were ways the Egyptians ensured their energy remained balanced and rooted in divine order.

The Egyptians believed in the Ka, the life force energy that connected the spiritual and physical bodies. The Ka was nourished by both physical sustenance and spiritual practices, such as grounding rituals. These rituals often included invoking the energies of specific deities, chanting sacred texts, or using tools like the ankh, which symbolized eternal life and the flow of energy between the heavens and the earth.

Grounding practices were also connected to the concept of energy centers, often symbolized by the serpent energy of the Uraeus (the cobra on the crowns of pharaohs). The Uraeus represented the activation and alignment of energy within the body, ensuring that one's spiritual essence was anchored in the physical realm while reaching toward higher consciousness.

The Nile River, the lifeblood of Egypt, played a crucial role in grounding practices. The Egyptians viewed the Nile as a divine entity, a source of renewal, and a bridge between the physical and spiritual realms. Ritual bathing, drinking its water, and meditating by its banks were grounding practices that connected individuals to the cycles of nature and the divine energy flowing through the earth.

Sacred natural spaces, such as the desert, were also considered grounding places for spiritual reflection and transformation. Pilgrimages to temples built in alignment with the earth's energy grids, such as those in Karnak and Abu Simbel, allowed individuals to attune themselves to the grounding energy of these sacred sites.

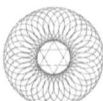

The Egyptians used sacred geometry in their temples and pyramids, which were designed to channel and amplify grounding energy. These structures were aligned with celestial bodies and the earth's magnetic fields to create spaces where individuals could meditate, pray, and connect with divine energies. The pyramids, in particular, were seen as energy hubs, grounding cosmic energy into the physical world.

By meditating or performing rituals within these spaces, the Egyptians believed they could align their energy with the universe and ground themselves in divine truth. These practices highlight the Egyptian understanding of the interconnectedness of the earth, the cosmos, and the human spirit.

Grounding was also practiced through the use of sacred tools and rituals, including:
- Incense and Oils: Frankincense and myrrh were commonly used to purify and ground energy during ceremonies, connecting the physical and spiritual realms.
- Amulets and Symbols: The ankh, djed pillar, and scarabs were worn or carried to ground the individual's energy and provide protection.
- Ritual Gestures: Specific postures and movements, such as standing with feet firmly planted and arms raised to the sky, symbolized the connection between the earth and the heavens.

In Egyptian spirituality, grounding was not just a practice, but a lifelong journey of balancing the material and spiritual worlds. The Egyptians saw humans as co-creators with the divine, responsible for maintaining harmony on Earth. Grounding practices ensured that individuals remained connected to their divine purpose while fulfilling their earthly responsibilities. By cultivating a deep connection with the earth and aligning with cosmic principles, the Egyptians believed that they could access higher states of consciousness while remaining firmly rooted in the stability and nourishment of the physical world. This balance, achieved through

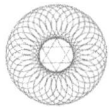

grounding, was key to living in accordance with Ma'at and achieving spiritual ascension.

Grounding in ancient Egyptian teachings was a holistic practice that integrated the physical, spiritual, and cosmic dimensions of life. It emphasized connection to Earth (Geb), alignment with divine order (Ma'at), and the nourishment of the life force (Ka). Through rituals, sacred geometry, nature, and mindfulness, the Egyptians developed a profound understanding of grounding as a way to achieve harmony with the universe and embody divine truth. These practices, rooted in ancient wisdom, continue to resonate with modern grounding techniques, revealing timeless principles of balance and connection.

In Tibetan teachings, grounding is a vital spiritual practice that emphasizes the integration of the body, mind, and spirit with the Earth's energy and the present moment. Grounding is viewed as essential for maintaining balance, stability, and clarity on the path to enlightenment. While many Tibetan practices focus on elevating consciousness and accessing higher spiritual states, grounding ensures that the practitioner remains connected to the physical body and the material world, facilitating harmony between the earthly and spiritual realms.

Tibetan Buddhism recognizes the prana (life force energy) flowing through the nadis (energy channels) and chakras of the subtle body. Grounding practices are used to anchor this energy within the lower chakras, particularly the root chakra, which is associated with stability, survival, and connection to the earth. Through grounding, practitioners ensure that the energetic body is balanced, preventing the overactivation of higher chakras, which can lead to feelings of disconnection or imbalance.

Tibetan meditation practices, such as shamatha (calm abiding), emphasize grounding as a foundation for deeper spiritual work. By focusing on the breath, the body, or a physical anchor like the sensation of sitting, practitioners center their awareness in the present moment, creating a stable base for higher states of

consciousness. Grounding through meditation allows practitioners to cultivate mindfulness and equanimity, ensuring that their spiritual insights are integrated into their daily lives.

Mantras, a cornerstone of Tibetan practice, are also used for grounding. Reciting mantras like "Om Mani Padme Hum" helps align the practitioner's energy with the earth while fostering a sense of connection to universal compassion. The vibrational resonance of these sacred sounds anchors the practitioner's energy while calming the mind and harmonizing the subtle body.

Tibetan practices often incorporate physical grounding techniques, such as prostrations and walking meditations. Prostrations are a dynamic way to connect the body to the earth while cultivating humility and reverence. Walking meditation encourages mindfulness of each step, creating a deep awareness of the physical connection to the earth and the present moment.

In Tibetan culture, nature is seen as a powerful ally for grounding. Mountains, rivers, and sacred landscapes are revered as living entities that offer grounding energy and spiritual guidance. Pilgrimages to sacred sites, such as Mount Kailash, are undertaken not only for spiritual elevation but also to harmonize one's energy with Earth's sacred vibrations.

Grounding in Tibetan teachings is also linked to bodhichitta (the awakened heart of compassion). Staying grounded allows practitioners to remain present with the suffering of others, fostering empathy and a commitment to alleviate it. By grounding their energy, practitioners maintain the balance needed to act with compassion and clarity, avoiding emotional overwhelm.

Tibetan teachings emphasize that true spiritual progress requires the integration of higher consciousness with everyday life. Grounding ensures that spiritual insights are not escapist but are instead embodied and applied in meaningful ways. It is a reminder that spiritual awakening is not separate from the physical world but is deeply intertwined with it.

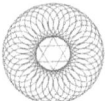

In Tibetan practice, grounding is seen as both a practical and spiritual discipline, ensuring stability, balance, and a strong foundation for the transformative journey toward enlightenment. By grounding their energy, practitioners remain deeply connected to the earth while expanding their awareness to higher realms, embodying the harmony between the physical and spiritual dimensions of existence.

Arcturian and Pleiadian teachings on grounding offer profound insights into balancing higher-dimensional energies with earthly existence. Both groups emphasize the importance of connecting with Earth's energy to create stability while integrating spiritual growth and ascension. The Arcturians, known for their mastery of energy and frequency, focus on grounding as a means of anchoring divine light into the physical body. They teach that visualization practices, such as imagining a column of golden or crystalline light descending through the body and into the earth's core, allow individuals to stabilize their energy while connecting to the planet's vibrational grid. Sacred geometry, such as the Merkaba or other geometric patterns, is often incorporated into their grounding practices to harmonize the physical and etheric bodies with Earth's energy fields. They also emphasize the importance of aligning with Earth's natural frequencies, such as the Schumann Resonance, to maintain coherence between body, mind, and spirit.

The Pleiadians, on the other hand, approach grounding through a more heart-centered and emotional perspective. They emphasize grounding as a way to anchor unconditional love and joy into the earth while fostering a nurturing connection with Gaia, the consciousness of the planet. Pleiadian teachings often involve connecting to Earth through the heart chakra, visualizing a flow of pink or green light extending from the heart into Earth's crystalline core. This practice fosters an exchange of energy that stabilizes emotions and enhances spiritual alignment. The Pleiadians also highlight the role of joy, play, and creative expression as natural grounding methods, reminding individuals to embrace the physical experience fully. They encourage engaging with nature—walking

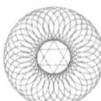

barefoot on the earth, meditating by water, or simply observing natural beauty—as a way to ground and harmonize with Gaia's energies.

Both Arcturians and Pleiadians emphasize the importance of multidimensional grounding, which involves anchoring not only the physical body but also the emotional, mental, and spiritual aspects of one's being. They stress the role of presence and mindfulness in grounding, encouraging individuals to remain in the "now" while navigating higher frequencies. Gratitude for the earth and the physical body is a shared cornerstone of their teachings, as it strengthens the connection to the planet and helps anchor higher vibrational energies. They also teach that grounding is essential for integrating the ascension process, ensuring that individuals remain balanced and avoid feeling overwhelmed or disconnected while working with higher-dimensional energies. By fostering this deep connection to Earth, both the Arcturians and Pleiadians guide humanity toward embodying its divine purpose while staying rooted in the beauty and stability of the physical world.

Biblical References
The concept of grounding, or connecting to the earth and balancing one's energy, can find support in biblical principles and passages that emphasize the relationship between humans, God, and creation. While the term "grounding" itself is not directly mentioned in the Bible, the idea of being deeply rooted in faith, connected to the earth, and aligned with God's natural order is a recurring theme. Below are scriptures and explanations that support the practice of grounding, both spiritually and physically.
- "Then the Lord God formed a man from the dust of the ground and breathed into his nostrils the breath of life, and the man became a living being" (Genesis 2:7) This verse highlights humanity's direct connection to the earth, as humans were formed from the dust of the ground. It emphasizes that the earth is part of our essence and a source of connection to God.
- "The earth is the Lord's, and everything in it, the world, and all who live in it; for he founded it on the seas and

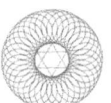

established it on the waters" (Psalm 24:1-2) This passage reminds us that the earth is sacred and belongs to God, encouraging believers to honor and connect with it as part of His creation.
- "All go to the same place; all come from dust, and to dust all return" (Ecclesiastes 3:20) This verse reinforces humanity's connection to the earth and the cyclical nature of life, reminding us of our grounding in God's creation.
- "So then, just as you received Christ Jesus as Lord, continue to live your lives in him, rooted and built up in him, strengthened in the faith as you were taught, and overflowing with thankfulness" (Colossians 2:6-7) Being "rooted" in Christ symbolizes a deep spiritual grounding that brings strength, stability, and growth.
- The following passage draws a parallel between spiritual grounding in God and the grounding of a tree with deep roots. It speaks to the importance of being deeply connected and stable to weather life's challenges:

  > But blessed is the one who trusts in the Lord, whose confidence is in him. They will be like a tree planted by the water that sends out its roots by the stream. It does not fear when heat comes; its leaves are always green. It has no worries in a year of drought and never fails to bear fruit. (Jeremiah 17:7-8)
- Grounding oneself in love and faith brings spiritual stability and the ability to remain steadfast:

  > I pray that out of his glorious riches he may strengthen you with power through his Spirit in your inner being, so that Christ may dwell in your hearts through faith. And I pray that you, being rooted and established in love ... (Ephesians 3:16-17)
- "He says, 'Be still, and know that I am God; I will be exalted among the nations, I will be exalted in the earth'" (Psalm 46:10) Grounding often involves stillness and mindfulness. This verse encourages believers to find peace and connection in the stillness of God's presence.
- "He makes me lie down in green pastures, he leads me beside quiet waters, he refreshes my soul. He guides me along the

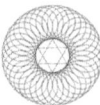

right paths for his name's sake" (Psalm 23:2-3) This passage highlights the restorative power of nature and God's creation. Spending time in natural settings can help believers feel grounded and refreshed spiritually.
- "Look at the birds of the air; they do not sow or reap or store away in barns, and yet your heavenly Father feeds them. Are you not much more valuable than they?" (Matthew 6:26) Observing and connecting with creation reminds us of God's providence and our place within the natural order.
- "Humble yourselves before the Lord, and he will lift you up" (James 4:10) Grounding involves humility, recognizing our dependence on God and our place in His creation.
- "He has shown you, O mortal, what is good. And what does the LORD require of you? To act justly and to love mercy and to walk humbly with your God" (Micah 6:8) Walking humbly with God reflects spiritual grounding—being aware of one's relationship with God and creation.
- The following passage reflects the interconnectedness of all life and the wisdom inherent in creation, supporting the idea of grounding in the earth as a way to reconnect with God's power:
    > But ask the animals, and they will teach you, or the birds in the sky, and they will tell you; or speak to the earth, and it will teach you, or let the fish in the sea inform you. Which of all these does not know that the hand of the LORD has done this? In his hand is the life of every creature and the breath of all mankind. (Job 12:7-10)
- "For since the creation of the world God's invisible qualities—his eternal power and divine nature—have been clearly seen, being understood from what has been made, so that people are without excuse" (Romans 1:20) Nature reveals God's divine qualities, and grounding in creation allows us to experience His power and presence more fully.

The Bible provides strong support for grounding, both in a physical and spiritual sense. Scripture encourages believers to:
- Connect with Earth as part of God's creation.

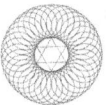

- Be rooted in faith, love, and God's truth for stability and spiritual strength.
- Find peace in nature, which reflects God's presence and restores the soul.

Grounding is a practice that aligns with biblical principles of humility, mindfulness, and connection to God through His creation. Whether through being still, walking in nature, or rooting oneself in faith, grounding helps believers realign their energy and spirit with the divine order established by God.

Grounding Implications in Western Medicine
Reduction of Inflammation
- Chronic inflammation is a root cause of many diseases, including autoimmune disorders, cardiovascular conditions, and arthritis.
- Research indicates that grounding may reduce inflammation by neutralizing free radicals in the body. This happens as electrons flow from the earth into the body, potentially stabilizing excess positive charges.
- A 2010 study published in the Journal of Alternative and Complementary Medicine reported reductions in inflammation markers after grounding practices.

Pain Relief
- Grounding has been linked to reduced chronic pain, including musculoskeletal pain and headaches. The anti-inflammatory effect of free electrons is believed to help alleviate pain over time.
- A 2004 pilot study showed improvements in chronic pain among participants using earthing mats.

Improved Sleep Quality
- Grounding may regulate cortisol levels, a stress hormone that disrupts sleep.
- A study found that participants who used grounding sheets during sleep experienced improved circadian rhythms and

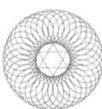

reduced night-time cortisol levels, leading to deeper and more restful sleep.

Stress and Mental Health Benefits
- Grounding practices reduce sympathetic nervous system activity (fight or flight) while increasing parasympathetic nervous system activity (rest and digest).
- This shift can help reduce stress, improve mood, and support mental well-being.
- The calming effects of physical contact with nature align with emerging practices like ecotherapy and forest bathing (Shinrin-yoku).

Improved Cardiovascular Health
- Grounding has been shown to improve blood flow and reduce blood viscosity, a risk factor for heart disease. Thinner blood is associated with a reduced risk of clots and cardiovascular events.

Immune System Regulation
- By reducing chronic inflammation and oxidative stress, grounding may improve immune function. This is particularly relevant for individuals with autoimmune conditions or chronic illnesses.

While grounding is still considered an alternative practice, studies are prompting interest in its mechanisms and potential integration into mainstream medicine. Western medicine demands robust clinical evidence. Existing studies on grounding are limited in sample size and methodology, which calls for further large-scale, peer-reviewed trials. Grounding aligns with the broader shift in Western medicine toward integrative approaches, emphasizing natural, low-risk, and cost-effective therapies to complement conventional treatments.

Grounding or earthing practices provide a bridge between ancient wisdom and modern science, offering a simple and accessible way to promote health and well-being. Emerging research in Western

medicine supports its potential to reduce inflammation, improve sleep, and alleviate pain. While more clinical validation is needed, grounding reflects a growing awareness of the mind-body-environment connection in modern healthcare.

Multidimensional Grounding Techniques

Multidimensional grounding is a holistic approach to staying present and centered across physical, emotional, mental, and spiritual dimensions. Using these practices together can provide a more robust grounding experience, balancing multiple dimensions of your being at once.

Physical Grounding

- Earthing: Spend time walking barefoot on natural surfaces like grass, soil, or sand to connect directly with the earth.

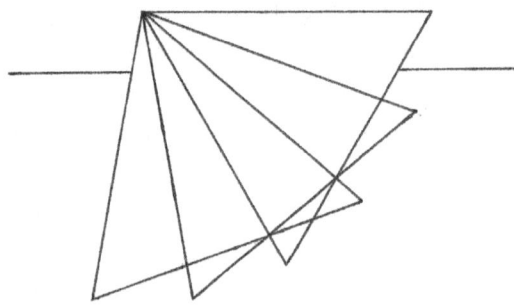

Rainbow Reiki Physical Grounding Symbol

- Breath-Body Scan: Sit or lie down and focus on each part of your body from head to toe while breathing deeply, releasing tension with each exhale.
- Weighted Objects: Holding a weighted blanket or item can help anchor the body and provide comfort.

Emotional Grounding
- Emotion Naming: Label what you are feeling without judgment. This can provide a sense of control and awareness.
- Journaling: Write out your emotions as they arise, helping you identify and process what's going on within you.
- Self-Compassion Mantras: Use affirmations that acknowledge your feelings and promote self-compassion, like, "It is okay to feel this way."

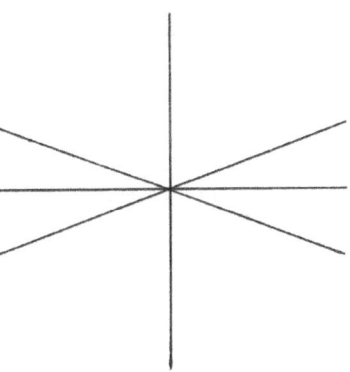

Rainbow Reiki
Emotional Grounding Symbol

Mental Grounding
- Mindful Breathing: Focus fully on your breath, observing each inhale and exhale, to bring awareness to the present moment.
- Counting Backwards: Count down slowly from 100 by 3 to focus the mind and shift it from racing thoughts.
- Visual Focus: Fix your gaze on an object and observe it in detail to break the cycle of anxious or intrusive thoughts.

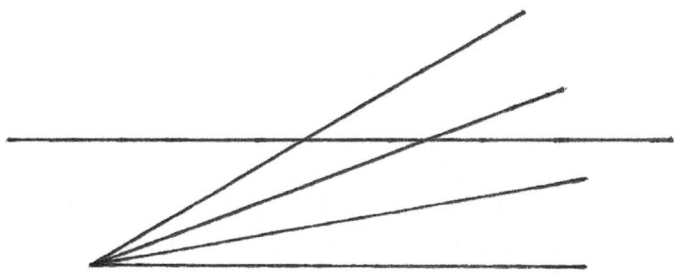

Rainbow Reiki Mental Grounding Symbol

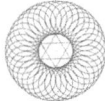

Energetic or Spiritual Grounding
- Visualize Roots: Imagine roots extending from your body into the earth, connecting you to its core, providing stability and strength.
- Connecting with Nature: Spending time outdoors, noticing the natural elements, can help you feel a deeper connection with the universe.
- Light Meditation: Picture a warm, grounding light entering your body, filling it with energy that grounds and balances you on a spiritual level.

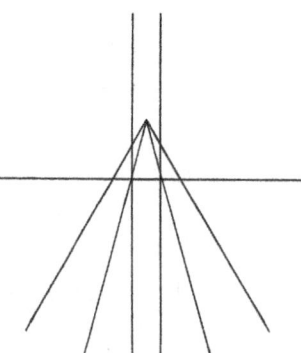

Rainbow Reiki Energetic/Spiritual Grounding Symbol

Relational Grounding
- Connecting with a Trusted Person: Have a grounding conversation with someone who offers you comfort and stability.
- Family or Ancestor Reflection: Reflect on the qualities or support of ancestors or loved ones, seeing them as a source of grounding energy.
- Physical Contact: Holding hands, hugging, or even gently tapping a loved one's shoulder can help create a grounded connection.

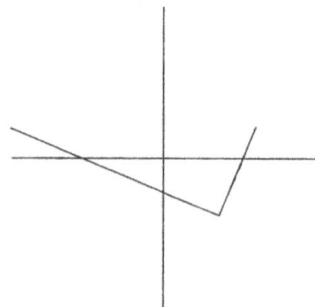

Rainbow Reiki Relational Grounding Symbol

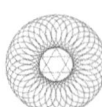

Creative Grounding
- Drawing or Painting: Create without specific goals; let your emotions flow onto the page, grounding you through creative expression.
- Music and Rhythm: Listening to or creating rhythmic sounds, like drumming, can ground you by connecting you to a steady beat.
- Dance or Movement: Move intuitively to music, allowing your body to express itself, creating a grounded connection with your physical and emotional self.

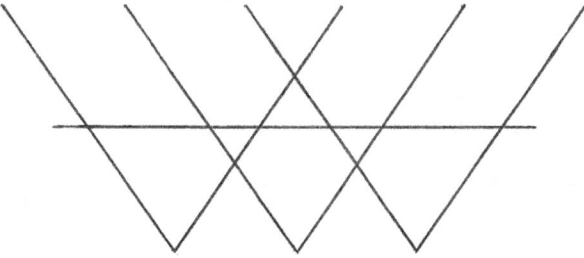

Rainbow Reiki Creative Grounding Symbol

Guided Meditation: Grounding Techniques for Beginners
Find a comfortable, quiet place where you will not be disturbed. Sit with your feet flat on the ground or lie down if that feels better. Close your eyes, take a deep breath in through your nose, and exhale slowly through your mouth. Let go of any tension and bring your focus to the present moment. Grounding is about connecting to the earth's energy to feel balanced, centered, and secure. This practice will guide you to release tension, anchor yourself, and regain a sense of calm and stability.

Awareness of the Body
Start by bringing your attention to your body. Feel the weight of your body pressing into the chair or floor. Notice the points of contact—your feet on the ground, your back against the chair, or your hands resting on your lap.
- Take a deep breath in, and as you exhale, feel yourself settling into the earth.
- Say to yourself: *"I am here. I am present. I am grounded."*

Root Visualization
Now, imagine roots growing from the soles of your feet and the base of your spine.
- See these roots extending downward, deep into the earth, through layers of soil and rock.
- Feel the earth's energy surrounding your roots, strong and nurturing.
- With each breath, visualize the roots growing deeper, anchoring you securely.

Energy Exchange with the Earth
Imagine the earth's energy rising through your roots.
- Feel this energy as a warm, golden light entering your feet and traveling up through your legs, into your body.
- As this energy flows upward, it clears away tension, negativity, or anything that does not serve you.
- On your exhale, imagine releasing any stress or heaviness through your roots back into the earth, where it is transformed into light.

Grounding Through Sensory Awareness
Bring your attention to your senses to deepen your grounding.
- Notice the temperature of the air on your skin.
- Listen to the sounds around you—whether it is silence, the hum of a fan, or distant noises.
- Focus on the scent of the air or any fragrances nearby.
- Wiggle your toes and feel the texture of the ground beneath you.

Affirmations for Grounding
Silently or aloud, repeat grounding affirmations:
- *"I am rooted and stable."*
- *"I release what no longer serves me."*
- *"I am connected to the earth's energy."*

Closing Visualization
Visualize your entire body surrounded by a cocoon of protective, grounding energy.
- See this energy as a shield that keeps you calm and centered throughout your day.
- Feel gratitude for the earth and its support and take a moment to thank yourself for taking this time to connect.

Gently bring your awareness back to your surroundings. Wiggle your fingers and toes, and slowly open your eyes. Take a few moments to stretch or move and carry this grounded energy with you as you go about your day.

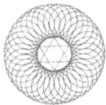

Advanced Guided Meditation: Grounding Without Chakra Focus

Find a quiet, comfortable place where you can sit or lie down. Close your eyes, take three deep breaths, and let go of any tension in your body. Feel yourself present and connected to the space you occupy. Grounding without chakra focus relies on sensory awareness, connection to nature, and visualization to anchor your energy. This meditation will guide you into a profound connection with the earth using imagery and sensory integration.

Rooting into the Earth

Begin by imagining your body as a strong, ancient tree.
- Visualize your legs and feet transforming into roots, growing downward into the soil.
- Feel these roots twisting and weaving through layers of the earth, stones, and water, until they reach the earth's core.
- Sense the strength and stability of these roots as they anchor you firmly to the planet.
- Take a deep breath in, and as you exhale, feel yourself sinking deeper into this grounded state.

Sensory Awareness

Bring your attention to your immediate physical surroundings.
- Focus on what you feel: the texture of the surface beneath you, the weight of your body, or the temperature of the air on your skin.
- Listen for subtle sounds in the environment—perhaps birdsong, wind, or the hum of silence.
- If possible, imagine the scent of earth after rain or the crisp freshness of nature.

Let these sensations connect you more deeply to the present moment and the Earth.

Connection to Nature's Elements

Imagine yourself in a serene natural setting, such as a forest, meadow, or by the ocean.
- *Earth:* Feel the stability of the ground beneath you, solid and unyielding. Imagine its weight supporting you fully.

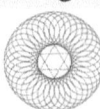

- *Water:* Picture a clear, flowing stream nearby. Imagine its gentle energy flowing through you, washing away tension, and refreshing your spirit.
- *Air:* Envision a soft breeze brushing against your skin, clearing mental clutter and bringing clarity.
- *Fire:* See the warm light of the sun above you, energizing and revitalizing your entire being.

Allow yourself to fully integrate the nurturing energy of these elements.

Magnetic Connection to the Earth
Visualize the earth's magnetic field surrounding you like an invisible embrace.
- Imagine this magnetic force pulling away any excess or chaotic energy from your body, leaving you balanced and calm.
- Feel your body aligning harmoniously with this field, as if you are resonating with the heartbeat of the planet.

With each breath, sense your connection to the earth growing stronger and more profound.

Releasing Through Visualization
Picture a golden thread of light extending from the top of your head down through your body, passing into your roots and deep into the earth.
- Imagine this thread carrying away any stress, negativity, or heaviness you may be holding.
- As these energies travel down the thread, see them dissolving into the earth, where they are transformed into neutral, nourishing energy.

Inhale deeply, feeling yourself grow lighter, and exhale fully, letting go of anything unnecessary.

Anchoring Energy with Breath
Begin a rhythmic breathing pattern: inhale for a count of four, hold for four, and exhale for four.
- With each inhale, imagine drawing in the strength and vitality of the earth.
- With each exhale, feel yourself sinking deeper into your connection with the ground.

Continue this for several cycles, feeling more anchored with every breath.

Energy Shielding and Integration
Visualize a layer of protective energy forming around you, like a bubble of light.
- This shield is connected to the earth, creating a steady flow of grounded energy.
- It allows you to feel calm and stable, no matter what happens in your external environment.

Take a deep breath and silently affirm: *"I am grounded. I am connected. I am stable and secure."*
Slowly bring your awareness back to your physical body. Wiggle your fingers and toes, roll your shoulders, and stretch gently. When you are ready, open your eyes, taking a moment to appreciate the calm and stability within you.

Carry this grounded energy with you, knowing you can return to this practice anytime you need balance and strength.

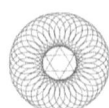

Guided Meditation: Discover Your Strongest Grounding Method

Find a quiet, comfortable space where you will not be disturbed. Sit or lie down in a relaxed position, close your eyes, and take a deep breath in through your nose. Exhale slowly through your mouth, letting go of any tension. Allow yourself to fully settle into the present moment.

Grounding connects us to stability, balance, and inner calm. Each person resonates with a unique method. In this meditation, we will explore a variety of grounding techniques to help you discover which feels most natural and powerful for you.

Breathing Into Presence
Take a deep breath, feeling the air fill your lungs, and exhale slowly.
- Repeat this breathing pattern, and as you do, imagine yourself entering a peaceful, open landscape filled with diverse grounding opportunities.
- Silently affirm: *"I am open to discovering the grounding method that aligns with my essence."*

Exploring Grounding Methods
In your mind's eye, you come across different grounding methods. Pause with each one and notice how it feels to connect with its energy.

Method 1: Mountains
Imagine yourself standing at the base of a massive, ancient mountain.
- Feel the solid, immovable strength beneath your feet.
- Sense the mountain's grounding energy rising into your body, providing stability and permanence.
- Ask yourself: *"Do I feel most grounded by this unshakable presence?"*

Method 2: Water
Picture yourself sitting by a calm, flowing river or serene lake.
- Hear the gentle movement of water and feel its cool, cleansing energy surrounding you.

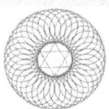

- Visualize the water washing away stress and anchoring you in a state of flow and peace.
- Ask yourself: *"Does the soothing, fluid energy of water feel like my strongest grounding method?"*

Method 3: Waterfalls
Stand before a powerful, cascading waterfall.
- Feel its dynamic, rushing energy grounding you in vitality and renewal.
- Imagine standing under the waterfall, letting its force cleanse and energize you.
- Ask yourself: *"Does the invigorating energy of the waterfall ground me most deeply?"*

Method 4: Roots
Visualize strong, thick roots growing from your feet and extending deep into the earth.
- Sense these roots anchoring you firmly, drawing nourishment and stability from the earth's core.
- Feel the organic connection grounding your entire being.
- Ask yourself: *"Does this natural, rooted connection resonate with me?"*

Method 5: Electrical Plug
Picture yourself as an electrical device connecting to a cosmic power outlet.
- See a bright cord extending from your body, plugging securely into a glowing energy source.
- Feel the steady, modern, and powerful energy flowing through you.
- Ask yourself: *"Does this efficient and empowering method ground me best?"*

Method 6: Sand
Imagine walking barefoot on soft, warm sand.
- Feel the grains shifting under your feet, connecting you to the earth in a comforting, tactile way.
- Sense the grounding warmth of the sun on your skin and the earth beneath you.

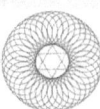

- Ask yourself: *"Do I feel most connected and grounded in this sandy, tactile environment?"*

Method 7: Trees
Visualize yourself leaning against a large, ancient tree.
- Feel its strong, solid trunk supporting your back and its roots extending deep into the earth.
- Imagine absorbing the tree's timeless wisdom and steady energy.
- Ask yourself: *"Does the energy of this living tree ground me most deeply?"*

Method 8: Stones
Picture yourself holding a smooth, heavy stone in your hands.
- Feel its solid weight, representing stability and endurance.
- Sense its cool, grounding energy calming your mind and body.
- Ask yourself: *"Does the presence of this stone help me feel the most grounded?"*

Method 9: Earth Embodiment
Imagine lying flat on the earth itself, feeling the soil, grass, or rock beneath you.
- Feel your body melting into the ground, fully supported by the planet.
- Sense a profound connection with the earth's energy enveloping and grounding you.
- Ask yourself: *"Do I feel most grounded when I embody the earth this way?"*

Reflecting on the Experience
Take a moment to consider which method resonated most deeply.
- Was there one visualization that made you feel calm, balanced, or more connected than the others?
- Reflect on the sensations, emotions, or energy shifts you experienced with each method.

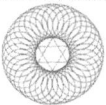

Anchoring Your Chosen Method
Return to the grounding method that felt the strongest for you.
- Spend a few moments fully immersed in its visualization.
- Allow its energy to flow through you, anchoring you deeply in stability and connection.
- Silently affirm: *"This is my grounding method. I can return to it whenever I need balance and calm."*

Take a deep breath in, feeling the grounding energy of your chosen method. As you exhale, bring your awareness back to your physical body. Wiggle your fingers and toes, stretch gently, and open your eyes when you are ready.

Carry this sense of grounding with you throughout your day and know that you can return to your chosen method anytime you need it.

Advanced Guided Meditation: Grounding Techniques with Chakra Introduction

Find a quiet, comfortable place where you can sit or lie down. Close your eyes, take a few deep breaths, and allow your body to relax. This meditation will combine grounding techniques with an advanced exploration of the chakra system to deepen your connection to the earth and your energetic body.

Grounding is the practice of connecting to the earth and balancing your energy. This meditation will guide you through advanced grounding techniques while introducing the main seven chakras. Each chakra plays a role in your energetic balance and connection to the earth.

Centering with Breath Awareness
Begin by taking a deep breath in, holding it for a moment, and exhaling slowly.
- With each breath, imagine yourself becoming more centered and present.
- Silently affirm: *"I am here. I am open. I am ready to connect."*

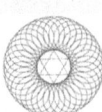

Aligning with the Chakras and Grounding Energy

Visualize a column of light running from the top of your head to the base of your spine, representing your chakra system. As you connect with each chakra, you will explore grounding techniques that harmonize with their energy.

Root Chakra (Muladhara): Grounding Through Roots

Located at the base of your spine, the root chakra represents stability and grounding.
- Imagine deep roots growing from the base of your spine and the soles of your feet, extending into the earth.
- Feel these roots connecting you to the earth's core, drawing up nourishing energy.
- Silently affirm: *"I am grounded. I am safe. I am supported."*

Sacral Chakra (Svadhisthana): Grounding Through Water

Located below your navel, the sacral chakra represents flow and emotions.
- Visualize yourself sitting by a calm, flowing river.
- Imagine the water cleansing and grounding your energy, bringing balance to your emotions.
- Silently affirm: *"I flow with life. I am in harmony with my energy."*

Solar Plexus Chakra (Manipura): Grounding Through the Sun

Located in your stomach area, the solar plexus represents confidence and power.
- Picture a warm, golden sun above you, its rays beaming down onto your body.
- Feel the sun's energy entering your core, radiating stability and personal strength.
- Silently affirm: *"I am strong. I am confident. I am steady."*

Heart Chakra (Anahata): Grounding Through Trees

Located in the center of your chest, the heart chakra represents love and connection.
- Imagine yourself leaning against a strong, ancient tree.

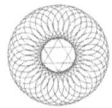

- Feel the tree's energy flowing into your heart, connecting you to nature and the earth.
- Silently affirm: *"I am connected. I am love. I am balanced."*

Throat Chakra (Vishuddha): Grounding Through Sound
Located at your throat, the throat chakra represents communication and expression.
- Visualize a gentle, vibrating tone resonating from your throat, grounding your voice and energy.
- Imagine the sound anchoring you deeply into the present moment.
- Silently affirm: *"I speak my truth. I am aligned with the earth."*

Third Eye Chakra (Ajna): Grounding Through Mountains
Located between your eyebrows, the third eye chakra represents insight and intuition.
- Visualize yourself standing at the base of a towering, ancient mountain.
- Feel the mountain's strength and wisdom grounding your intuition and mind.
- Silently affirm: *"I trust my vision. I am grounded in clarity."*

Crown Chakra (Sahasrara): Grounding Through Cosmic Light
Located at the top of your head, the crown chakra represents connection to the divine.
- Picture a beam of violet or white light descending from the cosmos into your crown.
- As the light travels through your body, it merges with the earth energy rising from your roots.
- Silently affirm: *"I am connected to the earth and the universe."*

Integrating and Balancing Energy
Now visualize all seven chakras glowing brightly in harmony, connected by the central column of light.
- Feel the grounding energy of the earth rising through your root, flowing up through each chakra, and merging with the cosmic energy at your crown.

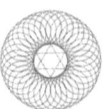

- Allow this balanced energy to expand outward, filling your entire aura with stability and connection.

Anchoring with Your Chosen Method
Reflect on the grounding technique or chakra that felt the strongest for you.
- Return to its visualization—whether roots, water, trees, the sun, or another element—and immerse yourself in its energy.
- Silently affirm: *"This is my grounding method. I can return to it whenever I need stability and balance."*

Take a deep breath in, feeling the grounded, balanced energy within you. As you exhale, bring your awareness back to your physical body. Wiggle your fingers and toes, stretch gently, and open your eyes when you are ready.

Carry this grounded and aligned energy with you and know you can revisit this practice whenever you need it.

Chakras

Traditional Chakras

Chakras are energy centers within the body, each associated with different aspects of physical, emotional, and spiritual well-being. The word "chakra" means "wheel" in Sanskrit, symbolizing the way these energy centers spin and flow. There are seven main chakras, aligned along the spine from the base to the crown of the head, each linked to different qualities and purposes.

1. *Root Chakra (Muladhara)*: Located at the base of the spine, this chakra is associated with stability, security, and basic needs. It is the foundation of grounding and feeling safe.

2. *Sacral Chakra (Svadhisthana)*: Located in the lower abdomen, it governs emotions, creativity, pleasure, and relationships.

3. *Solar Plexus Chakra (Manipura)*: Located in the stomach area, this chakra is tied to confidence, personal power, and self-discipline.

4. *Heart Chakra (Anahata)*: Positioned at the center of the chest, it is linked to love, compassion, and connection with others.

5. *Throat Chakra (Vishuddha)*: Found in the throat area, it governs communication, self-expression, and truth.

6. *Third Eye Chakra (Ajna)*: Located between the eyebrows, this chakra is associated with intuition, wisdom, and inner guidance.

7. *Crown Chakra (Sahasrara)*: Positioned at the top of the head, it is connected to spiritual awareness, higher consciousness, and unity with the universe.

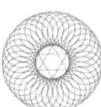

Each chakra influences different areas of life, and when they are balanced and open, energy flows freely, contributing to overall well-being. Imbalances or blockages in any chakra can lead to physical or emotional challenges, which is why many spiritual practices focus on aligning and balancing these energy centers.

Advanced Chakras

The advanced chakras extend beyond the seven main chakras and are part of a higher-dimensional system that can be accessed for deeper spiritual exploration and healing. These advanced chakras facilitate a deeper level of spiritual awakening, self-awareness, and alignment with universal consciousness. Working with them can help you explore profound spiritual realms, enhance intuitive abilities, and experience a greater sense of unity with Earth and the cosmos.

8. *Earth Gateway Chakra*: Located just below the Earth Star Chakra, this chakra connects deeply with the Earth's core energy. It is involved in grounding on a cosmic scale, offering access to Earth's ancient wisdom and nurturing energies, and is often connected to environmental awareness and Earth healing.

9. *Earth Star Chakra*: Located about 6-12 inches below the feet, this chakra connects your energy body with Earth, anchoring you and enhancing stability. It serves as a grounding portal and is associated with the soul's history, past lives, and connection to Earth's healing energy.

10. *Soul Star Chakra*: Situated 6-12 inches above the crown chakra, the Soul Star Chakra connects to the soul's higher purpose, spiritual gifts, and past-life wisdom. It is the gateway to the higher self and facilitates the release of karmic imprints, connecting you to divine purpose and spiritual ascension.

11. *Stellar Gateway Chakra*: Located above the Soul Star Chakra, the Stellar Gateway provides access to higher spiritual realms and the collective consciousness. It is associated with cosmic wisdom and

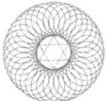

multidimensional awareness, often acting as a channel for higher knowledge and experiences beyond time and space.

12. *Universal Gateway Chakra*: Extending further beyond the Stellar Gateway, the Universal Gateway Chakra allows connection to universal energy and collective consciousness. It is linked to enlightenment, helping access universal truths and a deep understanding of oneness with all existence.

13. *Cosmic Gateway Chakra*: Situated even higher above the Universal Gateway, the Cosmic Gateway is the doorway to cosmic consciousness and universal wisdom, encompassing all dimensions and timelines. This chakra allows for full immersion in universal love and the realization of unity with the cosmos.

14. *Hand Chakras (Hrit)*: Located at the center of each palm, hand chakras are associated with giving and receiving energy. They are commonly activated for energy healing, such as Reiki, and are essential in channeling, creating, and sharing energy with others and the environment.

15. *Feet Chakras (Pada)*: Found in the soles of the feet, these chakras support grounding and the release of excess or stagnant energy into the earth. They help absorb Earth's energy, allowing balance, grounding, and a stronger connection to natural rhythms and stability.

16. *Knee Chakras*: Located in the knees, these chakras support flexibility and forward movement in life. They are connected to one's life path, resilience, and the ability to adapt and embrace change, allowing for balance between persistence and surrender.

17. *Chakra at the Base of the Skull*: Often called the "Mouth of God" or "Well of Dreams," this chakra is positioned at the base of the skull and is associated with spiritual insight, psychic abilities, and dream interpretation. It connects the higher spiritual realms with physical perception, supporting higher vision, intuition, and clear inner guidance.

18. *Telepathic Chakras*: These energy centers include the Third Eye Chakra, located at the center of the forehead, and subtle energy points around the temples and behind the ears. The telepathic chakras govern intuitive communication, mental clarity, and the ability to send and receive thoughts or emotions energetically. They enhance extrasensory perception, psychic abilities, and spiritual insight, fostering profound connection with others and the universal flow of wisdom.

Blocked Chakras
When the 18 chakras are blocked, it can create imbalances that affect various aspects of physical, emotional, mental, and spiritual health.

1. *Root Chakra*: Feelings of instability, insecurity, and anxiety, as well as physical issues in the lower body and adrenal fatigue.

2. *Sacral Chakra*: Creative blocks, emotional numbness, relationship issues, or reproductive and urinary health concerns.

3. *Solar Plexus Chakra*: Low self-esteem, lack of personal power, and issues with digestion and energy.

4. *Heart Chakra*: Difficulty with giving/receiving love, lack of compassion, and respiratory or circulatory issues.

5. *Throat Chakra*: Problems with self-expression, difficulty in communication, and issues with the throat and thyroid.

6. *Third Eye Chakra*: Poor intuition, difficulty concentrating, and headaches or vision problems.

7. *Crown Chakra*: Lack of purpose, disconnectedness from spirituality, and depression or alienation.

8. *Earth Gateway Chakra*: Lack of connection to environmental awareness and difficulty grounding spiritual practices, which can lead to feeling isolated from Earth.

9. *Earth Star Chakra*: Feelings of being ungrounded, unstable, or "lost" and struggling with life purpose or ancestral healing.

10. *Soul Star Chakra*: Karmic patterns or past life issues may feel unresolved, leading to a sense of disconnect from your higher self or true purpose.

11. *Stellar Gateway Chakra*: Difficulty connecting with higher dimensions or universal knowledge, potentially leading to a sense of limited spiritual awareness.

12. *Universal Gateway Chakra*: Blocked access to unity consciousness, creating a sense of separation from the universe and an inability to understand cosmic patterns.

13. *Cosmic Gateway Chakra*: A blocked cosmic gateway can prevent access to advanced states of consciousness, limiting spiritual growth and the ability to experience oneness.

14. *Hand Chakras*: Difficulty in giving or receiving energy, blocking the flow needed for healing or creative work; this can result in feeling creatively stagnant or disconnected from others.

15. *Feet Chakras*: Challenges with grounding and a sense of being "rooted" in life; may experience restlessness or feel unable to "put down roots" in any one area.

16. *Knee Chakras*: Resistance to change, rigidity in life, and difficulty moving forward; these blocks can manifest as physical stiffness or emotional inflexibility.

17. *Chakra at the Base of the Skull (Mouth of God or Well of Dreams)*: Blockages here can inhibit spiritual insights, restrict psychic abilities,

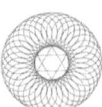

and make it hard to trust inner guidance. Physically, it can lead to tension in the neck and head.

18. *Telepathic Chakras*: Blockages here can result in mental fog, difficulty accessing intuition, and challenges with sending or receiving energy, thoughts, or emotions. Such blocks may hinder your connection to universal wisdom and higher realms, leaving you feeling disconnected from your intuitive and psychic abilities.

Implications of Widespread Blockages
When multiple chakras are blocked, especially across these advanced centers, it can create complex disruptions in the energy body, affecting emotional resilience, mental clarity, physical health, and spiritual growth.
- Physical and Mental Fatigue: Energy struggles to circulate, leading to low vitality.
- Emotional Instability: Difficulty processing or expressing emotions.
- Disconnection from Purpose: Sense of aimlessness or lack of meaning.
- Spiritual Confusion: Difficulty accessing higher consciousness and connecting with one's true self.
- Energetic Imbalance: Inability to ground or expand one's energy, leading to scattered focus and poor resilience against stress.

Each chakra, traditional or advanced, plays a role in keeping the system balanced, resilient, and flowing. Maintaining openness and alignment across all 17 chakras can support holistic well-being, promote spiritual evolution, and enhance connection with both Earth and the universe.

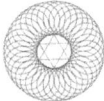

Guided Meditation: Clear and Re-align Blocked Chakras (Beginner Level)

Find a quiet, comfortable space where you will not be disturbed. Sit or lie down in a relaxed position. Close your eyes, take a few deep breaths, and allow your body to settle. This meditation will gently guide you through each chakra, clearing and balancing its energy. Take a deep breath in, and as you exhale, imagine letting go of any tension or stress. Visualize a column of light running from the top of your head to the base of your spine. This is your chakra system, your body's energetic highway. Together, we will clear and re-align each of these energy centers.

Root Chakra (Muladhara)
Located at the base of your spine, the root chakra represents stability and grounding.
- Visualize a glowing red light at the base of your spine.
- With each inhale, imagine this light growing brighter and stronger.
- With each exhale, release any fear, tension, or feelings of instability.
- Silently affirm: *"I am safe. I am grounded. I am supported."*

Sacral Chakra (Svadhisthana)
Located below your navel, the sacral chakra governs creativity and emotions.
- Picture a warm, orange light glowing in your lower abdomen.
- Breathe in, allowing this light to expand, filling the area with warmth and vitality.
- Exhale and let go of emotional blockages or creative stagnation.
- Silently affirm: *"I am creative. I am in flow. I embrace joy."*

Solar Plexus Chakra (Manipura)
Located in your stomach area, the solar plexus chakra is the center of confidence and personal power.
- Visualize a bright yellow light shining in your stomach.
- With each inhale, feel this light radiating outward like the sun.

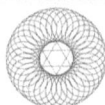

- With each exhale, release self-doubt, fear, or hesitation.
- Silently affirm: *"I am strong. I am confident. I am capable."*

Heart Chakra (Anahata)
Located in the center of your chest, the heart chakra is the seat of love and compassion.
- Picture a soft green light glowing at your heart center.
- Breathe deeply, feeling this light expanding and radiating love outward.
- Exhale and release past hurts, grief, or feelings of unworthiness.
- Silently affirm: *"I am love. I am compassionate. I give and receive freely."*

Throat Chakra (Vishuddha)
Located at your throat, the throat chakra governs communication and self-expression.
- Visualize a clear blue light glowing in your throat.
- Inhale, letting this light clear away any blockages to your voice.
- Exhale, releasing fear of speaking your truth or being misunderstood.
- Silently affirm: *"I speak my truth. I express myself clearly and authentically."*

Third Eye Chakra (Ajna)
Located between your eyebrows, the third eye chakra is your center of intuition and insight.
- Imagine an indigo light glowing at your third eye.
- With each inhale, feel this light expanding, opening your inner vision.
- Exhale and release doubt, confusion, or mental clutter.
- Silently affirm: *"I trust my intuition. I see clearly and wisely."*

Crown Chakra (Sahasrara)
Located at the top of your head, the crown chakra connects you to divine energy and universal wisdom.

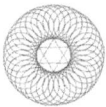

- Picture a violet or white light glowing at the crown of your head.
- Inhale, allowing this light to flow through your entire body, connecting you to the universe.
- Exhale and release feelings of disconnection or isolation.
- Silently affirm: *"I am connected. I am aligned with divine energy and wisdom."*

Closing: Full Chakra Alignment

Visualize all seven chakras glowing brightly, perfectly aligned, and connected by a column of light.
- Take a deep breath, imagining energy flowing freely through your entire body.
- Feel balanced, clear, and at peace.
- Silently affirm: *"My energy flows freely. I am balanced, aligned, and whole."*

Bring your awareness back to your breath. Gently wiggle your fingers and toes, and when you are ready, open your eyes. Take a moment to notice how you feel—calm, centered, and refreshed.

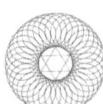

Advanced Guided Meditation: Clear and Re-align All 18 Chakras

Find a quiet, comfortable space where you can sit or lie down without interruption. Close your eyes and take three deep breaths, allowing yourself to relax fully. This advanced meditation will guide you through clearing and aligning all 18 chakras, from your foundational earth chakras to your highest cosmic connections. Imagine a column of brilliant light flowing from the highest realms of the cosmos, through your body, and into the earth. This light represents your energetic pathway, encompassing all 18 chakras. With each breath, you will bring this light into every chakra, clearing blockages and restoring balance.

Earth Gateway Chakra

Located about 12 inches below your feet, this chakra connects you to the earth's core.

- Visualize a glowing, rich brown or deep red orb beneath your feet.
- Imagine roots extending from this chakra, reaching into the heart of the earth.
- With each breath, feel the stabilizing energy of the earth rising into your body.
- Silently affirm: *"I am deeply connected to the earth's energy and wisdom."*

Feet Chakras

Located on the soles of your feet, these chakras facilitate grounding and energy flow.

- Visualize glowing orbs of light at the soles of your feet.
- With each inhale, draw Earth energy into these chakras.
- Exhale and release any energetic blockages or tension through your feet.
- Silently affirm: *"I walk my path with grounded clarity."*

Root Chakra (Muladhara)

Located at the base of your spine, this chakra represents stability.

- Visualize a radiant red light at the base of your spine.
- Allow this light to grow brighter with each breath, anchoring you firmly to the earth.

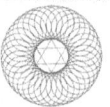

- Silently affirm: *"I am safe, secure, and grounded."*

Sacral Chakra (Svadhisthana)
Located below your navel, this chakra governs creativity and emotions.
- See a vibrant orange light swirling in your lower abdomen.
- Breathe into this area, releasing any emotional stagnation or creative blockages.
- Silently affirm: *"I am in flow with my emotions and creativity."*

Knee Chakras
Located at your knees, these chakras support flexibility and movement.
- Visualize warm, golden orbs of light at both knees.
- Inhale, allowing these lights to grow stronger, releasing stiffness or resistance.
- Silently affirm: *"I move forward in life with ease and grace."*

Solar Plexus Chakra (Manipura)
Located in your stomach, this chakra governs confidence and personal power.
- Visualize a glowing yellow sun in your stomach.
- Breathe into this area, releasing self-doubt or fear, and expanding your inner strength.
- Silently affirm: *"I am confident, capable, and empowered."*

Heart Chakra (Anahata)
Located in the center of your chest, this chakra represents love and compassion.
- Picture a green or pink light radiating from your heart.
- Breathe deeply, allowing this light to expand, clearing any grief or emotional blockages.
- Silently affirm: *"I am love. I give and receive with an open heart."*

Hand Chakras
Located in the palms of your hands, these chakras facilitate healing and giving.

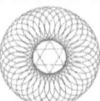

- Visualize bright white or golden orbs in the center of your palms.
- Breathe into these orbs, feeling warmth and energy flowing freely.
- Silently affirm: *"I use my hands to heal and create with love."*

Throat Chakra (Vishuddha)
Located at your throat, this chakra governs communication.
- See a glowing blue light at your throat.
- Breathe into this light, clearing blockages that prevent authentic self-expression.
- Silently affirm: *"I speak my truth clearly and confidently."*

Mouth of God Chakra
Located at the base of the skull, this chakra connects you to divine wisdom.
- Visualize a radiant silver or white light glowing at the back of your neck.
- Breathe deeply, allowing this light to open and flow freely.
- Silently affirm: *"I am aligned with divine truth and wisdom."*

Third Eye Chakra (Ajna)
Located between your eyebrows, this chakra represents intuition.
- Visualize an indigo light glowing at your third eye.
- Inhale clarity and insight and exhale any mental fog or doubt.
- Silently affirm: *"I trust my intuition and inner vision."*

Telepathic Chakras
Located at the Third Eye Chakra (center of the forehead), subtle points near the temples, and behind the ears, these chakras govern telepathic communication and intuitive connection.
- Visualize soft violet or shimmering indigo lights glowing at these points, interconnected by radiant streams of energy.
- Breathe deeply, drawing in clarity and universal wisdom, and exhale any mental blocks or resistance to intuitive connection.

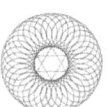

- Silently affirm: *"I am open to receive and transmit energy and thoughts with clarity, love, and alignment with the highest truth."*

Crown Chakra (Sahasrara)
Located at the top of your head, this chakra connects to divine energy.
- Picture a violet or white light at the crown of your head.
- Breathe deeply, feeling this light expand and connect to the universe.
- Silently affirm: *"I am connected to divine wisdom and oneness."*

Soul Star Chakra
Located about 6 inches above your head, this chakra connects to your higher self.
- Visualize a bright, golden-white orb above your head.
- Breathe into this chakra, allowing it to activate and align.
- Silently affirm: *"I am in harmony with my soul's purpose."*

Stellar Gateway Chakra
Located about 12 inches above your head, this chakra connects to universal energy.
- Imagine a shimmering, iridescent light far above your crown.
- Breathe deeply, feeling the expansive energy flowing into your body.
- Silently affirm: *"I am connected to the infinite universe."*

Universal Chakra
Located even higher, this chakra links to universal consciousness.
- Visualize a brilliant, multi-dimensional light above the Stellar Gateway.
- Inhale, drawing its wisdom into your entire being.
- Silently affirm: *"I am one with universal energy."*

Cosmic Gateway Chakra
The highest chakra, connecting to the source of all creation.
- Picture an infinite, glowing sphere of light far above you.

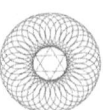

- Breathe deeply, allowing its energy to flow through all your chakras.
- Silently affirm: *"I am a channel for divine creation and universal love."*

Earth Star Chakra
Located below your feet, this chakra grounds your entire system.
- Visualize a deep, grounding energy beneath you, pulling everything into balance.
- Feel aligned, balanced, and supported.
- Silently affirm: *"I am deeply connected to the earth and the cosmos."*

Visualize all 18 chakras glowing brightly, connected by a column of light running through your body. Feel the harmony of their alignment. Take a deep breath in, and as you exhale, bring your awareness back to the present moment.

Wiggle your fingers and toes, stretch gently, and open your eyes when you are ready.

Chakra Color Theory

The 18 chakras, encompassing both the traditional and advanced energy centers, are each associated with specific colors. These colors represent the frequency and function of each chakra, helping to visualize and connect with them during spiritual practices. These colors can be visualized during meditation, energy healing, or chakra balancing to bring awareness to each chakra's unique qualities. Working with these colors can aid in balancing and clearing the chakras, enhancing connection to various aspects of consciousness and grounding in both Earth and cosmic energies.

Traditional Chakras		
Root Chakra	Red	Represents grounding, stability, and connection to Earth.
Sacral Chakra	Orange	Associated with creativity, sexuality, and emotional expression.
Solar Plexus Chakra	Yellow	Reflects personal power, confidence, and self-esteem.
Heart Chakra	Green or Pink	Signifies love, compassion, and healing.
Throat Chakra	Blue	Linked to communication, expression, and truth.
Third Eye Chakra	Indigo	Represents intuition, insight, and inner wisdom.
Crown Chakra	Violet or White	Associated with spirituality, higher consciousness, and unity with the universe.

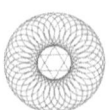

Advanced Chakras		
Earth Gateway Chakra	Deep Brown or Earth Tones	Symbolizes connection with Earth's core and environmental awareness.
Earth Star Chakra	Black or Dark Brown	Represents deep grounding, ancestral connection, and stability.
Soul Star Chakra	Magenta or Light Pink	Associated with soul purpose, divine love, and karmic connection.
Stellar Gateway Chakra	Gold or Platinum	Reflects high spiritual vibration, cosmic consciousness, and access to universal knowledge.
Universal Gateway Chakra	Silver or Clear White	Represents unity with the cosmos, universal consciousness, and wisdom.
Cosmic Gateway Chakra	Iridescent White or Rainbow	Reflects multidimensional awareness, higher states of consciousness, and cosmic energy.
Hand Chakras	White, Green, or Blue	Colors here often depend on the energy being channeled, as these chakras are involved in healing and energy work.
Feet Chakras	Brown or Dark Green	Linked to grounding energy from the earth,

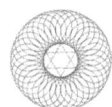

		connecting to natural rhythms and balance.
Knee Chakras	Silver or Light Blue	Represents flexibility, forward movement, and the ability to adapt to life changes.
Chakra at the Base of the Skull (Mouth of God or Well of Dreams)	Violet or Deep Blue	Associated with spiritual insight, psychic abilities, and access to inner guidance.
Telepathic Chakras	Indigo or Soft Violet	Intuitive communication, telepathy, and the ability to send and receive thoughts, emotions, and energy.

Advanced Chakra Color Theory Meditation

Find a quiet and comfortable space where you can relax without interruptions. Sit or lie down in a position that allows you to feel grounded yet open to receiving energy.

Close your eyes and take a few deep breaths. As you exhale, release any tension or stress from your body. With each inhale, imagine yourself drawing in a warm, glowing light of peace and clarity. Say silently or aloud: *"I open myself to connect with the energies of my chakras, bringing balance, awareness, and alignment to my body, mind, and spirit. I trust my intuition to guide me through this process."*

Earth Gateway Chakra

Visualize a deep, rich **brown** light at the base of your feet. Feel its grounding energy connecting you to Earth's core, anchoring you

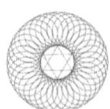

securely in the present moment. Breathe deeply and sense your connection with Earth's stability.

Earth Star Chakra
Imagine an orb of **black or dark brown** light slightly beneath your feet. This chakra connects you to your ancestral roots and deep grounding. Envision its energy spreading like roots through the earth.

Root Chakra
Move your awareness to the base of your spine. Visualize a vibrant **red** light, glowing steadily. Feel its strength as it provides security, stability, and connection to the physical world.

Sacral Chakra
Bring your focus to your lower abdomen. Picture a radiant **orange** light swirling, representing creativity, emotions, and pleasure. Allow this energy to flow freely.

Solar Plexus Chakra
Shift your awareness to your upper abdomen. See a **yellow** light glowing like the sun, representing personal power, confidence, and self-esteem. Breathe in its warmth and strength.

Heart Chakra
Visualize a glowing **green** or soft **pink** light in the center of your chest. Feel love, compassion, and healing emanating from this space, connecting you to others and yourself.

Throat Chakra
Move your focus to your throat. See a serene **blue** light, representing communication, truth, and expression. Imagine speaking your truth with clarity and confidence.

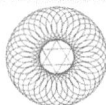

Third Eye Chakra
Bring your awareness to the space between your eyebrows. Visualize a deep **indigo** light, signifying intuition and inner wisdom. Feel your inner sight opening, allowing clarity and insight.

Crown Chakra
Picture a vibrant **violet** or **white** light at the top of your head, connecting you to universal consciousness. Feel this light expanding upward, uniting you with the divine and the cosmos.

Soul Star Chakra
Focus on an orb of **magenta** or **light pink** light above your head. This chakra connects you to your soul purpose and divine love. Visualize its energy descending into your being, aligning you with your higher self.

Stellar Gateway Chakra
Visualize a shimmering **gold** or **platinum** light above the Soul Star Chakra. Feel its high spiritual vibration connecting you to cosmic consciousness and the universe's wisdom.

Universal Gateway Chakra
Picture a glowing **silver** or **clear white** light above the Stellar Gateway Chakra. Envision its energy uniting all aspects of your consciousness and bringing clarity.

Cosmic Gateway Chakra
See an **iridescent white or rainbow** light far above your head. Sense its multidimensional awareness and cosmic energy cascading down, aligning all your chakras with the universe.

Hand Chakras
Bring your focus to the centers of your palms. Visualize **white, green, or blue** light radiating from your hands. Feel their healing energy and connection to the flow of life force.

Feet Chakras

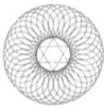

Shift awareness to the soles of your feet. See **brown or dark green** light glowing, connecting you to natural rhythms and balance.

Knee Chakras
Picture **silver or light blue** light at your knees. Sense flexibility and adaptability flowing through your body, encouraging forward movement in life.

Mouth of God (Base of Skull)
Bring your focus to the base of your skull. See a **violet or deep blue** light glowing, representing spiritual insight and psychic abilities. Feel its energy opening your connection to divine guidance.

Telepathic Chakras
Visualize **indigo or soft violet** light above your Third Eye. Sense its energy supporting intuitive communication and telepathic awareness.
- Take a deep breath, and as you exhale, imagine all the colors blending together, creating a harmonious and vibrant energy field around you.
- Feel balanced, aligned, and connected to Earth and the cosmos.
- Say silently or aloud: *"I am grateful for the wisdom and healing of my chakras. I am balanced, whole, and in alignment with my highest purpose."*

When ready, gently wiggle your fingers and toes, returning to full awareness. Open your eyes and take a moment to appreciate the calm and clarity within you.

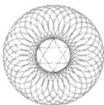

Aura

The human aura is an electromagnetic energy field that surrounds and penetrates the body, reflecting a person's physical, emotional, mental, and spiritual states. It is often visualized as layers of light extending from the body, with each layer or "body" corresponding to a different level of consciousness and interacting with the chakras.

These layers create a structured energy system, with each layer having its own unique function but working in harmony with others to support overall well-being.

Rainbow Reiki Aura Symbol

Grounding helps stabilize the energy field, ensuring that the lower auric layers (Etheric, Emotional, and Mental) remain clear and balanced. When grounded, the aura becomes more resilient and can more effectively support the body's needs and the flow of energy between layers. Grounding also helps release stagnant or negative energy through the earth, supporting clarity and focus.

Each layer of the aura is associated with a corresponding chakra, creating a flow of energy between the chakra system and the aura. Balanced chakras help maintain a healthy aura, allowing energy to flow freely. When a chakra is blocked or imbalanced, it can create disruptions in the corresponding auric layer, which might lead to physical, emotional, or spiritual issues.

In essence, the aura, chakras, and grounding work together in a dynamic energy system that supports holistic well-being. Grounding strengthens the lower layers, while balanced chakras keep the aura vibrant and aligned. This harmony allows for a stable, resilient energy field, fostering health, clarity, and spiritual growth.

The Seven Layers of the Aura Etheric Body (Physical Layer):

Closest to the body, this layer is connected to physical health and sensations. It is associated with the Root Chakra and relates to survival, grounding, and basic physical needs. This layer mirrors the physical body and is impacted by physical health and vitality.

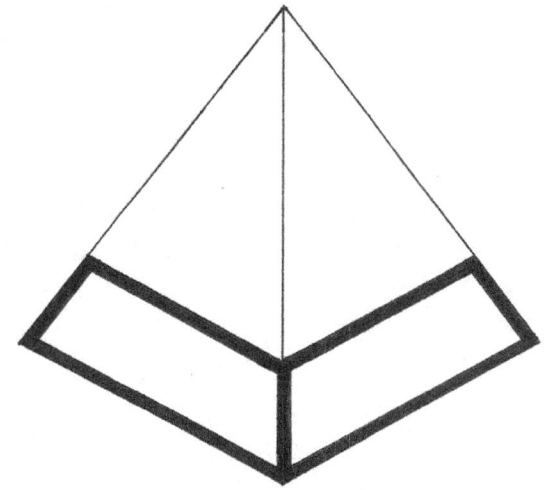

Rainbow Reiki Aura Etheric Body Symbol

The Etheric Body, also known as the Physical Layer, is the closest layer of the aura to the physical body. Deeply connected to physical health and sensations, this layer serves as the energetic blueprint of the body, mirroring its structure, organs, and systems. Rooted in the energy of the Root Chakra, the Etheric Body governs survival, grounding, and the fulfillment of basic physical needs, directly influencing vitality and well-being. Across various traditions, the significance of this layer is universally acknowledged.

In Egyptian teachings, the Etheric Body is likened to the "Ka," or the life-force energy, which is sustained through balance and rituals that connect the individual to Earth and divine forces. Tibetan practices emphasize the importance of the subtle energy channels (nadis) and prana flows, using techniques like breathwork and physical movements to strengthen this foundational layer. Arcturian and Pleiadean perspectives view the Etheric Body as a multidimensional energy field where advanced light codes and frequencies can be integrated to enhance physical health and awaken dormant potential.

Biblical scripture, such as Genesis 2:7, which states, "Then the LORD God formed a man from the dust of the ground and breathed into his nostrils the breath of life, and the man became a living being," aligns with the understanding that the Etheric Body is the carrier of divine breath and life-force energy. Together, these ancient and cosmic teachings highlight the importance of nurturing the Etheric Body through practices that ground, cleanse, and restore its vitality, thereby supporting overall health and spiritual evolution.

Emotional Body: The second layer extends beyond the physical and reflects emotions. Linked to the Sacral Chakra, it holds emotional experiences, desires, and creativity. This layer often shows color changes depending on a person's current emotional state.

The Emotional Body, also known as the Astral Layer, is the second layer of the aura and is deeply connected to emotions, desires, and energetic impressions from experiences. It is the bridge between the physical and mental bodies, storing emotional imprints, memories, and unresolved traumas. Governed by the Sacral Chakra, this layer influences creativity,

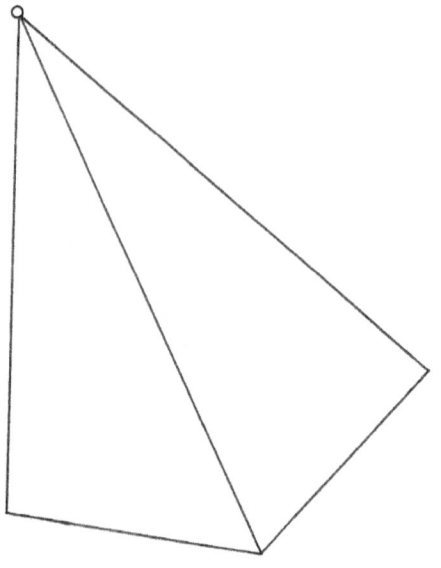

Rainbow Reiki
Aura Emotional Body Symbol

relationships, and the ability to feel and express emotions authentically. The vibrancy and movement of the Emotional Body reflect one's emotional state—when balanced, it radiates harmonious, flowing energy, but when burdened by unprocessed emotions, it may appear dense or fragmented.

Across various traditions, the significance of the Emotional Body is widely recognized. In Egyptian teachings, it is akin to the Ba, the individual's personality and emotional essence that continues beyond physical death. The Egyptians believed that emotional purification was necessary for the soul's ascension, achieved through sacred rites, anointing, and the practice of heka (divine words of power) to release emotional burdens. Tibetan Buddhism connects this layer to the winds (lung) of consciousness, acknowledging that unbalanced emotions create turbulence in the subtle body. Through meditation, mantra recitation, and energy clearing practices, the Emotional Body is harmonized to cultivate inner peace and detachment from suffering.

From an Arcturian and Pleiadian perspective, the Emotional Body is viewed as a fluid crystalline energy field that is particularly responsive to high-frequency healing. Emotional blockages can manifest as distortions in the auric structure, which these star beings assist in dissolving through vibrational recalibration, color healing, and sound frequencies. Arcturians emphasize the integration of higher emotional intelligence, while Pleiadians encourage heart-centered activation, allowing for deeper emotional connection and self-love.

Biblical scripture also acknowledges the importance of emotional energy in shaping one's spiritual state. Proverbs 4:23 states, "Above all else, guard your heart, for everything you do flows from it." This aligns with the understanding that the Emotional Body is the wellspring of one's energetic output, influencing thoughts, actions, and spiritual alignment. The Psalms and other biblical texts often reference the necessity of emotional purification through faith, forgiveness, and surrendering burdens to the divine.

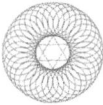

Together, these ancient and cosmic teachings highlight the Emotional Body's vital role in one's overall well-being. By engaging in practices that process emotions, release stagnant energy, and cultivate emotional balance, individuals can maintain a fluid and vibrant Emotional Body. Whether through grounding, breathwork, energy healing, or spiritual reflection, nurturing this auric layer allows for greater emotional resilience, spiritual clarity, and a deeper connection to oneself and others.

Mental Body: Connected with thoughts and beliefs, this layer is associated with the Solar Plexus Chakra. It governs logic, intellect, and analytical thought, showing patterns related to how a person thinks and perceives the world.

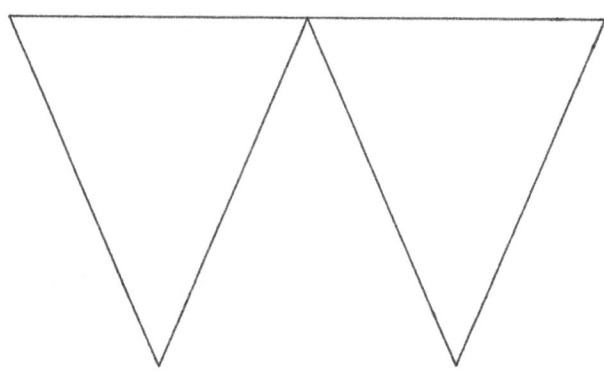

Rainbow Reiki Aura Mental Body Symbol

The Mental Body, also known as the Mental Layer, is the third layer of the aura, associated with thoughts, beliefs, perception, and cognitive processes. It serves as the energetic framework for mental clarity, logic, and the formation of ideas. Governed by the Solar Plexus Chakra, the Mental Body influences personal will, self-discipline, and the ability to manifest intentions into reality. When balanced, this layer radiates with structured, organized energy, supporting rational thinking and emotional intelligence. However, when overloaded with negative thought patterns, limiting beliefs, or mental stress, it can become clouded, fragmented, or rigid, restricting one's ability to receive higher wisdom.

Across various traditions, the Mental Body is recognized as an essential aspect of spiritual and psychological well-being. In

Egyptian teachings, this layer is closely related to the sahu, the refined spiritual mind that transcends ordinary thought and aligns with higher divine intelligence. The Egyptians believed that intellectual purification was necessary for ascension, achieved through sacred study, hieroglyphic wisdom, and meditative contemplation of universal laws. The Book of Thoth, attributed to the god of wisdom, emphasized mastering the mind to unlock the mysteries of creation.

In Tibetan Buddhism, the Mental Body is linked to rigpa, the state of pure awareness beyond conceptual thought. Tibetan practices such as Dzogchen meditation and Mahamudra cultivate an expansive, non-dual mind, dissolving mental illusions and attachments. The concept of manas (discriminative consciousness) highlights the importance of mental discipline, encouraging mindfulness to maintain clarity and detachment from ego-driven narratives.

From an Arcturian and Pleiadian perspective, the Mental Body is seen as a bioelectric field of thought frequency, with each thought pattern creating holographic imprints that shape reality. Arcturians teach that mental coherence is essential for activating higher intelligence, often using light technology and geometric codes to realign distorted mental fields. Pleiadians emphasize the Heart-Mind connection, teaching that when mental energy is synchronized with the emotional and spiritual layers, one can access multidimensional wisdom and intuitive knowledge.

Biblical scripture also underscores the power of thought and belief in shaping reality. Romans 12:2 states, "Do not conform to the pattern of this world, but be transformed by the renewing of your mind …" This aligns with the understanding that mental energy must be consciously refined to access divine wisdom. Proverbs states, "For as he thinketh in his heart, so is he …" (Proverbs 23:7, King James Version) emphasizing the Mental Body's role in manifestation and spiritual transformation. Biblical traditions advocate for prayer, meditation, and scripture study to cleanse and elevate the mind.

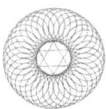

Together, these ancient and cosmic teachings highlight the Mental Body's critical role in shaping one's consciousness and reality. By clearing limiting beliefs, practicing mindfulness, and aligning thoughts with higher truths, individuals can cultivate a luminous and structured Mental Body. Whether through philosophical study, meditation, energy recalibration, or spiritual discipline, maintaining clarity in this auric layer enhances personal empowerment, discernment, and the ability to manifest one's divine purpose.

Astral Body: Also called the "bridge layer," the astral body connects the lower physical energies with higher spiritual ones. Aligned with the Heart Chakra, it reflects love, compassion, and relationships, bridging personal and universal love.

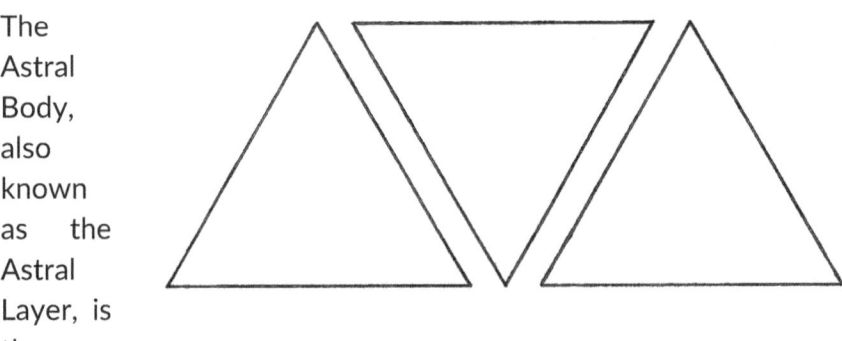

Rainbow Reiki Aura Astral Body Symbol

The Astral Body, also known as the Astral Layer, is the fourth layer of the aura and serves as the bridge between the physical and spiritual realms. It is the seat of higher emotions, spiritual connection, and the ability to experience love, compassion, and unity consciousness. Governed by the Heart Chakra, the Astral Body facilitates deep emotional bonds, intuition, and multidimensional travel, allowing individuals to access higher planes of existence. When balanced, this layer radiates harmony, divine love, and a sense of interconnectedness with all beings. However, when clouded by unresolved trauma, grief, or emotional wounds, it can manifest as energetic blockages, preventing the free flow of love and spiritual insight.

Across various traditions, the Astral Body is recognized as a vital conduit for spiritual evolution. In Egyptian teachings, it is akin to the

Ba, the aspect of the soul that possesses free will and travels between the earthly and divine realms. The Ba was often depicted as a bird with a human head, symbolizing the soul's ability to move beyond the physical form during dreams, meditation, and after death. The Egyptians believed that by engaging in sacred rites, anointing with essential oils, and invoking divine energies, one could purify the Astral Body and ascend to higher realms.

In Tibetan Buddhism, the Astral Body corresponds to the Dream Body, or illusory body (gyulu), which enables conscious astral projection and lucid dreaming. Tibetan monks practice Dream Yoga, a discipline designed to develop awareness during sleep states, ultimately leading to control over the Astral Body's movements beyond the physical world. The Bardo Thödol (Tibetan Book of the Dead) describes how the soul navigates the intermediate realms after death, emphasizing the importance of training the Astral Body to remain conscious during transitions between life and death.

From an Arcturian and Pleiadian perspective, the Astral Body is viewed as a fluid crystalline light field capable of interdimensional travel. Arcturians assist in auric repair and astral alignment through advanced energy healing, ensuring that distortions in this layer do not interfere with soul ascension. Pleiadians describe the Astral Body as a holographic bridge, allowing individuals to access past-life memories, Akashic Records, and cosmic guidance. Both civilizations emphasize the Heart-Centered Expansion Technique, which strengthens the Astral Body's ability to maintain coherence while navigating higher dimensions.

Biblical scripture also references the spiritual body and the existence of other realms. 1 Corinthians 15:44 states, "it is sown a natural body; it is raised a spiritual body. If there is a natural body, there is also a spiritual body." This suggests that beyond the physical form, there exists a luminous body capable of higher experiences. Genesis 28:12 describes Jacob's vision of a ladder reaching to Heaven, symbolizing the ability of the soul to travel between earthly and divine dimensions. Biblical traditions encourage prayer, fasting,

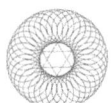

and divine communion to purify and strengthen the Astral Body, allowing for deeper spiritual revelations.

Together, these ancient and cosmic teachings highlight the Astral Body's role as the gateway to higher consciousness. By engaging in heart-centered healing, dreamwork, meditation, and spiritual devotion, individuals can maintain a vibrant and expansive Astral Body. Whether through Egyptian soul rites, Tibetan dream practices, energy healing, or biblical prayer, nurturing this auric layer enhances one's ability to connect with divine love, navigate multidimensional realities, and deepen their spiritual evolution.

Etheric Template: This layer serves as a blueprint for the physical body and holds the energetic template of the physical form. It is linked to the Throat Chakra, governing self-expression and communication. This layer is where healing and energy work often start, as it sets the energetic foundation for physical health.

The Etheric Template Body, also known as the Etheric Blueprint Layer, is the fifth layer of the aura and serves as the divine matrix or holographic blueprint of the physical body. It holds the perfect energetic template from which the physical and etheric bodies are formed, governing structural integrity, cellular regeneration, and the alignment of one's physical form with higher frequencies.

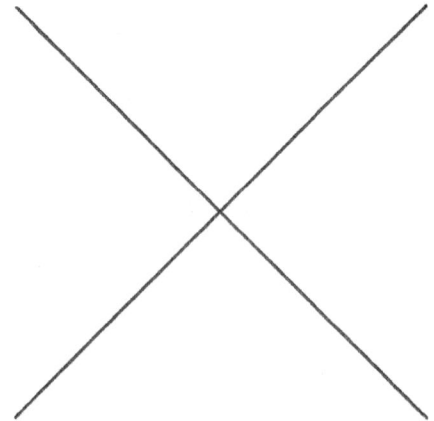

Rainbow Reiki Aura Etheric Template Symbol

Governed by the Throat Chakra, this layer is deeply connected to expression, truth, and divine will. When balanced, the Etheric Template Body vibrates with clarity, strength, and the potential for self-healing, but when disrupted, it can lead to distortions in physical and energetic structure, manifesting as chronic misalignments or dis-ease.

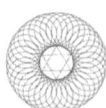

In Egyptian tradition, this layer is akin to the sekhem, the divine energetic pattern that sustains and governs the body's structure. sekhem healing, an ancient Egyptian energy system, was used to restore the original blueprint of wholeness when distortions occurred due to trauma, negative energy, or karmic interference. The Pyramid Texts describe the Etheric Template as a celestial double, imprinted with divine perfection, which priests and healers accessed through sacred rituals and temple initiations. The gods Thoth and Ptah were often invoked to realign one's energetic template with cosmic harmony.

In Tibetan Buddhism, the Etheric Template corresponds to the Vajra Body, an indestructible energetic structure that serves as the framework for enlightenment. Through practices such as Tummo (Inner Fire Meditation) and Yantra Yoga, practitioners refine their energy fields, working to activate and align their perfect blueprint with higher states of being. The Vajra Body is said to remain intact beyond death, serving as the basis for reincarnation and the manifestation of the Rainbow Body (Jalü), where the physical form dissolves into pure light.

From an Arcturian and Pleiadian perspective, the Etheric Template is a geometric light structure that encodes the original, uncorrupted DNA sequence before earthly distortions take place. Arcturians use holographic light recalibration to correct any misalignments, working with sacred geometry and vibrational frequency adjustments to restore coherence. Pleiadians view the Etheric Template as a crystalline lattice, capable of holding and transmitting high-frequency light codes. This is why light healing, sound frequencies, and DNA activations are essential for restoring the body's original divine pattern.

Biblical scripture acknowledges the existence of a divine template governing creation. Genesis 1:27 states, "So God created mankind in His own image ..." This reflects the idea that humans possess an inherent divine pattern, an energetic blueprint that aligns with God's original design. Psalm 139:13 further supports this concept, declaring, "For You created my inmost being; You knit me together

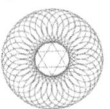

in my mother's womb." This suggests that the human form is structured through an intelligent divine matrix. Biblical traditions emphasize prayer, fasting, and divine surrender as ways to reconnect with and restore the Etheric Template to its original divine perfection.

Together, these ancient and cosmic teachings highlight the Etheric Template Body as the divine architectural structure of the human form. By engaging in energy healing, vibrational recalibration, sacred rituals, and spiritual devotion, individuals can realign with their perfect energetic blueprint. Whether through Egyptian Sekhem, Tibetan Vajra practices, Arcturian light technology, Pleiadian DNA activation, or biblical spiritual purification, nurturing this auric layer supports physical health, energetic integrity, and the full embodiment of one's divine potential.

Celestial Body: The Celestial Body is the spiritual-emotional plane, connecting to the Third Eye Chakra. It represents intuition, higher emotions, and divine love. Here, people experience spiritual joy, connection, and insights that reach beyond the physical realm.

The Celestial Body, also known as the Higher Mental Layer, is the sixth layer of the aura and serves as the bridge between personal consciousness and divine intelligence. This layer holds the vibrations of enlightenment, divine love, and universal wisdom, allowing one to access higher realms of thought, intuition, and spiritual insight. Governed by the Third Eye Chakra, the Celestial Body is deeply connected to spiritual vision, mystical experiences, and the ability to perceive beyond the limitations of the physical world. When balanced, this layer emanates a radiant, golden or opalescent light, signifying an open connection to the divine. When clouded by doubt, fear, or

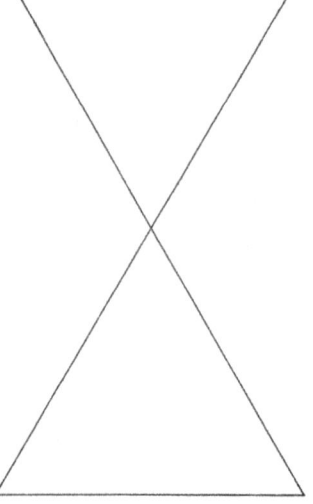

Rainbow Reiki Aura
Celestial Body Symbol

disconnection from higher consciousness, it may become dim or fragmented, limiting one's ability to receive spiritual guidance.

In Egyptian tradition, this layer corresponds to the Akhu, or "Luminous Spirit," which represents the divine aspect of the self that merges with cosmic consciousness. The Akhu was believed to be the immortal, shining essence of a person, fully awakened and able to communicate with higher realms. Ancient texts describe ritual purification, prayer, and initiatory rites as pathways to activate the Celestial Body and achieve enlightenment. The temples of Thoth, the god of wisdom, were places where initiates practiced higher thought mastery, sacred writing, and divine oracular visions, aligning the Celestial Body with the divine order of Ma'at.

In Tibetan Buddhism, this layer is closely linked to the Dharmakaya, the "Truth Body," representing the state of pure, boundless awareness beyond form and duality. Advanced practitioners engage in Dzogchen and Mahamudra meditation, which dissolve mental constructs and expand the mind into its original luminous state. The clear light of the mind, experienced during deep meditation and at the time of death, is considered a direct encounter with the Celestial Body. Tibetan monks also practice Tögal (Spontaneous Presence), a technique that strengthens the Celestial Body by dissolving the illusions of ego and self-identity, allowing one to perceive the universe as pure light.

From an Arcturian and Pleiadian perspective, the Celestial Body is perceived as an interdimensional light field composed of fractal intelligence, serving as a direct link to higher consciousness. Arcturians describe it as the Gateway to the Oversoul, where the higher aspects of the self converge into a single, luminous intelligence. They utilize advanced light frequency recalibration and celestial sound harmonics to activate and expand this layer, allowing individuals to access multidimensional awareness. Pleiadians emphasize the Heart-Mind-Soul connection, where the Celestial Body is strengthened through sacred geometric activations, star-coded transmissions, and deep meditative states that align one's vibration with the Source frequency.

Biblical scripture also acknowledges the concept of an illuminated, divine body that transcends earthly existence. Philippians 3:20-21 states, "But our citizenship is in heaven. And we eagerly await a Savior from there, the Lord Jesus Christ, who, by the power that enables him to bring everything under his control, will transform our lowly bodies so that they will be like his glorious body." This passage suggests that through spiritual purification and divine alignment, the Celestial Body becomes fully activated, enabling one to merge with divine consciousness. Matthew 6:22 reinforces this idea, stating, "The eye is the lamp of the body. If your eyes are healthy, your whole body will be full of light." Biblical traditions encourage prayer, contemplation, and devotion as ways to strengthen and purify the Celestial Body, allowing one to embody divine wisdom and spiritual illumination.

Together, these ancient and cosmic teachings highlight the Celestial Body as the radiant bridge between personal consciousness and universal intelligence. By engaging in higher states of meditation, divine contemplation, light activations, and sacred knowledge, individuals can expand their Celestial Body and awaken their full spiritual potential. Whether through Egyptian Akhu initiations, Tibetan Dzogchen practices, Arcturian frequency recalibrations, Pleiadian star activations, or biblical spiritual devotion, nurturing this auric layer allows one to access divine guidance, heightened intuition, and the purest form of enlightenment.

Ketheric (Causal) Body: This outermost layer corresponds to the Crown Chakra and represents the soul and divine connection. It holds the accumulated knowledge of past lives and the soul's purpose. This layer is the gateway to higher consciousness and unity with the universe.

The Ketheric Body, also known as the Causal Body, is the seventh and outermost layer of the aura, encompassing all other layers and serving as the divine connection to Source, cosmic consciousness, and the eternal self. This layer holds the records of the soul's journey across lifetimes, containing karmic imprints, divine purpose, and the

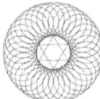

purest vibrations of enlightenment. Governed by the Crown Chakra, the Ketheric Body is associated with oneness, transcendence, and the dissolution of ego, allowing individuals to merge with the infinite. When balanced, it radiates as a golden or white luminescent energy field, expanding beyond the physical body and unifying the entire auric system. When misaligned, it may appear thin or fragmented, signifying a disconnection from divine awareness and spiritual purpose.

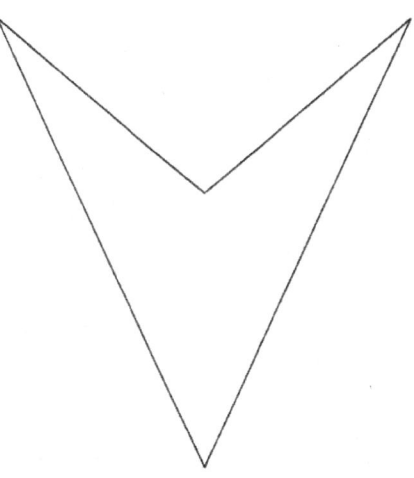
Rainbow Reiki Subtle Aura Ketheric Body Symbol

In Egyptian tradition, the Ketheric Body is aligned with the Ren, the "Eternal Name," which carries the essence of one's divine identity beyond physical existence. The Ba and Akhu, aspects of the soul, integrate into this highest body, enabling spiritual transcendence and unification with the Neteru (divine cosmic forces). Egyptian teachings emphasize that through sacred rituals, divine invocations, and initiations in the temples of Isis, Osiris, and Thoth, one could activate the Ketheric Body and achieve full enlightenment. The Pyramid Texts reference the final spiritual ascension where the soul, purified and radiant, becomes one with the cosmos, completing its cycle of reincarnation.

In Tibetan Buddhism, the Ketheric Body corresponds to the Adi-Buddha, the Primordial Awareness, which is the purest expression of ultimate reality. It is the state of absolute emptiness and infinite potential, where all individual consciousness dissolves into the limitless field of enlightenment. Advanced meditation techniques such as Mahamudra, Dzogchen, and the practice of Phowa (Conscious Death Transition) help practitioners connect to this supreme layer, guiding the soul into the Dharmakaya (the Body of Truth) upon physical death. The Rainbow Body phenomenon, where

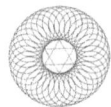

an enlightened master's physical body dissolves into light, represents the complete activation and transcendence of the Ketheric Body.

From an Arcturian and Pleiadian perspective, the Ketheric Body is described as the Universal Oversoul Field, the highest vibrational layer of human consciousness, which exists in direct alignment with the Source energy of the cosmos. Arcturians teach that this layer holds the Akashic Records and cosmic blueprints, providing access to infinite wisdom and interdimensional reality shifts. They assist in activating the Ketheric Body through light grid recalibrations, crystalline energy infusions, and high-frequency transmissions. Pleiadians view it as the Sacred Cosmic Gateway, enabling souls to travel across star systems, access universal memory, and integrate fully into divine consciousness. They emphasize that through deep meditative union, crystalline activations, and solar light coding, one can merge their Ketheric Body with the divine Source and embody cosmic awareness.

Biblical scripture also supports the idea of an eternal, divine essence that transcends physical existence. Ecclesiastes 12:7 states, "and the dust returns to the ground it came from, and the spirit returns to God who gave it." This verse suggests that the highest body, the eternal spirit, ultimately reunites with its divine origin. John 17:21 reinforces this, with Jesus saying, "that they may all be one, Father, just as you are in me and I am in you. May they also be in us …" This reflects the Ketheric Body's function as the unifying bridge between the soul and the Divine. Biblical traditions emphasize prayer, divine communion, and surrender to God's will as ways to align the Ketheric Body with the eternal light of creation.

Together, these ancient and cosmic teachings highlight the Ketheric Body as the final gateway to divine consciousness and enlightenment. By engaging in deep meditation, spiritual devotion, cosmic attunement, and karmic purification, individuals can fully activate and harmonize this auric layer. Whether through Egyptian soul ascension rituals, Tibetan Dzogchen practices, Arcturian crystalline activations, Pleiadian star-gate experiences, or biblical

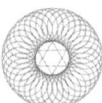

divine union, nurturing the Ketheric Body allows one to transcend duality, embrace infinite wisdom, and return to the eternal Source in pure, luminous wholeness.

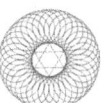

Guided Meditation: Clearing Auric Blockages and Grounding the Layers of the Aura

Find a quiet, comfortable space where you can sit or lie undisturbed. Close your eyes, take a few deep breaths, and allow your body to relax. This meditation will guide you in clearing blockages from your aura and grounding each layer into the earth, creating balance, clarity, and stability. Take a deep breath in, and as you exhale, imagine yourself surrounded by a glowing, multi-layered field of energy—your aura. This energy field reflects and protects your physical, emotional, mental, and spiritual states. Together, we will clear any blockages in these layers and ground them into the earth for renewal and stability.

Centering and Creating Sacred Space
- Visualize a column of white light descending from above, surrounding your body and aura.
- This light creates a sacred, protective space for your energy work.
- Silently affirm: *"I am safe, supported, and open to clearing and grounding my energy."*

Clearing Blockages in the Physical Layer (Etheric Body)
- Focus on the innermost layer of your aura, the physical or etheric body, closest to your skin.
- Visualize this layer as a glowing silver or white field hugging your body.
- Scan this layer for any areas that feel heavy, dark, or stagnant.
- Imagine the white light dissolving these blockages and flushing them downward, through your feet, into the earth.
- Breathe deeply, allowing the earth to transmute the energy into light.
- Silently affirm: *"I release all blockages from my physical energy. I am strong, clear, and grounded."*

Clearing Blockages in the Emotional Layer (Astral Body)
- Shift your focus outward to the emotional or astral body, representing your feelings and emotional patterns.

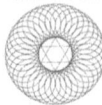

- Visualize this layer as a soft, shifting field of pink, orange, or yellow light.
- Scan this layer for any dense or turbulent areas.
- Imagine the white light flowing through, calming and dissolving these blockages.
- With each breath, release unresolved emotions into the earth for transformation.
- Silently affirm: *"I release emotional blockages and invite balance and peace into my aura."*

Clearing Blockages in the Mental Layer (Mental Body)
- Move your awareness to the mental body, which governs thoughts, beliefs, and mental patterns.
- Visualize this layer as a bright, golden field of energy.
- Scan for any areas of overactivity, confusion, or mental clutter.
- Allow the white light to sweep through this layer, clearing away negativity and self-limiting beliefs.
- Exhale deeply, releasing mental tension into the earth.
- Silently affirm: *"I release mental blockages. My mind is clear, focused, and grounded."*

Clearing Blockages in the Spiritual Layer (Causal Body)
- Shift your focus to the spiritual or causal body, the outermost layer connecting you to higher realms and your soul's essence.
- Visualize this layer as a radiant, iridescent field of light surrounding your entire energy field.
- Scan for areas of disconnection or heaviness.
- Allow the white light to flow through, restoring harmony and connection to your higher self.
- Silently affirm: *"I release spiritual blockages and align with my divine purpose."*

Grounding the Layers of the Aura
- Now, visualize each layer of your aura—physical, emotional, mental, and spiritual—glowing brightly, free of blockages.

- Imagine roots extending from every layer, traveling deep into the earth.
- With each inhale, draw up the earth's nourishing energy, filling every layer of your aura.
- With each exhale, release any residual tension or imbalance into the earth for transformation.
- Silently affirm: *"I ground all layers of my aura into the earth. I am balanced, aligned, and whole."*

Sealing and Strengthening the Aura
- Visualize a golden, shimmering light surrounding your aura, sealing it with protection and stability.
- This light acts as a shield, allowing only positive, supportive energy to enter your field.
- Silently affirm: *"My aura is strong, grounded, and protected. I am safe and aligned."*

Returning to the Present Moment
- Take a deep breath in, feeling your aura glowing brightly and your energy fully grounded.
- Wiggle your fingers and toes, stretch gently, and open your eyes when you are ready.

Take a moment to notice how your body, mind, and emotions feel after this meditation. Repeat this practice whenever you sense blockages or feel the need to ground and clear your energy.

Aura Colors

Aura colors can be diverse and reflect various aspects of a person's energy, personality, emotions, and even health. Aura colors can change over time and even within a day, reflecting current emotional, mental, or physical states. People often have a "base" color that aligns with their core personality traits, but temporary colors may appear based on mood or external influences.

Understanding aura colors can be valuable for gaining insight into a person's energy field, current life situation, and areas that may need healing or attention. Regular practices like grounding, meditation, and chakra balancing can help maintain a bright, balanced, and harmonious aura.

Red
- Meaning: Energy, strength, passion, and physical vitality.
- Bright Red: Indicates a strong, active, and passionate personality.
- Dark or Murky Red: May suggest anger, stress, or unresolved emotional issues.

Orange
- Meaning: Creativity, sociability, and joy.
- Bright Orange: Shows enthusiasm, excitement, and an active social life.
- Dull or Brownish Orange: Can indicate emotional stress or resistance to change.

Yellow
- Meaning: Optimism, intellect, and personal power.
- Bright Yellow: Reflects a cheerful, confident, and positive attitude.
- Pale Yellow: Can suggest caution, analytical thinking, or emerging clarity.

Green
- Meaning: Healing, balance, and compassion.

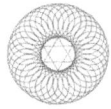

- Bright Green: Shows a person with healing energy, empathy, and a balanced heart.
- Muddy or Dark Green: May reflect jealousy, insecurity, or imbalance in relationships.

Blue
- Meaning: Calmness, communication, and truth.
- Light Blue: Represents peace, good communication, and clarity of thought.
- Deep Blue: Reflects strong intuition, introspection, and spiritual wisdom.
- Muddy Blue: Can indicate blocked communication or emotional sadness.

Indigo
- Meaning: Intuition, psychic abilities, and introspection.
- Bright Indigo: Reflects heightened intuition, inner wisdom, and deep insight.
- Dark Indigo: May suggest escapism or an overreliance on fantasy.

Purple or Violet
- Meaning: Spirituality, wisdom, and higher consciousness.
- Bright Violet or Purple: Suggests a person who is spiritually aware and creative.
- Dull Violet: Can indicate confusion or disconnection from one's spiritual self.

Pink
- Meaning: Love, compassion, and nurturing.
- Bright Pink: Shows strong love energy, gentleness, and kindness.
- Pale Pink: Represents a tender, innocent, and sensitive personality.
- Muddy Pink: May indicate emotional vulnerability or imbalance in relationships.

White

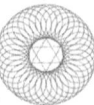

- Meaning: Purity, spiritual connection, and protection.
- Bright White: Indicates spiritual focus, high vibration, and divine connection.
- Grayish White: Can suggest a lack of grounding or over-focus on the spiritual realm.

Black
- Meaning: Protection, shielding, or unresolved issues.
- Black Spots or Patches: Often represent emotional blockages, pain, or repressed emotions.

Gold
- Meaning: Enlightenment, divine protection, and wisdom.
- Bright Gold: Indicates high spiritual awareness, wisdom, and a generous heart.
- Dull or Dirty Gold: Can suggest a need to focus on self-care and alignment.

Silver
- Meaning: Intuition, abundance, and adaptability.
- Bright Silver: Reflects intuition, psychic abilities, and adaptability.
- Grayish Silver: May suggest caution, introspection, or hidden fears.

Brown
- Meaning: Grounding and practicality.
- Rich Brown: Represents a strong connection to the Earth and a grounded personality.
- Muddy Brown: Can suggest stagnation, material attachment, or lack of movement.

Gray
- Meaning: Uncertainty, caution, or fear.
- Light Gray: Suggests introspection and contemplation.
- Dark or Cloudy Gray: May indicate worry, sadness, or confusion.

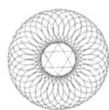

Turquoise
- Meaning: Healing, communication, and empathy.
- Bright Turquoise: Indicates a natural healer, someone empathetic and creative.
- Pale or Cloudy Turquoise: May reflect hesitancy in self-expression or a need for emotional release.

Guided Meditation: Channeling Colors into Your Aura to Understand Aura Color Theory

Find a quiet, comfortable space where you can sit or lie down without distraction. Close your eyes and take a few deep breaths, allowing your body to relax. This meditation will guide you through channeling different colors into your aura to deepen your understanding of how each color influences your emotional, mental, physical, and spiritual states. Take a deep breath in, and as you exhale, visualize a soft, glowing light surrounding your body. This is your aura, your energy field that reflects your inner and outer states of being. With each color we introduce, you'll explore how it feels, what emotions it evokes, and its impact on your mental, physical, and spiritual states.

Grounding with Red

Begin by visualizing your aura filling with a deep, vibrant red light.
- Emotional State: Feel the energy of strength, passion, and vitality.
- Mental State: Notice a sense of focus, determination, and alertness.
- Physical Sensation: Experience warmth and grounding, as though your body is rooted firmly to the earth.
- Spiritual State: Feel connected to your primal instincts and the foundational energy of life.
- Silently affirm: *"I am strong, grounded, and full of vitality."*

Awakening Creativity with Orange

Let the red light gently fade as your aura fills with a bright, warm orange glow.
- Emotional State: Feel joy, playfulness, and creativity flowing through you.
- Mental State: Notice a spark of inspiration and openness to new ideas.
- Physical Sensation: Experience a gentle stirring of energy in your lower abdomen, like flowing water.
- Spiritual State: Feel your inner passion and creativity connecting you to the flow of life.

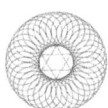

- Silently affirm: *"I embrace joy and creativity in all aspects of my life."*

Empowering Confidence with Yellow

Allow the orange light to transform into a radiant yellow, surrounding your body.
- Emotional State: Feel confidence, happiness, and optimism rising within you.
- Mental State: Experience mental clarity and a heightened sense of personal power.
- Physical Sensation: Feel warmth and a sense of strength radiating from your core.
- Spiritual State: Sense your inner light shining brightly, illuminating your path.
- Silently affirm: *"I am confident, capable, and filled with light."*

Cultivating Love with Green

Watch as the yellow light transitions into a soothing green hue, surrounding your heart center.
- Emotional State: Feel a deep sense of love, compassion, and balance.
- Mental State: Notice a sense of calm, acceptance, and harmony in your thoughts.
- Physical Sensation: Experience a gentle expansion in your chest, as though your heart is opening wide.
- Spiritual State: Feel connected to the natural flow of love and the interconnectedness of all beings.
- Silently affirm: *"I am love, compassion, and balance."*

Expressing Truth with Blue

Let the green light fade into a tranquil blue that surrounds your throat.
- Emotional State: Feel a sense of peace and authenticity.
- Mental State: Notice clarity and ease in your communication and self-expression.
- Physical Sensation: Experience a cool, calming energy around your throat.

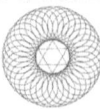

- Spiritual State: Feel aligned with your truth and empowered to share your voice.
- Silently affirm: *"I speak my truth with clarity and confidence."*

Enhancing Intuition with Indigo

The blue light deepens into a mystical indigo, filling the area around your third eye.
- Emotional State: Feel a sense of inner wisdom and deep understanding.
- Mental State: Notice clarity in your thoughts and an openness to intuition.
- Physical Sensation: Sense a gentle pressure or tingling between your eyebrows.
- Spiritual State: Feel connected to your inner vision and higher consciousness.
- Silently affirm: *"I trust my intuition and see with clarity."*

Connecting to Divinity with Violet

Watch the indigo light transform into a radiant violet that surrounds the top of your head.
- Emotional State: Feel a sense of serenity, wholeness, and oneness.
- Mental State: Experience a quiet, expansive awareness beyond ordinary thought.
- Physical Sensation: Sense a gentle, upward pull at the top of your head.
- Spiritual State: Feel deeply connected to divine energy and universal wisdom.
- Silently affirm: *"I am connected to the divine and in harmony with the universe."*

Integrating White Light for Unity

Visualize all the colors blending into a brilliant white light that encompasses your entire aura.
- Emotional State: Feel balanced and at peace.
- Mental State: Experience clarity, alignment, and focus.
- Physical Sensation: Sense lightness and harmony throughout your body.

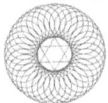

- Spiritual State: Feel a deep connection to the infinite and the unity of all energies.
- Silently affirm: *"I am whole, balanced, and aligned with universal energy."*

Take a deep breath in, feeling the white light sealing your aura, harmonizing all the colors within it. As you exhale, bring your awareness back to your body. Gently wiggle your fingers and toes, and when you are ready, open your eyes.

Take a moment to reflect on how each color felt and what insights arose about your emotional, mental, physical, and spiritual states.

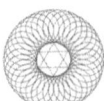

Advanced Guided Meditation: Channeling Unique Colors into Your Aura

Find a quiet, comfortable space where you can sit or lie undisturbed. Close your eyes and take several deep breaths, allowing your body and mind to relax. This meditation will guide you in channeling non-traditional colors into your aura, helping you explore how these unique energies influence your emotional, mental, physical, and spiritual states. Visualize your aura as a glowing, flexible field of energy surrounding your body. It is a canvas that can shift and adapt as you invite new colors into it. With each color, focus on its unique qualities, and observe how it interacts with your energy, emotions, thoughts, physical sensations, and spiritual awareness.

Silver: Reflection and Clarity
Imagine your aura filling with a soft, shimmering silver light.
- Emotional State: Feel a sense of neutrality and emotional detachment, as though you can observe your feelings without being overwhelmed.
- Mental State: Notice an enhanced clarity, as if your mind is a polished mirror reflecting only what is essential.
- Physical Sensation: Sense coolness or lightness, as though tension is dissipating.
- Spiritual State: Feel connected to higher guidance and reflective wisdom, as though the silver light is a bridge to divine insights.
- Silently affirm: *"I am clear, reflective, and open to wisdom."*

Gold: Empowerment and Radiance
Now, allow the silver light to transition into a radiant golden glow.
- Emotional State: Feel a surge of confidence, empowerment, and joy.
- Mental State: Experience clarity and purpose, with an ability to focus on your goals.
- Physical Sensation: Sense warmth spreading through your body, like sunlight on your skin.
- Spiritual State: Feel deeply connected to divine abundance and the universal flow of prosperity.

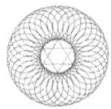

- Silently affirm: *"I am radiant, empowered, and aligned with divine energy."*

Turquoise: Balance and Expression
Visualize your aura shifting to a bright, refreshing turquoise.
- Emotional State: Feel a blend of calmness and creative energy, balancing emotions with joy.
- Mental State: Notice openness and flexibility in your thinking, with ideas flowing freely.
- Physical Sensation: Sense a soothing, cooling energy, as if washing away tension.
- Spiritual State: Feel connected to authentic self-expression and harmonious communication.
- Silently affirm: *"I express myself with balance, creativity, and clarity."*

Lavender: Tranquility and Subtle Awareness
Allow your aura to soften into a gentle lavender hue.
- Emotional State: Feel a deep sense of calm and tranquility, releasing stress and worry.
- Mental State: Notice subtle awareness and intuitive insights emerging naturally.
- Physical Sensation: Sense a light, tingling sensation, like a gentle breeze.
- Spiritual State: Feel connected to subtle realms of consciousness and spiritual peace.
- Silently affirm: *"I am tranquil, intuitive, and aligned with higher awareness."*

Peach: Warmth and Nurturing
Now, visualize your aura filling with a soft peach-colored glow.
- Emotional State: Feel warmth, nurturing, and a sense of gentle comfort.
- Mental State: Experience ease and compassion in your thoughts, letting go of harsh self-judgment.
- Physical Sensation: Sense a soft, enveloping warmth, like being wrapped in a cozy blanket.

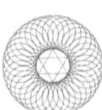

- Spiritual State: Feel deeply connected to the energy of unconditional love and kindness.
- Silently affirm: *"I am warm, nurtured, and surrounded by gentle love."*

Charcoal Gray: Grounding and Introspection

Allow your aura to darken slightly into a smooth charcoal gray.
- Emotional State: Feel a sense of introspection and detachment, allowing you to process emotions without judgment.
- Mental State: Notice a grounding of your thoughts, with a focus on practicality and clarity.
- Physical Sensation: Sense a calming heaviness, like being anchored securely to the earth.
- Spiritual State: Feel connected to deep inner wisdom and the ability to reflect without distraction.
- Silently affirm: *"I am grounded, introspective, and deeply centered."*

Pearl: Purity and Wholeness

Visualize your aura shifting into a luminous pearlescent light.
- Emotional State: Feel a sense of purity, peace, and renewal.
- Mental State: Notice clarity and alignment, as though your thoughts are in perfect harmony.
- Physical Sensation: Sense lightness and purity, like a soft breeze cleansing your energy.
- Spiritual State: Feel connected to your true essence, whole and untouched by external influences.
- Silently affirm: *"I am pure, whole, and connected to my essence."*

Copper: Strength and Transformation

Now, visualize a warm copper tone filling your aura.
- Emotional State: Feel resilience and adaptability, as though you can handle anything with grace.
- Mental State: Notice creative and transformative thoughts emerging, with an openness to new possibilities.

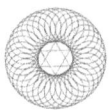

- Physical Sensation: Sense a strengthening energy coursing through your body, invigorating and revitalizing you.
- Spiritual State: Feel deeply rooted in transformative growth and aligned with the cycles of life.
- Silently affirm: *"I am resilient, transformative, and aligned with my inner strength."*

Soft Pink: Tenderness and Harmony
Finally, visualize your aura glowing with a gentle, soft pink light.
- Emotional State: Feel tender love and compassion, both for yourself and others.
- Mental State: Notice gentle and harmonious thoughts, free from criticism or conflict.
- Physical Sensation: Sense a delicate, soothing energy washing over you, like a soft embrace.
- Spiritual State: Feel deeply aligned with the vibration of universal love and emotional healing.
- Silently affirm: *"I am tender, compassionate, and surrounded by love."*

Integration: Blending the Colors
Now visualize all these unique colors blending harmoniously into your aura, creating a dynamic and multifaceted energy field.
- Observe how each color contributes to your overall emotional, mental, physical, and spiritual balance.
- Silently affirm: *"I am a vibrant, balanced being, aligned with the full spectrum of my energy."*

Take a deep breath in, feeling your aura glowing brightly with all the colors you have experienced. Exhale slowly, sealing this energy field around you. Bring your awareness back to your physical body. Wiggle your fingers and toes, stretch gently, and open your eyes when you are ready.

Advanced Guided Meditation: Comprehensive Energy Clearing, Cleansing, and Realignment

This meditation will guide you through the advanced clearing, cleansing, and realignment of all 18 chakras, the 7 layers of your aura, and the grounding and reinforcement of your entire energetic system for a deep, in-depth energy reset.

Find a quiet, comfortable space where you will not be disturbed. Sit or lie down in a relaxed position. Close your eyes, take several deep breaths, and allow your body to settle. Set an intention for the meditation, such as: *"I clear, cleanse, and realign my chakras and aura for balance, clarity, and harmony."*

<u>Entering Sacred Space</u>
- Visualize a column of white light descending from above, surrounding your entire body.
- Feel this light forming a protective and sacred space for your energy work.
- Silently affirm: *"I am safe, supported, and open to receiving this deep energy cleanse and alignment."*

<u>Part 1: Clearing and Realigning the 18 Chakras</u>
Earth Gateway Chakra
- Located 12 inches below your feet, this chakra anchors your connection to the earth.
- Visualize a deep, rich brown light glowing beneath your feet.
- Breathe in stability and strength and exhale any stagnant energy.
- Silently affirm: *"I am deeply connected to the earth's core and grounded in its wisdom."*

Feet Chakras
- Visualize glowing orbs at the soles of your feet.
- Imagine earth energy flowing upward, clearing and opening these chakras.
- Silently affirm: *"I walk my path with clarity and purpose."*

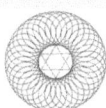

Root Chakra
- Located at the base of your spine, this chakra grounds your physical energy.
- Visualize a vibrant red light spinning and clearing away fear or instability.
- Silently affirm: *"I am safe, secure, and grounded."*

Sacral Chakra
- Below your navel, this chakra governs creativity and emotions.
- Visualize a glowing orange light swirling gently, releasing emotional blockages.
- Silently affirm: *"I flow with joy and creative energy."*

Knee Chakras
- Located in both knees, these chakras support flexibility in movement and life.
- Visualize warm golden lights at your knees, dissolving resistance and stiffness.
- Silently affirm: *"I move forward with grace and ease."*

Solar Plexus Chakra
- In your stomach area, this chakra radiates confidence and personal power.
- Picture a bright yellow sun shining, clearing away self-doubt.
- Silently affirm: *"I am empowered and confident in my purpose."*

Heart Chakra
- At the center of your chest, this chakra holds love and compassion.
- Visualize a soft green or pink light expanding outward, healing emotional wounds.
- Silently affirm: *"I give and receive love freely and openly."*

Hand Chakras
- Located in your palms, these chakras facilitate healing and creation.

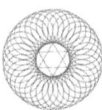

- Visualize bright orbs of light in your hands, glowing with warmth and energy.
- Silently affirm: *"I create and heal with love and intention."*

Throat Chakra
- At your throat, this chakra governs communication.
- See a bright blue light clearing and opening, allowing authentic expression.
- Silently affirm: *"I speak my truth with clarity and confidence."*

Mouth of God Chakra
- Located at the base of the skull, this chakra connects to divine wisdom.
- Visualize a radiant silver light glowing and opening this connection.
- Silently affirm: *"I am aligned with divine wisdom and truth."*

Telepathic Chakras
- Located at the Third Eye Chakra (center of the forehead), subtle points near the temples, and behind the ears, these chakras govern telepathic communication and intuitive connection.
- Visualize soft indigo or violet lights glowing in these areas, connected by streams of radiant energy.
- Breathe deeply, drawing in clarity and universal wisdom, and exhale any mental blocks or resistance to intuitive connection.
- Silently affirm: *"I am open to receive and transmit energy and thoughts with clarity, love, and alignment with universal truth."*

Third Eye Chakra
- Between your eyebrows, this chakra enhances intuition.
- Picture an indigo light glowing brightly, opening inner vision and insight.
- Silently affirm: *"I trust my intuition and inner wisdom."*

Crown Chakra

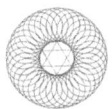

- At the top of your head, this chakra connects you to the divine.
- Visualize a violet or white light expanding upward, linking you to universal energy.
- Silently affirm: *"I am one with divine energy and wisdom."*

Soul Star Chakra
- Above your head, this chakra connects to your higher self.
- Visualize a golden-white orb glowing, harmonizing with your soul's purpose.
- Silently affirm: *"I align with my higher self and divine purpose."*

Stellar Gateway Chakra
- Located further above, this chakra links to universal consciousness.
- Visualize a shimmering iridescent light expanding infinitely.
- Silently affirm: *"I am connected to universal wisdom and infinite possibilities."*

Universal Chakra
- Connecting all realms, this chakra links your energy to the cosmos.
- Visualize a multidimensional light clearing and aligning this space.
- Silently affirm: *"I am one with the infinite universe."*

Cosmic Gateway Chakra
- The highest chakra, connecting to divine source energy.
- Visualize a brilliant, infinite sphere of light above your head, infusing your entire system.
- Silently affirm: *"I am a channel for divine creation and universal love."*

Earth Star Chakra
- Located beneath your feet, this chakra anchors your entire energetic system.
- Visualize a deep grounding energy pulling all other chakras into alignment with the earth.

- Silently affirm: *"I am deeply rooted and balanced in the earth's energy."*

Part 2: Clearing and Grounding the 7 Layers of the Aura

Physical Layer
- Visualize a glowing white light clearing blockages closest to your body.
- Silently affirm: *"My physical energy is cleansed and grounded."*

Emotional Layer
- Picture a soft pink light soothing and balancing your emotions.
- Silently affirm: *"My emotional energy flows freely and peacefully."*

Mental Layer
- Imagine a bright golden light clearing mental clutter and overthinking.
- Silently affirm: *"My thoughts are clear and grounded."*

Astral Layer
- Visualize a serene blue light connecting and harmonizing your relationships.
- Silently affirm: *"I am in harmony with my external connections."*

Etheric Template Layer
- Picture an indigo light repairing and strengthening your energetic blueprint.
- Silently affirm: *"My energy template is whole and aligned."*

Celestial Layer
- Imagine a radiant violet light aligning your spiritual connection.
- Silently affirm: *"I am connected to divine love and light."*

Ketheric Layer
- Visualize a shimmering golden-white light sealing and protecting your aura.

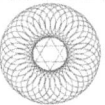

- Silently affirm: *"My entire aura is cleansed, grounded, and protected."*

Part 3: Grounding and Sealing the Energy
- Visualize your entire chakra system and aura glowing brightly, fully aligned and grounded.
- Imagine roots extending from every chakra and auric layer into the earth.
- Silently affirm: *"I am balanced, grounded, and in perfect harmony."*

Take a deep breath, feeling the harmony and alignment within you. Slowly bring your awareness back to your body, wiggle your fingers and toes, and open your eyes when ready.

Subtle Bodies

The concept of the mental, emotional, physical, and spiritual bodies refers to different aspects or dimensions of a person's existence and well-being, often called the "subtle bodies" or "energy bodies". These bodies are like layers or dimensions that define various aspects of our experience and are not necessarily identical to the aura layers, although there is overlap in energy practices.

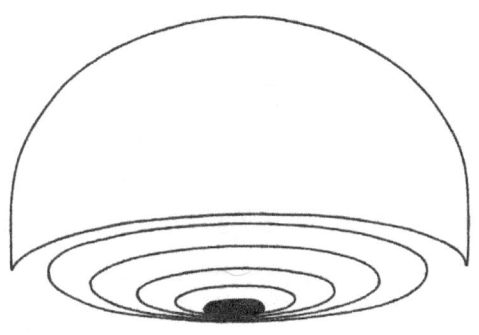

Rainbow Reiki Subtle Bodies Symbol

While the aura layers reflect a structured, layered energy field surrounding the body, the subtle bodies are more like multi-dimensional aspects that influence the core of our physical, emotional, mental, and spiritual experiences.

The aura layers serve as an outward expression of the state of these subtle bodies:
- Physical Body ↔ Etheric Layer: Physical health and vitality are reflected in the aura's etheric layer.
- Emotional Body ↔ Emotional Layer: Emotional states manifest in the emotional layer of the aura.
- Mental Body ↔ Mental Layer: Thoughts and beliefs are mirrored in the aura's mental layer.
- Spiritual Body ↔ Celestial and Ketheric Layers: Spiritual insights and connection to higher consciousness are expressed in these higher aura layers.

Aura Layers are focused on the vibrational "layers" that extend from the physical body outward. These are seen as a structured energy field surrounding the body and associated with different chakras and frequencies.

Subtle Bodies refers to the dimensions of human experience—physical, emotional, mental, and spiritual—that form the core of our existence. They are more about the "essence" of our being and influence how we experience life on all levels.

Energy practices such as grounding, chakra balancing, and aura cleansing work on harmonizing both the aura layers and the subtle bodies. While the aura layers help visualize the energy field's structure, the subtle bodies emphasize the internal dimensions and levels of awareness that guide overall well-being.

Understanding both concepts helps provide a holistic view of energy work and healing, supporting balance, alignment, and an integrated sense of well-being across all levels of existence.

Subtle Bodies Across Traditions
The concept of the subtle bodies—the physical, emotional, mental, and spiritual aspects of existence—has been understood and explored across various spiritual traditions, each offering unique insights into their function and interconnection.

While modern energy healing often emphasizes the relationship between the aura layers and the chakras, ancient traditions have long recognized these multi-dimensional aspects of human consciousness as essential to overall well-being.

In ancient Egyptian wisdom, the subtle bodies were deeply intertwined with the Ka (vital energy body), Ba (soul consciousness), and Akh (spirit body). The Ka was akin to the etheric body, representing life force, vitality, and the energetic double of a person, sustaining physical existence. The Ba, often depicted as a human-headed bird, embodied the emotional and mental bodies, carrying personal consciousness and identity beyond death. The Akh, the highest form of spiritual transformation, aligned with the spiritual body, merging with divine cosmic forces and the afterlife realms. Egyptian spiritual practices involved sacred geometry, temple initiations, and energy purification rituals to balance these bodies,

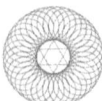

ensuring harmonious passage between dimensions and higher states of consciousness.

In Tibetan philosophy, the concept of subtle bodies is foundational in esoteric Buddhism, particularly in the study of the prana (life force), nadis (energy channels), and bindu (spiritual essence). Tibetan teachings describe three primary energy channels—Ida (left, lunar), Pingala (right, solar), and Sushumna (central channel)—which correspond to the mental, emotional, and spiritual bodies. The physical body is understood as a manifestation of karmic imprints, while the emotional and mental bodies hold attachments and aversions that influence reincarnation cycles. The spiritual body is cultivated through tantric practices, breathwork, and deep meditation, aiming for complete transcendence of duality into the state of rigpa (pure awareness). Tibetan monks practice dream yoga, energy work, and deity visualizations to harmonize the subtle bodies and dissolve illusions of separation from the divine.

The Arcturian perspective views the subtle bodies as bio-electromagnetic layers of consciousness, each acting as a frequency bandwidth that interfaces with higher-dimensional intelligence. The physical body is seen as a densified light form, structured by vibrational patterns from higher realms. The emotional and mental bodies are understood as holographic imprints, carrying the soul's encoded experiences across lifetimes. The spiritual body is recognized as an interstellar bridge, connecting an individual's higher self to the cosmic grid of universal consciousness. Arcturian healing involves light infusion, DNA recalibration, and photonic frequency adjustments to ensure that all subtle bodies remain synchronized with Earth's ascension process and multidimensional evolution.

From a Pleiadian viewpoint, the subtle bodies are seen as fluid, harmonic fields of consciousness, continuously shifting in response to emotional resonance, energetic intention, and planetary frequencies. The physical body is not viewed as separate but as an expression of energy crystallized into form. The emotional and mental bodies function as vibrational regulators, determining how a

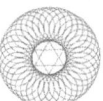

person interacts with different timelines and parallel realities. The spiritual body is understood as a frequency bridge, allowing for soul integration, ancestral healing, and interstellar communication. Pleiadians emphasize harmonic attunement, light activations, and sound frequencies to align the subtle bodies, enabling individuals to experience greater ease in multidimensional awareness and embodiment of their divine potential.

The Bible contains references to the subtle bodies as aspects of divine creation and consciousness. 1 Thessalonians 5:23 states, "May God himself, the God of peace, sanctify you through and through. May your whole spirit, soul and body be kept blameless at the coming of our Lord Jesus Christ." This verse acknowledges the spiritual, emotional (soul), and physical dimensions of a person as distinct yet interwoven elements of divine wholeness. Hebrews 4:12 further supports this idea: "For the word of God is alive and active. Sharper than any double-edged sword, it penetrates even to dividing soul and spirit, joints and marrow; it judges the thoughts and attitudes of the heart." This passage reflects the ability of divine consciousness to discern between the mental, emotional, and spiritual bodies, recognizing them as integral parts of a unified existence.

Across these traditions, the subtle bodies are consistently described as multi-dimensional aspects of human existence, essential for spiritual growth, healing, and energetic harmony. While Egyptians viewed them as aspects of the soul's divine journey, Tibetans focused on their purification for enlightenment, Arcturians perceived them as cosmic energy interfaces, and Pleiadians recognized them as vibrational fluidity, all perspectives align in acknowledging their profound role in shaping human consciousness.

Understanding and working with the subtle bodies allows individuals to experience greater balance, intuitive clarity, and a deeper connection to their highest potential.

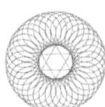

Physical Body

The physical layer of the subtle bodies, often referred to as the etheric body, is the energetic blueprint of the physical form and the closest layer to the body in the auric field. It serves as a bridge between the physical and energetic realms, maintaining the health and vitality of the physical body by channeling universal life force energy to every organ, tissue, and cell. This layer vibrates just beyond the skin and mirrors the physical form in its structure, extending slightly outward and encompassing the physical anatomy. It acts as a protective shield, filtering and absorbing energy from the environment and other subtle layers while grounding this energy into the physical body.

Rainbow Reiki Subtle Body Physical Body Symbol

The physical layer is integral to overall well-being, as imbalances or blockages in this layer can manifest as physical discomfort, illness, or fatigue. It interacts with the chakras and energy meridians, distributing life force energy throughout the body and maintaining equilibrium. Advanced energy practices, such as Rainbow Reiki, focus on cleansing and harmonizing the etheric body to enhance its connection to higher vibrational frequencies while grounding it firmly in Gaia's energy. Techniques like energy clearing, vibrational upgrades, and multidimensional alignments ensure the physical layer remains resilient, vibrant, and aligned with the universal flow of energy.

This layer also serves as a key interface for healing work, providing a gateway for practitioners to address physical ailments by influencing their energetic root causes. By working with the etheric body, individuals can experience improved vitality, strengthened immunity, and an enhanced connection to their physical form. Understanding and engaging with this subtle body layer allows for deeper self-awareness, a greater sense of embodiment, and a holistic approach to physical and energetic well-being.

Advanced Subtle Body Physical Layer Guided Meditation

The physical layer of the subtle body, often referred to as the etheric body, is the energetic double of the physical form. It governs vitality, supports the health of the physical body, and serves as the bridge between the physical and subtle dimensions. This advanced guided meditation integrates the multidimensional frequencies of Rainbow Reiki—including Usui, Shadow, Arcturian, Pleiadian, Egyptian Sekhem-Seichim, and Magdalene/Yeshua Reiki—to cleanse, strengthen, and help you connect deeply with the energy of the subtle body's physical layer.

Find a quiet and comfortable space to sit or lie down. Close your eyes and take several deep breaths, inhaling deeply through your nose and exhaling slowly through your mouth. Allow your body to relax, releasing tension and inviting calmness into your being.

Set your intention: *"I welcome the advanced energies of Rainbow Reiki to cleanse, balance, and deepen my connection to the physical layer of my subtle body, enhancing vitality, alignment, and well-being."*

<u>Grounding and Cosmic Alignment</u>
Visualize roots extending from your feet deep into the Earth's crystalline core. Feel Gaia's grounding energy rising through these roots, flowing into your body and energizing every cell and tissue. At the same time, imagine a column of radiant rainbow light descending from the cosmos, entering your crown chakra, and cascading throughout your physical body and subtle body's physical layer.

Feel the merging of Earth and cosmic energies within and around you, creating a harmonious flow for cleansing and healing.

<u>Activating the Physical Layer of the Subtle Body</u>
Bring your awareness to the space just beyond your physical skin, where the physical layer of the subtle body resides. Visualize it as a shimmering, glowing layer of energy that mirrors the outline of your physical form. It radiates health, vitality, and connection to the universal life force.

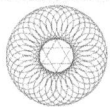

Notice its texture, movement, and brightness. Allow yourself to sense the unique energetic feeling of this subtle body layer—its warmth, vibration, or gentle pulsation.

Affirm: *"I am deeply connected to the physical layer of my subtle body, which radiates health and vitality."*

Cleansing the Physical Layer of the Subtle Body
Visualize a deep indigo light from Shadow Reiki surrounding the physical layer of your subtle body. This light gently dissolves blockages, stagnant energy, or imbalances that may interfere with the natural flow of energy. Feel this indigo light clearing away tension, fatigue, or illness from your energetic field.

Once the cleansing feels complete, imagine a soft rose-gold light from Magdalene/Yeshua Reiki infusing the physical layer of your subtle body. This light brings love, harmony, and renewal, restoring balance and radiance to this energetic layer.

Affirm: *"I release all blockages and imbalances, allowing the physical layer of my subtle body to flow freely and harmoniously."*

Strengthening and Energizing
Visualize intricate geometric patterns of golden and emerald-green light from Egyptian Sekhem-Seichim Reiki weaving through the physical layer of your subtle body. These sacred patterns stabilize and fortify its structure, enhancing its ability to support and protect your physical health.

Next, see vibrant rainbow light from Pleiadian and Arcturian Reiki streaming into this layer. This light activates its multidimensional connections, aligning it with universal energy grids and cosmic frequencies.

Feel the physical layer of your subtle body becoming more vibrant, balanced, and connected to the infinite flow of universal energy.

Affirm: *"The physical layer of my subtle body is vibrant, balanced, and aligned with the flow of universal life force energy."*

Becoming Familiar with the Energetic Feeling of the Physical Layer
Spend a few moments focusing on the unique energetic sensation of the physical layer of your subtle body. Notice its texture, warmth, or pulsation as it surrounds and interacts with your physical form. Observe how it feels when it is cleansed, balanced, and aligned with your health and vitality. Deepen your awareness of its energy and its role in supporting your well-being.

Affirm: *"I am attuned to the energy of the physical layer of my subtle body, vibrant and aligned with universal health and vitality."*

Integration and Multidimensional Alignment
Expand your awareness to include the energetic connections of the physical layer of your subtle body to your emotional, mental, and spiritual layers. Visualize its energy harmonizing with your auric field and connecting to the Earth Star Chakra, Heart Chakra, and universal grids.

Imagine the physical layer of your subtle body aligning with Gaia's crystalline grid and cosmic frequencies. Feel its energy integrating with your divine blueprint, enhancing your vitality and creating balance across all aspects of your being.

Affirm: *"The physical layer of my subtle body is fully integrated, balanced, and aligned with my highest potential and universal flow."*

Bring your awareness back to your heart center. Visualize a glowing orb of rainbow light within your chest, pulsating with gratitude and healing energy. Allow this light to radiate outward, integrating all the healing energies you have received.

Take a moment to thank the physical layer of your subtle body for its role in supporting your health and vitality. Express gratitude for the Rainbow Reiki energies and your ability to heal and align with universal life force energy.

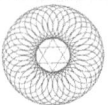

When you feel ready, gently bring your awareness back to the present moment. Wiggle your fingers and toes, stretch lightly, and open your eyes.

Post-Meditation Care
- Hydration: Drink water to support the integration of healing energies and the release of any residual blockages.
- Reflection: Journal any sensations, insights, or shifts you experienced, noting how your physical and subtle body layers feel.
- Body-Centric Practices: Engage in physical activities like yoga, walking, or stretching to reinforce your connection to your physical and subtle layers.

This meditation can be practiced regularly to maintain the strength, balance, and vitality of your physical layer of the subtle body while deepening your connection to its energy and the multidimensional frequencies of Rainbow Reiki.

Emotional Body

The emotional body layer of the subtle bodies is intricately tied to feelings, desires, and emotional experiences, serving as a dynamic and fluid energy field that directly impacts the mental and physical states. Located beyond the physical layer, the emotional body radiates in vibrant, shifting colors that reflect an individual's emotional state, such as love, anger, joy, or sadness. This layer acts as the energetic repository for unresolved emotional patterns, trauma, and deeply held feelings, influencing the chakras and shaping one's perception of the world. The emotional body's health is critical for overall well-being, as imbalances or distortions can manifest as emotional instability, stress, or even physical symptoms.

Rainbow Reiki Subtle Body Emotional Body Symbol

Advanced energy practices like Rainbow Reiki work with the emotional body to cleanse and harmonize this layer, facilitating the release of stored emotions and the resolution of patterns that may hinder growth. Techniques include using high-frequency energies to dissolve emotional blockages, recalibrating the vibrational flow, and activating the heart and sacral chakras for emotional balance and creative expression. The emotional body is a conduit for cultivating self-love, empathy, and emotional resilience, allowing individuals to process their emotions constructively and align with their higher self.

This subtle body layer also connects to the astral plane, influencing dreams, intuition, and interdimensional emotional experiences. By healing and strengthening the emotional body, individuals can achieve a greater sense of inner peace, improve their relationships, and develop a deeper connection to their authentic emotions. Engaging with the emotional body fosters personal transformation, unlocking the potential for emotional freedom, harmonious living, and expanded spiritual awareness.

Advanced Subtle Body Emotional Layer Guided Meditation

The emotional layer of the subtle body governs the flow of feelings, desires, and emotional experiences, influencing the physical, mental, and spiritual aspects of one's being. This layer radiates vibrant colors that shift with emotional states and serves as a repository for emotional energy, including unresolved patterns and traumas.

This advanced guided meditation integrates the multidimensional frequencies of Rainbow Reiki—including Usui, Shadow, Arcturian, Pleiadian, Egyptian Sekhem-Seichim, and Magdalene/Yeshua Reiki—to cleanse, balance, and harmonize the emotional body while deepening your connection to its energy.

Find a quiet, comfortable space to sit or lie down. Close your eyes and take several deep breaths, inhaling deeply through your nose and exhaling slowly through your mouth. Allow your body to relax, releasing tension with each exhale, and opening your energy field to receive healing.

Set your intention: *"I invite the advanced energies of Rainbow Reiki to cleanse, heal, and align my emotional body, releasing old patterns and fostering balance, harmony, and emotional freedom."*

<u>Grounding and Cosmic Connection</u>
Visualize roots extending from your feet deep into the Earth's crystalline core. Feel Gaia's nurturing energy rising through these roots, flowing upward to support and stabilize your emotional body. Simultaneously, imagine a radiant column of rainbow light descending from the cosmos, entering through your crown chakra, and spreading outward to envelop your emotional body in a cocoon of high-frequency light.

Feel the merging of Earth's grounding energy and cosmic frequencies within your emotional body, creating a harmonious flow for healing.

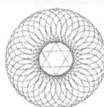

Activating the Emotional Body

Bring your awareness to the space surrounding your physical body, where the emotional body radiates its energy. Visualize it as a vibrant, fluid layer of shifting colors—soft pink, warm orange, calming green, or any hues that resonate with your emotional state. Allow yourself to sense the unique energetic feeling of this layer—its flow, warmth, or gentle vibration.

Affirm: *"I am connected to the energy of my emotional body, which reflects my feelings, desires, and inner harmony."*

Cleansing the Emotional Body

Visualize a deep indigo light from Shadow Reiki flowing through your emotional body. This light gently dissolves emotional blockages, unresolved patterns, or stagnant energies that may cloud your emotional field. As the indigo light moves, feel the release of old fears, grief, anger, or any emotions that no longer serve you.

Once the cleansing feels complete, imagine a soft rose-gold light from Magdalene/Yeshua Reiki infusing your emotional body. This light radiates unconditional love, emotional balance, and a sense of inner peace, restoring the natural harmony of this layer.

Affirm: *"I release all emotional blockages and patterns, allowing my emotional body to flow freely and harmoniously."*

Strengthening and Energizing

Visualize intricate golden and orange geometric patterns from Egyptian Sekhem-Seichim Reiki weaving through your emotional body. These sacred patterns stabilize its energetic structure, enhancing its resilience and capacity to process emotions constructively.

Next, see vibrant rainbow light from Pleiadian and Arcturian Reiki streaming into your emotional body. This light activates its multidimensional aspects, aligning it with higher vibrational frequencies and cosmic emotional balance.

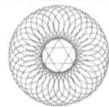

Feel your emotional body becoming more vibrant, balanced, and deeply connected to the flow of universal love and emotional harmony.

Affirm: *"My emotional body is vibrant, balanced, and aligned with universal harmony and emotional freedom."*

<u>Becoming Familiar with the Energetic Feeling of the Emotional Body</u>
Spend a few moments focusing on the unique energetic sensations of your emotional body. Notice its fluidity, warmth, or pulsation as it interacts with your physical form.

Observe how it feels when it is cleansed, balanced, and aligned with the universal flow of energy. Deepen your awareness of its role in processing emotions and supporting your well-being.

Affirm: *"I am attuned to the energy of my emotional body, aligned with balance, harmony, and emotional freedom."*

<u>Integration and Multidimensional Alignment</u>
Expand your awareness to include the energetic connections of your emotional body to your physical, mental, and spiritual layers. Visualize its energy harmonizing with your auric field and connecting seamlessly to your Heart Chakra, Sacral Chakra, and universal grids.

Imagine your emotional body aligning with Gaia's nurturing energy and cosmic frequencies. Feel its energy integrating with your divine blueprint, enhancing your capacity for self-love, emotional resilience, and authentic expression.

Affirm: *"My emotional body is fully integrated, balanced, and aligned with my highest potential and the universal flow of love and harmony."*

Bring your awareness back to your heart center. Visualize a glowing orb of rainbow light within your chest, pulsating with gratitude and healing energy. Allow this light to radiate outward, integrating all the healing energies you have received.

Take a moment to thank your emotional body for its role in processing your feelings and supporting your growth. Express gratitude for the Rainbow Reiki energies and your ability to heal and align with universal harmony.

When you feel ready, gently bring your awareness back to the present moment. Wiggle your fingers and toes, stretch lightly, and open your eyes.

Post-Meditation Care
- Hydration: Drink water to support the release of emotional blockages and enhance the flow of energy.
- Reflection: Journal any emotions, sensations, or insights you experienced, noting how your emotional body feels.
- Emotional Nurturing: Engage in self-care practices such as journaling, meditation, or creative expression to reinforce the healing and balance of your emotional body.

This meditation can be practiced regularly to maintain the strength, balance, and vitality of your emotional body while deepening your connection to its energy and the multidimensional frequencies of Rainbow Reiki.

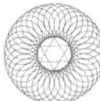

Mental Body

The mental body layer of the subtle bodies is the energetic field associated with thoughts, beliefs, and cognitive processes, shaping an individual's perception of reality and their capacity for logic, creativity, and intuition. Positioned beyond the emotional body, the mental body appears as a structured, radiant field of light that often emanates patterns, forms, and symbols corresponding to a person's mental activity. This layer serves as the interface between conscious and subconscious thought, housing deeply ingrained belief systems, habitual thinking patterns, and intellectual knowledge. It is intricately linked to the third eye and crown chakras, playing a vital role in processing information, decision-making, and connecting to higher wisdom.

Rainbow Reiki Subtle Body Mental Body Symbol

In advanced energy practices like Rainbow Reiki, the mental body is a focal point for clearing limiting beliefs, reframing negative thought patterns, and harmonizing the vibrational resonance of the mind. Energetic techniques work to dissolve mental blockages, recalibrate the flow of energy within this layer, and integrate higher frequencies that align the mind with universal truth and clarity. This process supports enhanced mental clarity, greater focus, and the ability to access higher states of consciousness.

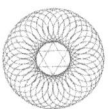

The mental body also connects to the collective consciousness, making it a pathway for receiving insights, universal wisdom, and creative inspiration. Balancing and strengthening this layer allows individuals to transcend mental constructs that no longer serve them, unlocking new potentials for innovation, intuition, and spiritual growth. A healthy mental body promotes an aligned mindset, fostering a harmonious relationship between thoughts, emotions, and the physical body while enabling a deeper connection to one's soul purpose and universal knowledge.

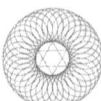

Advanced Subtle Body Mental Layer Guided Meditation
The mental layer of the subtle body governs thoughts, beliefs, and mental patterns, shaping how you perceive and interact with the world. It is the energetic field where conscious and subconscious thought resides, and it plays a vital role in mental clarity, creativity, and alignment with universal wisdom. This advanced guided meditation integrates the multidimensional frequencies of Rainbow Reiki—including Usui, Shadow, Arcturian, Pleiadian, Egyptian Sekhem-Seichim, and Magdalene/Yeshua Reiki—to cleanse, balance, and align the mental layer while deepening your connection to its energy.

Find a quiet and comfortable space to sit or lie down. Close your eyes and take several deep breaths, inhaling deeply through your nose and exhaling slowly through your mouth. Allow your body to relax, releasing tension with each exhale, and opening your energy field to receive healing.

Set your intention: *"I invite the advanced energies of Rainbow Reiki to cleanse, balance, and align the mental layer of my subtle body, releasing limiting beliefs and fostering clarity, creativity, and universal wisdom."*

<u>Grounding and Cosmic Connection</u>
Visualize roots extending from your feet deep into the Earth's crystalline core. Feel Gaia's stabilizing energy rising through these roots, flowing upward into your body and supporting the mental layer of your subtle body. Simultaneously, imagine a radiant column of rainbow light descending from the cosmos, entering your crown chakra, and expanding outward to envelop the mental layer in high-frequency light.

Feel the merging of Earth's grounding energy and cosmic wisdom within the mental layer, creating a harmonious flow for healing and alignment.

<u>Activating the Mental Layer</u>
Bring your awareness to the space surrounding your emotional body, where the mental layer radiates. Visualize it as a structured, luminous field of light filled with patterns, symbols, or streams of

vibrant energy that represent your thoughts and beliefs. Allow yourself to sense the unique energetic feeling of this layer—its clarity, structure, or flow.

Affirm: *"I am connected to the mental layer of my subtle body, which reflects my thoughts, beliefs, and mental clarity."*

Cleansing the Mental Layer
Visualize a deep indigo light from Shadow Reiki flowing through your mental layer. This light gently dissolves mental blockages, negative thought patterns, or limiting beliefs that no longer serve your highest good. Feel the indigo light clearing away confusion, overthinking, or mental rigidity, leaving your mental body calm and open.

Once the cleansing is complete, imagine a soft golden light from Magdalene/Yeshua Reiki infusing the mental layer. This light radiates peace, harmony, and divine wisdom, restoring balance and clarity to your thoughts and beliefs.

Affirm: *"I release all limiting thoughts and beliefs, allowing my mental body to flow freely with clarity and wisdom."*

Strengthening and Energizing
Visualize intricate geometric patterns of gold and silver light from Egyptian Sekhem-Seichim Reiki weaving through your mental layer. These sacred patterns stabilize and fortify its structure, enhancing its capacity to channel universal truth and higher guidance.

Next, see vibrant rainbow light from Pleiadian and Arcturian Reiki streaming into the mental layer. This light activates its multidimensional aspects, aligning it with cosmic intelligence and the infinite flow of universal energy.

Feel your mental body becoming more vibrant, balanced, and aligned with universal clarity, creativity, and insight.

Affirm: *"My mental body is vibrant, balanced, and aligned with divine wisdom and creative potential."*

Becoming Familiar with the Energetic Feeling of the Mental Layer
Spend a few moments focusing on the unique energetic sensations of your mental body. Notice its structure, brightness, or pulsation as it interacts with your thoughts and beliefs. Observe how it feels when it is cleansed, balanced, and aligned with universal truth and clarity. Deepen your awareness of its role in supporting mental clarity and creative expression.

Affirm: *"I am attuned to the energy of my mental body, aligned with clarity, creativity, and universal wisdom."*

Integration and Multidimensional Alignment
Expand your awareness to include the energetic connections of your mental body to your physical, emotional, and spiritual layers. Visualize its energy harmonizing with your auric field and connecting seamlessly to your Third Eye Chakra, Crown Chakra, and universal grids.

Imagine your mental body aligning with Gaia's stabilizing energy and cosmic frequencies. Feel its energy integrating with your divine blueprint, enhancing your ability to think clearly, create intuitively, and access higher states of consciousness.

Affirm: *"My mental body is fully integrated, balanced, and aligned with universal flow and my highest potential."*

Bring your awareness back to your heart center. Visualize a glowing orb of rainbow light within your chest, pulsating with gratitude and healing energy. Allow this light to radiate outward, integrating all the healing energies you have received.

Take a moment to thank your mental body for its role in supporting your clarity and alignment. Express gratitude for the Rainbow Reiki energies and your ability to heal and align with universal truth.

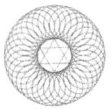

When you feel ready, gently bring your awareness back to the present moment. Wiggle your fingers and toes, stretch lightly, and open your eyes.

Post-Meditation Care
- Hydration: Drink water to support the release of mental blockages and enhance the flow of energy.
- Reflection: Journal any insights, sensations, or shifts you experienced, noting changes in mental clarity or creativity.
- Mindful Practices: Engage in activities that stimulate your mind and creativity, such as meditation, writing, or problem-solving, to reinforce the healing and balance of your mental body.

This meditation can be practiced regularly to maintain the strength, balance, and vitality of your mental body while deepening your connection to its energy and the multidimensional frequencies of Rainbow Reiki.

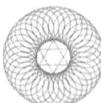

Spiritual Body

The spiritual body layer, the most expansive and transcendent of the subtle bodies, connects an individual to their soul, higher self, and universal consciousness. Encompassing all other layers, it radiates a luminous, infinite energy that reflects one's divine essence and alignment with the higher realms. This layer serves as the bridge between the individual and Source energy, holding the blueprint for spiritual growth, life purpose, and multidimensional awareness. It is associated with the crown chakra, as well as higher chakras such as the Soul Star, Stellar Gateway, and Cosmic Gateway, facilitating access to divine guidance, cosmic wisdom, and universal love.

Rainbow Reiki Subtle Body
Spiritual Body Symbol

In advanced energy practices like Rainbow Reiki, the spiritual body is a focal point for aligning with one's highest potential and integrating multidimensional energies. Techniques involve clearing distortions in this layer, recalibrating it to resonate with higher frequencies, and anchoring cosmic energies into the lower layers to support holistic healing. By harmonizing the spiritual body, practitioners enable deeper connections to the divine, fostering inner peace, spiritual awakening, and alignment with the greater flow of universal energy.

The spiritual body is also the key to understanding and navigating the ascension process, as it holds the energetic imprints of past lifetimes, karmic patterns, and the evolutionary path of the soul. Working with this layer supports the dissolution of separation, helping individuals transcend egoic limitations and embrace their oneness with the universe. A balanced and vibrant spiritual body enhances intuitive abilities, amplifies spiritual gifts, and aligns the individual with their soul mission, enabling them to embody their authentic essence and experience profound spiritual fulfillment.

Advanced Subtle Body Spiritual Layer Guided Meditation

The spiritual layer of the subtle body is the most expansive, connecting you to your higher self, soul purpose, and universal consciousness. This layer encompasses all other subtle body layers and serves as the bridge to divine realms, cosmic wisdom, and multidimensional awareness. Through this advanced guided meditation, the multidimensional frequencies of Rainbow Reiki—including Usui, Shadow, Arcturian, Pleiadian, Egyptian Sekhem-Seichim, and Magdalene/Yeshua Reiki—are utilized to cleanse, balance, and align your spiritual body, deepening your connection to your divine essence and Source energy.

Find a quiet, comfortable space to sit or lie down. Close your eyes and take several deep breaths, inhaling deeply through your nose and exhaling slowly through your mouth. Allow your body and mind to relax with each exhale, releasing any tension or distractions, and opening yourself to the flow of universal energy.

Set your intention: *"I invite the advanced energies of Rainbow Reiki to cleanse, balance, and align my spiritual body, connecting me to my higher self, soul purpose, and universal consciousness."*

Grounding and Cosmic Alignment
Visualize roots extending from your feet deep into the Earth's crystalline core. Feel Gaia's nurturing energy rising through these roots, grounding and stabilizing your physical and energetic bodies. At the same time, imagine a radiant column of rainbow light descending from the cosmos, entering your crown chakra, and expanding outward to encompass your spiritual body in a cocoon of infinite light.

Feel the merging of Earth's grounding energy and cosmic light within your spiritual body, creating a harmonious foundation for healing and alignment.

Activating the Spiritual Body
Bring your awareness to the space surrounding your mental body, where the spiritual body radiates its energy. Visualize it as a luminous, infinite field of pure, radiant light—golden, silver, and

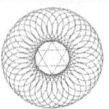

iridescent hues shimmering and pulsating. This field expands far beyond your physical body, connecting you to the vastness of the universe.

Allow yourself to sense the unique energetic feeling of the spiritual body—its expansiveness, transcendence, and profound sense of connection to Source energy.

Affirm: *"I am connected to the infinite light and wisdom of my spiritual body, which aligns me with my soul purpose and universal truth."*

<u>Cleansing the Spiritual Body</u>
Visualize a deep indigo light from Shadow Reiki flowing through your spiritual body. This light gently dissolves any blockages, distortions, or dense energies that hinder your connection to your higher self and divine realms. Feel the indigo light clearing away old karmic imprints, limiting beliefs, or energetic debris that no longer serve your spiritual growth.

Once the cleansing is complete, imagine a soft golden light from Magdalene/Yeshua Reiki infusing your spiritual body. This light radiates unconditional love, divine peace, and a profound sense of unity with the universe, restoring the vibrancy and alignment of this layer.

Affirm: *"I release all limitations and blockages, allowing my spiritual body to radiate divine light and wisdom."*

<u>Strengthening and Energizing</u>
Visualize intricate geometric patterns of golden and crystalline light from Egyptian Sekhem-Seichim Reiki weaving through your spiritual body. These sacred patterns stabilize and fortify its structure, enhancing its ability to channel Source energy and universal frequencies.

Next, see vibrant rainbow light from Pleiadian and Arcturian Reiki streaming into the spiritual body. This light activates its

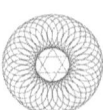

multidimensional aspects, aligning it with the universal grids, cosmic wisdom, and the infinite flow of divine energy.

Feel your spiritual body becoming more radiant, expansive, and aligned with your highest vibrational potential and the infinite wisdom of the universe.

Affirm: *"My spiritual body is vibrant, balanced, and fully aligned with divine light and universal consciousness."*

<u>Becoming Familiar with the Energetic Feeling of the Spiritual Body</u>
Spend a few moments focusing on the unique energetic sensation of your spiritual body. Notice its vastness, luminous quality, and profound connection to Source energy. Observe how it feels when it is cleansed, balanced, and aligned with universal truth and divine flow. Deepen your awareness of its role as the bridge to higher realms and your soul's essence.

Affirm: *"I am attuned to the energy of my spiritual body, aligned with infinite wisdom, universal love, and my divine purpose."*

<u>Integration and Multidimensional Alignment</u>
Expand your awareness to include the connections of your spiritual body to your physical, emotional, and mental layers. Visualize its energy radiating outward, harmonizing your entire auric field and seamlessly connecting with your Crown Chakra, Soul Star Chakra, and Cosmic Gateway Chakra.
Imagine your spiritual body aligning with Gaia's crystalline grid and the multidimensional grids of the universe. Feel its energy integrating with your divine blueprint, enhancing your spiritual awareness, cosmic alignment, and connection to Source.

Affirm: *"My spiritual body is fully integrated, balanced, and aligned with the infinite flow of divine energy and my highest potential."*

Bring your awareness back to your heart center. Visualize a glowing orb of rainbow light within your chest, pulsating with gratitude and

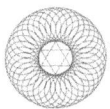

peace. Allow this light to radiate outward, integrating all the healing energies you have received.

Take a moment to thank your spiritual body for its role in connecting you to your divine essence and the universe. Express gratitude for the Rainbow Reiki energies and your ability to align with infinite love and universal consciousness.

When you feel ready, gently bring your awareness back to the present moment. Wiggle your fingers and toes, stretch lightly, and open your eyes.

Post-Meditation Care
- Hydration: Drink water to support the release of energetic blockages and the integration of divine energy.
- Reflection: Journal any insights, sensations, or shifts you experienced, noting how your connection to your higher self and Source feels.
- Spiritual Practices: Engage in meditation, prayer, or journaling to deepen your alignment with your spiritual body and maintain its balance and vibrancy.

This meditation can be practiced regularly to maintain the strength, balance, and vitality of your spiritual body while deepening your connection to its energy and the multidimensional frequencies of Rainbow Reiki.

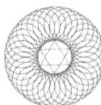

Guided Meditation for Balancing Subtle Bodies

Begin by finding a comfortable seated or lying position. Close your eyes gently and take a deep breath in through your nose, holding it briefly, then exhale slowly through your mouth. Repeat this three times, allowing your body to settle and your mind to become still.

Body Awareness

Bring your attention to your physical body. Mentally scan from the top of your head to the tips of your toes. Notice areas of tension or discomfort without judgment and imagine them softening with each exhale.

Affirm: *"I honor my physical body as the sacred vessel for my soul."*

Emotional Awareness

Shift your focus to your heart space. Observe any emotions present—joy, sadness, peace, frustration. Allow yourself to feel without attaching labels or stories. Picture a gentle golden light expanding from your heart, soothing and embracing these emotions.

Affirm: *"I embrace my emotions as guides to my inner truth."*

Mental Clarity

Turn your awareness to your thoughts. Imagine them as clouds drifting across the sky—some light and fluffy, others dark and heavy. Let them float by, knowing you don't need to hold on to any one thought.

Affirm: *"I cultivate a clear and focused mind."*

Spiritual Connection

Visualize a stream of white or violet light pouring into the crown of your head, connecting you to a higher source of wisdom and love. Feel this light filling your body, merging with your subtle bodies, creating harmony.

Affirm: *"I am connected to the divine essence within and around me."*

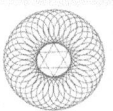

Integration and Gratitude

Envision all four subtle bodies (physical, emotional, mental, spiritual) aligning like layers of a radiant sphere surrounding you. Breathe deeply into this alignment, feeling balanced and whole. Offer gratitude for this moment of self-awareness and connection. Slowly bring your awareness back to the room. Wiggle your fingers and toes, and when you are ready, open your eyes. Take a moment to reflect on how you feel before moving on with your day.

Advanced Guided Meditation: Harmonizing the Subtle Bodies

Sacred Space & Centering

Begin in a quiet, sacred space. Light a candle, burn incense, or set up crystals if desired. Take a deep breath, and on the exhale, set the intention to harmonize your subtle bodies for higher alignment. Visualize a protective sphere of golden-white light surrounding you, ensuring only energies of the highest vibration enter this space.

Activation of the Physical Body (Grounding)

Sit or lie down comfortably, connecting to the earth beneath you. Imagine roots growing from your base (tailbone, feet, or spine), deep into Earth's crystalline core. Feel Earth's nurturing energy rising, infusing your body with vitality.

Affirm: *"I am grounded, and my physical body is a temple for divine energy."*

Take a few moments to feel each cell of your body activating with life force energy.

Emotional Body (Heart Activation)

Shift your focus to your heart space. Picture a lotus flower blooming at the center of your chest, radiating gentle, iridescent light. Invite any emotional residues—old wounds, suppressed feelings, or joy—to rise into your awareness. Use your breath to release heavy energies on the exhale and amplify love and gratitude on the inhale.

Affirm: *"I flow with the frequency of unconditional love and emotional balance."*

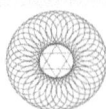

Mental Body (Alignment and Clarity)

Visualize your mind as a calm, still lake. Each thought becomes a ripple, dissolving as it touches the edges of the lake. Call in a beam of indigo light, entering through your third eye (brow center). This light clears mental clutter and enhances intuitive clarity. If you feel called, invite a specific guide, archetype, or higher aspect of yourself to communicate through insight.

Affirm: *"My mind is aligned with the wisdom of the cosmos and my divine truth."*

Spiritual Body (Expansion)

Draw your awareness to your crown chakra and feel it opening like a thousand-petaled lotus, connecting to infinite Source energy. Envision a column of pure white or golden light descending from above, integrating into every layer of your being. As this light merges with your energy, allow your awareness to expand beyond your physical form. Sense the interconnectedness of all life.

Affirm: *"I am a luminous being of light, unified with the universal consciousness."*

Subtle Body Integration (Multidimensional Harmony)

Picture the four layers of your subtle bodies (physical, emotional, mental, spiritual) as interlocking orbs of light, each vibrating at its unique frequency. Envision these orbs spinning and aligning, harmonizing as one radiant sphere around you. Tune into this sphere's vibration, sensing any imbalances being healed, upgraded, and recalibrated to your highest good.

Cosmic Connection and Intentional Manifestation

From this aligned state, set an intention or ask for guidance on your spiritual journey. Allow the energy of your intention to ripple outward, planting seeds in the infinite field of possibility. Trust that these energies will return in divine timing, perfectly aligned with your highest purpose. Slowly draw your awareness back to your body. Visualize the light gently sealing into your subtle bodies, anchoring your expanded awareness into the present moment.

Gently press your palms together at your heart center and express gratitude for this connection and the sacred work you have just completed.

Rainbow Reiki History

Reiki, a Japanese energy healing modality founded by Mikao Usui, is rooted in the principles of channeling universal life force energy for physical, emotional, and spiritual healing. Traditionally, Usui Reiki is structured into three levels: Level 1 (Shoden), focusing on self-healing and hands-on practice; Level 2 (Okuden), introducing distance healing and symbols; and Level 3 (Shinpiden), which includes the Master level for teaching and deeper spiritual work. Over time, additional levels have been developed, expanding Reiki into 20 levels in some advanced systems. These additional levels often involve attunements to higher frequencies, advanced symbols, and work on multidimensional healing, aligning practitioners with the needs of contemporary spiritual evolution.

Beyond Usui Reiki, alternative and complementary systems such as Egyptian Sekhem-Seichim Reiki integrate ancient Egyptian energy healing practices, invoking Sekhem (a term for universal energy) for profound transformation and connection to divine archetypes. Shadow Reiki delves into the subconscious and unacknowledged aspects of the self, helping practitioners address and transmute shadow energies into healing and integration. Pleiadian Crystalline Reiki connects practitioners to the high-vibrational energies of the Pleiadian star beings, channeling crystalline light to activate DNA and raise spiritual consciousness. Similarly, Arcturian Reiki draws upon the wisdom of Arcturian star beings, focusing on interdimensional healing and aligning the practitioner with advanced spiritual frequencies.

Magdalene/Yeshua Reiki centers on the energies associated with Mary Magdalene and Yeshua (Jesus), embodying compassion, divine love, and spiritual awakening. This modality facilitates heart-centered healing, divine feminine and masculine balance, and a deep connection to Christ consciousness. Together, these diverse Reiki

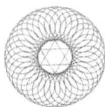

systems provide an advanced, multidimensional framework for energy healing, tailored to the unique vibrational needs and spiritual paths of practitioners and recipients.

The integration of these diverse Reiki systems into what is now referred to as Rainbow Reiki represents a groundbreaking evolution in energy healing, combining the unique strengths of each modality to meet the advancing vibrational needs of humanity and the planet. As the collective consciousness shifts toward the Age of Aquarius and Gaia ascends into a fifth-dimensional (5D) frequency, traditional and standalone methods are no longer sufficient to sustain the profound healing and transformation required for this new era. Rainbow Reiki weaves together the foundational principles of Usui Reiki with the ancient wisdom of Egyptian Sekhem-Seichim, the shadow work of Shadow Reiki, and the multidimensional alignments offered by Pleiadian, Arcturian, and Magdalene/Yeshua Reiki. This unified approach creates a holistic and advanced healing framework designed to activate higher consciousness, align with universal unity, and catalyze the ascension of both individuals and the collective.

This evolution is essential because each method, while powerful in its own right, addresses only specific aspects of healing and spiritual growth. In isolation, these systems no longer provide the expansive results they once did, as humanity now requires more integrated and multidimensional approaches to match the accelerated pace of energetic shifts on Earth. Rainbow Reiki bridges the gap by unifying the strengths of these modalities, enabling practitioners to address healing on every level—physical, emotional, mental, and spiritual—while also working in alignment with the cosmic energies that govern the planet's evolution. Through this unity, Rainbow Reiki empowers individuals to clear ancestral and karmic patterns, activate crystalline DNA, balance divine feminine and masculine energies, and access the wisdom of higher-dimensional guides.

As we enter the Golden Age, Rainbow Reiki serves as a vital tool for aligning with the energies of love, unity, and harmony that characterize the 5D frequency. It fosters a deeper connection

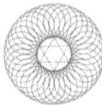

between humanity and Gaia, supporting not only personal ascension but also the collective evolution of consciousness. This modality represents a call to unity, reminding us that collaboration, integration, and the synthesis of diverse traditions are key to navigating this new era. By embracing Rainbow Reiki, we honor the richness of our shared spiritual heritage while stepping into the limitless potential of the future, co-creating a world aligned with the highest frequencies of peace, compassion, and enlightenment.

Traditional Usui Reiki
Traditional Usui Reiki is a spiritual and energetic healing system founded by Mikao Usui in the early 20th century. It is rooted in the principles of universal life force energy and serves as a method for self-healing, personal growth, and channeling healing energy to others. Usui Reiki is typically structured into three progressive levels: Level 1 (Shoden), Level 2 (Okuden), and Level 3 (Shinpiden), each offering deeper attunements, practices, and spiritual understanding. Together, these levels create a holistic framework for healing, personal development, and connection to the universal energy that sustains all life.

Level 1: Shoden focuses on personal healing and introduces the practitioner to Reiki energy. At this stage, students receive their first attunement, a sacred energetic process conducted by a Reiki Master that opens the practitioner's energy channels and connects them to the universal life force. This attunement allows the practitioner to channel Reiki energy through their hands for self-healing and to share it with others through direct touch. The primary focus at Level 1 is on self-care, grounding, and becoming familiar with the flow of Reiki energy. Students are also introduced to the foundational principles of Reiki, known as the gokai (Five Precepts), which encourage mindfulness, compassion, and a harmonious way of living. This level lays the groundwork for developing energetic sensitivity, emotional balance, and an understanding of how Reiki facilitates physical and spiritual well-being.

Level 2: Okuden deepens the practitioner's connection to Reiki energy and expands their ability to work with others. At this level,

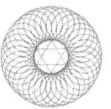

practitioners receive additional attunements and are introduced to the first three sacred Reiki symbols: the Power Symbol (Cho Ku Rei), the Harmony Symbol (Sei He Ki), and the Distance Symbol (Hon Sha Ze Sho Nen). These symbols act as keys to focus and amplify Reiki energy, enabling the practitioner to address specific issues such as emotional healing, mental clarity, or clearing energetic blockages. The Distance Symbol, in particular, empowers the practitioner to send Reiki across time and space, making it possible to perform distance healing or address past and future events energetically. Okuden emphasizes a deeper spiritual commitment, encouraging practitioners to cultivate intuition and explore the broader applications of Reiki in their daily lives and healing practices.

Level 3: Shinpiden, also known as the Master Level, represents the culmination of Usui Reiki training and is both a path of mastery and a spiritual journey. At this stage, practitioners receive the Master Symbol (Dai Ko Myo), the most powerful of the Reiki symbols, which facilitates spiritual awakening, deep healing, and connection to divine consciousness. The Master Symbol is often described as the gateway to enlightenment, amplifying the practitioner's ability to channel universal energy and align with their higher self. Shinpiden training often includes teachings on how to perform attunements, enabling the practitioner to pass on Reiki energy to others as a Master Teacher. However, not all who complete Level 3 choose to teach; some pursue mastery solely for personal growth and to deepen their spiritual connection. Shinpiden emphasizes the practitioner's role as a vessel for universal energy, fostering humility, gratitude, and alignment with the interconnectedness of all life.

Throughout the progression from Level 1 to Level 3, Traditional Usui Reiki nurtures a holistic transformation, balancing the physical, emotional, mental, and spiritual aspects of the individual. It is not only a healing practice but also a way of life, guiding practitioners to embody peace, compassion, and alignment with universal energy. Each level builds upon the last, offering tools and insights that empower practitioners to heal themselves, assist others, and contribute to the collective evolution of consciousness. Traditional

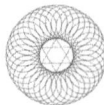

Usui Reiki remains one of the most accessible and profound systems for exploring the depths of energy healing and spiritual awakening.

Advanced Usui Reiki

Advanced Grand Master Levels 4–20 in Usui Reiki represent a significant evolution beyond the traditional three levels, expanding the scope of Reiki into multidimensional healing and advanced spiritual work. These levels were developed to address the growing spiritual needs of practitioners and the planet as humanity progresses into higher states of consciousness. Each level introduces practitioners to advanced attunements, symbols, and techniques designed to amplify their ability to work with universal energy and higher frequencies. While not part of Mikao Usui's original system, these Grand Master levels are a response to the spiritual and energetic demands of contemporary times, blending traditional Reiki principles with innovative energy work to support healing on a global and cosmic scale.

Levels 4–10 focus on the refinement of energy flow, advanced symbol work, and personal mastery. Practitioners receive attunements to higher-frequency symbols that resonate with cosmic energies, enabling them to access deeper layers of healing and spiritual insight. These levels often emphasize the development of intuitive abilities, such as clairvoyance, clairaudience, and clairsentience, to enhance the practitioner's connection to universal guidance. Additionally, practitioners are trained to work with the subtle bodies, including the astral, etheric, and causal layers, allowing them to facilitate profound healing that transcends the physical and emotional realms. This stage also introduces concepts of planetary healing, where practitioners channel energy to assist in Gaia's ascension process and the collective evolution of humanity.

Levels 11–16 represent a shift from personal mastery to cosmic and multidimensional work. These levels introduce practitioners to interdimensional Reiki techniques, including working with higher-dimensional beings, star energies, and crystalline grids. The focus here is on anchoring 5D and higher frequencies into the human energy field, activating dormant DNA, and aligning with divine

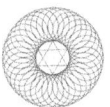

blueprints. Advanced symbols at this stage often carry light codes and sacred geometry, designed to harmonize the practitioner with universal consciousness. These levels also train practitioners in transmuting karmic imprints and ancestral patterns, facilitating liberation from cycles of limitation and enabling a greater alignment with one's soul mission.

Levels 17–20 culminate in the mastery of universal energy at its highest levels, often referred to as Grand Mastery. These levels are deeply spiritual and transformative, focusing on ascension, unity consciousness, and the practitioner's role as a conduit for global and cosmic healing. Practitioners are taught to work with the Akashic Records, access timelines, and integrate universal wisdom into their practice. These levels emphasize becoming a pure vessel for divine energy, embodying unconditional love, and radiating healing to all beings. Practitioners at this stage are often called to teach and mentor others, guiding them through the advanced levels of Reiki and supporting their own spiritual journeys.

The Grand Master levels of Usui Reiki are not just a continuation of the traditional system but an expansion that aligns with the accelerated spiritual evolution of humanity. They provide a framework for advanced practitioners to work with higher energies, integrate multidimensional healing, and play an active role in the ascension of the planet and its inhabitants. These levels challenge practitioners to transcend personal limitations, embrace their divine essence, and contribute to the collective awakening with wisdom, compassion, and mastery.

Egyptian Sekhem-Seichim Reiki
Egyptian Sekhem-Seichim Reiki is a multidimensional energy healing system that integrates the ancient Egyptian concept of Sekhem, the universal life force energy that flows through all creation, with modern frequency-based healing techniques. Rooted in the vibrational wisdom of ancient Egypt, this modality emphasizes the dynamic interplay of sound, vibration, and light frequencies to facilitate profound transformation on physical, emotional, mental, and spiritual levels. Practitioners channel Sekhem energy, often

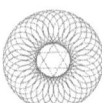

associated with the goddess Sekhmet, a symbol of power, healing, and protection, to bring balance and vitality to the energy body.

What sets Sekhem-Seichim Reiki apart is its advanced use of soundwaves and frequency healing in harmony with universal energy flow. Sound, considered a sacred tool in Egyptian cosmology, serves as a carrier for Sekhem energy, amplifying its potency and precision. Practitioners may use vocal toning, chanting ancient mantras, or instruments such as tuning forks, crystal singing bowls, and gongs to generate specific frequencies that resonate with the recipient's energy field. These frequencies penetrate deep into the cellular and energetic layers, breaking up stagnant energy, restoring coherence, and recalibrating the recipient's energetic blueprint.

In a Sekhem-Seichim Reiki session, the practitioner works with both the physical and subtle energy systems, focusing on the chakras, meridians, and auric layers. As the universal energy flows through the practitioner, sound vibrations act as a guide, targeting areas of energetic misalignment or blockages. This integration creates a dual healing effect: the frequencies address physical and energetic density, while Sekhem energy promotes spiritual expansion and connection to higher consciousness. The result is not only a release of physical and emotional imbalances but also an activation of the recipient's innate healing potential and a deeper alignment with their soul purpose.

This modality also emphasizes the role of sacred geometry and light codes embedded within the Sekhem energy. Practitioners often visualize or invoke energetic structures, such as pyramids or ankh symbols, to further amplify healing. Combined with the resonance of soundwaves, these symbols bridge the earthly and cosmic planes, creating a conduit for transformative energy flow. By harmonizing ancient Egyptian wisdom, sound frequency, and universal energy, Sekhem-Seichim Reiki provides a holistic, deeply restorative experience that facilitates personal evolution, spiritual awakening, and multidimensional healing.

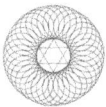

Shadow Reiki

Shadow Reiki is a transformative energy healing modality that delves into the depths of the subconscious and the unacknowledged aspects of the self, often referred to as the "shadow." The term "shadow" originates from the work of Carl Jung, who defined it as the parts of the psyche we suppress, deny, or reject—often due to societal conditioning, trauma, or fear. Shadow Reiki blends traditional Reiki energy work with psychological and spiritual techniques to illuminate and integrate these hidden aspects, fostering wholeness, healing, and self-awareness. Unlike traditional Reiki, which focuses on channeling universal life force energy for general balance and well-being, Shadow Reiki specifically targets the darker, unhealed, or repressed areas of a person's energy field, helping them confront and release deeply embedded patterns, fears, and emotional wounds.

At the core of Shadow Reiki is the understanding that the shadow is not inherently negative but rather a repository of unprocessed emotions, unresolved trauma, and untapped potential. By addressing the shadow, practitioners can help clients uncover the root causes of recurring patterns, self-sabotage, and limiting beliefs. During a session, the practitioner creates a safe, compassionate space for the client to explore their energetic and emotional depths. Using traditional Reiki techniques, symbols, and intuitive guidance, the practitioner channels healing energy to illuminate areas where the shadow is most active. This may include clearing energetic blockages, soothing emotional pain, and inviting the client to confront aspects of themselves they have long avoided.

Advanced Shadow Reiki often incorporates visualization, guided inner journeys, and energetic dialogue with the shadow self. Practitioners may guide clients to envision their shadow as a distinct presence within their energy field, often appearing as a symbolic figure, color, or feeling. Through this visualization, the client is encouraged to communicate with their shadow, asking what it needs to feel seen, heard, or healed. The practitioner supports this process by channeling Reiki energy to maintain a high vibrational container, allowing the client to face their shadow without fear or

judgment. Additionally, advanced Shadow Reiki sessions may include the use of specific symbols, such as the Sei He Ki (emotional and mental healing symbol), to deepen the clearing of subconscious blockages or to heal past-life trauma that contributes to the shadow's presence.

Shadow Reiki is particularly powerful for addressing patterns of guilt, shame, anger, and fear, as well as healing deep wounds related to trauma, abandonment, or betrayal. As the shadow is acknowledged and integrated, clients often experience a profound shift in their energy, gaining greater self-acceptance, inner peace, and empowerment. The integration of shadow aspects not only heals old wounds but also unlocks hidden strengths, creativity, and wisdom, transforming the shadow from a source of pain into a wellspring of growth. This modality is ideal for individuals committed to deep self-work, spiritual evolution, and authentic embodiment of their true selves. Shadow Reiki ultimately aligns clients with their higher self, enabling them to live more harmoniously and authentically by embracing all facets of their being.

Pleiadian Crystalline Reiki
Pleiadian Crystalline Reiki is an advanced energy healing modality that draws upon the high-frequency energies of the Pleiadian star beings, integrating them with crystalline light to facilitate deep spiritual transformation, energetic upgrades, and multidimensional healing. The Pleiadians, often regarded as compassionate and spiritually evolved beings, are known for their connection to humanity's ascension journey. This modality channels their wisdom and energy to activate crystalline codes within the body and energy field, aligning recipients with higher dimensions of consciousness and accelerating spiritual evolution. Pleiadian Crystalline Reiki focuses on raising the vibrational frequency of the individual, clearing blockages, and activating dormant DNA to enhance physical, emotional, and spiritual well-being.

At the heart of Pleiadian Crystalline Reiki is the concept of the crystalline grid, an energetic network believed to connect humanity

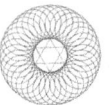

with higher-dimensional frequencies and Earth's ascension process. Practitioners work with crystalline light energy, visualized as luminous, multifaceted beams, often in hues of gold, silver, and iridescent blue, which carry the Pleiadian frequency. This energy penetrates the auric field and cellular structures, dissolving dense energies, clearing karmic imprints, and realigning the chakras to higher-dimensional frequencies. The crystalline light also acts as a carrier for Pleiadian light codes—energetic blueprints designed to awaken spiritual gifts, activate higher consciousness, and harmonize the energy body with the divine cosmic flow.

During a session, practitioners typically channel Pleiadian energy through advanced Reiki techniques, including specific hand positions, intuitive guidance, and visualization. They may also use sacred geometry and crystalline tools, such as clear quartz or celestite, to amplify the healing process. The energy flows into the recipient's energy field, targeting areas of stagnation or misalignment. One of the key aspects of this modality is its ability to integrate and harmonize multidimensional energy layers, allowing recipients to access deeper levels of healing that transcend time and space. This often includes past-life healing, ancestral clearing, and the release of energetic imprints that hinder spiritual growth.

Pleiadian Crystalline Reiki also emphasizes the activation of crystalline DNA, a concept that refers to the potential for human DNA to hold and express higher-dimensional frequencies. As the crystalline codes are activated, individuals may experience heightened intuition, enhanced connection to their soul purpose, and a deepened sense of unity with the cosmos. This process often brings about profound inner shifts, including emotional release, spiritual insights, and a greater capacity for unconditional love. Practitioners and recipients alike describe the energy as deeply loving, nurturing, and empowering, creating a safe and expansive space for healing and transformation.

This modality is ideal for those on a path of ascension, seeking to elevate their vibration, activate spiritual gifts, or connect more deeply with their cosmic origins. Pleiadian Crystalline Reiki aligns

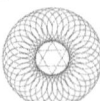

the recipient with the frequencies of the New Earth paradigm, fostering a sense of peace, clarity, and alignment with their higher self. It is both a healing and an activation process, awakening the soul's potential and anchoring the recipient into their divine blueprint for this lifetime. Through its integration of Pleiadian guidance, crystalline light, and universal energy flow, this advanced Reiki system offers a profound and transformative journey into higher consciousness.

Arcturian Reiki

Arcturian Reiki is an advanced energy healing modality rooted in the high-frequency guidance of Arcturian beings, renowned for their wisdom and technological advancements in energy healing and spiritual evolution. This system goes beyond traditional Reiki by addressing the multidimensional layers of human consciousness and integrating cutting-edge energetic techniques to facilitate profound healing and ascension. One of its hallmarks is its focus on cellular regeneration, neurotransmitter recalibration, mitochondrial DNA upgrades, and the activation of evolutionary pathways in human brain development, making it a transformative tool for those seeking deep physical, mental, and spiritual alignment.

At the core of advanced cellular regeneration in Arcturian Reiki is the activation of the body's innate healing mechanisms. Practitioners channel high-frequency Arcturian energy to restore cellular integrity, targeting areas of disease, dysfunction, or aging at the quantum level. This process involves clearing energetic imprints or trauma stored in the cells, allowing them to return to their natural, harmonious state. Visualizations of luminous geometric patterns and crystalline light are often used to restructure cellular function, promoting regeneration and vitality. This modality emphasizes the rejuvenation of tissues, organs, and systems, addressing issues ranging from chronic illnesses to accelerated aging. The energy works in concert with the recipient's divine blueprint, ensuring the healing is tailored to their highest potential.

Neurotransmitter protocols in Arcturian Reiki focus on balancing and enhancing the brain's chemistry to support optimal mental and emotional well-being. These protocols target the energetic patterns influencing neurotransmitter production, such as serotonin, dopamine, and GABA, which are crucial for regulating mood, cognition, and sleep. Practitioners use specialized symbols and frequencies to clear blockages in neural pathways, recalibrate the brain's energetic circuits, and foster a state of mental clarity, emotional balance, and spiritual receptivity. This aspect of Arcturian Reiki is particularly effective for addressing conditions such as anxiety, depression, post-traumatic stress disorder, and neurodivergent challenges, helping to rewire the brain for higher functioning and inner peace.

A significant focus of Arcturian Reiki is mitochondrial DNA upgrades, which involve activating the mitochondria as energetic powerhouses to sustain higher frequencies in the physical body. The mitochondria, responsible for cellular energy production, are recalibrated through Arcturian light codes to enhance their efficiency and resilience. This process supports the integration of light energy into the body, enabling the recipient to hold higher vibrational states without experiencing fatigue or energetic overwhelm. Mitochondrial DNA upgrades are also associated with awakening dormant genetic codes, facilitating evolutionary shifts in the body's structure and function. These upgrades contribute to the embodiment of the crystalline light body, a state of being essential for thriving in higher-dimensional realities.

Lastly, evolutionary human brain development is a cornerstone of Arcturian Reiki, aimed at activating the latent potential of the brain. This includes stimulating regions such as the pineal gland, which governs spiritual insight and higher consciousness, and enhancing neural plasticity to support the brain's ability to adapt to new frequencies and paradigms. Practitioners use advanced Arcturian symbols and frequencies to align the brain with cosmic intelligence, fostering expanded awareness, intuitive abilities, and multidimensional perception. This work facilitates the integration of

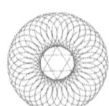

the divine mind, allowing recipients to access higher realms of wisdom and contribute to the collective evolution of humanity.

Arcturian Reiki is a pioneering modality for those on the cutting edge of spiritual and energetic evolution. By addressing the deepest layers of physical and energetic anatomy, it supports a seamless integration of advanced healing processes and ascension energies. Its unique focus on cellular regeneration, neurotransmitter recalibration, mitochondrial activation, and brain development positions it as a transformative tool for navigating humanity's leap into a higher dimensional state of being.

Magdalene/Yeshua Reiki
Magdalene/Yeshua Reiki is a profoundly heart-centered energy healing modality that draws upon the divine archetypal energies of Mary Magdalene and Yeshua (Jesus), combining the compassionate, nurturing essence of the Divine Feminine with the expansive, empowering frequency of the Divine Masculine. Rooted in Christ Consciousness, this system transcends traditional Reiki by focusing on awakening unconditional love, deep forgiveness, and spiritual unity. Magdalene/Yeshua Reiki is a pathway to personal and collective healing, helping practitioners and recipients embody their highest spiritual potential while integrating the sacred balance of feminine and masculine energies within themselves.

One of the core aspects of Magdalene/Yeshua Reiki is its focus on heart chakra activation and expansion, which serves as the foundation for profound healing and spiritual ascension. The energy channeled through this modality vibrates at the frequency of love and compassion, creating a sacred space for individuals to release emotional wounds, heal relational dynamics, and restore their connection to their own divinity. Practitioners often work with sacred symbols and light codes associated with Mary Magdalene and Yeshua, visualizing golden and rose-colored light to cleanse and amplify the heart's energy. This process not only facilitates personal healing but also activates the heart's ability to serve as a portal for accessing higher dimensions of consciousness, allowing individuals to align with their soul's purpose and Christ Consciousness.

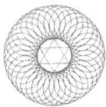

Magdalene/Yeshua Reiki also emphasizes karmic healing and the release of soul-level wounds. Practitioners work with the Akashic Records and the energetic imprints of past lives to clear patterns of suffering, guilt, and shame that have carried over into the present. By channeling the energies of Mary Magdalene and Yeshua, who embody unconditional love and forgiveness, practitioners guide recipients to release these burdens and embrace spiritual liberation. This aspect of the modality is particularly powerful for healing wounds related to betrayal, abandonment, and spiritual disconnection, as it provides an opportunity for profound transformation and reconnection to one's higher self. The integration of these energies fosters a state of grace, empowering individuals to move forward with clarity, authenticity, and renewed faith.

Another distinctive feature of Magdalene/Yeshua Reiki is its focus on sacred union and balance—both within the individual and in their external relationships. This modality emphasizes the importance of harmonizing the Divine Feminine and Divine Masculine energies, often depicted through the synergy of Mary Magdalene and Yeshua as spiritual equals. Practitioners are guided to channel energy that supports the integration of these polarities, enabling individuals to transcend duality and embody wholeness. This balance fosters deeper self-love, improved relationships, and the capacity to co-create in alignment with divine will. It also aligns recipients with the collective shift toward unity consciousness, a cornerstone of the ascension process.

Magdalene/Yeshua Reiki is not only a modality for healing but also a spiritual path that invites practitioners and recipients to embody the virtues of compassion, forgiveness, and divine love in their daily lives. It resonates deeply with the energies of the Age of Aquarius, supporting humanity's collective evolution toward a higher vibrational state of being. By merging the timeless wisdom of Mary Magdalene and Yeshua with the principles of Reiki, this system offers a powerful, multidimensional approach to healing and

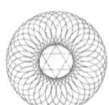

spiritual growth, guiding individuals to awaken their divine essence and radiate unconditional love into the world.

Advanced Guided Meditation for Receiving the Chi Ball Energy Frequency Attunement of Rainbow Reiki Symbols

Grounding
Find a quiet and comfortable place where you will not be disturbed. Sit or lie down with your spine straight, ensuring your body feels supported and relaxed. Close your eyes and take a few deep breaths, inhaling deeply through your nose and exhaling slowly through your mouth. Visualize roots growing from the base of your spine and feet, anchoring deep into Earth's crystalline core. As these roots connect, feel Earth's grounding energy flowing upward, stabilizing your body and mind.

Set your intention for this meditation: *"I open myself to receive the Chi Ball energy frequency attunement of all Rainbow Reiki symbols for my highest good, with ease, grace, and alignment with divine timing."*

Creating the Sacred Space
Visualize a protective sphere of golden-white light forming around you. This light is filled with divine love and purity, ensuring that only the highest vibrational energies enter your space. Call upon your spiritual guides, angels, ascended masters, and the benevolent beings associated with each Reiki system—Usui, Shadow, Arcturian, Pleiadian, Egyptian Sekhem-Seichim, and Magdalene/Yeshua Reiki—to support and guide you during this attunement.

Feel their presence surrounding you, their energies amplifying the sacredness of this moment.

Receiving the Chi Ball Attunement
Imagine a glowing Chi Ball of vibrant, multidimensional energy descending from above. This Chi Ball is infused with the frequencies, symbols, activations, and vibrational upgrades of all Rainbow Reiki systems. See it radiating with shimmering hues—gold, silver, violet, emerald green, deep blue, rose pink, and crystalline white—representing the spectrum of energies you are about to receive.

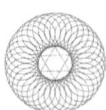

Visualize the Chi Ball gently hovering above your crown chakra, where it begins to dissolve into pure energy. Feel this energy flowing into your crown, activating your spiritual connection and opening your energy field to receive the attunement.

Activation of the Symbols
The energy from the Chi Ball now flows through your entire being, delivering the frequencies and activations of each Reiki system:

- Usui Reiki Symbols (Levels 1–20):
Visualize traditional Usui Reiki symbols, such as Cho Ku Rei, Sei He Ki, and Hon Sha Ze Sho Nen, alongside advanced Master symbols. Allow these symbols to illuminate your energy field, amplifying your ability to channel universal life force energy. Feel their balanced, foundational vibration anchoring within you.
- Shadow Reiki Symbols:
Sense a deep, grounding energy entering your subconscious. The Shadow Reiki symbols work gently, helping you transmute unacknowledged patterns, heal emotional wounds, and integrate aspects of your shadow self. You may perceive these as symbols, colors, or feelings.
- Arcturian and Pleiadian Reiki Symbols:
Feel the high-frequency vibrations of interdimensional energy activating your crystalline DNA, expanding your consciousness, and aligning your energy field with higher dimensions. These symbols may appear as geometric patterns, beams of light, or pure energetic pulses. Allow their advanced frequencies to recalibrate your physical and subtle bodies.
- Egyptian Sekhem-Seichim Reiki Symbols:
Golden and deep indigo energy flows through you, infused with sacred archetypal symbols representing ancient Egyptian wisdom. These frequencies activate regeneration, divine protection, and profound transformation, reconnecting you with the universal source energy of Sekhem.

- Magdalene/Yeshua Reiki Symbols:
  A wave of compassionate, heart-centered energy flows into your heart chakra. See or sense rose-pink and golden light, embodying divine love, forgiveness, and the sacred union of the feminine and masculine. These symbols open pathways for healing karmic wounds and aligning with Christ Consciousness.

Each symbol and frequency integrates into your being as a unique energetic blueprint, enhancing your ability to work with the Rainbow Reiki energy system.

<u>Anchoring and Integration</u>
Visualize the attunement energy flowing through all your chakras, balancing and harmonizing them. Imagine it anchoring deeply into your root chakra and extending into the earth through your grounding roots. Feel the attunement stabilizing within your body, mind, and spirit.

Affirm: *"I allow these energies and symbols to anchor, integrate, and align with my highest potential in divine timing. I trust this attunement process as it unfolds over the next 21 days."*

<u>Closing and Guidance</u>
Take a moment to thank the universal energy, the Chi Ball, and the spiritual guides who assisted you in this process. Visualize the protective sphere of light around you gently sealing in the attunement energy, ensuring it continues to integrate smoothly.

When you are ready, bring your awareness back to the present moment. Wiggle your fingers and toes, stretch gently, and open your eyes.

<u>Post-Attunement Recommendations</u>
- Drink an additional 20–30 ounces of water daily to support energetic detoxification.
- Eat a diet rich in fruits, vegetables, and clean foods to nourish your body during this process.

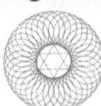

- Take weekly heavy metal detox baths, using Epsom salt, baking soda, or bentonite clay, to help clear toxins from your physical and energetic bodies.
- Journal your experiences over the 21-day integration period, noting any insights, dreams, or shifts in energy.

This attunement marks the beginning of a transformative journey into the advanced energies of Rainbow Reiki. Trust the process and allow the symbols and frequencies to anchor deeply into your being, guiding you toward alignment with your highest self and purpose.

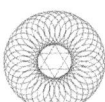

Rainbow Reiki Hand Placements Attunement Guided Meditation
Rainbow Reiki Hand Placements are a fusion of traditional Usui Reiki techniques and the advanced, multidimensional energies of Rainbow Reiki, incorporating the diverse frequencies and symbols of the integrated systems (Usui, Shadow, Arcturian, Pleiadian, Egyptian Sekhem-Seichim, and Magdalene/Yeshua Reiki). These placements serve as an intentional framework for channeling energy to the physical, emotional, mental, and spiritual bodies while addressing specific energy centers and multidimensional layers of the recipient. While traditional Reiki often focuses on the seven primary chakras, Rainbow Reiki hand placements expand this to include energetic grids, crystalline pathways, and interdimensional connections.

Crown and Higher Connection Hand Placements
Begin with one hand lightly resting on the crown chakra and the other positioned just above the head, connecting to the soul star chakra (a chakra located about six inches above the crown). This placement opens the recipient to receive universal life force energy and higher-dimensional frequencies, particularly from the Arcturian and Pleiadian energies. It aligns the recipient's energy field with their divine blueprint, activating crystalline DNA and enhancing their connection to cosmic intelligence. Visualize golden, silver, or violet light pouring into the crown, clearing blockages and facilitating mental clarity and spiritual expansion.

Heart-Centered Hand Placements
Move to the heart chakra, placing one hand directly over the chest and the other between the shoulder blades at the back heart center. This placement integrates the compassionate and nurturing energies of Magdalene/Yeshua Reiki and the transformative wisdom of Sekhem-Seichim Reiki. Visualize a glowing rose-pink and golden light expanding from the heart center, creating harmony and balance between the divine feminine and masculine within the recipient. This hand position is particularly effective for emotional healing, releasing grief, and fostering unconditional love.

Solar Plexus and Sacral Chakra Placements

For the solar plexus and sacral chakras, place one hand over the upper abdomen and the other just below the navel. This position works with Shadow Reiki to transmute emotional blockages, self-doubt, and suppressed fears. It also channels the powerful Sekhem-Seichim energy to activate personal power and creativity.

Visualize a vibrant golden or orange light swirling through these energy centers, clearing energetic stagnation and aligning the recipient with their authentic self. This placement is excellent for addressing confidence issues, creative blocks, and the integration of shadow aspects.

Root Chakra and Earth Connection

Place one hand over the root chakra at the base of the spine and the other on the recipient's feet (or a few inches above if not touching). This position grounds the recipient's energy, anchoring the high-frequency Rainbow Reiki energies into the earth through the crystalline grid. It also aligns the root with the heart of Gaia, supporting physical stability, vitality, and connection to Earth's ascension process. Use this placement to channel Arcturian and Sekhem-Seichim energies for cellular regeneration and clearing survival-based fears. Visualize a deep red or shimmering golden light flowing through the recipient, fostering security and resilience.

Multidimensional Energy Field Placement

Expand your focus beyond the physical body to the aura and energetic layers. Move your hands above and around the recipient's energy field, intuitively scanning for imbalances or blockages. Channel Reiki energy to the mental, emotional, and spiritual layers, addressing past-life imprints, karmic patterns, or interdimensional energies. Pleiadian Reiki is particularly effective here, infusing the energy field with crystalline light codes to activate DNA and align with higher-dimensional frequencies. Visualize a kaleidoscope of colors weaving through the aura, harmonizing and uplifting the recipient's entire energy system.

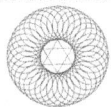

Integration and Closing
End the session with one hand on the heart chakra and the other on the solar plexus, creating a bridge between the upper and lower chakras. This placement integrates the healing energies and symbols, allowing them to anchor fully into the recipient's energy body. Visualize a unified rainbow light radiating throughout their being, signifying the completion of the healing process. Express gratitude for the energies channeled and seal the session with a protective, golden-white light around the recipient.

By combining these hand placements with the advanced symbols and frequencies of Rainbow Reiki, practitioners can address the multidimensional needs of the recipient while supporting their journey toward alignment, balance, and ascension. These placements are flexible and intuitive, allowing the practitioner to adapt to the unique energetic requirements of each session.

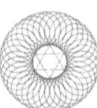

Basic Anatomy

A foundational understanding of basic anatomy and body systems is invaluable for Rainbow Reiki practitioners, as it enhances the precision and effectiveness of their energy healing work. While in-depth medical expertise is not required, knowledge of the body's systems—such as the skeletal, muscular, circulatory, nervous, endocrine, lymphatic, respiratory, and digestive systems—empowers practitioners to set clear, focused intentions during sessions. It enables them to energetically connect with specific organs, tissues, and physiological functions, offering tailored support that addresses the root causes of physical discomfort or energetic imbalances. For example, understanding the role of the nervous system in stress responses or the circulatory system in oxygenating the body allows practitioners to align their healing work with these critical functions, fostering more profound and effective outcomes.

This anatomical awareness also facilitates a holistic approach by integrating the physical, emotional, and energetic aspects of healing. Practitioners can better comprehend how physical symptoms may arise from emotional or energetic disruptions and vice versa, helping clients release stored trauma, tension, or blockages that impact their well-being. For instance, knowledge of the endocrine system's hormonal regulation might guide a practitioner in balancing energetic flow to support emotional stability or physical vitality. By addressing these connections, they can harmonize body, mind, and spirit, creating a more comprehensive healing experience.

Furthermore, this understanding helps practitioners communicate more effectively with clients, building trust and offering a clear explanation of how energy work interacts with their physical concerns. Whether focusing on a specific area like the lower back for pain relief or targeting the respiratory system to support

breathwork, this anatomical knowledge ensures that practitioners can deliver targeted, intentional, and results-driven sessions. It bridges the gap between traditional energy healing practices and the physical body, allowing practitioners to serve as conduits for holistic healing that integrates spiritual alignment with physical wellness.

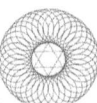

Basic Anatomy Guided Meditation for Cleansing and Clearing Physical Anatomy, Organs, Cells, and DNA

This meditation is designed to guide your awareness through the physical body's systems, structures, and energy fields, cleansing and clearing stagnant energies while aligning your cells and DNA with higher frequencies. The process integrates the multidimensional energies of Rainbow Reiki, utilizing the healing frequencies of its combined systems to address the physical body and beyond.

Find a quiet and comfortable position where you will not be disturbed. Close your eyes and take three deep breaths, inhaling deeply through your nose and exhaling slowly through your mouth. Feel your body relax more deeply with each breath. Imagine roots growing from your feet, anchoring you firmly into Gaia's crystalline core, drawing Earth's grounding energy upward into your body.

Set your intention: *"I allow the healing energies of Rainbow Reiki to cleanse, clear, and align my physical body, organs, cells, and DNA with my highest potential for health and vitality."*

Full Body Activation and Grounding
Visualize a brilliant rainbow light descending from above, entering your crown chakra. This light flows gently through your entire body, illuminating every cell and organ as it moves downward. Feel it anchoring into your root chakra and extending into the earth through your grounding roots. This rainbow light forms a protective, cleansing field around you, creating a safe and sacred space for healing.

Nervous System Cleansing
Shift your awareness to your nervous system, beginning with the brain and spinal cord. Visualize the rainbow light flowing through your brain, clearing any energetic stagnation in your neurons and activating optimal communication pathways. Let this light move down your spine, soothing the nerves that extend to every part of your body. Imagine the entire nervous system glowing with vitality.

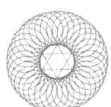

Affirm: *"My nervous system is clear, calm, and functioning in perfect harmony with my body and spirit."*

Circulatory System Renewal
Bring your focus to your heart and circulatory system. See the rainbow light entering your heart, filling it with love, strength, and vitality. Imagine this energy flowing through your arteries, veins, and capillaries, purifying your blood and infusing it with high-frequency energy. Sense this renewed energy being carried to every part of your body.

Affirm: *"My heart and circulatory system are strong, vibrant, and aligned with the flow of universal life force energy."*

Respiratory System Purification
Shift your attention to your lungs and respiratory system. Visualize the rainbow light filling your lungs with a radiant glow. Imagine this light cleansing every breath you take, removing toxins and bringing in fresh, high-vibrational energy. Sense the light moving through your bronchial tubes and alveoli, renewing your capacity for life.

Affirm: *"My lungs and respiratory system are clear, vital, and effortlessly support my life force energy."*

Digestive System Clearing
Focus on your digestive system, beginning with your stomach, intestines, liver, pancreas, and kidneys. Visualize the rainbow light flowing through these organs, dissolving any blockages, toxins, or stagnant energy. See the digestive system glowing with renewed health and efficiency, perfectly processing and assimilating nourishment.

Affirm: *"My digestive system is balanced, cleansed, and nourished by the universal energy flowing through me."*

Muscular and Skeletal Systems Healing
Move your awareness to your muscles and skeletal system. Visualize the rainbow light flowing through every muscle, tendon, and

ligament, releasing tension and restoring strength. Allow the light to penetrate your bones and bone marrow, clearing dense energies and activating regeneration. Sense the strength and resilience of your body being amplified.

Affirm: *"My muscles and bones are strong, aligned, and vibrantly healthy."*

Cellular and DNA Alignment
Bring your focus to your cells and DNA. Imagine the rainbow light entering each cell in your body, cleansing it of toxins and restoring its natural vitality. See the double helix of your DNA glowing with crystalline light as the energy clears inherited patterns, repairs damage, and activates dormant potential. Visualize your cells functioning in perfect harmony, aligned with the highest blueprint of health.

Affirm: *"Every cell in my body is vibrant, healthy, and aligned with my divine blueprint for perfect health."*

Endocrine System Balance
Shift your attention to your endocrine system, including the pineal gland, thyroid, adrenal glands, and pancreas. Visualize the rainbow light flowing through these glands, balancing hormone production and restoring energetic harmony. Sense this system supporting your body's optimal functioning and spiritual connection.

Affirm: *"My endocrine system is balanced and supports my physical, emotional, and spiritual well-being."*

Integration and Aura Cleansing
Expand your awareness to your entire body and its surrounding aura. See the rainbow light radiating outward, cleansing and harmonizing your energy field. Imagine this light sealing your body and aura in a protective, nurturing cocoon, allowing the healing energies to integrate fully.

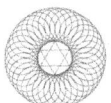

Affirm: *"My body, cells, and DNA are cleansed, clear, and aligned with the frequencies of health, vitality, and divine perfection."*

Slowly bring your awareness back to your breath. Wiggle your fingers and toes, grounding yourself in the present moment. When ready, open your eyes and take a few moments to reflect on your experience.

Post-Meditation Recommendations
- Hydration: Drink plenty of water to support detoxification and energetic integration.
- Nourishment: Focus on clean eating, incorporating fresh fruits, vegetables, and whole foods.
- Gentle Movement: Engage in light stretching or yoga to further support energy flow.
- Reflection: Journal any insights, sensations, or shifts you experienced during the meditation.

This guided meditation can be practiced regularly to maintain balance, health, and alignment in your physical and energetic systems.

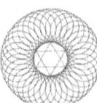

Skeletal System

The skeletal system, comprising all the bones and joints in the body, is the structural framework that supports and shapes the human form. It provides critical protection for vital organs, such as the heart and lungs shielded by the ribcage and the brain encased within the skull. In conjunction with the muscular system, the skeletal system facilitates movement and physical activity, allowing the body to perform everything from simple gestures to complex motions. Key areas of focus include the spine, which houses and protects the spinal cord while supporting posture; the pelvis, which stabilizes the lower body and supports reproductive and abdominal organs; the skull, which safeguards the brain and sensory organs; the ribs, which protect the thoracic cavity; and the bones of the arms and legs, which enable mobility and dexterity.

From a Reiki perspective, the skeletal system can be an essential focal point for energy healing, as it not only represents physical support but also serves as a metaphor for energetic stability and resilience. Reiki can be directed to bones and joints to promote alignment, relieve pain, and encourage healing from injuries, fractures, or chronic conditions such as arthritis. For example, focusing Reiki energy on the spine can help release tension, realign vertebrae energetically, and support the nervous system housed within it. Similarly, targeting areas like the knees or hips can address joint discomfort, restore mobility, and promote structural balance.

Energetically, bones are considered dense, grounding elements in the body, holding both physical strength and ancestral memory. Reiki practitioners often work with this density to infuse energy into deeper layers of the body, facilitating long-term healing and reinforcing the body's foundation. By promoting structural balance and addressing disruptions in the skeletal system's energy flow, Reiki can enhance the body's overall harmony, improve posture and movement, and create a sense of stability and support on physical, emotional, and spiritual levels. This approach allows the skeletal system to act not just as a physical framework but as an energetic channel for resilience, grounding, and alignment.

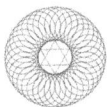

Reiki Hand Placement

Crown of the Head (Skull and Spine Alignment)
Placement: Place both hands gently on the top of the head.
Purpose: Supports alignment of the skull, cervical spine, and cranial tension release.

Base of the Skull (Cervical Spine)
Placement: Place both hands at the base of the skull (occiput area).
Purpose: Addresses the upper spine and neck, relieving tension and promoting skeletal alignment.

Shoulders (Clavicle and Shoulder Joints)
Placement: Rest one hand on each shoulder, covering the collarbone area.
Purpose: Supports the alignment of the clavicle and shoulder joints, often relieving tension from poor posture.

Chest (Thoracic Spine and Rib Cage)
Placement: Place hands on the chest, one above the heart and the other just below the collarbone.
Purpose: Balances the thoracic spine and ribcage, supporting skeletal alignment in the upper torso.

Lower Back (Lumbar Spine and Pelvis)
Placement: Position hands on the lower back, just above the hips, or on either side of the spine.
Purpose: Addresses the lumbar spine, sacrum, and pelvic alignment, relieving lower back discomfort.

Hips (Hip Joints and Pelvis)
Placement: Rest hands on the hip joints, with fingers pointing toward the pelvis.
Purpose: Balances the pelvic region and aligns the hip joints.

Knees
Placement: Place one hand gently over each knee.
Purpose: Supports joint health, alignment, and energy flow through the legs.

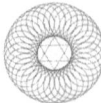

Feet (Ankles and Grounding)
Placement: Rest hands on the tops of the feet or cup the ankles.
Purpose: Grounds the energy and supports skeletal structure from the base, addressing issues like alignment and balance.

Full Spine (Back Body Integration)
Placement: Run your hands slowly down the client's back, stopping at key points along the spine (cervical, thoracic, lumbar, and sacrum).
Purpose: Provides overall support to the entire spinal column and encourages energetic flow through the skeletal framework.

Guided Meditation for Strengthening and Healing the Skeletal System

Grounding
- Find a quiet and comfortable position. Sit or lie down, ensuring your body is fully supported.
- Close your eyes gently and take three deep breaths. Inhale through your nose, hold for a moment, and exhale slowly through your mouth.
- Feel yourself grounding into the earth, imagining roots growing from your spine or feet deep into Earth's core.

Connection to the Bones (Awareness)
- Bring your awareness to your skeletal system, the framework that supports your entire body.
- Imagine your bones glowing softly within you, representing their strength and resilience.
- Sense the interconnectedness of your skeleton, from the top of your skull to the tips of your toes.

Healing Visualization
- Golden Light Activation
  - Visualize a warm, golden light entering the top of your head. This light represents healing energy and vitality.
  - Let this light flow through your body, moving into every bone. Picture it filling your skull, spine, ribcage, arms, pelvis, and legs.
- Restoration and Renewal
  - See this golden light strengthening your bones, repairing any weak or damaged areas.
  - Imagine the light activating your bone marrow, boosting its natural regenerative abilities.
- Crystal-Like Radiance
  - Picture your bones becoming crystalline in structure, glowing with vitality, strength, and flexibility.
  - Feel a deep sense of stability and grounding as this energy works through you.

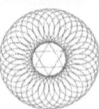

Affirmations for the Skeletal System
Repeat the following affirmations silently or out loud:
- *"My bones are strong, resilient, and filled with vibrant energy."*
- *"I release any tension or blockages stored in my skeletal system."*
- *"My body knows how to heal, and my bones are regenerating with ease."*
- *"I am fully supported by my inner and outer structure."*

Energy Clearing
- Imagine a gentle wave of pure white light sweeping through your skeletal system, washing away any residual pain, tension, or stagnant energy.
- See this light carrying away anything that no longer serves you, leaving your bones vibrant and healthy.

Gratitude and Connection to Earth Energy
- Place your hands on your lower belly or thighs (if comfortable).
- Visualize Earth's energy rising into your body, merging with your skeletal system, offering grounding and support.
- Thank your bones for their strength, protection, and role in your physical health.

Closing and Integration
- Gradually bring your awareness back to your breath. Feel the inhale nourishing your body and the exhale releasing any lingering tension.
- Wiggle your fingers and toes, stretch gently if needed, and open your eyes when ready.
- Carry this sense of stability, strength, and healing with you throughout your day.

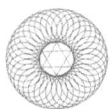

Advanced Guided Meditation for Strengthening and Healing the Skeletal System

This guided meditation is designed to focus the multidimensional energies of Rainbow Reiki on the skeletal system. It integrates the vibrational frequencies of Usui, Shadow, Arcturian, Pleiadian, Egyptian Sekhem-Seichim, and Magdalene/Yeshua Reiki to support cellular regeneration, bone density, and energetic alignment of the skeletal structure.

Find a quiet and comfortable space to sit or lie down. Close your eyes and take three deep breaths, inhaling deeply through your nose and exhaling slowly through your mouth. Allow your body to relax with each breath, feeling your muscles release tension and your mind becoming calm.

Set your intention: *"I open myself to the healing energies of Rainbow Reiki to strengthen and restore my skeletal system, aligning it with divine health and vitality."*

Grounding and Connection
Visualize roots extending from your feet into Earth's crystalline core. Feel Gaia's nurturing energy rising through these roots, infusing your body with stability and grounding. At the same time, visualize a column of rainbow light descending from above, entering through your crown chakra and flowing into your body.

Feel Earth's energy merging with the rainbow light, creating a harmonious flow that supports and grounds you while aligning your energy with higher-dimensional frequencies.

Activating the Skeletal System
Bring your awareness to your skeletal system. Visualize your entire skeletal structure glowing with a soft, golden-white light. See this light traveling through your skull, spine, ribs, arms, pelvis, and legs. Acknowledge the strength and support your bones provide, even if they feel weakened or strained.

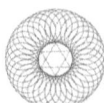

Affirm: *"My skeletal system is the foundation of my strength and vitality, fully supported by universal energy."*

Cellular Regeneration
Focus on the cells within your bones. Imagine a crystalline energy, infused with Pleiadian and Arcturian light codes, flowing into the bone marrow. This energy activates cellular regeneration, clearing old or damaged cells and promoting the growth of healthy new ones.

Visualize the energy working like a soft, radiant pulse within your bones, restoring density and flexibility. Feel the energy filling every part of your skeletal system, from the smallest joints to the largest bones.

Affirm: *"My bones are renewed, strong, and resilient, regenerating with ease and perfection."*

Strengthening the Structural Integrity
Shift your attention to the spine, the central pillar of your skeletal system. Visualize a vibrant rainbow light flowing through each vertebra, aligning and strengthening your entire spinal column. See the light extending into your ribs, creating a web of luminous energy that supports your core.

From here, imagine the rainbow light spreading into your arms, pelvis, and legs, reinforcing the structural integrity of your entire skeleton. Visualize your skeletal system glowing with a unified energy, solid yet flexible.

Affirm: *"My skeletal system is strong, aligned, and capable of supporting me in every aspect of my life."*

Clearing Energetic Imprints
Bring your focus to any areas of pain or weakness in your skeletal system. With your mind's eye, visualize Shadow Reiki energy entering these areas as a deep indigo or black light. This energy dissolves any emotional or energetic imprints held within your bones, such as trauma, fear, or ancestral patterns.

Feel the energy clearing away blockages, making space for healing and renewal. Once the clearing is complete, see a soft rose-pink light from Magdalene/Yeshua Reiki flowing into these spaces, filling them with love, compassion, and restoration.

Affirm: *"I release all energetic blockages from my skeletal system and allow divine healing to restore my bones."*

Infusing Crystalline Energy
Visualize the Egyptian Sekhem-Seichim energy entering your skeletal system as a golden, crystalline light. See this energy forming intricate geometric patterns within your bones, reinforcing their strength and connecting them to Earth's crystalline grid.

Feel the energy stabilizing and energizing your skeletal system, aligning it with the frequencies of Earth and the cosmos.

Affirm: *"My skeletal system is aligned with the divine blueprint of health and strength, connected to the crystalline energies of Gaia."*

Integration and Anchoring
Bring your awareness to your entire skeletal system. See it glowing with a radiant rainbow light, perfectly aligned and fully restored. Visualize this light anchoring into your energy field and connecting with Earth's core, stabilizing the healing energies.

Affirm: *"I am deeply grounded, supported, and strengthened. My skeletal system is healthy, vibrant, and aligned with universal energy."*

Closing and Gratitude
Take a few deep breaths, feeling the strength and vitality flowing through your skeletal system. Express gratitude to the Rainbow Reiki energies, your body, and the universal life force for supporting your healing.

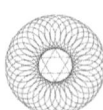

When you are ready, bring your awareness back to the present moment. Wiggle your fingers and toes, stretch gently, and open your eyes.

Post-Meditation Care
- Drink plenty of water to support detoxification and energetic integration.
- Incorporate foods rich in calcium, magnesium, and vitamin D to nourish your bones physically.
- Consider journaling any insights or sensations experienced during the meditation.
- Repeat this meditation as often as needed to maintain and strengthen your skeletal system.

This meditation combines the multidimensional energies of Rainbow Reiki to create a holistic and profound healing experience, ensuring your skeletal system is supported on all levels.

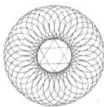

Muscular System

The muscular system encompasses all the muscles in the body, forming an intricate network that works in harmony with the skeletal system to enable movement, maintain posture, and facilitate essential functions like circulation and respiration. Comprising three types of muscle—skeletal, smooth, and cardiac—the muscular system plays a vital role in both voluntary actions, such as walking and lifting, and involuntary processes, such as the rhythmic contraction of the heart and the movement of food through the digestive system. Key areas of focus within this system include the neck and shoulders, which are prone to tension from stress and poor posture; the back, which supports the spine and bears much of the body's weight; the arms and legs, which provide strength and mobility; and the abdominal muscles, which stabilize the core and protect internal organs.

From a Reiki perspective, the muscular system often reflects the physical manifestations of emotional or energetic imbalances. Stress, anxiety, and unprocessed emotions frequently lead to muscle tension, spasms, or pain, particularly in areas like the shoulders and lower back, where stress tends to accumulate. Reiki can be directed to these areas to promote relaxation, release stagnant energy, and ease physical discomfort. The gentle flow of Reiki energy helps muscles release their tight grip, allowing blood flow and oxygenation to improve, which aids in natural healing and recovery.

Additionally, the muscular system serves as a bridge between the physical body and emotional experiences, often holding energetic imprints of trauma or suppressed feelings. By channeling Reiki to tense or fatigued muscles, practitioners can not only address physical symptoms but also encourage the release of emotional burdens stored within these tissues. This approach fosters holistic healing, where relaxation of the muscular system leads to greater mobility, reduced pain, and a deeper sense of overall well-being. Reiki's ability to harmonize the body's energy field makes it a powerful tool for restoring balance, alleviating stress, and

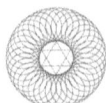

supporting the muscular system's vital role in maintaining the body's strength, flexibility, and functionality.

Reiki Hand Placement

Crown of the Head (Tension Release in Face and Neck Muscles)
Placement: Place hands gently on the top of the head.
Purpose: Relieves tension in the face, jaw, and upper neck muscles, especially for stress-related tightness.

Base of the Skull and Neck (Cervical Muscles)
Placement: Rest hands at the base of the skull, with fingers pointing downward along the neck.
Purpose: Eases tension in the neck muscles, especially from posture issues or strain.

Shoulders (Trapezius and Shoulder Muscles)
Placement: Place one hand on each shoulder, covering the trapezius area.
Purpose: Relaxes tight shoulder muscles, commonly associated with stress or repetitive movements.

Chest (Pectoral Muscles and Upper Back Support)
Placement: Position one hand on the upper chest and the other hand on the upper back.
Purpose: Balances the energy flow in the pectoral muscles and supports the upper back, relieving chest tightness.

Arms and Hands
Placement: Place hands along the upper arm (biceps and triceps) or on the forearms and hands.
Purpose: Addresses tension in the arms and promotes energy flow in areas affected by repetitive strain or overuse.

Abdomen (Core and Oblique Muscles)
Placement: Rest hands on the upper abdomen, just below the ribcage.
Purpose: Releases tension in core muscles, aiding in relaxation of the torso and supporting posture.

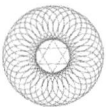

Lower Back (Lumbar Muscles and Erector Spinae)
Placement: Place hands on the lower back, with fingers pointing toward the spine.
Purpose: Relieves tightness in the lumbar muscles and promotes relaxation in the lower back area.

Hips and Thighs (Gluteal and Quadriceps Muscles)
Placement: Rest hands on the hips or directly on the thighs, just above the knees.
Purpose: Relaxes the gluteal muscles and promotes energy flow in the upper legs.

Knees
Placement: Place one hand over each knee.
Purpose: Supports joint mobility and addresses tension in the surrounding muscles, including the quadriceps and hamstrings.

Feet and Calves
Placement: Rest hands on the tops of the feet or gently on the calves.
Purpose: Grounds the energy and supports the calf muscles, relieving tension from standing or walking.

Full Body Sweep (Overall Muscular Relaxation)
Placement: Sweep hands gently down the client's body, from head to feet, pausing at areas where muscle tension is concentrated.
Purpose: Promotes full-body relaxation and energy alignment.

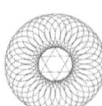

Basic Guided Meditation for Strengthening and Healing the Muscular System

This meditation focuses on bringing awareness and healing energy to the muscular system, promoting relaxation, strength, and vitality.

Find a quiet, comfortable position where you can sit or lie down. Close your eyes and take three deep breaths, inhaling deeply through your nose and exhaling slowly through your mouth. With each breath, allow your body to relax, letting go of any tension.

Set your intention for the meditation: *"I invite healing energy to strengthen and restore my muscular system, allowing my body to move with ease and vitality."*

Grounding
Visualize roots growing from your feet into the earth. Feel Earth's grounding energy rising through these roots and flowing into your body. This energy provides stability and support, anchoring you in the present moment.

Bringing Awareness to the Muscular System
Bring your attention to your muscles. Imagine your entire muscular system as a glowing network within your body, connecting every part of you. Starting at the top of your head, slowly move your awareness down through your face, neck, shoulders, arms, chest, back, abdomen, hips, legs, and feet.

As you focus on each area, imagine it relaxing and softening. Allow any tension or tightness to melt away, replaced by a feeling of lightness and ease.

Visualizing Healing Light
Visualize a warm, golden light flowing into your body from above. See this light moving into your muscles, filling them with healing energy. Imagine the light spreading through every muscle, tendon, and ligament, bringing strength, flexibility, and vitality.

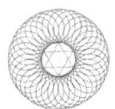

Feel the light cleansing and renewing your muscles, removing any fatigue or stress. Allow this energy to restore your muscles to their natural, balanced state.

Affirm: *"My muscles are relaxed, strong, and filled with life force energy."*

Releasing Tension
Focus on any areas where you may feel tension or discomfort. Visualize the golden light concentrating in these areas, dissolving any tightness or blockages. Imagine the tension melting away with each exhale, leaving the muscles soft, relaxed, and restored.

Affirm: *"I release all tension and allow my muscles to relax and heal completely."*

Strengthening and Energizing
Visualize the golden light becoming brighter and stronger, infusing your muscles with energy and vitality. See your muscles glowing with strength and resilience, ready to support your body with ease and flexibility.

Affirm: *"My muscles are healthy, strong, and full of energy."*

Closing and Gratitude
Take a moment to express gratitude for your body and its ability to heal and support you. Thank the energy for assisting in the healing process.

When you feel ready, gently bring your awareness back to the present moment. Wiggle your fingers and toes, stretch if needed, and open your eyes.

Post-Meditation Care
- Hydration: Drink water to support the healing process.
- Stretching: Consider light stretches to reinforce the relaxation and strength of your muscles.

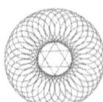

- Reflection: Take a moment to reflect on how your body feels after the meditation.

This simple meditation can be practiced regularly to support the health and vitality of your muscular system.

Advanced Guided Meditation for Strengthening and Healing the Muscular System

This meditation is designed to channel the multidimensional energies of Rainbow Reiki into the muscular system, promoting strength, flexibility, and recovery on a physical, energetic, and cellular level. It integrates the healing frequencies of Usui, Shadow, Arcturian, Pleiadian, Egyptian Sekhem-Seichim, and Magdalene/Yeshua Reiki.

Find a quiet, comfortable space where you can sit or lie down undisturbed. Close your eyes and take several deep breaths, inhaling deeply through your nose and exhaling slowly through your mouth. With each exhale, feel your body softening and releasing tension.

Set your intention for this meditation: *"I open myself to the advanced healing energies of Rainbow Reiki to strengthen and restore my muscular system, aligning it with optimal health and divine vitality."*

Grounding and Sacred Connection
Visualize roots extending from your feet into Earth's crystalline core. Feel the grounding energy of Gaia rising through these roots, entering your body, and anchoring you securely. At the same time, imagine a column of rainbow light descending from the cosmos, entering through your crown chakra, and filling your body.

As these energies merge, they create a harmonious flow within you, balancing and preparing your energy field to receive advanced healing.

Activating the Muscular System
Bring your awareness to your muscular system. Visualize a glowing grid of light over your body, representing the network of muscles, tendons, and ligaments. Imagine this grid becoming illuminated with a vibrant rainbow light, energizing and activating every muscle group.

Start at the top of your head, moving awareness down through your face, neck, shoulders, arms, chest, back, abdomen, hips, legs, and

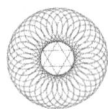

feet. Allow the rainbow light to flow through each area, cleansing and energizing your muscles as it moves.

Affirm: *"My muscular system is vibrant, strong, and perfectly aligned with universal life force energy."*

Cellular Healing and Regeneration
Shift your focus to the cells within your muscles. Visualize each cell glowing with crystalline light, infused with Arcturian and Pleiadian energy codes. See these light codes entering the mitochondria—the energy centers of your cells—activating optimal energy production and cellular repair.

Imagine this light expanding through every cell in your muscles, clearing toxins, removing energetic blockages, and promoting regeneration. Sense the vibrational frequencies of these advanced energies recalibrating your cells to their highest potential.

Affirm: *"Each cell in my muscular system is infused with light, strength, and perfect health."*

Clearing Stagnant Energy
Focus on areas of tightness, pain, or discomfort within your muscles. Envision Shadow Reiki energy flowing into these areas as a deep indigo light. This energy works to dissolve emotional and physical tension, releasing any blockages or stored trauma within your muscles.

As the indigo light clears these areas, visualize a soft rose-pink light from Magdalene/Yeshua Reiki entering, filling the space with love, compassion, and healing. Feel the muscles in these areas softening, relaxing, and becoming more flexible.

Affirm: *"I release all tension and stored emotions from my muscular system, creating space for healing and renewal."*

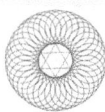

Strengthening and Energizing

Visualize the Egyptian Sekhem-Seichim energy flowing into your muscles as golden, crystalline patterns. These patterns weave through every tendon, ligament, and muscle fiber, strengthening the structural integrity of your muscular system. Feel your muscles becoming more resilient and elastic, fully supported by this sacred energy.

Next, sense a vibrant rainbow light flowing into your muscles, bringing the frequencies of vitality, flexibility, and divine alignment. Allow this light to permeate your entire muscular system, creating a protective energetic layer around it.

Affirm: *"My muscular system is infused with strength, resilience, and the ability to move with ease and grace."*

Aligning with the Divine Blueprint

Expand your awareness to include your entire body. Visualize your muscular system as a glowing, vibrant network of light, perfectly aligned with your divine blueprint. Sense the multidimensional energies of Rainbow Reiki anchoring deeply into your muscles, harmonizing them with Earth's crystalline grid and cosmic frequencies.

Feel the connection between your muscles and your skeletal system, creating a seamless flow of strength, support, and balance.

Affirm: *"My muscular system is aligned with the divine blueprint of health and vitality, fully integrated with my physical and energetic bodies."*

Integration and Closing

Bring your focus back to your heart center. Visualize a radiant orb of rainbow light within your chest, pulsating and sending waves of healing energy throughout your body. This light integrates all the healing energies you have received, anchoring them into your being.

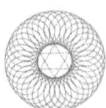

Take a few deep breaths, feeling gratitude for your body and the healing energies that have supported this process. Express thanks to the Rainbow Reiki frequencies, your spiritual guides, and your own body for its strength and resilience.

When you feel ready, bring your awareness back to the present moment. Wiggle your fingers and toes, stretch gently, and open your eyes.

Post-Meditation Care
- Hydrate: Drink plenty of water to support the release of toxins and energy integration.
- Nourish: Eat foods rich in proteins and nutrients to support muscle repair and recovery.
- Move: Engage in gentle stretches or yoga to enhance flexibility and reinforce the healing process.
- Reflect: Journal any sensations, insights, or changes you noticed during the meditation.

By combining the advanced energies of Rainbow Reiki, this meditation offers a comprehensive and multidimensional approach to strengthening, healing, and aligning your muscular system with divine health and vitality.

Nervous System

The nervous system, consisting of the brain, spinal cord, and peripheral nerves, is the body's master control and communication network. It processes sensory input, regulates motor functions, and maintains homeostasis by coordinating vital processes such as breathing, heart rate, and digestion. The central nervous system (CNS), comprising the brain and spinal cord, acts as the processing hub for all information, while the peripheral nervous system (PNS) connects the CNS to the rest of the body, enabling sensory and motor responses. Key areas of focus include the brain, which governs thought, memory, and voluntary actions; the spinal cord, which transmits signals between the brain and body; and the peripheral nerves, which carry messages to and from muscles, skin, and organs.

Reiki is particularly effective in supporting the nervous system, as it promotes a deep state of relaxation and helps regulate the body's stress response. Chronic stress, anxiety, and tension can overstimulate the nervous system, leading to symptoms such as headaches, fatigue, and muscle tightness. By channeling Reiki energy to key areas such as the brain and spine, practitioners can encourage the nervous system to shift from the fight-or-flight state (sympathetic dominance) to a state of rest and repair (parasympathetic activation). This allows the body to release stress, reduce cortisol levels, and restore balance to its natural rhythms.

Additionally, Reiki's gentle, harmonizing energy can help alleviate neurological discomfort, such as migraines or nerve pain, by soothing energetic imbalances in the nervous system. It supports the flow of energy along neural pathways, promoting clarity, focus, and emotional resilience. The nervous system is deeply connected to both physical and emotional well-being, and Reiki's calming influence helps address the underlying energetic patterns contributing to imbalances. By fostering relaxation and restoring equilibrium, Reiki aids in enhancing the nervous system's ability to communicate, regulate, and heal, creating a foundation for overall health and harmony.

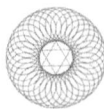

Reiki Hand Placement

Crown of the Head (Central Nervous System Connection)
Placement: Place hands gently on the top of the head.
Purpose: Calms the mind, balances brain activity, and supports the central nervous system (CNS).

Base of the Skull (Brainstem and Autonomic Nervous System)
Placement: Rest hands at the base of the skull (occiput area), with fingers pointing downward.
Purpose: Eases tension around the brainstem, which regulates involuntary functions such as breathing and heartbeat.

Forehead and Back of the Head (Mind-Body Connection)
Placement: Place one hand on the forehead (third eye area) and the other hand at the back of the head.
Purpose: Promotes clarity, reduces stress, and soothes the nervous system by integrating mental and physical harmony.

Shoulders (Connection to Peripheral Nervous System)
Placement: Rest hands on the tops of the shoulders.
Purpose: Relieves tension in the neck and shoulders, areas that hold stress affecting the peripheral nerves.

Heart and Upper Back (Vagus Nerve Stimulation)
Placement: Place one hand on the heart (center of the chest) and the other between the shoulder blades.
Purpose: Activates the vagus nerve, encouraging relaxation and reducing the fight-or-flight response.

Solar Plexus (Autonomic Nervous System Hub)
Placement: Rest hands just below the ribcage over the solar plexus.
Purpose: Balances the autonomic nervous system (sympathetic and parasympathetic), promoting emotional and physical relaxation.

Lower Back (Spinal Cord and Nerve Roots)
Placement: Place hands on the lower back, near the sacrum or lumbar region.

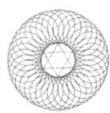

Purpose: Supports the spinal cord and calms the nerve roots extending into the lower body.

Hips and Sacrum (Nerve Bundle Release)
Placement: Rest hands on the hips or directly over the sacrum.
Purpose: Relaxes the sacral plexus, a key area for nerve communication to the legs and pelvic region.

Hands and Feet (Peripheral Nervous System Relaxation)
Placement: Gently hold the client's hands or place hands over the tops of the feet.
Purpose: Grounds the energy, calms the peripheral nervous system, and enhances circulation of energy through the extremities.

Full Spine Sweep (Central Nervous System Support)
Placement: Slowly run hands along the client's spine, starting at the base of the skull and moving toward the sacrum.
Purpose: Balances energy flow through the entire spinal cord and supports the central nervous system.

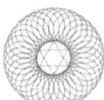

Basic Guided Meditation for Strengthening and Healing the Nervous System

This meditation is designed to bring calm, balance, and vitality to your nervous system, supporting both its physical and energetic well-being.

Find a quiet, comfortable position where you can sit or lie down. Close your eyes and take three deep breaths, inhaling deeply through your nose and exhaling slowly through your mouth. Allow your body to relax with each exhale.

Set your intention for the meditation: *"I invite healing energy to soothe, strengthen, and restore my nervous system, bringing calm and balance to my body and mind."*

Grounding and Centering
Visualize roots growing from your feet deep into the earth. Feel Earth's grounding energy rising through these roots and flowing into your body, anchoring you in the present moment. This energy provides stability and support, creating a sense of calm.

Affirm: *"I am grounded, safe, and supported by Earth's energy."*

Calming the Nervous System
Bring your awareness to your breath. Take slow, deep breaths, allowing each inhale to fill you with calm and each exhale to release tension. Visualize a soft, golden light flowing into your body with each breath. This light moves through your entire nervous system, starting at your brain and traveling down your spinal cord and out through your nerves.

As the light flows, imagine it soothing and calming your nervous system. Feel any overactivity or stress melting away, replaced by a gentle, peaceful energy.

Affirm: *"My nervous system is calm, balanced, and at peace."*

Healing and Strengthening

Visualize the golden light becoming brighter and warmer. See it entering your brain, nourishing your neurons and restoring balance to your thoughts. Imagine the light traveling down your spinal cord, strengthening the communication pathways between your brain and body.

As the light flows through your peripheral nerves, visualize it repairing and energizing each connection, ensuring your entire body feels supported and strong.

Affirm: *"My nervous system is strong, healthy, and functioning in perfect harmony."*

Releasing Tension

Focus on any areas where you may feel tension or discomfort, such as your head, neck, or back. Visualize the golden light concentrating in these areas, dissolving any blockages or stress. Imagine the tension flowing out of your body with each exhale, leaving you feeling lighter and more at ease.

Affirm: *"I release all tension from my nervous system and allow healing energy to flow freely."*

Energizing and Harmonizing

Picture the golden light expanding throughout your entire body, filling every nerve with vitality. See your nervous system glowing with radiant energy, functioning smoothly and effortlessly. Feel a sense of connection and harmony between your body and mind.

Affirm: *"My nervous system is fully restored, vibrant, and perfectly balanced."*

Closing and Gratitude

Take a moment to express gratitude to your body for its resilience and ability to heal. Thank the golden light for its healing energy.

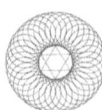

When you feel ready, gently bring your awareness back to your breath and the present moment. Wiggle your fingers and toes, stretch gently if needed, and open your eyes.

Post-Meditation Care
- Hydration: Drink water to support your nervous system's function.
- Mindful Rest: Allow yourself a few moments of quiet reflection to deepen the sense of calm.
- Light Stretching: Gentle yoga or stretching can complement this meditation, enhancing relaxation.

This meditation can be practiced regularly to maintain a calm and resilient nervous system.

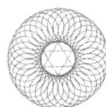

Advanced Rainbow Reiki Guided Meditation for Strengthening and Healing the Nervous System

This advanced guided meditation combines the multidimensional energies of Rainbow Reiki with the intention to heal, strengthen, and balance the nervous system. It integrates the healing frequencies of Usui, Shadow, Arcturian, Pleiadian, Egyptian Sekhem-Seichim, and Magdalene/Yeshua Reiki, addressing the physical, energetic, and spiritual aspects of the nervous system.

Find a quiet, comfortable space where you can sit or lie down. Close your eyes and take a few deep breaths, inhaling deeply through your nose and exhaling slowly through your mouth. Allow your body to relax with each exhale, releasing any tension or stress.

Set your intention: *"I invite the advanced energies of Rainbow Reiki to strengthen, restore, and balance my nervous system, aligning it with optimal health and higher vibrational frequencies."*

Grounding and Cosmic Connection

Visualize roots extending from your feet deep into Earth's crystalline core. Feel Gaia's grounding energy rising through these roots, entering your body, and stabilizing your energy field. At the same time, imagine a column of rainbow light descending from the cosmos, entering your crown chakra, and filling your body with high-frequency energy.

Feel the merging of these energies within you, creating a harmonious flow that grounds and elevates your nervous system.

Illuminating the Nervous System

Bring your awareness to your nervous system, beginning with the brain. Visualize a golden light gently flowing into your brain, illuminating every neuron and connection. See this light traveling down your spinal cord, lighting up the intricate web of your peripheral nerves.

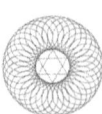

As the light moves through your entire nervous system, imagine it cleansing away tension, overactivity, or blockages, leaving behind a calm and harmonious glow.

Affirm: *"My nervous system is calm, clear, and illuminated by universal healing energy."*

Cellular Repair and Regeneration
Shift your focus to the cellular level of your nervous system. Visualize crystalline light codes from Arcturian and Pleiadian Reiki entering your neurons and synapses, repairing and optimizing their function. See these codes activating the mitochondria within each cell, enhancing energy flow and restoring vitality.

Imagine your entire nervous system glowing with crystalline energy, perfectly tuned to its highest potential.

Affirm: *"Each cell in my nervous system is restored, energized, and aligned with my divine blueprint."*

Releasing Emotional and Energetic Imprints
Focus on areas of emotional or energetic tension within your nervous system. Visualize Shadow Reiki energy as a deep indigo light flowing into these areas, gently dissolving old patterns, fears, or stress imprints stored in your neural pathways.

Once the clearing is complete, see a soft pink light from Magdalene/Yeshua Reiki filling these spaces, infusing them with compassion, peace, and love. Feel the nervous system releasing its burdens and returning to a state of balance.

Affirm: *"I release all emotional and energetic imprints from my nervous system, allowing peace and balance to flow freely."*

Strengthening and Energizing
Visualize Egyptian Sekhem-Seichim Reiki energy entering your nervous system as a radiant golden light, weaving sacred geometric patterns through your brain, spinal cord, and peripheral nerves. This

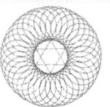

energy strengthens the structural and energetic integrity of your nervous system, enhancing its resilience and functionality.

Next, imagine a vibrant rainbow light flowing into your nervous system, bringing flexibility, harmony, and vitality. Feel this light connecting your nervous system to your chakras and auric field, aligning your entire being.

Affirm: *"My nervous system is resilient, strong, and fully aligned with universal energy flow."*

Integration and Multidimensional Alignment
Expand your awareness to include the energetic layers of your nervous system, reaching into your auric field and multidimensional grids. Visualize the advanced Rainbow Reiki energies anchoring into these layers, aligning your nervous system with the cosmic and crystalline grids of Gaia and the universe.

Feel the interconnectedness of your nervous system with your physical, emotional, mental, and spiritual bodies. Allow the energies to harmonize and integrate fully.

Affirm: *"My nervous system is a harmonious bridge between my physical and spiritual essence, fully aligned with the divine flow of life."*

Closing and Gratitude
Bring your awareness back to your heart center. Visualize a glowing orb of rainbow light within your chest, pulsating and sending waves of gratitude and peace throughout your body and energy field.

Express gratitude for your nervous system, the Rainbow Reiki energies, and your ability to heal and align with higher vibrations. Gently return your awareness to your breath and the present moment. When you are ready, wiggle your fingers and toes, stretch gently, and open your eyes.

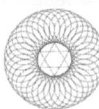

Post-Meditation Care
- Hydration: Drink plenty of water to support energy integration and detoxification.
- Nourishment: Focus on foods that nourish the nervous system, such as those rich in omega-3s, magnesium, and antioxidants.
- Rest: Allow yourself time to relax and integrate the healing energies.
- Reflection: Journal any sensations, insights, or changes you noticed during the meditation.

This advanced meditation can be practiced regularly to maintain the strength, balance, and vitality of your nervous system, aligning it with the multidimensional energies of Rainbow Reiki.

Circulatory System

The circulatory system, comprising the heart, arteries, veins, and capillaries, is a vital network responsible for transporting blood throughout the body. This system delivers oxygen and nutrients to cells while removing waste products like carbon dioxide, playing a critical role in maintaining overall health and homeostasis.

The heart serves as the central pump, ensuring a continuous flow of blood, while the arteries carry oxygen-rich blood to tissues, and the veins return deoxygenated blood to the heart for reoxygenation. The capillaries, as the smallest blood vessels, enable the exchange of oxygen, nutrients, and waste between blood and tissues, making them essential for cellular health.

Reiki is particularly effective in supporting the circulatory system by promoting relaxation, reducing stress, and improving energetic flow. Stress and tension can constrict blood vessels and impair circulation, increasing the risk of issues such as high blood pressure or cardiovascular strain. Reiki's gentle, harmonizing energy can encourage the relaxation of blood vessels, helping to lower blood pressure and enhance blood flow throughout the body. By focusing on the heart, Reiki practitioners can channel energy to support its rhythmic function and emotional connection, fostering a sense of warmth, vitality, and love.

Energetically, the circulatory system is deeply linked to the heart chakra, representing love, compassion, and life force. Imbalances in this system may reflect emotional challenges such as grief or blocked expression of love. Reiki helps to release these energetic blockages, restoring the harmonious flow of energy in the heart and throughout the circulatory pathways. By addressing both the physical and energetic aspects of the circulatory system, Reiki supports the body's natural ability to heal, bringing balance, vitality, and a renewed sense of well-being. This holistic approach nurtures both physical heart health and emotional resilience, creating harmony between the body, mind, and spirit.

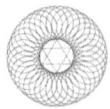

Reiki Hand Placement

<u>Crown of the Head (Brain Circulation)</u>
Placement: Place hands gently on the top of the head.
Purpose: Encourages optimal blood flow to the brain, promoting mental clarity and relaxation.

<u>Forehead and Back of the Head (Cranial Circulation)</u>
Placement: Place one hand on the forehead and the other on the back of the head.
Purpose: Balances circulation to and from the brain, reducing stress and tension.

<u>Throat (Carotid Arteries and Circulation to the Brain)</u>
Placement: Place hands gently on either side of the neck.
Purpose: Enhances blood flow through the carotid arteries and supports healthy oxygen delivery to the brain.

<u>Heart Center (Primary Circulatory System Focus)</u>
Placement: Rest hands over the chest, directly above the heart.
Purpose: Supports the heart's function, enhances emotional balance, and promotes healthy blood flow throughout the body.

<u>Solar Plexus (Major Blood Vessels and Relaxation)</u>
Placement: Place hands on the upper abdomen, just below the ribcage.
Purpose: Encourages relaxation, reduces tension in the body, and supports blood flow through major vessels like the aorta.

<u>Lower Abdomen (Pelvic Circulation and Grounding)</u>
Placement: Rest hands on the lower abdomen.
Purpose: Promotes circulation to the pelvic area and grounds the energy flow for overall balance.

<u>Upper Back (Heart and Lung Circulation)</u>
Placement: Place hands on the upper back, between the shoulder blades.
Purpose: Supports the back of the heart and lungs, facilitating better oxygenation and blood flow.

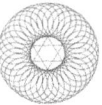

Lower Back (Kidney and Circulatory Support)
Placement: Rest hands over the lower back, near the kidneys.
Purpose: Supports kidney function, which plays a role in regulating blood pressure and filtering blood.

Hands and Arms (Peripheral Circulation)
Placement: Gently hold the client's hands or place hands on the forearms.
Purpose: Enhances circulation to the extremities, relieving tension from repetitive use or poor circulation.

Hips and Thighs (Major Arteries)
Placement: Place hands on the hips or thighs, just above the knees.
Purpose: Supports circulation through the femoral arteries and promotes energy flow in the lower body.

Feet (Grounding and Venous Return)
Placement: Rest hands on the tops of the feet or gently cup the ankles.
Purpose: Grounds energy and supports blood flow back to the heart, relieving tension in the lower extremities.

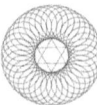

Basic Guided Meditation for Strengthening and Healing the Circulatory System

This guided meditation is designed to bring awareness, healing energy, and restoration to your circulatory system, promoting vitality and flow throughout your body.

Find a comfortable position, either sitting or lying down. Close your eyes and take three deep breaths, inhaling deeply through your nose and exhaling slowly through your mouth. Allow your body to relax with each exhale, releasing tension and stress.

Set your intention for the meditation: *"I welcome healing energy to strengthen and restore my circulatory system, promoting healthy flow and vitality throughout my body."*

Grounding and Connection
Visualize roots extending from your feet deep into the earth. Feel Earth's stabilizing energy rising through these roots, grounding and supporting you. Imagine this energy flowing upward, filling your body with a sense of security and balance.

Affirm: *"I am grounded, safe, and connected to the nurturing energy of the earth."*

Bringing Awareness to the Heart
Shift your focus to your heart, the central organ of your circulatory system. Visualize your heart as a radiant orb of golden light, glowing brightly in the center of your chest. Feel its steady rhythm as it pumps blood throughout your body, nourishing every cell.

Imagine this golden light expanding outward from your heart, filling your chest with warmth and vitality.

Affirm: *"My heart is strong, steady, and filled with vibrant energy."*

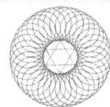

Visualizing Blood Flow
Bring your attention to your arteries, veins, and capillaries, the intricate network through which blood flows. Visualize the golden light from your heart flowing into these vessels, traveling through your body like a warm, gentle wave.

Imagine this light cleansing and clearing your circulatory pathways, dissolving any blockages or stagnation. Feel the energy restoring balance and flow, allowing your blood to carry oxygen and nutrients effortlessly to every part of your body.

Affirm: *"My blood flows freely and effortlessly, bringing life and vitality to every cell."*

Strengthening the Circulatory System
Focus on the strength and resilience of your circulatory system. See the golden light fortifying the walls of your blood vessels and energizing your heart. Visualize this energy enhancing the function of your entire system, promoting balance and harmony.

Affirm: *"My circulatory system is healthy, strong, and functions in perfect harmony with my body."*

Full Body Integration
Expand your awareness to your entire body. Imagine the golden light circulating through every part of you, infusing your muscles, organs, and cells with vitality. See your whole body glowing with radiant energy, a reflection of your healthy and balanced circulatory system.

Affirm: *"My body is energized and nourished by the healthy flow of my circulatory system."*

Closing and Gratitude
Take a moment to express gratitude for your heart, blood vessels, and the life-giving energy of your circulatory system. Thank your body for its strength and resilience, and thank the healing energy for its support.

When you are ready, gently bring your awareness back to your breath. Wiggle your fingers and toes, stretch lightly, and open your eyes.

Post-Meditation Care
- Hydration: Drink plenty of water to support your circulatory health and energy flow.
- Movement: Consider light physical activity, such as stretching or walking, to encourage circulation.
- Reflection: Spend a few moments reflecting on how your body feels after the meditation.

This simple meditation can be practiced regularly to support the health and vitality of your circulatory system.

Advanced Guided Meditation for Strengthening and Healing the Circulatory System

This advanced guided meditation channels the multidimensional energies of Rainbow Reiki to strengthen and heal the circulatory system. It incorporates the combined frequencies of Usui, Shadow, Arcturian, Pleiadian, Egyptian Sekhem-Seichim, and Magdalene/Yeshua Reiki to address the physical, energetic, and spiritual aspects of your circulatory system.

Find a quiet, comfortable space where you can sit or lie down undisturbed. Close your eyes and take several deep breaths, inhaling deeply through your nose and exhaling slowly through your mouth. With each exhale, allow your body to relax more deeply.

Set your intention: *"I invite the advanced energies of Rainbow Reiki to cleanse, strengthen, and restore my circulatory system, aligning it with optimal health and divine harmony."*

Grounding and Cosmic Alignment
Visualize roots extending from your feet deep into the crystalline core of the earth. Feel Gaia's grounding energy rising through these roots, anchoring and supporting your body. Simultaneously, imagine a column of vibrant rainbow light descending from the cosmos, entering through your crown chakra, and filling your entire being.

Feel the merging of these energies within your body, harmonizing and preparing your circulatory system to receive advanced healing.

Illuminating the Heart
Bring your awareness to your heart, the central organ of your circulatory system. Visualize your heart as a radiant orb of golden and rose-pink light, pulsing gently in your chest. This light embodies the nurturing frequencies of Magdalene/Yeshua Reiki, filling your heart with love, compassion, and vitality.

Feel this energy expanding outward, creating a harmonious rhythm that resonates throughout your circulatory system.

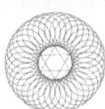

Affirm: *"My heart is strong, open, and aligned with the divine flow of life."*

Cleansing and Balancing Blood Flow
Shift your focus to your arteries, veins, and capillaries, the pathways through which your blood flows. Visualize a shimmering rainbow light entering these vessels from your heart, flowing effortlessly through your entire body.

See this light clearing any blockages or stagnation, dissolving toxins, and energizing your blood with life-giving energy. Imagine the light harmonizing with your body, ensuring every cell receives the oxygen and nutrients it needs to thrive.

Affirm: *"My blood flows freely and harmoniously, carrying vitality and nourishment to every cell in my body."*

Cellular Regeneration and DNA Activation
Bring your awareness to the cells within your blood and vessels. Visualize crystalline light codes from Arcturian and Pleiadian Reiki entering your cells, activating and restoring them to their highest potential. See these codes working within the mitochondria, enhancing energy production and cellular health.

Imagine this energy weaving through your circulatory system, upgrading your DNA and aligning your body with its divine blueprint for health and vitality.

Affirm: *"Each cell in my circulatory system is vibrant, healthy, and aligned with my highest potential."*

Strengthening and Energizing
Focus on your circulatory system as a whole. Visualize Egyptian Sekhem-Seichim Reiki energy entering as golden geometric patterns, strengthening the walls of your arteries and veins, and enhancing the elasticity of your vessels. See this energy supporting the structural integrity of your circulatory system.

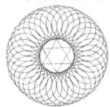

Next, feel a vibrant rainbow light flowing through your heart and vessels, bringing resilience, balance, and divine harmony to your entire system.

Affirm: *"My circulatory system is strong, resilient, and perfectly aligned with the flow of universal energy."*

Releasing Emotional and Energetic Imprints
Focus on areas of emotional or energetic tension within your circulatory system. Visualize a deep indigo light from Shadow Reiki flowing into these areas, dissolving old patterns, emotional blockages, or stress stored in your heart and vessels.

Once these blockages are cleared, see a soft rose-pink light from Magdalene/Yeshua Reiki filling these spaces, infusing them with love, forgiveness, and peace.

Affirm: *"I release all emotional and energetic imprints from my circulatory system, allowing peace and harmony to flow freely."*

Full Body Integration and Divine Flow
Expand your awareness to your entire body. Visualize your circulatory system glowing with a unified rainbow light, perfectly balanced and fully restored. Feel this energy connecting your circulatory system with the energetic layers of your aura and the multidimensional grids of Earth and cosmos.

Sense the alignment of your physical and energetic systems, creating a seamless flow of vitality and life force energy throughout your being.

Affirm: *"My circulatory system is fully integrated, flowing effortlessly with divine life force energy."*

Closing and Gratitude
Bring your awareness back to your heart center. Visualize a radiant orb of rainbow light within your chest, pulsating and sending waves of gratitude and healing throughout your body.

Take a moment to thank your circulatory system for its strength and resilience, and thank the advanced energies of Rainbow Reiki for their healing support. When you feel ready, gently return your awareness to your breath and the present moment.

Post-Meditation Care
- Hydration: Drink plenty of water to support the cleansing and detoxification process.
- Nourishment: Incorporate heart-healthy foods, such as leafy greens, berries, and omega-3-rich foods, into your diet.
- Reflection: Journal any sensations, insights, or changes you noticed during the meditation.

This advanced meditation can be practiced regularly to maintain the strength, flow, and vitality of your circulatory system, aligning it with the high frequencies of Rainbow Reiki.

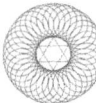

Respiratory System

The respiratory system is essential for life, enabling the intake of oxygen and the removal of carbon dioxide through the process of breathing. This system comprises the lungs, which facilitate gas exchange; the trachea, which serves as the main airway; the bronchi, which distribute air into the lungs; and the diaphragm, the primary muscle responsible for breathing. Together, these structures ensure that oxygen is delivered to the bloodstream to nourish cells and that waste gases like carbon dioxide are expelled efficiently. Proper functioning of the respiratory system is not only vital for physical health but also closely tied to emotional and energetic well-being, as the breath serves as a bridge between the body and mind.

Reiki can play a transformative role in supporting the respiratory system by promoting relaxation, reducing tension in the chest, and encouraging deep, rhythmic breathing. Stress and anxiety often result in shallow or erratic breathing patterns, which can reduce oxygen intake and create a sense of unease in the body. Reiki's gentle, harmonizing energy helps release tension in the diaphragm and chest muscles, allowing for a more natural and expansive breath. This not only enhances the physical flow of oxygen but also calms the nervous system, fostering a profound sense of relaxation and inner peace.

Energetically, the respiratory system is connected to the throat chakra and heart chakra, symbolizing communication, expression, and the breath of life. Imbalances in the respiratory system can reflect unresolved emotions, unexpressed truths, or suppressed grief. Reiki can assist in clearing these energetic blockages, helping individuals release emotional burdens and restore the harmonious flow of life force energy. By addressing both the physical and energetic dimensions of breathing, Reiki nurtures the respiratory system's natural functions, supporting vitality, emotional clarity, and a deeper connection to the present moment. This holistic approach fosters not just physical well-being but also a greater sense of alignment between the body, mind, and spirit.

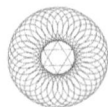

Reiki Hand Placement

Crown of the Head (Respiratory-Brain Connection)
Placement: Place hands gently on the top of the head.
Purpose: Enhances the mind-body connection and supports the brain's role in regulating breathing.

Forehead and Back of the Head (Nervous System and Breathing)
Placement: Place one hand on the forehead and the other at the base of the skull.
Purpose: Balances the nervous system, which influences the respiratory rhythm.

Throat (Trachea and Airway Support)
Placement: Place hands gently over the throat, ensuring light touch or just above the skin.
Purpose: Clears energetic blockages in the airways and supports the throat chakra, which governs expression and breath.

Upper Chest (Lung Health and Heart-Lung Connection)
Placement: Rest both hands on the upper chest, covering the area over the lungs.
Purpose: Directs healing energy to the lungs, promoting deeper, clearer breathing and oxygenation.

Rib Cage (Diaphragm and Respiratory Expansion)
Placement: Place hands on the sides of the ribcage, just below the chest.
Purpose: Supports the diaphragm and encourages full respiratory expansion.

Solar Plexus (Breath and Emotional Release)
Placement: Rest hands on the upper abdomen, just below the ribcage.
Purpose: Helps release emotional blockages that can restrict breathing, fostering a deeper sense of calm.

Upper Back (Lung and Rib Cage Support)

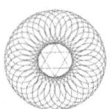

Placement: Place hands on the upper back, between the shoulder blades.
Purpose: Supports the back of the lungs and addresses tension that might restrict breathing.

Hands on Sides of the Neck (Lymphatic and Respiratory Flow)
Placement: Rest hands lightly on the sides of the neck.
Purpose: Supports the lymphatic system, which works closely with the respiratory system to clear toxins.

Lower Abdomen (Grounding Breath)
Placement: Place hands over the lower abdomen.
Purpose: Encourages deep, diaphragmatic breathing and supports grounding energy.

Feet (Grounding and Whole-System Connection)
Placement: Place hands on the tops of the feet or gently cup the ankles.
Purpose: Grounds the energy and integrates the healing work done on the respiratory system.

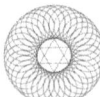

Guided Meditation for Respiratory Healing and Strengthening
Find a quiet, comfortable space where you will not be disturbed. Sit or lie down in a relaxed position and let us begin.

Take a moment to settle in. Close your eyes gently and take a deep breath in through your nose ... and slowly exhale through your mouth. Allow your body to begin to relax.

Let us focus on your breath, the life force that flows through you, nourishing every cell. With each breath, we will strengthen and heal the respiratory system, bringing vitality and peace.

<u>Body Awareness</u>
Bring your awareness to your body. Notice how you are supported by the surface beneath you. Feel yourself held, safe, and grounded.

Shift your attention to your chest and lungs. Notice the rise and fall as you breathe in and out. There is no need to change anything right now—just observe.

<u>Guided Breathing</u>
Now, let us begin a healing breathing pattern:
- Inhale deeply for a count of four. Feel your lungs expand fully.
- Hold your breath gently for a count of four, allowing oxygen to infuse your body.
- Exhale slowly and completely for a count of six. Let go of any tension or stagnation.
- Repeat this pattern for a few cycles, imagining your breath clearing and revitalizing your lungs.

<u>Visualization for Healing</u>
As you breathe, visualize a gentle, warm light entering your body with each inhale. This light represents healing energy.
- Imagine this light filling your lungs, expanding and strengthening them.

- With each exhale, visualize releasing any tension, congestion, or negativity. Let it flow out like a soft, gray mist, dissolving into the air.
- Feel your lungs becoming clearer, more vibrant, and full of life with each breath.

Affirmations for Health

As you breathe, silently repeat these affirmations to yourself:
- *"My lungs are strong and healthy."*
- *"Every breath I take nourishes my body and soul."*
- *"I release all tension and embrace vitality."*
- *"My respiratory system is resilient and thriving."*

Feel the truth of these affirmations resonating deeply within you.

Begin to bring your awareness back to your surroundings. Wiggle your fingers and toes, and when you are ready, open your eyes.

Take a moment to notice how you feel—calmer, more centered, and deeply connected to your breath.

Remember, your breath is always with you, a tool for healing and presence.

Advanced Guided Meditation for Strengthening and Healing the Respiratory System

This guided meditation channels the advanced, multidimensional energies of Rainbow Reiki to heal, strengthen, and align the respiratory system. It integrates the frequencies of Usui, Shadow, Arcturian, Pleiadian, Egyptian Sekhem-Seichim, and Magdalene/Yeshua Reiki, addressing the physical, energetic, and spiritual dimensions of your breath and lung health.

Find a quiet, comfortable place where you can sit or lie down undisturbed. Close your eyes and take several deep breaths, inhaling deeply through your nose and exhaling slowly through your mouth. Allow your body to relax with each exhale.

Set your intention: *"I open myself to the advanced healing energies of Rainbow Reiki to cleanse, strengthen, and align my respiratory system, promoting vitality, ease, and harmony."*

<u>Grounding and Cosmic Connection</u>
Visualize roots extending from your feet into the crystalline core of Earth. Feel Gaia's grounding energy rising through these roots, anchoring and stabilizing your energy. Simultaneously, envision a column of vibrant rainbow light descending from the cosmos, entering through your crown chakra, and filling your body.

Feel the harmonious blending of Earth and cosmic energies within you, creating a stable and elevated foundation for respiratory healing.

<u>Illuminating the Respiratory System</u>
Shift your focus to your respiratory system, beginning with your lungs. Visualize your lungs glowing with a soft, golden light. Imagine this light filling your nasal passages, throat, windpipe, and bronchial tubes, traveling into every air sac and alveolus.

See this golden light flowing like a gentle breeze through your entire respiratory system, cleansing and energizing every structure.

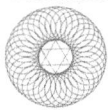

Affirm: *"My respiratory system is open, clear, and illuminated with healing light."*

Cellular Healing and Regeneration
Bring your awareness to the cells within your respiratory system. Visualize crystalline light codes from Arcturian and Pleiadian Reiki entering each cell. See these codes activating the mitochondria, boosting cellular repair and renewal. Imagine your lung tissue glowing with vitality, strong and flexible.

Envision this crystalline energy clearing toxins, repairing damaged tissue, and optimizing oxygen exchange. Feel your entire respiratory system revitalized.

Affirm: *"Every cell in my respiratory system is vibrant, healthy, and aligned with my highest potential."*

Clearing Stagnant Energy
Focus on areas of heaviness, tightness, or tension in your respiratory system. Visualize a deep indigo light from Shadow Reiki flowing into these areas, dissolving old patterns of grief, fear, or stagnation that may be stored in your lungs and chest.

Once these blockages are cleared, see a soft rose-pink light from Magdalene/Yeshua Reiki filling the space, infusing your respiratory system with love, peace, and emotional release.

Affirm: *"I release all tension, grief, and stagnant energy from my respiratory system, creating space for healing and harmony."*

Strengthening and Energizing
Visualize Egyptian Sekhem-Seichim Reiki energy entering your respiratory system as golden, geometric patterns. These sacred patterns weave through your lungs, bronchial tubes, and diaphragm, strengthening the structural and energetic integrity of your respiratory system.

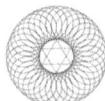

Next, imagine a vibrant rainbow light flowing into your respiratory system, bringing resilience, vitality, and ease. Feel this light spreading throughout your body with each inhale, nourishing your entire being.

Affirm: *"My respiratory system is strong, resilient, and filled with life force energy."*

Aligning Breath with Life Force
Shift your focus to your breath. With each inhale, imagine breathing in pure, healing energy from the universe. With each exhale, release any tension, toxins, or energy that no longer serves you.

Feel the rhythm of your breath aligning with the universal life force, creating a flow of vitality and peace within you. Sense your breath connecting your physical body with your energetic and spiritual essence.

Affirm: *"Each breath I take is filled with healing energy, aligning my body, mind, and spirit with divine harmony."*

Multidimensional Integration
Expand your awareness to include the energetic layers of your respiratory system, extending into your auric field. Visualize the advanced Rainbow Reiki energies anchoring into these layers, aligning your breath with the multidimensional grids of Earth and the cosmos.

Feel the interconnectedness of your respiratory system with your entire energy body, creating a seamless flow of vitality, balance, and divine alignment.

Affirm: *"My breath flows effortlessly, connecting me to Earth, the cosmos, and my divine essence."*

Closing and Gratitude
Bring your awareness back to your heart center. Visualize a glowing orb of rainbow light within your chest, pulsating with gratitude and

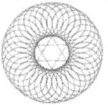

healing energy. Allow this light to radiate outward, integrating all the healing energies you have received.

Take a moment to thank your respiratory system for its resilience and strength, and express gratitude for the Rainbow Reiki energies and your ability to heal.

When you feel ready, gently bring your awareness back to the present moment. Wiggle your fingers and toes, stretch lightly, and open your eyes.

Post-Meditation Care
- Hydration: Drink plenty of water to support detoxification and energy flow.
- Deep Breathing: Practice slow, deep breathing exercises throughout the day to enhance the healing effects.
- Reflection: Journal any sensations, insights, or shifts you experienced during the meditation.

This advanced meditation can be practiced regularly to maintain the strength, balance, and vitality of your respiratory system while aligning it with the high frequencies of Rainbow Reiki.

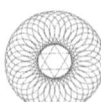

Digestive System

The digestive system is responsible for breaking down food, absorbing essential nutrients, and eliminating waste, making it a cornerstone of overall health and vitality. Key components of this system include the stomach, where initial digestion occurs; the intestines, which further break down food and absorb nutrients into the bloodstream; the liver, which processes toxins and produces bile to aid fat digestion; the pancreas, which secretes digestive enzymes and regulates blood sugar levels; and the gallbladder, which stores and releases bile as needed. Together, these organs ensure the body receives the nutrients it needs to function efficiently while maintaining detoxification and waste removal processes.

Reiki is particularly effective in supporting the digestive system by promoting relaxation, reducing inflammation, and addressing energetic imbalances that may disrupt digestive health. Stress, anxiety, and emotional turmoil are often linked to digestive issues such as irritable bowel syndrome (IBS), acid reflux, or bloating. Reiki's calming energy helps activate the parasympathetic nervous system, also known as the "rest-and-digest" state, which encourages optimal digestion and nutrient absorption. By focusing Reiki energy on areas like the stomach and intestines, practitioners can alleviate physical discomfort, ease tension, and promote a smoother digestive process.

Energetically, the digestive system is closely associated with the solar plexus chakra, the center of personal power, will, and self-confidence. Digestive imbalances can often reflect unresolved emotions, feelings of being overwhelmed, or difficulty processing life experiences. Reiki can help release these energetic blockages, allowing the digestive system to function more harmoniously. By addressing both the physical and energetic dimensions of digestion, Reiki fosters a sense of balance, vitality, and overall well-being, helping individuals feel nourished on both a physical and emotional level. This holistic approach to digestive health enables the body to process not only food but also life's challenges with greater ease and alignment.

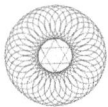

Reiki Hand Placement

Crown of the Head (Mind-Gut Connection)
Placement: Place hands gently on the top of the head.
Purpose: Supports the connection between the brain and the gut, addressing the mind's influence on digestion.

Forehead and Back of the Head (Stress Relief)
Placement: Place one hand on the forehead and the other on the back of the head.
Purpose: Calms the nervous system, reducing stress that can affect digestion.

Throat (Esophagus and Swallowing)
Placement: Place hands lightly on the throat area.
Purpose: Clears energetic blockages in the esophagus and supports smooth swallowing.

Upper Abdomen (Stomach and Upper Digestive Tract)
Placement: Rest hands just below the ribcage, over the stomach area.
Purpose: Promotes energy flow to the stomach, easing issues like indigestion, acid reflux, or nausea.

Solar Plexus (Digestive Organs and Emotional Stress)
Placement: Place hands on the solar plexus, just above the navel.
Purpose: Balances the energy in this area, which governs the digestive organs and stores stress and emotions.

Lower Abdomen (Intestines and Lower Digestive Tract)
Placement: Rest hands on the lower abdomen, below the navel.
Purpose: Supports the intestines and lower digestive processes, promoting relaxation and flow.

Lower Back (Kidneys and Digestive Support)
Placement: Place hands on the lower back, near the kidney area.
Purpose: Assists with detoxification and supports the body's ability to process nutrients and waste.

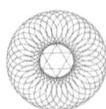

Sides of the Abdomen (Colon and Large Intestine)
Placement: Place hands gently on the sides of the abdomen.
Purpose: Stimulates energy flow through the large intestine, encouraging natural elimination and detoxification.

Hands on Hips (Grounding Digestive Energy)
Placement: Rest hands over the hip bones.
Purpose: Grounds energy and supports the sacral chakra, which is connected to digestion and fluid balance.

Feet (Grounding and Whole-Body Integration)
Placement: Rest hands on the tops of the feet or gently cup the ankles.
Purpose: Grounds the energy and integrates the healing work throughout the entire digestive system.

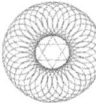

Guided Meditation for Digestive Healing and Strengthening
Find a calm, comfortable space where you can sit or lie down without distractions. When you are ready, close your eyes and take a deep breath.

Begin by noticing your breath. Take a deep inhale through your nose, and exhale slowly through your mouth. With each breath, allow your body to relax. Release any tension in your shoulders, your jaw, and your abdomen.

Let us focus on your digestive system—your body's powerful center of nourishment and transformation. Through visualization and intention, we will support its healing and optimal functioning.

<u>Body Awareness</u>
Bring your attention to your belly. Place a hand gently on your abdomen if that feels comfortable for you. Notice the rise and fall of this area as you breathe in and out.

With each inhale, feel your abdomen expand gently like a balloon. With each exhale, feel it relax, releasing any tension or tightness.

<u>Healing Breathing</u>
Now let us deepen the breath:
- Breathe in slowly through your nose for a count of four. Imagine fresh energy flowing to your digestive organs.
- Hold your breath for a count of four, allowing this energy to nourish and strengthen your system.
- Exhale slowly through your mouth for a count of six, releasing any blockages, discomfort, or tension.
- Repeat this cycle for several breaths, letting your digestive system feel supported and calm.

<u>Visualization for Digestive Healing</u>
As you continue to breathe, imagine a warm golden light glowing in the center of your belly. This light represents healing energy, warmth, and vitality.

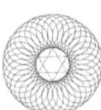

- See this light expanding with each inhale, gently surrounding your stomach, intestines, and other digestive organs.
- Visualize this light dissolving any discomfort, blockages, or stress, replacing it with soothing, nourishing energy.
- With each exhale, release anything that no longer serves you, letting it flow out like a soft mist.
- Feel your digestive system becoming balanced, calm, and strong.

<u>Affirmations for Digestive Health</u>
As you breathe, silently or softly repeat these affirmations:
- *"My digestion is healthy and harmonious."*
- *"I trust my body's ability to process and absorb nourishment."*
- *"I release all tension and embrace balance in my digestive system."*
- *"My body is healing, strong, and thriving."*

Let these words sink into your consciousness, affirming the health and strength of your digestive system.

Begin to bring your awareness back to your surroundings. Wiggle your fingers and toes, and when you feel ready, open your eyes.

Take a moment to notice how you feel—a sense of ease, calm, and connection to your body. Remember, your digestive system thrives when you create space for rest and mindfulness.

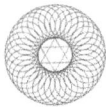

Advanced Guided Meditation for Strengthening and Healing the Digestive System

This guided meditation integrates the multidimensional energies of Rainbow Reiki to heal, strengthen, and align the digestive system. It combines the frequencies of Usui, Shadow, Arcturian, Pleiadian, Egyptian Sekhem-Seichim, and Magdalene/Yeshua Reiki to address the physical, energetic, and spiritual aspects of digestion.

Find a quiet, comfortable space where you can sit or lie down undisturbed. Close your eyes and take a few deep breaths, inhaling deeply through your nose and exhaling slowly through your mouth. Allow your body to relax with each exhale.

Set your intention: *"I invite the advanced healing energies of Rainbow Reiki to cleanse, strengthen, and align my digestive system, promoting balance, vitality, and ease."*

<u>Grounding and Cosmic Connection</u>
Visualize roots extending from your feet deep into Earth's crystalline core. Feel Earth's stabilizing energy rising through these roots, grounding and supporting you. At the same time, envision a vibrant column of rainbow light descending from the cosmos, entering your crown chakra, and filling your body.
Sense the harmonious blending of Earth and cosmic energies within you, creating a foundation for digestive healing.

<u>Illuminating the Digestive System</u>
Shift your focus to your digestive system, starting with your stomach. Visualize your stomach glowing with a soft, golden light. See this light spreading through your esophagus, intestines, liver, pancreas, and all parts of your digestive tract.

As the light flows, imagine it cleansing and energizing every part of your digestive system, clearing away blockages, toxins, or stagnant energy.

Affirm: *"My digestive system is illuminated with healing light, functioning in harmony and ease."*

Cellular Healing and Regeneration
Focus on the cells within your digestive system. Visualize crystalline light codes from Arcturian and Pleiadian Reiki entering each cell. These codes activate the mitochondria, promoting cellular repair and renewal. See your digestive lining glowing with vitality and resilience.

Imagine this crystalline energy enhancing the production of digestive enzymes, improving nutrient absorption, and supporting optimal function at every level.

Affirm: *"Each cell in my digestive system is vibrant, healthy, and aligned with my highest potential."*

Clearing Emotional and Energetic Imprints
Focus on areas where you may hold emotional tension or stress in your digestive system, such as your stomach or gut. Visualize a deep indigo light from Shadow Reiki entering these areas, dissolving any stored emotions, such as worry, anxiety, or fear.

Once these blockages are cleared, imagine a soft rose-pink light from Magdalene/Yeshua Reiki filling the space, infusing your digestive system with love, peace, and emotional balance.

Affirm: *"I release all emotional and energetic imprints from my digestive system, creating space for healing and renewal."*

Strengthening and Energizing
Visualize Egyptian Sekhem-Seichim Reiki energy flowing into your digestive system as radiant golden geometric patterns. These patterns weave through your digestive organs, strengthening their structure and enhancing their function.

Next, see a vibrant rainbow light flowing through your digestive system, bringing vitality, balance, and ease. Feel this light harmonizing your entire digestive process, from ingestion to elimination.

Affirm: *"My digestive system is strong, resilient, and functions effortlessly in perfect harmony."*

Aligning with Life Force Energy
Shift your focus to the flow of life force energy through your digestive system. Visualize the rainbow light aligning your digestive organs with your body's energetic pathways, ensuring that your digestive system is nourished and supported by universal energy.

Sense your digestive system working in harmony with your body's overall energy flow, creating a seamless connection between your physical and energetic bodies.

Affirm: *"My digestive system is nourished and aligned with the divine flow of life force energy."*

Full Integration and Multidimensional Alignment
Expand your awareness to include the energetic layers of your digestive system, reaching into your auric field. Visualize the advanced Rainbow Reiki energies anchoring into these layers, connecting your digestive system to Earth's crystalline grid and the cosmic frequencies.

Feel the alignment of your digestive system with the multidimensional aspects of your being, creating a state of wholeness and balance.

Affirm: *"My digestive system is fully integrated, balanced, and aligned with my highest vibrational potential."*

Closing and Gratitude
Bring your awareness back to your heart center. Visualize a glowing orb of rainbow light within your chest, pulsating with gratitude and healing energy. Allow this light to radiate outward, integrating all the healing energies you have received.

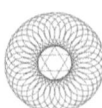

Take a moment to thank your digestive system for its resilience and strength, and express gratitude for the Rainbow Reiki energies and your ability to heal.

When you feel ready, gently bring your awareness back to the present moment. Wiggle your fingers and toes, stretch lightly, and open your eyes.

Post-Meditation Care
- Hydration: Drink plenty of water to support the cleansing and detoxification process.
- Nourishment: Focus on whole, nutrient-dense foods to support your digestive health.
- Reflection: Journal any sensations, insights, or changes you noticed during the meditation.

This advanced meditation can be practiced regularly to maintain the strength, balance, and vitality of your digestive system while aligning it with the high frequencies of Rainbow Reiki.

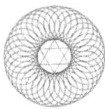

Endocrine System

The endocrine system is a network of glands that produce and release hormones, acting as the body's chemical messengers to regulate critical functions such as metabolism, growth, development, mood, and reproduction. Key components of this system include the thyroid gland, which governs metabolism and energy levels; the adrenal glands, which produce stress hormones like cortisol and adrenaline to manage the body's response to stress; the pancreas, which regulates blood sugar through insulin production; and the reproductive glands (ovaries and testes), which control reproductive health and influence hormonal balance. The endocrine system works in harmony with the nervous system, maintaining homeostasis and ensuring that the body's processes operate in a balanced and synchronized manner.

Reiki can provide powerful support for the endocrine system by promoting relaxation, reducing stress, and helping to restore energetic balance to glands that may be overworked or underfunctioning. Chronic stress, emotional strain, and energetic blockages often disrupt hormonal balance, leading to issues such as fatigue, mood swings, weight imbalances, or reproductive challenges. Reiki's calming and harmonizing energy encourages the body to enter a state of relaxation, alleviating the stress that places strain on glands like the thyroid and adrenals. By focusing on these key areas, Reiki helps to reduce inflammation, enhance energy flow, and promote the optimal functioning of the endocrine system.

Energetically, the endocrine system is interconnected with various chakras, such as the throat chakra (thyroid), sacral chakra (reproductive glands), and solar plexus chakra (pancreas). Imbalances in these energy centers often manifest as hormonal issues or mood disturbances. Reiki facilitates the clearing of these blockages, helping to align the physical and energetic aspects of the endocrine system. This holistic approach not only supports physical health but also fosters emotional resilience, mood stability, and overall well-being. By addressing the root causes of stress and imbalance, Reiki enhances the body's ability to self-regulate,

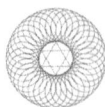

creating harmony across all systems and empowering individuals to live with greater vitality and balance.

Reiki Hand Placement

Crown of the Head (Pineal and Pituitary Glands)
Placement: Place hands gently on the top of the head.
Purpose: Supports the pineal gland, which regulates sleep and circadian rhythms, and the pituitary gland, the "master gland" that controls other endocrine glands.

Forehead and Third Eye (Pituitary and Hypothalamus)
Placement: Rest hands lightly on the forehead, covering the third eye area.
Purpose: Balances the pituitary gland and hypothalamus, which govern the nervous and endocrine systems.

Throat (Thyroid and Parathyroid Glands)
Placement: Place hands gently over the throat area.
Purpose: Supports the thyroid and parathyroid glands, which regulate metabolism, calcium balance, and energy levels.

Upper Chest (Thymus Gland)
Placement: Rest hands over the center of the chest, just above the heart.
Purpose: Balances the thymus gland, which plays a role in immune function and energy flow in the body.

Solar Plexus (Adrenal Glands)
Placement: Place hands on the upper abdomen, just below the ribcage.
Purpose: Supports the adrenal glands, which regulate stress hormones like cortisol and adrenaline, promoting relaxation and balance.

Lower Abdomen (Pancreas)
Placement: Rest hands on the lower abdomen, between the navel and the ribcage.

Purpose: Balances the pancreas, which regulates blood sugar levels and digestion.

Lower Abdomen (Ovaries or Testes)
Placement: Rest hands just below the navel over the reproductive area.
Purpose: Supports hormonal balance in the ovaries or testes, aiding reproductive health and energy flow.

Lower Back (Kidney-Adrenal Connection)
Placement: Place hands on the lower back, over the kidney area.
Purpose: Energizes and balances the adrenal glands and kidneys, supporting hormonal and energy balance.

Hands and Feet (Overall Hormonal Flow)
Placement: Gently hold the hands or place hands over the tops of the feet.
Purpose: Grounds and integrates the work done on the endocrine system, promoting balance throughout the body.

Entire Spine (Central Nervous System and Endocrine Balance)
Placement: Sweep hands along the spine, stopping at the base of the skull, between the shoulder blades, and the lower back.
Purpose: Aligns the energy flow between the central nervous system and the endocrine glands.

Guided Meditation for Endocrine System Healing

Find a quiet, comfortable place where you can sit or lie down. Close your eyes and allow yourself to settle into stillness.

Take a deep breath in through your nose, and slowly exhale through your mouth. With each breath, allow your body to relax. Let go of any tension in your jaw, shoulders, and belly.

The endocrine system is a network of glands that communicate and regulate essential body functions. This meditation will focus on restoring balance, vitality, and harmony to this intricate system.

<u>Body Awareness</u>
Bring your attention to your entire body. Notice where you feel tension or ease. Now, gently shift your focus to the major glands of the endocrine system.
- Begin at the top of your head, the pineal gland, associated with sleep and intuition.
- Move to the center of your forehead, the pituitary gland, the master regulator.
- Bring your attention to your throat, the home of the thyroid and parathyroid glands, governing energy and metabolism.
- Focus on your chest, where the thymus gland supports immunity.
- Move down to your abdomen, connecting to the pancreas, which balances blood sugar.
- Finally, bring awareness to your pelvis, where the adrenal glands and reproductive glands support vitality and creation.

<u>Healing Breathing</u>
Let us deepen the breath for healing and balance:
- Breathe in slowly through your nose for a count of four. Imagine fresh, calming energy entering your body.
- Hold the breath gently for a count of four, allowing this energy to circulate through your endocrine glands.
- Exhale slowly and completely for a count of six, releasing any tension or imbalance.

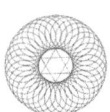

- Repeat this cycle, imagining your breath bringing nourishment and harmony to your entire system.

Visualization for Healing

As you breathe, visualize a gentle, radiant light entering your body. This light is pure healing energy, warm and soothing.
- Imagine this light flowing first to your head, energizing your pineal and pituitary glands.
- Let it move down your throat, bathing the thyroid and parathyroid glands in warmth.
- See the light radiating through your chest, nurturing the thymus gland.
- Feel it flowing into your abdomen, revitalizing your pancreas and digestion.
- Finally, let the light settle in your pelvis, strengthening your adrenal and reproductive glands.

This light balances and heals, leaving your endocrine system in harmony.

Affirmations for Endocrine Health

As you continue breathing and visualizing, silently repeat these affirmations:
- "My endocrine system is balanced and vibrant."
- "My hormones are in perfect harmony."
- "My body knows how to heal and thrive."
- "Every cell in my body supports my vitality and balance."

Feel these affirmations resonating throughout your body, creating a deep sense of well-being.

Begin to bring your awareness back to your surroundings. Wiggle your fingers and toes, and when you are ready, open your eyes.

Take a moment to notice how you feel—lighter, more balanced, and deeply connected to your body's natural rhythms.

Advanced Guided Meditation for Strengthening and Healing the Endocrine System

This advanced guided meditation channels the multidimensional energies of Rainbow Reiki to strengthen, balance, and heal the endocrine system. It integrates the frequencies of Usui, Shadow, Arcturian, Pleiadian, Egyptian Sekhem-Seichim, and Magdalene/Yeshua Reiki to address the physical, energetic, and spiritual dimensions of the glands and hormonal functions within the body.

Find a quiet, comfortable space to sit or lie down. Close your eyes and take several deep breaths, inhaling deeply through your nose and exhaling slowly through your mouth. With each exhale, feel your body releasing tension and relaxing further.

Set your intention: *"I invite the advanced healing energies of Rainbow Reiki to cleanse, strengthen, and align my endocrine system, supporting balance, vitality, and divine harmony."*

Grounding and Cosmic Connection
Visualize roots growing from your feet deep into the crystalline core of Earth. Feel Gaia's stabilizing energy rising through these roots, entering your body, and grounding you. At the same time, envision a column of vibrant rainbow light descending from the cosmos, entering your crown chakra, and filling your entire body.

Feel the harmonious blending of Earth and cosmic energies, grounding and elevating your endocrine system for healing.

Illuminating the Endocrine System
Bring your awareness to your endocrine system. Visualize each gland glowing with golden light as you move your focus through the system:
- Pineal Gland (center of the brain): A radiant violet light awakens and activates this gland, enhancing your connection to divine consciousness.
- Pituitary Gland (beneath the brain): A soft indigo light balances this gland, aligning it as the master regulator of hormonal activity.

- Thyroid and Parathyroid Glands (throat): A soothing blue light harmonizes these glands, supporting metabolism and calcium balance.
- Thymus Gland (upper chest): A glowing green light infuses the thymus, strengthening your immune system and heart energy.
- Adrenal Glands (above the kidneys): A warm golden-orange light restores balance to these glands, releasing stored stress and enhancing resilience.
- Pancreas (upper abdomen): A golden-yellow light balances the pancreas, supporting blood sugar regulation and digestive harmony.
- Ovaries/Testes (lower abdomen): A soft red light energizes these glands, balancing reproductive hormones and creative energy.

Affirm: *"My endocrine system is illuminated with healing light, functioning in harmony and balance."*

Cellular Healing and Regeneration
Visualize crystalline light codes from Arcturian and Pleiadian Reiki entering the cells of each gland. See these codes activating the mitochondria, enhancing cellular repair and regeneration. Imagine each gland glowing with renewed vitality, perfectly calibrated to support hormonal balance.

Feel the energy clearing any stagnation, optimizing communication between the glands, and restoring harmony throughout your body.

Affirm: *"Each gland in my endocrine system is vibrant, healthy, and aligned with my highest potential."*

Clearing Emotional and Energetic Imprints
Focus on areas within your endocrine system that may hold emotional or energetic blockages. Visualize Shadow Reiki energy as a deep indigo light entering these areas, dissolving any stored stress, fear, or tension. Feel the release of old patterns and emotions that no longer serve you.

Once cleared, see a soft rose-pink light from Magdalene/Yeshua Reiki filling these spaces, infusing your endocrine system with love, peace, and divine balance.

Affirm: *"I release all emotional and energetic imprints from my endocrine system, creating space for healing and renewal."*

Strengthening and Energizing
Visualize the sacred geometric patterns of Egyptian Sekhem-Seichim Reiki flowing into your endocrine system as radiant golden light. These patterns weave through each gland, strengthening its structure and optimizing its function.

Next, imagine a vibrant rainbow light flowing through your endocrine system, bringing vitality, balance, and harmony. Feel this light connecting each gland in a seamless flow, ensuring smooth communication and energy exchange.

Affirm: *"My endocrine system is strong, resilient, and perfectly aligned with the flow of universal energy."*

Aligning with Life Force Energy
Focus on your breath as a carrier of life force energy. With each inhale, visualize the rainbow light entering your endocrine system, nourishing and energizing each gland. With each exhale, release any remaining tension, toxins, or blockages.

Feel the rhythm of your breath aligning your endocrine system with your body's energetic pathways, creating balance and harmony throughout your being.

Affirm: *"My endocrine system is nourished and aligned with the divine flow of life force energy."*

Multidimensional Integration
Expand your awareness to the energetic layers of your endocrine system, extending into your auric field. Visualize the advanced

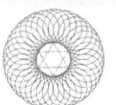

Rainbow Reiki energies anchoring into these layers, connecting your endocrine system to Earth's crystalline grid and the cosmic frequencies.

Feel the alignment of your endocrine system with the multidimensional aspects of your being, fostering wholeness and balance.

Affirm: *"My endocrine system is fully integrated, balanced, and aligned with my highest vibrational potential."*

Closing and Gratitude
Bring your awareness back to your heart center. Visualize a glowing orb of rainbow light within your chest, pulsating with gratitude and healing energy. Allow this light to radiate outward, integrating all the healing energies you have received.

Take a moment to thank your endocrine system for its resilience and strength, and express gratitude for the Rainbow Reiki energies and your ability to heal.

When you feel ready, gently bring your awareness back to the present moment. Wiggle your fingers and toes, stretch lightly, and open your eyes.

Post-Meditation Care
- Hydration: Drink plenty of water to support the cleansing and energy flow within your endocrine system.
- Nourishment: Focus on foods that support glandular health, such as nuts, seeds, leafy greens, and adaptogenic herbs.
- Reflection: Journal any sensations, insights, or shifts you experienced during the meditation.

This advanced meditation can be practiced regularly to maintain the strength, balance, and vitality of your endocrine system while aligning it with the high frequencies of Rainbow Reiki.

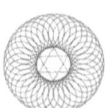

Lymphatic/Immune System
The lymphatic system is a vital part of the body's immune system and detoxification process, working to remove toxins, waste, and excess fluids while playing a crucial role in defending the body against infections and diseases. This system includes lymph nodes, which filter harmful substances and produce immune cells; lymph vessels, which transport lymph fluid throughout the body; the spleen, which filters blood and helps fight infections; and the tonsils, which provide a first line of defense against airborne and ingested pathogens. Unlike the circulatory system, the lymphatic system lacks a central pump like the heart and relies on muscle movement and breathing to keep lymph fluid flowing, making it particularly sensitive to blockages and stagnation.

Reiki can provide significant support for the lymphatic system by promoting relaxation, enhancing energy flow, and encouraging the body's natural detoxification processes. Stress and energetic blockages can lead to stagnation within the lymphatic system, reducing its efficiency in removing toxins and maintaining immune health. By focusing Reiki energy on key areas such as the lymph nodes and spleen, practitioners can help facilitate lymphatic drainage, reduce inflammation, and stimulate the body's immune response. This gentle, yet profound, energetic support helps to clear physical and energetic blockages, allowing the lymphatic system to function more effectively.

Energetically, the lymphatic system is linked to the heart and solar plexus chakras, representing compassion, vitality, and the body's ability to protect and heal itself. Imbalances in these chakras may manifest as weakened immunity or feelings of vulnerability. Reiki helps restore balance to these energy centers, empowering the lymphatic system to cleanse and regenerate with greater efficiency.

This holistic approach not only supports physical detoxification and immunity but also fosters a sense of lightness and vitality, enabling the body to release not just physical waste but also emotional and energetic burdens. By harmonizing the lymphatic system, Reiki

promotes a healthier, more resilient body and mind, supporting overall well-being and longevity.

Reiki Hand Placement

Crown of the Head (Immune System Regulation)
Placement: Place hands gently on the top of the head.
Purpose: Supports the brain's regulation of the immune response and promotes overall energetic balance.

Forehead and Back of the Head (Stress Relief and Hypothalamus)
Placement: Rest one hand on the forehead and the other on the back of the head.
Purpose: Reduces stress that can compromise immunity and supports the hypothalamus, which regulates immune and lymphatic functions.

Throat (Lymph Nodes and Thymus)
Placement: Place hands gently on the throat.
Purpose: Clears blockages in the lymph nodes around the neck and supports immune function regulated by the thymus.

Upper Chest (Thymus Gland and Lungs)
Placement: Rest hands over the center of the chest, just above the heart.
Purpose: Activates the thymus gland (a key player in immune function) and supports lymph flow in the chest area.

Underarms (Axillary Lymph Nodes)
Placement: Place hands on the sides of the chest, near the underarms.
Purpose: Encourages lymphatic drainage and clears energy blockages in the axillary lymph nodes.

Solar Plexus (Emotional Immune Connection)
Placement: Place hands on the upper abdomen, just below the ribcage.
Purpose: Balances emotional energy, which significantly impacts the immune system.

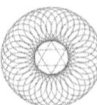

Lower Abdomen (Digestive-Immune Link)
Placement: Rest hands on the lower abdomen, just below the navel.
Purpose: Supports the gut-associated lymphoid tissue (GALT), which plays a major role in immune defense.

Lower Back (Kidneys and Lymphatic Support)
Placement: Place hands on the lower back, near the kidney area.
Purpose: Supports kidney function and lymphatic detoxification.

Sides of the Neck (Cervical Lymph Nodes)
Placement: Rest hands lightly on the sides of the neck.
Purpose: Encourages lymph flow through the cervical lymph nodes, which help filter toxins.

Hands and Feet (Lymphatic Grounding)
Placement: Hold the client's hands or place hands on the tops of their feet.
Purpose: Grounds the energy and promotes lymphatic circulation throughout the body.

Entire Spine (Immune-Nervous System Connection)
Placement: Sweep hands along the spine, pausing at key points (base of the skull, between the shoulder blades, and lower back).
Purpose: Aligns the energy flow between the nervous and immune systems, fostering balance and resilience.

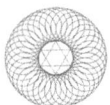

Guided Meditation for Lymphatic and Immune System Healing

Find a quiet, comfortable place to sit or lie down. Close your eyes gently and allow your body to relax.

Take a deep breath in through your nose, and exhale slowly through your mouth. Let your shoulders drop, your jaw relax, and your entire body begin to feel supported and at ease.

The lymphatic system is a vital part of your immune system, clearing toxins and maintaining balance. Together, we'll focus on activating its natural flow and enhancing your body's innate ability to heal.

Body Awareness

Bring your attention to your body. Start at your feet and slowly scan upward, noticing any sensations, areas of tension, or ease.
- Focus on your neck and under your jawline—key areas of lymphatic activity.
- Bring awareness to your chest, where the thymus gland helps support immunity.
- Shift your focus to your abdomen, where lymph nodes and the spleen work to cleanse and protect your body.
- Lastly, focus on your arms, legs, and groin—areas rich with lymphatic flow.

Feel a sense of gratitude for the work your lymphatic and immune systems do every day.

Healing Breathing

Let us engage the breath to stimulate lymphatic flow and healing:
- Breathe in deeply through your nose for a count of four, imagining clean, fresh energy entering your body.
- Hold the breath for a count of four, allowing this energy to flow through your lymphatic pathways.
- Exhale completely for a count of six, releasing any tension or toxins.

Repeat this breathing cycle for a few moments, feeling your body relax and energize with each breath.

Visualization for Lymphatic Healing

As you continue to breathe, visualize a gentle, cooling, blue-green light entering your body. This light represents healing and renewal.
- Imagine this light flowing into your lymphatic vessels and nodes, gently flushing away toxins and stagnation.
- See the light moving to your neck, chest, and abdomen, activating your thymus gland and spleen with vibrant energy.
- Picture the light traveling to your arms and legs, circulating through every lymph node, cleansing and revitalizing.

Feel this light supporting your body's natural detoxification and immunity, leaving you energized and balanced.

Affirmations for Immune Health

As you breathe deeply, silently or softly repeat these affirmations:
- *"My lymphatic system flows freely, supporting my health and vitality."*
- *"My immune system is strong and resilient."*
- *"My body releases what no longer serves me with ease."*
- *"I am vibrant, balanced, and whole."*

Let these words resonate deeply, reinforcing your body's ability to heal and thrive.

Self-Massage (Optional)

If you feel comfortable, gently massage the areas where lymph nodes are concentrated:
- Use light, circular motions under your jawline and around your neck.
- Gently rub your chest and underarms, imagining energy flowing freely.
- Massage your abdomen and the creases of your legs, encouraging circulation.

This optional step can enhance lymphatic flow and deepen your connection to your body.

Begin to bring your awareness back to the present moment. Wiggle your fingers and toes, and when you are ready, open your eyes.

Take a moment to notice how you feel—a sense of lightness, clarity, and inner strength. Remember, your lymphatic and immune systems thrive when you prioritize rest, mindfulness, and self-care.

Advanced Guided Meditation for Strengthening and Healing the Lymphatic and Immune System

This advanced guided meditation integrates the multidimensional energies of Rainbow Reiki to heal, strengthen, and align the lymphatic and immune systems. It utilizes the combined frequencies of Usui, Shadow, Arcturian, Pleiadian, Egyptian Sekhem-Seichim, and Magdalene/Yeshua Reiki to support physical health, energetic clearing, and spiritual vitality.

Find a quiet, comfortable place where you can sit or lie down undisturbed. Close your eyes and take several deep breaths, inhaling deeply through your nose and exhaling slowly through your mouth. With each exhale, release any tension, allowing your body to relax.

Set your intention: *"I open myself to the advanced healing energies of Rainbow Reiki to cleanse, strengthen, and align my lymphatic and immune systems, promoting balance, vitality, and optimal health."*

<u>Grounding and Cosmic Connection</u>
Visualize roots extending from your feet into the crystalline core of Earth. Feel Gaia's stabilizing energy rising through these roots, anchoring and grounding your energy. At the same time, envision a vibrant column of rainbow light descending from the cosmos, entering your crown chakra, and filling your entire body.

Feel the merging of Earth and cosmic energies within you, creating a harmonious flow to support your lymphatic and immune systems.

<u>Illuminating the Lymphatic System</u>
Bring your awareness to your lymphatic system. Visualize the major lymph nodes in your body glowing with a soft, golden light—at the throat, armpits, chest, abdomen, and groin. See this light flowing through the network of lymphatic vessels, cleansing and energizing them.

Imagine this light moving lymph fluid effortlessly through your body, clearing toxins and enhancing your immune response.

Affirm: *"My lymphatic system is clear, balanced, and flowing with vitality and ease."*

Cellular Healing and Regeneration
Shift your focus to the immune cells within your body. Visualize crystalline light codes from Arcturian and Pleiadian Reiki entering your immune cells. See these codes activating the mitochondria, enhancing cellular repair, renewal, and the efficient functioning of your immune response.

Feel the crystalline energy strengthening your body's ability to protect and heal itself, supporting optimal health at the cellular level.

Affirm: *"Every cell in my lymphatic and immune systems is vibrant, healthy, and aligned with my highest potential."*

Clearing Emotional and Energetic Imprints
Focus on areas within your lymphatic and immune systems where emotional or energetic blockages may reside. Visualize a deep indigo light from Shadow Reiki entering these areas, gently dissolving any stored stress, fear, or stagnant energy.

Once cleared, see a soft rose-pink light from Magdalene/Yeshua Reiki flowing into these spaces, filling them with love, peace, and renewal. Feel your lymphatic and immune systems releasing their burdens, creating space for vitality and balance.

Affirm: *"I release all emotional and energetic imprints from my lymphatic and immune systems, allowing healing and harmony to flow freely."*

Strengthening and Energizing
Visualize Egyptian Sekhem-Seichim Reiki energy entering your lymphatic and immune systems as radiant golden geometric patterns. These sacred patterns weave through your lymph nodes, vessels, and immune cells, strengthening their structure and enhancing their function.

Next, see a vibrant rainbow light flowing through your lymphatic and immune systems, bringing resilience, vitality, and divine alignment. Feel this light harmonizing your body's defenses and restoring its natural balance.

Affirm: *"My lymphatic and immune systems are strong, resilient, and perfectly aligned with the flow of universal energy."*

Aligning with Life Force Energy
Focus on your breath as a carrier of life force energy. With each inhale, visualize the rainbow light entering your lymphatic and immune systems, nourishing and energizing every cell. With each exhale, release any remaining tension, toxins, or blockages.

Feel the rhythm of your breath aligning your lymphatic and immune systems with the universal life force energy, promoting vitality and health throughout your being.

Affirm: *"My lymphatic and immune systems are nourished and aligned with the divine flow of life force energy."*

Multidimensional Integration
Expand your awareness to include the energetic layers of your lymphatic and immune systems, extending into your auric field. Visualize the advanced Rainbow Reiki energies anchoring into these layers, connecting your systems to Earth's crystalline grid and the cosmic frequencies.

Feel the alignment of your lymphatic and immune systems with the multidimensional aspects of your being, fostering wholeness, balance, and optimal health.

Affirm: *"My lymphatic and immune systems are fully integrated, balanced, and aligned with my highest vibrational potential."*

Closing and Gratitude
Bring your awareness back to your heart center. Visualize a glowing orb of rainbow light within your chest, pulsating with gratitude and

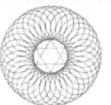

healing energy. Allow this light to radiate outward, integrating all the healing energies you have received.

Take a moment to thank your lymphatic and immune systems for their resilience and strength, and express gratitude for the Rainbow Reiki energies and your ability to heal.

When you feel ready, gently bring your awareness back to the present moment. Wiggle your fingers and toes, stretch lightly, and open your eyes.

Post-Meditation Care
- Hydration: Drink plenty of water to support the cleansing and detoxification process within your lymphatic system.
- Movement: Engage in light stretching, yoga, or walking to encourage lymphatic flow.
- Nourishment: Focus on nutrient-dense foods, including leafy greens, citrus fruits, and antioxidant-rich options, to support your immune health.
- Reflection: Journal any sensations, insights, or shifts you experienced during the meditation.

This advanced meditation can be practiced regularly to maintain the strength, balance, and vitality of your lymphatic and immune systems while aligning them with the high frequencies of Rainbow Reiki.

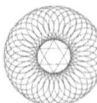

Urinary System

The urinary system plays a critical role in maintaining the body's internal balance by removing waste products, regulating fluid levels, and maintaining electrolyte and pH balance. This system consists of the kidneys, which filter blood to remove toxins and excess substances while retaining essential nutrients; the ureters, which transport urine from the kidneys to the bladder; the bladder, which stores urine until elimination; and the urethra, which carries urine out of the body. Together, these organs ensure that the body's waste products are effectively removed, preventing the buildup of harmful substances and maintaining homeostasis.

Reiki can be a powerful tool in supporting the urinary system by promoting relaxation, reducing stress, and addressing energetic imbalances that may affect elimination. Chronic stress, anxiety, and unprocessed emotions can contribute to urinary issues, such as frequent urination, bladder discomfort, or kidney strain. By directing Reiki energy to key areas like the kidneys and bladder, practitioners can help release tension, encourage healthy energy flow, and support the body's natural detoxification processes. Reiki also aids in reducing inflammation and alleviating discomfort associated with urinary system imbalances.

Energetically, the urinary system is closely connected to the sacral chakra, which governs emotions, creativity, and the flow of life. Blockages in this chakra can manifest as difficulty in releasing not only physical waste but also emotional or energetic burdens. Reiki helps clear these blockages, fostering a sense of ease and flow within both the physical and subtle energy systems. By supporting the urinary system in its role of elimination and purification, Reiki helps the body release toxins, maintain fluid balance, and restore harmony. This holistic approach nurtures physical health while creating space for emotional clarity and energetic renewal, supporting overall vitality and well-being.

Reiki Hand Placement
<u>Crown of the Head (Mind-Body Connection)</u>
Placement: Place hands gently on the top of the head.

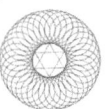

Purpose: Supports the mind-body connection and promotes relaxation, which can influence kidney and bladder function.

Forehead and Back of the Head (Stress Relief and Hormonal Regulation)
Placement: Place one hand on the forehead and the other on the back of the head.
Purpose: Reduces stress and balances the hypothalamus, which regulates hormones that affect the urinary system.

Throat (Energy Pathways and Communication)
Placement: Place hands lightly over the throat area.
Purpose: Opens energy pathways connected to the kidneys and urinary system and balances the throat chakra, linked to fluid communication in the body.

Lower Ribcage (Kidney Placement)
Placement: Rest hands on either side of the lower ribcage, toward the back.
Purpose: Energizes and balances the kidneys, which are vital for filtering blood and maintaining fluid balance.

Lower Abdomen (Bladder and Urinary Tract)
Placement: Rest hands on the lower abdomen, just above the pelvic area.
Purpose: Directs healing energy to the bladder and urinary tract, supporting elimination and flow.

Sacral Area (Pelvic Region)
Placement: Place hands on the sacrum, just above the tailbone.
Purpose: Balances the energy flow in the pelvic area, supporting the bladder, urethra, and urinary system as a whole.

Lower Back (Kidney-Adrenal Support)
Placement: Rest hands on the lower back, near the kidney area.
Purpose: Provides energy to the kidneys and adrenal glands, promoting detoxification and hormonal balance.

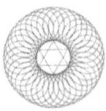

Hips (Grounding and Flow)
Placement: Place hands over the hips on either side.
Purpose: Supports energy flow through the pelvic region and grounds the work being done on the urinary system.

Hands and Feet (Lymphatic and Urinary Connection)
Placement: Hold the client's hands or place hands on the tops of their feet.
Purpose: Grounds the energy and supports lymphatic drainage, which works closely with the urinary system to remove waste.

Entire Spine (Urinary-Nervous System Connection)
Placement: Sweep hands along the spine, pausing at key areas such as the lower back and sacrum.
Purpose: Aligns energy pathways between the nervous and urinary systems, supporting relaxation and detoxification.

Guided Meditation for Urinary System Healing
Find a quiet, comfortable place where you can sit or lie down. When you are ready, close your eyes and take a deep breath.

Take a deep inhale through your nose and a slow exhale through your mouth. Allow your body to begin relaxing. Let your shoulders drop, your jaw soften, and your belly rise and fall gently with each breath.

Your urinary system works tirelessly to filter and remove toxins, maintaining your body's balance. This meditation will focus on supporting its health and vitality.

Body Awareness
Bring your attention to your body, starting at the top of your head and slowly scanning downward. Notice any tension or sensations in your body.
- Focus on your lower back, where your kidneys are located. Feel gratitude for their vital role in filtering and balancing your body's fluids.

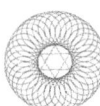

- Shift your attention to your lower abdomen, where your bladder stores and releases waste. Imagine this area feeling calm, strong, and at ease.
- Bring awareness to your pelvis, where the ureters and urethra guide the flow of cleansing energy through your body.

Healing Breathing

Let us engage in a cleansing breath to activate healing for your urinary system:
- Breathe in deeply through your nose for a count of four, imagining fresh, healing energy entering your body.
- Hold your breath gently for a count of four, allowing this energy to circulate through your kidneys, bladder, and urinary pathways.
- Exhale slowly through your mouth for a count of six, releasing any tension or toxins.
- Repeat this cycle for a few moments, feeling calmness and renewal flow through your body.

Visualization for Healing

As you continue to breathe, visualize a soothing, clear-blue light entering your body with each inhale. This light represents cleansing and healing.
- See this light flowing into your kidneys, gently purifying them and restoring their balance.
- Imagine the light traveling through your ureters, flowing smoothly like a peaceful stream.
- Visualize the light filling your bladder, cleansing and strengthening its walls.
- Finally, see the light exiting your body as you exhale, taking with it any impurities, discomfort, or tension.

Feel this flow of energy restoring your urinary system, leaving it clear, healthy, and strong.

Affirmations for Urinary Health

As you breathe deeply, silently or softly repeat these affirmations:

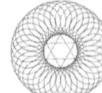

- *"My urinary system is strong and functions with ease."*
- *"My kidneys, bladder, and pathways are healthy and balanced."*
- *"I release toxins and negativity effortlessly."*
- *"My body is in perfect harmony and supports my well-being."*

Let these words resonate deeply within you, affirming your body's natural capacity for healing.

<u>Closing and Gratitude</u>
Take a moment to silently thank your urinary system for the work it does every day to keep you healthy. Feel gratitude for its ability to cleanse and restore balance to your body.

Begin to bring your awareness back to the present moment. Wiggle your fingers and toes, stretch gently if you like, and when you are ready, open your eyes.

Notice how you feel—a sense of ease, clarity, and connection to your body. Remember, your urinary system thrives when you hydrate, rest, and care for your well-being.

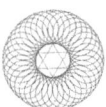

Advanced Guided Meditation for Strengthening and Healing the Urinary System

This advanced guided meditation channels the multidimensional energies of Rainbow Reiki to heal, strengthen, and align the urinary system. It combines the powerful frequencies of Usui, Shadow, Arcturian, Pleiadian, Egyptian Sekhem-Seichim, and Magdalene/Yeshua Reiki to address the physical, energetic, and spiritual layers of this vital system.

Find a quiet, comfortable space to sit or lie down. Close your eyes and take several deep breaths, inhaling deeply through your nose and exhaling slowly through your mouth. With each exhale, feel your body relaxing and releasing tension.

Set your intention: *"I invite the advanced healing energies of Rainbow Reiki to cleanse, strengthen, and align my urinary system, supporting balance, vitality, and ease."*

<u>Grounding and Cosmic Alignment</u>
Visualize roots extending from your feet deep into the crystalline core of Earth. Feel Gaia's nurturing energy rising through these roots, anchoring and grounding you. Simultaneously, envision a vibrant column of rainbow light descending from the cosmos, entering your crown chakra, and filling your body.

Feel these energies merging in your lower abdomen, creating a harmonious flow to support your urinary system's healing and alignment.

<u>Illuminating the Urinary System</u>
Bring your awareness to your urinary system: the kidneys, ureters, bladder, and urethra. Visualize a soft, golden light flowing into your kidneys, cleansing and energizing them. See this light traveling through the ureters, reaching the bladder, and finally flowing through the urethra.

Imagine this golden light washing away toxins, blockages, and any stagnant energy, leaving your urinary system clear and rejuvenated.

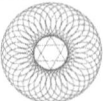

Affirm: *"My urinary system is cleansed, balanced, and flowing effortlessly."*

Cellular Healing and Regeneration
Shift your focus to the cells within your urinary system. Visualize crystalline light codes from Arcturian and Pleiadian Reiki entering each cell. See these codes activating the mitochondria, boosting cellular repair, renewal, and detoxification.

Imagine this crystalline energy restoring the filtration and purification functions of your kidneys, as well as optimizing the storage and release capabilities of your bladder.

Affirm: *"Every cell in my urinary system is vibrant, healthy, and aligned with my highest potential."*

Clearing Emotional and Energetic Imprints
Focus on any areas in your urinary system that may hold emotional tension, such as fear, anxiety, or frustration. Visualize a deep indigo light from Shadow Reiki entering these areas, dissolving old patterns and stagnant energies.

Once these blockages are cleared, see a soft rose-pink light from Magdalene/Yeshua Reiki filling the space, infusing your urinary system with love, peace, and renewal.

Affirm: *"I release all emotional and energetic imprints from my urinary system, creating space for healing and renewal."*

Strengthening and Energizing
Visualize the golden geometric patterns of Egyptian Sekhem-Seichim Reiki flowing through your urinary system. These patterns strengthen the structural and energetic integrity of your kidneys, bladder, and connecting pathways.

Next, see a vibrant rainbow light flowing through your urinary system, bringing resilience, harmony, and vitality. Feel this light

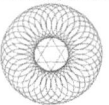

enhancing your body's ability to release toxins and maintain a balanced flow of fluids.

Affirm: *"My urinary system is strong, resilient, and functioning in perfect harmony."*

Aligning with Life Force Energy

Focus on your breath as a carrier of life force energy. With each inhale, visualize the rainbow light entering your urinary system, nourishing and energizing every organ and pathway. With each exhale, release any remaining tension, toxins, or blockages.

Feel the rhythm of your breath aligning your urinary system with the universal life force energy, promoting flow and balance throughout your being.

Affirm: *"My urinary system is nourished and aligned with the divine flow of life force energy."*

Multidimensional Integration

Expand your awareness to include the energetic layers of your urinary system, extending into your auric field. Visualize the advanced Rainbow Reiki energies anchoring into these layers, connecting your urinary system to Earth's crystalline grid and the cosmic frequencies.

Feel the alignment of your urinary system with the multidimensional aspects of your being, fostering wholeness and balance.

Affirm: *"My urinary system is fully integrated, balanced, and aligned with my highest vibrational potential."*

Closing and Gratitude

Bring your awareness back to your heart center. Visualize a glowing orb of rainbow light within your chest, pulsating with gratitude and healing energy. Allow this light to radiate outward, integrating all the healing energies you have received.

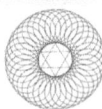

Take a moment to thank your urinary system for its resilience and strength, and express gratitude for the Rainbow Reiki energies and your ability to heal.

When you feel ready, gently bring your awareness back to the present moment. Wiggle your fingers and toes, stretch lightly, and open your eyes.

Post-Meditation Care
- Hydration: Drink plenty of water to support the detoxification and energy flow within your urinary system.
- Nourishment: Incorporate foods that support kidney and urinary health, such as cranberries, watermelon, and leafy greens.
- Reflection: Journal any sensations, insights, or shifts you experienced during the meditation.

This advanced meditation can be practiced regularly to maintain the strength, balance, and vitality of your urinary system while aligning it with the high frequencies of Rainbow Reiki.

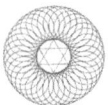

Reproductive System

The reproductive system is essential for human reproduction and plays a pivotal role in pregnancy and childbirth. This system includes the ovaries, which produce eggs and hormones like estrogen and progesterone; the uterus, where a fertilized egg can develop into a fetus; the testes, which produce sperm and testosterone; and the prostate, which contributes to seminal fluid and supports sperm health. Beyond its biological functions, the reproductive system is deeply intertwined with emotional, hormonal, and energetic aspects of well-being, influencing identity, intimacy, and creativity.

Reiki offers profound support for the reproductive system by addressing physical, emotional, and energetic dimensions of health. Energetically, this system is closely connected to the sacral chakra, which governs creativity, sexuality, and emotional expression. Imbalances in this chakra can manifest as hormonal disruptions, menstrual irregularities, fertility challenges, or emotional struggles related to intimacy or reproductive experiences. Reiki helps clear blockages in this energy center, restoring balance and harmony to both the physical and energetic bodies.

Reiki can also alleviate physical discomfort associated with the reproductive system, such as menstrual pain, pelvic tension, or stress-related imbalances. By directing energy to key areas like the ovaries, uterus, or prostate, Reiki can reduce inflammation, promote relaxation, and support the body's natural healing processes. Additionally, Reiki can help balance hormones by reducing stress, which often disrupts endocrine function and impacts reproductive health.

Emotionally, the reproductive system often holds energetic imprints of past experiences, including trauma, loss, or unprocessed emotions related to sexuality or childbirth. Reiki assists in releasing these stored energies, fostering emotional healing and a deeper sense of connection to the self.

This holistic approach not only supports physical reproductive health but also nurtures emotional well-being, enhancing self-

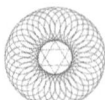

awareness, intimacy, and creative expression. Through Reiki, individuals can find balance, empowerment, and harmony within their reproductive system and its associated energies.

Reiki Hand Placement
Crown of the Head (Hormonal Regulation)
Placement: Place hands gently on the top of the head.
Purpose: Supports the hypothalamus and pituitary gland, which regulate reproductive hormones and maintain balance in the endocrine system.

Forehead and Back of the Head (Stress and Hormonal Connection)
Placement: Place one hand on the forehead and the other on the back of the head.
Purpose: Calms the nervous system and balances the hypothalamus, which influences the hormonal cycles governing reproduction.

Throat (Thyroid and Communication)
Placement: Rest hands lightly over the throat.
Purpose: Supports the thyroid gland, which plays a role in hormonal balance and communication within the endocrine and reproductive systems.

Heart Center (Emotional Healing)
Placement: Place hands over the chest, directly above the heart.
Purpose: Supports emotional healing and releases energy blockages that may impact the reproductive system.

Solar Plexus (Emotional and Hormonal Link)
Placement: Rest hands on the upper abdomen, just below the ribcage.
Purpose: Addresses emotional energy stored in this area, which often impacts reproductive health.

Lower Abdomen (Primary Reproductive Focus)
Placement: Place hands on the lower abdomen, just below the navel.

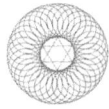

Purpose: Directs healing energy to the ovaries, uterus, fallopian tubes, or testes and prostate, supporting reproductive organ function and hormonal balance.

Sacral Area (Pelvic Support)
Placement: Place hands on the sacrum, just above the tailbone.
Purpose: Balances the sacral chakra, which governs creativity, sexual energy, and reproductive health.

Lower Back (Kidney and Reproductive Connection)
Placement: Rest hands on the lower back near the kidney area.
Purpose: Supports energy flow to the reproductive organs through their connection with the kidneys and adrenal glands.

Hips (Grounding and Energy Flow)
Placement: Place hands on both hips.
Purpose: Promotes energy flow through the pelvic area and aligns the sacral energy pathways.

Hands and Feet (Energy Integration and Grounding)
Placement: Hold the client's hands or place hands on the tops of the feet.
Purpose: Grounds and integrates the energy work done on the reproductive system while supporting overall balance.

Entire Spine (Reproductive-Nervous System Connection)
Placement: Sweep hands along the spine, pausing at the base of the skull, between the shoulder blades, and lower back.
Purpose: Aligns energy flow between the nervous and reproductive systems, promoting balance and harmony.

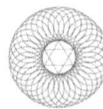

Guided Meditation for Reproductive System Healing

Find a quiet, comfortable place where you can sit or lie down. Close your eyes and allow your body to settle.

Take a deep breath in through your nose, and slowly exhale through your mouth. With each breath, let go of tension and invite a sense of calm into your body.

Your reproductive system plays a vital role in creation, renewal, and balance. Together, we will focus on nurturing this system, fostering health, and supporting its natural rhythms.

Body Awareness
Bring your attention to your body, starting at the top of your head and slowly scanning downward. Notice any areas of tension or ease.

Now, gently shift your focus to your pelvis, the home of your reproductive system. Whether you are focusing on the uterus, ovaries, testes, or other reproductive organs, imagine this area as a center of vitality and creation.

Feel a sense of gratitude for all the ways your reproductive system supports your body, whether it is through hormone regulation, cycles of renewal, or nurturing life.

Healing Breathing
Let us use the breath to invite healing and balance:
- Breathe deeply through your nose for a count of four, imagining fresh, nourishing energy entering your pelvis.
- Hold the breath for a count of four, letting this energy settle and restore balance.
- Exhale slowly through your mouth for a count of six, releasing any tension, discomfort, or negative emotions.
- Repeat this cycle, feeling more connected and grounded with each breath.

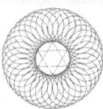

Visualization for Healing

As you continue to breathe deeply, visualize a warm, soft pink or golden light forming in your pelvis. This light represents healing, love, and vitality.

- Imagine this light enveloping your reproductive organs, soothing and restoring balance.
- See it flowing to areas that may feel heavy or stagnant, dissolving tension and creating a sense of renewal.
- Allow this light to expand, radiating outward into your entire body, connecting your reproductive system to the rest of your being.

Feel this healing light bringing harmony and vitality to your reproductive system.

Affirmations for Reproductive Health

Silently or softly repeat the following affirmations:

- *"My reproductive system is strong, healthy, and vibrant."*
- *"I honor my body's cycles and rhythms."*
- *"I release any tension, fear, or imbalance."*
- *"I trust my body's ability to heal and thrive."*

Let these words settle into your consciousness, reaffirming your connection to your body and its natural wisdom.

Closing and Gratitude

Take a moment to thank your reproductive system for all it does for you, whether you are aware of its processes or not. Feel a sense of appreciation for this system's role in your overall well-being and vitality.

Slowly bring your awareness back to the present moment. Wiggle your fingers and toes, stretch gently if you like, and when you are ready, open your eyes.

Notice how you feel—a sense of calm, connection, and renewed energy. Remember, your reproductive system is part of the beautiful, intricate system that makes up your whole being.

Advanced Guided Meditation for Strengthening and Healing the Reproductive System

This guided meditation channels the multidimensional energies of Rainbow Reiki to strengthen, heal, and align the reproductive system. It incorporates the powerful frequencies of Usui, Shadow, Arcturian, Pleiadian, Egyptian Sekhem-Seichim, and Magdalene/Yeshua Reiki to address physical, emotional, energetic, and spiritual layers of the reproductive organs and their connection to creative and life force energy.

Find a quiet and comfortable place to sit or lie down. Close your eyes and take several deep breaths, inhaling deeply through your nose and exhaling slowly through your mouth. Allow your body to relax with each exhale, releasing tension and inviting calmness into your being.

Set your intention: *"I open myself to the advanced healing energies of Rainbow Reiki to cleanse, strengthen, and align my reproductive system, enhancing balance, vitality, and divine creativity."*

Grounding and Cosmic Connection
Visualize roots extending from your feet deep into the crystalline core of Earth. Feel Gaia's nurturing energy rising through these roots, anchoring and grounding you. At the same time, imagine a vibrant column of rainbow light descending from the cosmos, entering your crown chakra, and filling your body.

Feel these energies merging in your sacral region, creating a harmonious flow to support the healing and alignment of your reproductive system.

Illuminating the Reproductive System
Bring your awareness to your reproductive system. Visualize a warm, golden light flowing into your reproductive organs, whether they are ovaries, uterus, fallopian tubes, or testes, prostate, and associated structures. Let this light cleanse and energize each organ, filling it with vitality.

Imagine the light traveling through the reproductive pathways, clearing any blockages or stagnant energy, and restoring balance to your creative and life force energy.

Affirm: *"My reproductive system is illuminated with healing light, functioning in harmony and ease."*

Cellular Healing and Regeneration
Shift your focus to the cells within your reproductive organs. Visualize crystalline light codes from Arcturian and Pleiadian Reiki entering each cell. See these codes activating the mitochondria, enhancing cellular repair, renewal, and vitality.

Imagine this crystalline energy regenerating tissue, optimizing hormonal balance, and supporting the natural cycles and functions of your reproductive system.

Affirm: *"Each cell in my reproductive system is vibrant, healthy, and aligned with my divine blueprint."*

Clearing Emotional and Energetic Imprints
Focus on any emotional or energetic tension stored in your reproductive system, such as fear, guilt, shame, or grief. Visualize a deep indigo light from Shadow Reiki entering these areas, gently dissolving and clearing old patterns and imprints.

Once these blockages are cleared, see a soft rose-pink light from Magdalene/Yeshua Reiki filling these spaces, infusing your reproductive system with unconditional love, peace, and divine compassion.

Affirm: *"I release all emotional and energetic imprints from my reproductive system, creating space for healing and renewal."*

Strengthening and Energizing
Visualize the golden geometric patterns of Egyptian Sekhem-Seichim Reiki flowing through your reproductive system. These

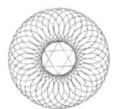

sacred patterns strengthen the structural and energetic integrity of your reproductive organs, enhancing their resilience and vitality.

Next, see a vibrant rainbow light flowing through your reproductive system, harmonizing its functions and connecting it to your creative life force energy. Feel this light igniting your divine creative potential.

Affirm: *"My reproductive system is strong, resilient, and harmonized with the universal flow of creative energy."*

Aligning with Creative and Life Force Energy
Focus on your sacral chakra, the energy center associated with creation and emotional flow. Visualize the rainbow light expanding from this chakra, connecting your reproductive system to the universal energy of creation. Feel this energy flowing freely, empowering your creativity and grounding it in divine alignment.

Affirm: *"My reproductive system is aligned with my creative life force energy, supporting balance and divine creation."*

Multidimensional Integration
Expand your awareness to include the energetic layers of your reproductive system, extending into your auric field. Visualize the advanced Rainbow Reiki energies anchoring into these layers, connecting your reproductive system to Earth's crystalline grid and the cosmic frequencies.

Feel the alignment of your reproductive system with the multidimensional aspects of your being, fostering wholeness, balance, and divine harmony.

Affirm: *"My reproductive system is fully integrated, balanced, and aligned with my highest vibrational potential."*

Closing and Gratitude
Bring your awareness back to your heart center. Visualize a glowing orb of rainbow light within your chest, pulsating with gratitude and

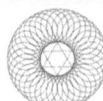

healing energy. Allow this light to radiate outward, integrating all the healing energies you have received.

Take a moment to thank your reproductive system for its resilience and strength, and express gratitude for the Rainbow Reiki energies and your ability to heal.

When you feel ready, gently bring your awareness back to the present moment. Wiggle your fingers and toes, stretch lightly, and open your eyes.

Post-Meditation Care
- Hydration: Drink plenty of water to support detoxification and energy flow.
- Nourishment: Focus on foods that support reproductive health, such as seeds, nuts, leafy greens, and antioxidant-rich fruits.
- Reflection: Journal any sensations, insights, or shifts you experienced during the meditation.

This advanced meditation can be practiced regularly to maintain the strength, balance, and vitality of your reproductive system while aligning it with the high frequencies of Rainbow Reiki.

Body Systems and Traditional Chakras

The seven traditional chakras are energy centers aligned along the spine, each representing distinct physical, emotional, and spiritual aspects of human existence. Originating in ancient Indian traditions, particularly Hinduism and Tantric Buddhism, the word "chakra" means "wheel" in Sanskrit, symbolizing spinning vortexes of energy. These dynamic centers act as conduits for energy flow, responding to emotional states, thoughts, and spiritual practices. They influence the body's health and vitality, the mind's clarity, and the spirit's alignment, forming a holistic framework for healing and growth. Associated with specific colors, locations, elements, and vibrational qualities, chakras serve as bridges between the physical and spiritual realms.

Each chakra corresponds to particular anatomical areas and physiological functions. The Root Chakra (Muladhara), located at the base of the spine, is symbolized by the color red and represents grounding, stability, and survival. It influences the skeletal system, legs, and adrenal glands, offering a sense of security and connection to Earth. The Sacral Chakra (Svadhisthana), just below the navel, radiates orange energy and governs emotions, creativity, and sexuality. It is linked to the reproductive organs and the flow of life force. The Solar Plexus Chakra (Manipura), in the upper abdomen, is depicted as yellow and symbolizes personal power, confidence, and transformation. It regulates the digestive system, liver, and pancreas, supporting vitality and self-esteem.

The Heart Chakra (Anahata), at the center of the chest, is a green energy wheel that bridges the physical and spiritual realms. It governs love, compassion, and emotional balance, influencing the heart and lungs. The Throat Chakra (Vishuddha), located at the throat, is blue and governs communication and self-expression, empowering authenticity and influencing the thyroid and vocal cords. The Third Eye Chakra (Ajna), situated between the eyebrows, shines indigo and symbolizes intuition and insight. It governs the brain, eyes, and pineal gland, enhancing spiritual vision and perception. Lastly, the Crown Chakra (Sahasrara), at the top of the head, is represented by violet or white light and connects to divine

consciousness and spiritual enlightenment, transcending physicality and influencing the nervous system.

Chakras are connected to physical systems and their functions, creating a direct link between energy flow and physical health. For example, the root chakra is tied to the skeletal system and lower body, providing stability and grounding. Imbalances can manifest as lower back pain or adrenal fatigue. Similarly, the sacral chakra influences the reproductive system and emotional flow, while the solar plexus chakra governs digestive health and self-esteem. The heart chakra connects to cardiovascular and respiratory health, and the throat chakra governs communication and thyroid function. The third eye chakra supports brain function and intuition, and the crown chakra links to the nervous system and spiritual connection.

Cultures and religions worldwide have embraced variations of the chakra system for healing and spiritual development. In Taoism, energy centers like the Dantians align with chakras to cultivate vitality and enlightenment. In Tibetan Buddhism, chakras are central to meditative practices for liberation, visualized as lotuses or energy channels (nadis). Sufi traditions reference lata'if, subtle centers purifying the heart and connecting to the divine. Similarly, Native American traditions harmonize human energy with nature, and Chinese medicine employs meridians and acupuncture points to balance Qi, akin to chakra work.

Practices such as Reiki, yoga, sound therapy, mantra chanting, meditation, and color visualization cleanse, activate, and harmonize these energy centers. Systems like Rainbow Reiki expand on traditional chakra work, incorporating multidimensional energies and advanced techniques from Usui, Shadow, Arcturian, Pleiadian, Egyptian Sekhem-Seichim, and Magdalene/Yeshua Reiki. These methods link chakras to cosmic frequencies, addressing imbalances across physical, emotional, mental, and spiritual layers. By working with chakras, individuals align their energies, support holistic health, and foster self-awareness and unity with the cosmos. The widespread adoption of chakra systems demonstrates a universal

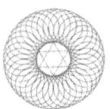

desire to integrate body, mind, and spirit for healing and spiritual growth.

Rainbow Reiki Chakra Symbols

The chakra symbols used in Rainbow Reiki differ significantly from the traditional chakra symbols, reflecting the evolving consciousness of humanity and the collective shift toward higher vibrational states. While traditional chakra symbols are rooted in ancient systems and designed to correspond to specific energy centers in the body, Rainbow Reiki chakra symbols have been updated to align with the heightened energetic frequencies and spiritual advancements of the modern era. These symbols are imbued with sacred geometry, which amplifies their energetic resonance and creates a multidimensional framework for healing and transformation. Additionally, they integrate advanced Egyptian and Tibetan healing frequencies, which are known for their profound ability to access deeper layers of the subtle energy body and promote balance at a soul level.

The innovative design and energetic structure of Rainbow Reiki symbols serve as activators of higher consciousness. Simply gazing upon these symbols can initiate healing and catalyze positive change in the energy fields and energy centers. Their vibrational potency works beyond the physical plane, influencing emotional, mental, and spiritual dimensions to harmonize and elevate one's overall energy. This evolutionary approach acknowledges humanity's growth and readiness for more sophisticated tools in energy healing, supporting individuals in their journey toward self-realization and alignment with the universal flow of love and light. By merging ancient wisdom with contemporary spiritual advancements, Rainbow Reiki chakra symbols embody a bridge between the past and the future, inviting us to step into our highest potential.

Advanced civilizations, such as the Arcturians and Pleiadians, communicate through highly evolved methods that transcend verbal language. Their communication relies on telepathy and holographic

visual transmissions, allowing for instant and multidimensional exchanges of knowledge, emotions, and frequencies. These advanced beings operate on higher vibrational planes and utilize their third eye and higher consciousness to transmit and receive information in the form of symbols, light codes, and sacred geometries. This method of interaction not only conveys information but also energetically aligns the receiver with higher states of awareness and healing.

When you engage with Rainbow Reiki symbols through third-eye visualization, ocular gazing, or meditative focus, you begin to harmonize with these advanced methods of communication. By doing so, you are actively raising your vibrational frequency and increasing the light quotient in your energy field. This elevation is not an isolated event; it ripples outward, impacting everyone who enters your energy field. As your personal frequency rises, you naturally emit higher vibrations that interact with others, transferring the frequencies necessary for their own growth and evolution. This collective energetic exchange facilitates humanity's readiness for the next stage of evolution, preparing us for deeper contact and collaboration with galactic civilizations.

The power of Rainbow Reiki symbols extends beyond individual healing, touching the soul and oversoul layers of a person. These symbols act as catalysts for profound spiritual transformation, aligning one's entire being with the universal flow of ascension. Moreover, their effects radiate outward, creating a healing resonance that touches everyone in your orbit. This interconnectedness means that every person you encounter—physically or energetically—is influenced by the frequencies of these symbols. In essence, by embodying their energy, you contribute to raising the collective vibration of humanity, accelerating the planetary shift toward ascension for those who are ready and choose this path. These symbols are not merely tools for individual evolution; they are instruments for the healing and elevation of all, weaving a network of light that unites and uplifts humanity on a global scale.

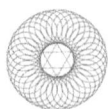

Bridging Ancient Wisdom, Modern Science, and Galactic Healing

Lemuria, also known as the Land of Mu, and Atlantis are often regarded as advanced ancient civilizations that existed tens of thousands of years ago, embodying profound spiritual wisdom and technological advancements. Lemuria is said to have been a peaceful society, deeply attuned to Earth's natural rhythms and the interconnectedness of all life. Its people possessed advanced healing techniques, working with crystalline energies, vibrational medicine, and a profound understanding of subtle energy bodies. Atlantis, on the other hand, was a civilization of immense technological innovation and exploration, known for its mastery of energy manipulation, sacred geometry, and integration of spiritual and scientific pursuits.

The destruction of both civilizations is often attributed to their respective imbalances. Lemuria's downfall is linked to Earth's geological shifts, while Atlantis fell due to the misuse of power, particularly with energy technologies that destabilized the environment. Despite their physical demise, the spiritual and energetic wisdom of these civilizations was preserved in the collective consciousness, seeding future civilizations such as ancient Egypt, Tibet, and other spiritually advanced cultures.

Rainbow Reiki acts as a modern bridge to the ancient wisdom of Lemuria and Atlantis, facilitating the rebirth of their higher vibrational states in what is often referred to as New Lemuria and New Jerusalem. These terms symbolize the evolution of humanity into a golden age of harmony, balance, and unity consciousness. New Lemuria represents the re-emergence of spiritual alignment with Earth's energies, emphasizing holistic healing and the restoration of natural balance. New Jerusalem symbolizes a collective ascension into higher dimensions of awareness, integrating spiritual and technological advancements in harmony. Rainbow Reiki embodies this fusion by incorporating ancient healing frequencies—such as Egyptian energy alchemy and Tibetan spiritual practices—with modern scientific understandings of quantum energy and vibrational medicine. It channels higher-dimensional

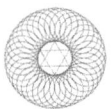

energies, helping individuals access the wisdom of advanced civilizations and align with their highest potential.

The Lemurians and Atlanteans employed advanced healing techniques that were deeply connected to Earth and cosmos. Lemurians utilized crystalline healing, working with crystals as conduits for energy to harmonize the physical, emotional, and spiritual bodies. Both civilizations understood the power of sound waves and frequency therapy to realign energy fields, dissolve blockages, and restore balance. Atlanteans, in particular, used sacred geometry to harness universal energies, creating powerful tools for healing and manifestation. They also worked with light codes and symbols, which are precursors to modern light language, transmitting frequencies that activated healing at both cellular and soul levels. These techniques resonate with modern approaches like vibrational medicine, biofield tuning, and quantum healing, demonstrating the timeless nature of these methods.

Rainbow Reiki bridges ancient and modern approaches to healing by embracing quantum physics, neuroscience, and energy psychology. Ancient healing techniques are now understood through the lens of quantum energy fields, where thoughts, emotions, and symbols influence the vibrational reality of matter. Similarly, modern neuroscience supports ancient practices of visualization, meditation, and mantra, demonstrating their ability to rewire neural pathways for healing through neuroplasticity. Additionally, Rainbow Reiki works with the body's electromagnetic field, aligning with biofield science to restore energetic coherence and balance.

Beyond its terrestrial origins, Rainbow Reiki is also connected to the healing methodologies of advanced galactic civilizations like the Pleiadians, Arcturians, and Sirians. These beings often transmit light codes, sound frequencies, and holographic healing techniques to support humanity's ascension. Through Rainbow Reiki, individuals access these galactic frequencies, raising their vibrational state and enhancing their ability to heal themselves and others. This practice not only awakens dormant healing abilities but also prepares humanity for contact and collaboration with advanced civilizations.

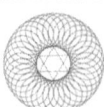

Ultimately, Rainbow Reiki is a convergence of ancient wisdom, modern science, and galactic frequencies, creating a comprehensive system of healing that transcends time and space. By integrating the techniques of Lemuria, Atlantis, Egypt, Tibet, and beyond, Rainbow Reiki serves as a powerful tool for individual and collective transformation, supporting humanity's journey into a new golden age of unity, harmony, and ascension. In embracing Rainbow Reiki, we align with the vision of New Lemuria and New Jerusalem, becoming conduits of light and healing for ourselves, our communities, and the planet.

Energy Meridians
Energy meridians are pathways through which life energy, or Qi (pronounced "chee"), flows throughout the body. These meridians are a foundational concept in Traditional Chinese Medicine (TCM), acupuncture, and acupressure. Similar to how blood circulates through blood vessels, energy flows through meridians, supporting the balance and health of organs, systems, and overall well-being.

Qi is the vital life force energy that flows through meridians, supporting the body's physical, mental, and emotional health. Balanced Qi flow is essential for health, while blockages or imbalances can lead to illness or discomfort.

In TCM, the meridians and organs are categorized as yin or yang. Yin meridians are more nurturing and cooling, while yang meridians are warming and energizing. This balance is crucial for maintaining harmony in the body.

Along each meridian are acupoints, specific points where Qi can be accessed or influenced. In acupuncture and acupressure, these points are stimulated to balance energy flow, release blockages, or address various health issues.

Energy meridians are closely connected to emotions, with each meridian associated with specific emotional states. In Traditional Chinese Medicine (TCM), emotions are seen as both a cause and

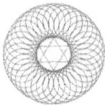

result of imbalances in the body's Qi (energy) flow. When energy becomes blocked or stagnant in a meridian, it can lead to specific emotional issues, and unresolved emotions can also disrupt the flow of Qi within that meridian.

Energy meridians play a crucial role in understanding and working with the body's energetic systems, making them an essential focus in holistic practices like Rainbow Reiki. These pathways, fundamental in TCM, serve as channels for the flow of Qi, the life force energy that sustains physical, emotional, and mental health. In Rainbow Reiki, the concept of meridians complements the chakra system, allowing practitioners to address energy flow in both the vertical axis of chakras and the intricate web of pathways that govern organ systems, emotional states, and subtle energy dynamics. Recognizing the interconnectedness of chakras and meridians enhances the ability to harmonize energy across multiple layers of the body and spirit, facilitating deeper healing and multidimensional alignment.

Understanding meridians is particularly important in Rainbow Reiki, as this advanced system integrates the energetic principles of TCM with the high-frequency energies of Usui Reiki, Shadow Reiki, Arcturian, Pleiadian, Egyptian Sekhem-Seichim, and Magdalene/Yeshua modalities. By working with meridians, practitioners can identify and release blockages that may not be fully addressed through chakra work alone, allowing for a more comprehensive approach to balancing energy flow. For example, stimulating specific acupoints along meridians during a Rainbow Reiki session can enhance the energy flow to organs, release emotional patterns stored in the body, and align the individual with higher frequencies for healing and spiritual growth.

Moreover, meridians bridge the gap between physical and energetic anatomy, offering insights into how emotions, physical health, and energy imbalances interact. For instance, the liver meridian, associated with anger in TCM, can hold energetic stagnation that manifests as physical symptoms like tension or digestive issues. In Rainbow Reiki, addressing such imbalances through both meridian and chakra work provides a holistic path to healing. The integration of meridian pathways into Rainbow Reiki enables practitioners to work with the body's energetic blueprints at a more nuanced level, fostering balance, vitality, and harmony across all dimensions of being. This synthesis of ancient wisdom and multidimensional energy systems underscores the transformative potential of Rainbow Reiki in promoting health and spiritual alignment.

The 12 Primary Meridians
In Rainbow Reiki, understanding the 12 main meridians is essential for comprehensively addressing the body's energetic flow and supporting holistic healing. These meridians, foundational to Traditional Chinese Medicine (TCM), are pathways through which Qi, or life force energy, flows. Each meridian is associated with a specific organ or function and is categorized as either yin or yang. The yin meridians, which are more internal, include the lung, spleen, heart, kidney, pericardium, and liver meridians. They are nurturing and cooling, regulating the body's restorative and balancing functions. The yang meridians, which are more external, include the large intestine, stomach, small intestine, bladder, triple burner, and gallbladder meridians. These are energizing and warming, supporting dynamic processes like movement and transformation. Together, the yin and yang meridians create a harmonious energetic balance that is critical for health and vitality.

In Rainbow Reiki, the integration of meridian knowledge enhances traditional chakra work by expanding the scope of energy alignment to include the intricate network of pathways that govern physical and emotional health. Each meridian not only corresponds to an organ but also has specific emotional and energetic associations. For example, the lung meridian, a yin meridian, is linked to grief and the ability to let go, while the liver meridian, another yin meridian, is associated with anger and the flow of energy and emotions. Blockages in these meridians can manifest as physical discomfort or emotional imbalances, such as respiratory issues for the lung meridian or frustration for the liver meridian. Understanding these dynamics allows Rainbow Reiki practitioners to target specific

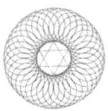

energy pathways, releasing stagnation, restoring balance, and addressing the root causes of physical or emotional challenges.

Rainbow Reiki further enhances meridian work by incorporating high-frequency energies and advanced healing techniques from modalities such as Usui, Shadow, Arcturian, Pleiadian, Egyptian Sekhem-Seichim, and Magdalene/Yeshua Reiki. These energies enable practitioners to work with meridians not only on the physical and emotional levels but also across multidimensional layers of the energy body. For instance, directing Rainbow Reiki energy through the kidney meridian—a yin meridian associated with fear and the adrenal glands—can help alleviate stress, support hormonal balance, and promote a sense of grounding and security.

By combining the meridian system with the chakra system, Rainbow Reiki provides a multidimensional approach to energy healing, addressing vertical energy centers and horizontal energy pathways simultaneously. This holistic framework allows practitioners to work with the body's energy flow at a profound level, supporting physical health, emotional resilience, mental clarity, and spiritual alignment. Understanding the 12 main meridians and their yin-yang dynamics not only deepens the practitioner's knowledge but also enhances the effectiveness of Rainbow Reiki in promoting balance and harmony across all aspects of life.

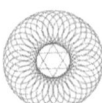

Guided Meditation to Become Aware of the Energy Flow Through the 12 Primary Meridians

Find a comfortable seated or lying position. Close your eyes and take a few deep breaths. Inhale deeply through your nose, allowing your belly to expand, and exhale softly through your mouth, releasing tension. Feel your body settle, your mind quiet, and your awareness shift inward.

Begin by focusing on your breath. Imagine each inhale drawing in pure, revitalizing energy and each exhale releasing any tension or stagnant energy from your body. Feel yourself becoming grounded and centered, present in this moment.

Now, bring your awareness to the center of your body, just below your navel, the area known as your energetic core. Visualize a gentle, glowing light here, representing your life force energy, or Qi. This light pulses softly, radiating warmth and vitality throughout your body.

From this core, imagine your energy beginning to flow through your meridians, the intricate network of pathways that carry your life force energy to every part of your being. Let your focus travel through these meridians, one by one, as you tune in to the sensations of energy moving through your body.

- Lung Meridian (LU): Bring your awareness to your chest, where the Lung Meridian begins. Feel the energy flowing from your lungs, traveling down the inner side of your arms to your thumbs. This pathway governs your breath and immune system. With each inhale, sense energy flowing smoothly through this meridian, connecting you to the rhythm of life.
- Large Intestine Meridian (LI): Shift your focus to your index fingers, where the Large Intestine Meridian begins. Feel the energy move upward along the outer arms to your shoulders and neck, supporting the elimination of what no longer serves you. Imagine this flow releasing physical and emotional waste, creating space for renewal.

- Stomach Meridian (ST): Move your awareness to the area below your eyes, where the Stomach Meridian begins. Visualize energy flowing downward along the front of your torso and legs to your second toes. This meridian supports digestion and nourishment. Sense the grounding energy of the earth element stabilizing and revitalizing you.
- Spleen Meridian (SP): Bring your focus to your big toes, where the Spleen Meridian begins. Feel energy moving upward along the inner legs to the chest, nourishing your body and mind. This meridian governs emotional balance and clarity, helping you process and transform life's experiences.
- Heart Meridian (HT): Shift your awareness to your chest again, where the Heart Meridian resides. Feel energy flowing from your heart down the inner side of your arms to your little fingers. This meridian supports love, joy, and emotional warmth. Imagine its energy radiating outward, filling you with compassion and connection.
- Small Intestine Meridian (SI): Focus on your little fingers, where the Small Intestine Meridian begins. Sense the energy traveling upward along the outer arms to your shoulders. This meridian governs discernment, helping you sort through experiences and emotions. Feel clarity and understanding flowing through this pathway.
- Bladder Meridian (BL): Bring your attention to the corners of your eyes, where the Bladder Meridian begins. Visualize energy flowing over the top of your head, down your back, and along the back of your legs to your little toes. This meridian releases fear and tension, grounding you in safety and security.
- Kidney Meridian (KI): Move your awareness to the soles of your feet, where the Kidney Meridian begins. Sense the energy rising along the inner legs to the chest. This meridian stores your life force energy and supports vitality and resilience. Feel its energy strengthening and grounding you.
- Pericardium Meridian (PC): Focus on your chest, where the Pericardium Meridian begins. Visualize energy flowing down the inner side of your arms to your middle fingers. This

meridian protects your heart, balancing emotional boundaries and vulnerability. Feel its energy creating a sense of emotional safety and connection.
- San Jiao/Triple Burner Meridian (SJ): Bring your awareness to your ring fingers, where the San Jiao Meridian begins. Feel the energy moving along the outer arms to your shoulders. This meridian harmonizes your body's energy, regulating warmth and fluid balance. Sense its flow bringing connection and cohesion throughout your body.
- Gallbladder Meridian (GB): Focus on the outer corners of your eyes, where the Gallbladder Meridian begins. Visualize energy flowing over your head, down the sides of your body, and along the outer legs to your fourth toes. This meridian supports decision-making and courage. Feel its energy inspiring clarity and action.
- Liver Meridian (LV): Finally, bring your attention to your big toes, where the Liver Meridian begins. Sense energy traveling along the inner legs to your chest. This meridian governs detoxification and emotional flow. Feel its energy cleansing and renewing you, promoting patience and balance.

Now, imagine all your meridians flowing in harmony, creating a network of glowing pathways within you. Feel the balance of yin and yang energies and the seamless flow of Qi throughout your body. With each breath, this energy becomes stronger, clearer, and more vibrant, filling you with vitality and peace.

Take a moment to express gratitude for your body and its energy system. When you are ready, slowly bring your awareness back to the present moment. Wiggle your fingers and toes, and open your eyes, carrying this sense of connection and harmony with you into your day.

Yin Meridian - Lung Meridian (LU)

The Lung Meridian (LU) plays a vital role in supporting both physical health and emotional well-being by addressing the energetic flow associated with respiration, immunity, and emotional release. The Lung Meridian, which belongs to the yin meridians, governs the lungs, skin, and immune system, influencing the body's ability to breathe deeply and protect itself from external pathogens. It is connected to the element of metal, symbolizing clarity, strength, and the ability to let go of what no longer serves. The meridian's pathway begins in the chest, extends along the inner arm, and ends at the thumb, linking it to the movement of energy through the upper body.

Emotionally, the Lung Meridian is associated with grief and sadness, making it a key focus for addressing unresolved emotions and enhancing resilience. In Traditional Chinese Medicine, unprocessed grief can create energetic stagnation in the lung meridian, manifesting as physical symptoms such as shallow breathing, a weakened immune system, or tightness in the chest. In Rainbow Reiki, practitioners work with this meridian to clear blockages, allowing the energy to flow freely and supporting the release of emotional burdens. By integrating multidimensional energies from modalities such as Shadow Reiki, which addresses hidden emotional patterns, and Magdalene/Yeshua Reiki, which offers deep compassion and healing, Rainbow Reiki provides a powerful approach to restoring balance in the Lung Meridian.

The Lung Meridian's role in letting go is crucial for maintaining a sense of lightness and emotional freedom. Energetic imbalances here can result in difficulty releasing attachments, whether emotional, mental, or physical, leading to a sense of heaviness, stagnation, or even depression. Rainbow Reiki practitioners may focus on this meridian to facilitate the release of grief, cultivate resilience, and enhance the ability to embrace new beginnings. Techniques such as Reiki-infused breathwork, visualization of metallic colors (like silver or white, associated with the element of metal), and directing high-frequency energy along the meridian's

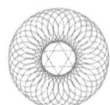

pathway can deeply support the process of emotional release and renewal.

Additionally, Rainbow Reiki enhances the healing potential of the Lung Meridian by connecting it to broader energetic systems, such as the heart chakra, which governs love and emotional balance, and the Earth Star Chakra, which grounds the energy into stability. This multidimensional approach aligns the lung meridian with the chakras, universal grids, and cosmic frequencies, facilitating not only physical and emotional healing but also spiritual integration. By working with the Lung Meridian, Rainbow Reiki practitioners help clients achieve a harmonious balance between resilience, release, and renewal, supporting a healthier and more aligned state of being.

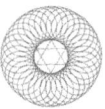

Advanced Guided Meditation to Clear Blockages and Restore Energy Flow to the Lung Meridian (LU)

Find a quiet space where you can sit or lie comfortably. Close your eyes and take a few deep breaths, allowing your body to relax with each exhale. Begin to connect with your breath, letting it flow naturally and deeply.

Take a deep inhale and visualize the air you breathe in as pure, radiant light. Let this light fill your lungs, expanding your chest and bringing a sense of peace and vitality. As you exhale, imagine releasing any tension, heaviness, or stagnant energy. With each breath, feel yourself becoming more grounded and present.

Now, shift your focus to your Lung Meridian. Begin at your chest, where the energy of the Lung Meridian originates. Visualize a gentle, white light glowing in the center of your chest, representing the pure and vital energy of the lungs. This light carries the essence of life force, or Qi, supporting your ability to breathe deeply, connect, and let go.

As you focus on this light, imagine it expanding and flowing downward along the inner side of your arms to your thumbs. See this pathway illuminated with bright, healing light, clearing any blockages along the way. If you notice any areas of tension, darkness, or stagnation, gently send your breath and this radiant light to dissolve them.

<u>Rainbow Reiki Activation</u>

Now, call in the energy of Rainbow Reiki to amplify the healing process. Visualize a stream of multicolored light descending from above, entering your chest, and merging with the white light of the Lung Meridian. This vibrant energy flows through your entire Lung Meridian pathway, carrying higher frequencies of love, healing, and renewal.

Each color of the Rainbow Reiki light represents a specific aspect of healing:

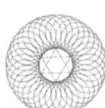

- Red for grounding and vitality, anchoring the energy into your body.
- Orange for emotional release, helping you let go of grief or sadness.
- Yellow for clarity and confidence, strengthening your ability to breathe deeply and freely.
- Green for balance and renewal, revitalizing your lungs and immune system.
- Blue for calming and soothing energy, bringing peace to your breath.
- Indigo for intuition and connection, deepening your awareness of your body's energy.
- Violet for spiritual alignment, linking the flow of your breath to your higher self.

Feel this Rainbow Reiki light infusing the Lung Meridian, harmonizing its flow, and restoring its vitality.

Emotional Release and Affirmation
Take a moment to connect with any emotions tied to your lungs, such as grief, sadness, or difficulty letting go. Allow these emotions to surface gently, without judgment. Imagine the Rainbow Reiki energy wrapping these emotions in light, transforming them into a sense of peace and release.

Silently or aloud, repeat the following affirmations:
- *"I release all grief and sadness; I welcome peace and renewal."*
- *"I breathe deeply and freely, connecting with the life force within me."*
- *"I let go of what no longer serves me, making space for joy and vitality."*

With each affirmation, feel the energy of the Lung Meridian becoming clearer, stronger, and more aligned.

Integration and Flow
Visualize the Rainbow Reiki energy settling into a steady, harmonious flow throughout your Lung Meridian. See the pathway

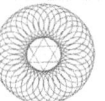

glowing brightly, flowing smoothly from your chest down your arms to your thumbs. Feel your lungs expanding effortlessly, drawing in the pure, life-giving energy of the universe with every breath.

Take a moment to imagine this clear, vibrant energy radiating outward, connecting your breath to every cell in your body. Let this energy flow not only through your lungs but also through your entire being, filling you with vitality, peace, and balance.

Closing and Gratitude
When you are ready, gently bring your awareness back to your breath. Take a few deep inhales and exhales, anchoring this renewed energy into your body. Visualize the Rainbow Reiki light gently integrating into your energy field, continuing its healing work.

Express gratitude for the energy of your lungs and the flow of the Lung Meridian. Thank the Rainbow Reiki energy for its support and healing.

When you feel ready, slowly wiggle your fingers and toes, and open your eyes. Carry this sense of openness, vitality, and ease with you into the rest of your day.

Yin Meridian – Heart Meridian (HT)

The Heart Meridian (HT) holds profound significance as it governs the flow of energy related to circulation, emotional health, and the expression of joy and love. As a yin meridian linked to the fire element, the Heart Meridian represents warmth, vitality, and the dynamic power of emotional connection. Physically, it influences the heart, blood vessels, and circulation, ensuring that life force energy flows harmoniously throughout the body. The pathway of this meridian begins in the chest, flows along the inner arm, and ends at the little finger, symbolically connecting the heart's energy to the hands, which are instruments of both physical and emotional expression.

Emotionally, the Heart Meridian is associated with joy, love, and emotional warmth. It acts as the central axis of emotional stability, allowing individuals to cultivate meaningful relationships and experience the fullness of life. However, when the energy of the Heart Meridian becomes blocked or imbalanced, it can result in emotional instability, anxiety, restlessness, or a sense of emptiness. These imbalances may manifest as physical symptoms, such as palpitations, chest tightness, or poor circulation, as well as difficulties in connecting with others or finding joy in life's experiences.

Rainbow Reiki works with the Heart Meridian to restore balance and harmony, integrating its energy with high-frequency healing modalities such as Magdalene/Yeshua Reiki, which fosters deep compassion, and Pleiadian Reiki, which uplifts emotional resonance. Practitioners may channel Rainbow Reiki energy along the Heart Meridian's pathway, clearing blockages and infusing it with vitality to promote emotional stability and a sense of inner peace. Visualization of radiant red or golden light, reflective of the fire element, is often used to re-energize the meridian and support its natural vibrancy.

Beyond emotional healing, Rainbow Reiki emphasizes the spiritual dimension of the Heart Meridian by aligning it with the heart chakra and broader energetic grids. This alignment enhances the

individual's ability to connect with universal love and divine compassion, fostering a sense of oneness with the cosmos. Techniques such as Reiki-infused affirmations, heart-focused breathwork, and multidimensional energy transmissions help clients release emotional pain, resolve patterns of disconnection, and rediscover the joy and warmth inherent in their being.

By working with the Heart Meridian, Rainbow Reiki practitioners facilitate a holistic healing process that addresses physical circulation, emotional expression, and spiritual alignment. This approach not only alleviates symptoms of imbalance, such as anxiety or restlessness, but also nurtures the individual's capacity to love, connect, and experience the transformative power of joy. Through the synergy of meridian work, chakra alignment, and multidimensional energy healing, the Heart Meridian becomes a conduit for profound emotional and spiritual growth, promoting harmony and vitality at every level.

Advanced Guided Meditation to Clear Blockages and Restore Energy Flow to the Heart Meridian (HT)

Find a comfortable seated or lying position. Close your eyes and take a deep breath, inhaling peace and exhaling tension. Allow your body to relax with each exhale. Begin to connect with your heartbeat, gently placing your awareness in the center of your chest.

Take a moment to focus on your heart center. Visualize a warm, emerald-green light radiating gently from the area. This light represents the life-giving energy of your Heart Meridian, flowing from your chest along the inner side of your arms to your little fingers. This meridian governs joy, love, and emotional warmth, and clearing it helps restore balance, connection, and vitality.

Now, imagine this green light expanding outward, creating a protective and soothing glow around your heart. With each breath, the light becomes stronger and more vibrant, preparing the Heart Meridian to release any blockages and restore its natural flow.

<u>Activating Rainbow Reiki Energy</u>
Visualize a stream of Rainbow Reiki energy descending from above, flowing into your heart center. This light contains all the colors of the rainbow, each carrying a specific frequency of healing:
- Red for grounding, anchoring the energy of love into your body.
- Orange for emotional release, allowing stored grief or pain to flow out gently.
- Yellow for confidence, brightening your emotional resilience.
- Green for renewal, harmonizing the heart's rhythm.
- Blue for calm and clarity, soothing any emotional turbulence.
- Indigo for insight, deepening your understanding of your emotional patterns.
- Violet for spiritual connection, linking your heart to universal love.

Feel this multicolored light entering your heart and flowing along the pathway of the Heart Meridian. Visualize it traveling from your

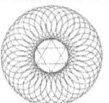

chest, down the inner arms, and into your little fingers, clearing blockages and illuminating the entire meridian.

Releasing Blockages and Emotional Healing
As the Rainbow Reiki energy moves through the Heart Meridian, tune in to any areas of tension or stagnation along the pathway. These may appear as dark patches, knots, or heaviness. Visualize the rainbow light dissolving these blockages, transforming them into clear, flowing energy.

Allow yourself to connect with any emotions stored in the Heart Meridian, such as grief, sadness, or resentment. With compassion, acknowledge these feelings and imagine them being wrapped in the Rainbow Reiki light. As the light works, these emotions gently dissolve, leaving a sense of peace and emotional balance.

Affirmations
Repeat the following affirmations silently or aloud:
- *"I open my heart to love and joy."*
- *"I release all pain and resentment, making space for connection and compassion."*
- *"My heart is a vessel of peace, warmth, and vitality."*

With each affirmation, feel the energy in your Heart Meridian flowing more freely, creating a sense of lightness and expansion.

Restoring Energy Flow
Now, visualize the Heart Meridian glowing with vibrant green light, flowing smoothly from your chest down your arms to your little fingers. This light carries the frequencies of love, warmth, and renewal, infusing your body and energy field with vitality. Sense the joy and emotional balance returning to your heart as this flow becomes steady and harmonious.

Let the Rainbow Reiki energy expand beyond the Heart Meridian, radiating outward into your entire body. Feel it connecting your heart to every cell, filling you with a sense of unity, openness, and peace.

Connecting to Universal Love

Allow the Rainbow Reiki energy to connect your heart to the greater universal flow of love. Visualize your heart center glowing brighter, a beacon of love and compassion that connects you to the world and the divine. Feel the interconnectedness of all life, knowing that your heart is a vital part of this web of energy.

Breathe deeply, feeling the infinite flow of love moving through you, cleansing, healing, and renewing.

Closing and Gratitude

When you feel ready, begin to draw your awareness back to your physical body. Visualize the Rainbow Reiki energy gently integrating into your Heart Meridian, continuing to support its flow. Thank your heart for its strength, love, and resilience. Express gratitude to the Rainbow Reiki energy for its healing and support.

Take a deep breath in, anchoring the sense of love and balance into your body, and exhale fully. Wiggle your fingers and toes, slowly returning to the present moment. When you are ready, open your eyes, carrying this renewed sense of warmth, love, and vitality with you into your day.

Yin Meridian – Pericardium Meridian (PC)

The Pericardium Meridian (PC) plays a vital role in fostering emotional balance and maintaining healthy boundaries, earning its title as the "heart protector." This yin meridian, associated with the fire element, extends from the chest down the inner arm to the middle finger, symbolically linking the heart's energy to emotional interaction and physical expression. Physically, the Pericardium Meridian influences circulation and the protective functions of the pericardium, the membrane surrounding the heart. Energetically, it acts as a shield for the heart, regulating emotional openness and vulnerability to maintain a healthy balance between connection and protection.

Emotionally, the Pericardium Meridian is closely tied to emotional boundaries and protection, offering resilience against emotional overwhelm and supporting the ability to trust and connect authentically. When this meridian is blocked or imbalanced, individuals may feel overly guarded, excessively worried about emotional safety, or hesitant to trust others. Conversely, a lack of balance may manifest as emotional vulnerability, difficulty establishing boundaries, or a tendency to overextend oneself in relationships, leading to burnout or emotional exhaustion.

Rainbow Reiki works with the Pericardium Meridian by clearing blockages and restoring its natural flow, enabling individuals to experience both emotional protection and connection in harmony. Using high-frequency energies from modalities such as Shadow Reiki, practitioners can help address hidden fears or past emotional wounds that contribute to over-guarding or emotional shutdown. Simultaneously, Magdalene/Yeshua Reiki can infuse the meridian with compassion and healing, fostering trust, emotional warmth, and a sense of safety.

The fire element connection of the Pericardium Meridian is emphasized in Rainbow Reiki practices through visualizations of warm, golden light or flame-like energy flowing along its pathway. This energizes the meridian, reigniting vitality and balance while dissolving fear-based blockages. Rainbow Reiki also integrates the meridian's energy with the heart chakra, aligning it with universal love and promoting emotional equilibrium. This alignment helps individuals release patterns of emotional defensiveness and build healthier, more fulfilling relationships.

Through Rainbow Reiki, the Pericardium Meridian becomes a powerful channel for developing emotional resilience, self-trust, and balanced vulnerability. Techniques such as energy transmissions, affirmations focused on safety and trust, and Reiki-infused breathwork empower individuals to embrace their emotional authenticity while maintaining boundaries that protect their well-being. By harmonizing the Pericardium Meridian with multidimensional energies and the broader energetic system, Rainbow Reiki supports a holistic healing process that nurtures emotional health, spiritual alignment, and the freedom to engage with life and relationships from a place of strength and love.

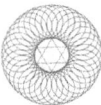

Advanced Guided Meditation to Clear Blockages and Restore Energy Flow to the Pericardium Meridian (PC)

Find a quiet and comfortable place to sit or lie down. Close your eyes and take a deep breath, allowing your body to relax with each exhale. Begin to center your awareness on your heart area, connecting with its rhythm and energy.

Take a few deep breaths, inhaling peace and exhaling tension. Visualize a gentle, rose-gold light forming in the center of your chest, symbolizing the loving, protective energy of the Pericardium Meridian—often called the "heart protector." This meridian extends from your chest along the inner side of your arms to your middle fingers. It governs emotional boundaries, vulnerability, and the ability to connect authentically while remaining protected.

Imagine the rose-gold light growing brighter and more vibrant, surrounding your heart and chest. This light represents the healing, protective energy of the Pericardium Meridian, ready to clear blockages and restore harmony.

<u>Activating Rainbow Reiki Energy</u>
Visualize a radiant stream of Rainbow Reiki energy descending from above, entering your heart center and merging with the rose-gold light. This multicolored energy carries the frequencies of love, compassion, and renewal. Allow each color of the Rainbow Reiki light to flow into the Pericardium Meridian, enhancing its healing properties:
- Red for grounding, strengthening emotional stability.
- Orange for emotional release, helping you let go of fear or guardedness.
- Yellow for clarity, encouraging confidence in emotional boundaries.
- Green for balance, promoting harmony and openness.
- Blue for calm, soothing emotional turbulence.
- Indigo for intuition, deepening your connection to inner wisdom.
- Violet for spiritual alignment, linking your heart to divine protection.

Feel this light infusing the Pericardium Meridian, moving from your chest down the inner arms to your middle fingers, clearing away blockages and revitalizing its flow.

Releasing Emotional Blockages
As the Rainbow Reiki energy flows through the Pericardium Meridian, tune in to any areas of tension or heaviness along its pathway. These might appear as dark spots, knots, or sluggish energy. Visualize the rainbow light gently dissolving these blockages, transforming them into clear, radiant energy.
Connect with any emotions tied to the Pericardium Meridian, such as fear, emotional exhaustion, or difficulty trusting. Allow these emotions to surface without judgment. Visualize the Rainbow Reiki energy wrapping these feelings in light, transmuting them into a sense of safety, compassion, and emotional freedom.

Affirmations
Repeat the following affirmations silently or aloud:
- *"I am emotionally protected and open to love."*
- *"I release fear and embrace trust and connection."*
- *"My heart is safe, balanced, and supported."*

With each affirmation, feel the energy of the Pericardium Meridian becoming lighter, freer, and more aligned.

Restoring Energy Flow
Now, visualize the Pericardium Meridian glowing with rose-gold light, flowing smoothly from your chest, down your arms, to your middle fingers. This radiant light represents emotional resilience, healthy boundaries, and the ability to connect authentically without losing your sense of self.

Let this energy ripple outward from the Pericardium Meridian, filling your entire body with love, peace, and balance. Feel a renewed sense of connection to your heart, as well as a strong, protective boundary that allows you to navigate the world with confidence and compassion.

Connecting to Universal Love and Protection
Visualize the Rainbow Reiki energy expanding from your heart, connecting you to the universal flow of love and protection. Imagine your Pericardium Meridian acting as a shield of light, allowing love and positive energy to flow freely while gently filtering out anything that does not serve your highest good.

Feel a deep sense of alignment with the energy of the universe, knowing that your heart is both open and protected.

Closing and Gratitude
When you feel ready, begin to bring your awareness back to your breath. Visualize the Rainbow Reiki energy settling into your Pericardium Meridian, continuing its healing work. Thank your heart and the Pericardium Meridian for their strength and resilience. Express gratitude to the Rainbow Reiki energy for its support and guidance.

Take a deep breath in, anchoring this renewed sense of emotional protection and balance into your body, and exhale fully. Wiggle your fingers and toes, slowly bringing your awareness back to the present moment. When you are ready, open your eyes, carrying the sense of safety, trust, and emotional alignment with you into the rest of your day.

Yin Meridian - Spleen Meridian (SP)

The Spleen Meridian (SP) holds a central role in balancing both physical and emotional energies, as it governs digestion, blood production, and fluid regulation while supporting mental clarity and emotional nurturing. This yin meridian, associated with the Earth element, flows from the big toe up the inner leg to the torso, energetically connecting the physical processes of nourishment with the emotional need for stability and grounding. Physically, the Spleen Meridian influences the transformation and transportation of nutrients, ensuring the body has the energy it needs for vitality and well-being. Energetically, it represents the nurturing and stabilizing qualities of the Earth element, providing a foundation for emotional security and balance.

Emotionally, the Spleen Meridian is associated with worry, overthinking, and rumination, making it crucial for addressing mental and emotional patterns that create stagnation. When energy in the Spleen Meridian is blocked or depleted, individuals may feel mentally burdened, anxious, or stuck in repetitive thought cycles. This imbalance can also manifest physically as digestive issues, fluid retention, or fatigue, reflecting the interconnectedness of physical and emotional health. The Spleen's role in emotional nurturing highlights its connection to self-care, the ability to give and receive support, and finding balance between productivity and rest.

Rainbow Reiki supports the Spleen Meridian by harmonizing its energy flow, addressing both physical and emotional imbalances. High-frequency energies, such as those from Pleiadian Reiki, can uplift the heavy, stagnant energy often associated with worry and overthinking, promoting mental clarity and emotional lightness. Simultaneously, Shadow Reiki helps uncover and release subconscious patterns contributing to rumination or self-doubt, allowing individuals to cultivate a sense of trust in themselves and their ability to navigate life's challenges. Reiki techniques are often combined with grounding practices, visualizing the nurturing energy of the Earth element—symbolized by warm, golden light—flowing along the Spleen Meridian to reestablish stability and connection.

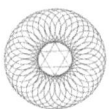

In addition to its emotional benefits, working with the Spleen Meridian in Rainbow Reiki supports physical digestion and energy transformation, aligning it with the solar plexus chakra, the center of personal power and vitality. By integrating meridian and chakra work, practitioners can address the root causes of energy depletion, whether physical, emotional, or spiritual. This multidimensional approach promotes not only digestive health but also a sense of emotional and mental harmony, empowering individuals to move beyond worry and embrace a grounded, balanced perspective.

Through Rainbow Reiki, the Spleen Meridian becomes a powerful pathway for cultivating self-nurturing, clarity, and resilience. Practitioners may use Reiki-infused affirmations, breathwork, and energy transmissions to clear blockages and strengthen the meridian, allowing for smoother energy flow and emotional equilibrium. By balancing the Spleen Meridian, Rainbow Reiki fosters a deeper connection to the Earth element and the qualities of stability, nourishment, and inner peace, supporting a holistic sense of well-being.

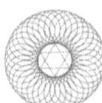

Advanced Guided Meditation to Clear Blockages and Restore Energy Flow to the Spleen Meridian (SP)

Sit or lie down comfortably in a quiet space. Close your eyes and take a few slow, deep breaths, letting your body relax and your mind settle. Bring your awareness to your lower abdomen, just below your navel, as you prepare to connect with the energy of your Spleen Meridian.

Focus on your breath, inhaling deeply through your nose and exhaling fully through your mouth. With each exhale, release any tension, fatigue, or stress. Begin to feel grounded and present in your body.

Now, bring your awareness to the Spleen Meridian, which begins at the inside of your big toes, flows upward along the inner legs, and extends to the chest. This meridian governs digestion, nourishment, emotional balance, and mental clarity, aligning with the Earth element that provides stability and grounding. Visualize a soft, golden-yellow light forming at the soles of your feet, representing the nurturing energy of the Spleen Meridian.

As you breathe in, imagine this golden-yellow light flowing upward through your feet and legs, traveling along the pathway of the Spleen Meridian. With each breath, this light becomes stronger, illuminating the entire meridian and preparing it for healing and renewal.

<u>Activating Rainbow Reiki Energy</u>
Call in the energy of Rainbow Reiki, visualizing a radiant stream of multicolored light descending from above. This light enters your lower abdomen, merging with the golden-yellow light of the Spleen Meridian. Each color of the Rainbow Reiki energy contributes to the healing process:
- Red for grounding and stability, anchoring your energy.
- Orange for emotional release and creative flow.
- Yellow for clarity, vitality, and mental focus.
- Green for balance and renewal, harmonizing the body and mind.

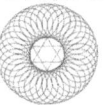

- Blue for calm and peace, soothing any emotional turbulence.
- Indigo for insight and intuition, helping you understand emotional patterns.
- Violet for spiritual alignment, connecting you to universal nourishment.

Feel this multicolored light infusing the Spleen Meridian, clearing away any blockages or stagnant energy and restoring its natural flow.

Releasing Blockages and Emotional Healing
As the Rainbow Reiki energy moves through the Spleen Meridian, tune into any areas of heaviness or tension along the pathway. These blockages might appear as dark spots, sluggish movement, or sensations of tightness. Allow the golden-yellow and Rainbow Reiki light to dissolve these blockages gently, transforming them into clear, radiant energy.

Connect with the emotional aspects of the Spleen Meridian, which may hold worry, overthinking, or feelings of lack. Acknowledge any emotions that surface without judgment. Visualize the Rainbow Reiki energy wrapping these emotions in light, releasing them from your body and replacing them with a sense of peace, stability, and trust.

Affirmations
Silently or aloud, repeat these affirmations:
- *"I release worry and embrace trust in the flow of life."*
- *"I am deeply nourished and supported by Earth."*
- *"I think clearly, act confidently, and feel balanced in all I do."*

Feel the energy of the Spleen Meridian becoming lighter, freer, and more harmonious with each affirmation.

Restoring Energy Flow
Visualize the Spleen Meridian glowing with vibrant golden-yellow light, flowing smoothly from your big toes up your inner legs to your

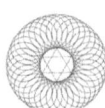

chest. This light represents nourishment, balance, and a deep connection to the grounding energy of Earth.

Allow the Rainbow Reiki energy to expand beyond the Spleen Meridian, filling your entire body with vitality and balance. Feel this energy harmonizing your digestion, emotions, and mental clarity, aligning all aspects of your being with stability and peace.

Connecting to the Earth Element
Bring your awareness to the Earth beneath you, feeling its grounding energy rise to support you. Imagine roots extending from your feet deep into the Earth, connecting you to its stabilizing and nurturing energy. Allow this connection to further strengthen the flow of the Spleen Meridian, creating a continuous cycle of grounding, nourishment, and renewal.

Closing and Gratitude
When you feel ready, begin to draw your awareness back to your breath. Visualize the Rainbow Reiki energy settling into the Spleen Meridian, continuing its healing and balancing work. Thank your body, the Spleen Meridian, and the Rainbow Reiki energy for their support and vitality.

Take a deep breath in, anchoring this renewed energy and stability into your being, and exhale fully. Gently wiggle your fingers and toes, bringing yourself back to the present moment. When you are ready, open your eyes, carrying this sense of nourishment, clarity, and balance with you into your day.

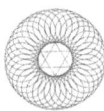

Yin Meridian - Kidney Meridian (KI)

The Kidney Meridian (KI) is recognized as a vital channel for accessing and harmonizing the body's life force energy, essential for growth, reproduction, and overall vitality. This yin meridian, associated with the water element, flows from the soles of the feet along the inner legs to the torso, symbolizing the upward flow of grounding and nourishing energy that supports survival and longevity. Physically, the Kidney Meridian governs fluid balance, the function of the kidneys, and reproductive health, playing a key role in maintaining the body's reserves of energy and vitality. It also influences bone health, hair quality, and the production of marrow, connecting it deeply to foundational life force.

Emotionally, the Kidney Meridian is tied to the emotion of fear and the body's survival instincts. When the energy of this meridian is balanced, it fosters courage, resilience, and a sense of inner security. However, when Qi becomes blocked or depleted in the Kidney Meridian, individuals may experience excessive fear, anxiety, and feelings of insecurity. Over time, these emotional imbalances can manifest physically as fatigue, weakened kidney function, reproductive challenges, or a sense of inadequacy, reflecting the depletion of the body's foundational energy reserves. Chronic stress, trauma, or unresolved fears can further strain this meridian, amplifying both physical and emotional symptoms.

Rainbow Reiki provides a powerful framework for working with the Kidney Meridian by combining traditional meridian healing with advanced multidimensional energy techniques. Practitioners may direct Reiki energy along the meridian's pathway, from the feet to the torso, to restore the flow of Qi and release energetic stagnation. High-frequency energies such as those from Pleiadian Reiki can infuse the Kidney Meridian with vitality, while Shadow Reiki can help uncover and release deeply rooted fears and subconscious patterns that contribute to energetic blockages. Visualizing the soothing and cleansing properties of the water element, represented by flowing blue light, further supports the harmonization of the Kidney Meridian, allowing for the release of fear and the restoration of emotional balance.

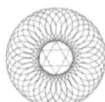

The Kidney Meridian's connection to life force energy also aligns it with the root chakra and sacral chakra, amplifying its role in grounding, survival, and creative potential. By integrating these energetic systems, Rainbow Reiki practitioners can address not only immediate physical and emotional imbalances but also the deeper spiritual dimensions of insecurity and resilience. Techniques such as Reiki-infused affirmations, breathwork, and grounding exercises help clients reconnect with their inner strength, cultivating a sense of trust in their ability to navigate life's challenges.

Working with the Kidney Meridian in Rainbow Reiki supports both short-term relief from fear and anxiety and long-term restoration of vitality and confidence. By harmonizing the meridian and aligning it with the broader energetic system, practitioners empower individuals to move beyond fear, embrace courage, and reconnect with their inherent life force energy. This holistic approach nurtures the body, mind, and spirit, fostering resilience, balance, and a renewed sense of self-assurance.

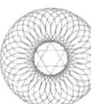

Advanced Guided Meditation to Clear Blockages and Restore Energy Flow to the Kidney Meridian (KI)

Find a quiet and comfortable position to sit or lie down. Close your eyes and take a deep breath, inhaling calmness and exhaling any tension. Place your awareness at the base of your spine and the soles of your feet, grounding yourself into the present moment.

Begin by focusing on your breath. With each inhale, draw in the energy of renewal, and with each exhale, release fear, tension, or stress. As you settle into this rhythm, bring your attention to your Kidney Meridian, which begins at the soles of your feet, flows upward along the inner legs, and travels to the chest. The Kidney Meridian governs life force energy, fluid balance, growth, and resilience, and it is deeply connected to the water element and the emotion of fear.

Visualize a deep blue light at the soles of your feet, symbolizing the healing energy of the Kidney Meridian. This light is soothing, pure, and vibrant. With each inhale, imagine this blue light flowing upward, gently illuminating the pathway of the Kidney Meridian, preparing it for healing.

<u>Activating Rainbow Reiki Energy</u>

Now, call in the powerful energy of Rainbow Reiki, envisioning a radiant stream of multicolored light descending from above. This light flows into your body, merging with the deep blue light of the Kidney Meridian. Each color of the Rainbow Reiki energy carries a unique vibration to assist in the healing process:
- Red for grounding and vitality, anchoring your energy.
- Orange for emotional release and creative flow.
- Yellow for clarity, confidence, and courage.
- Green for balance, harmony, and renewal.
- Blue for calmness and inner peace, soothing any fear or anxiety.
- Indigo for intuitive insight, helping you understand emotional patterns.
- Violet for spiritual connection, aligning you with universal wisdom.

Feel this Rainbow Reiki light infusing the Kidney Meridian, filling it with healing, clearing any blockages, and restoring the natural flow of Qi.

Releasing Blockages and Emotional Healing
As the Rainbow Reiki energy flows through the Kidney Meridian, tune into any areas of tension, heaviness, or stagnation along the pathway. These blockages might feel like dark spots or sluggish movement. Visualize the Rainbow Reiki light gently dissolving these blockages, transforming them into flowing, radiant energy.

Connect with any emotional patterns stored in the Kidney Meridian, such as fear, insecurity, or stress. Acknowledge these emotions with compassion, and as you exhale, imagine them being carried away by the flowing blue and Rainbow Reiki light. Feel these emotions dissolve, replaced by a sense of trust, security, and resilience.

Affirmations
Silently or aloud, repeat these affirmations:
- *"I release fear and embrace the flow of life."*
- *"I am supported, resilient, and deeply connected to my inner strength."*
- *"My energy flows freely, filling me with vitality and peace."*

With each affirmation, sense the energy of the Kidney Meridian becoming lighter, clearer, and more vibrant.

Restoring Energy Flow
Visualize the Kidney Meridian glowing with brilliant blue light, flowing smoothly from the soles of your feet up your inner legs to your chest. This vibrant light carries the energy of renewal, grounding, and resilience, harmonizing the flow of life force energy throughout your body.

Allow the Rainbow Reiki energy to expand beyond the Kidney Meridian, filling your entire being with vitality, balance, and peace.

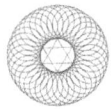

Feel this energy harmonizing not only your physical body but also your emotional and spiritual layers, aligning all aspects of your being.

Connecting to the Water Element
Bring your awareness to the water element within and around you. Visualize a serene body of water—perhaps a calm lake or a flowing river. Imagine this water gently cleansing and rejuvenating your energy, washing away any remaining tension or fear. Feel its fluid, adaptive nature reminding you of your own inner strength and resilience.

Closing and Gratitude
When you are ready, begin to draw your awareness back to your breath. Visualize the Rainbow Reiki energy gently integrating into your Kidney Meridian, continuing to flow freely and support you. Thank your kidneys, the Kidney Meridian, and the Rainbow Reiki energy for their healing and alignment.

Take a deep breath in, anchoring this renewed sense of strength and balance into your being, and exhale fully. Wiggle your fingers and toes, bringing yourself back to the present moment. When you are ready, open your eyes, carrying this sense of vitality, trust, and peace with you into your day.

Yin Meridian - Liver Meridian (LV)
The Liver Meridian (LV) is essential for maintaining the smooth flow of energy throughout the body, supporting detoxification, hormone balance, and emotional harmony. This yin meridian, associated with the wood element, flows from the big toe along the inner leg to the torso, symbolizing upward growth, renewal, and the capacity for adaptability. Physically, the Liver Meridian governs the liver's role in processing toxins, regulating hormones, and supporting blood flow. Its influence extends to the eyes, muscles, and tendons, reflecting its importance in maintaining physical flexibility and strength. The liver's function as a detoxifying organ is mirrored energetically in its ability to clear emotional stagnation, making it a cornerstone of overall balance.

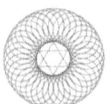

Emotionally, the Liver Meridian is tied to anger and frustration, as well as the ability to plan, envision, and adapt to life's changes. When the energy of this meridian is balanced, it fosters patience, clarity, and emotional control, enabling individuals to respond to challenges with grace and resilience. However, blockages or imbalances in the Liver Meridian can result in feelings of anger, irritability, or resentment. These emotional disruptions may manifest physically as tension in the body, headaches, hormonal imbalances, or digestive issues. Chronic stress or unprocessed emotions can further strain the Liver Meridian, amplifying its impact on both emotional and physical health.

Rainbow Reiki works with the Liver Meridian by using advanced energy techniques to restore the flow of Qi, release emotional blockages, and harmonize the body's energetic system. Practitioners may channel Reiki energy along the meridian's pathway, infusing it with the healing and grounding qualities of the wood element, often visualized as vibrant green light representing growth and renewal. Shadow Reiki is particularly effective in addressing deeply held anger or frustration, helping to uncover and release the underlying emotional patterns contributing to stagnation. Meanwhile, Pleiadian and Arcturian Reiki energies can uplift and recalibrate the meridian, promoting emotional clarity and physical detoxification.

The Liver Meridian's connection to planning and vision also makes it a key focus for addressing issues related to indecision, lack of direction, or feeling "stuck" in life. In Rainbow Reiki, this meridian is often integrated with the solar plexus chakra, enhancing the individual's sense of personal power and the ability to make clear, confident decisions. Techniques such as Reiki-infused affirmations, guided visualizations of flowing energy, and breathwork that emphasizes release and renewal help clients reconnect with their sense of purpose and emotional balance.

Through its work with the Liver Meridian, Rainbow Reiki provides a holistic approach to emotional healing and physical detoxification, addressing both immediate symptoms and deeper energetic imbalances. By promoting the smooth flow of energy and releasing

emotional stagnation, Rainbow Reiki helps individuals cultivate patience, clarity, and a renewed sense of control over their lives. This multidimensional approach nurtures the body, mind, and spirit, fostering adaptability, resilience, and emotional harmony.

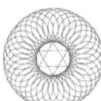

Advanced Guided Meditation to Clear Blockages and Restore Energy Flow to the Liver Meridian (LV)

Find a quiet, comfortable place to sit or lie down. Close your eyes and take a deep breath, allowing your body to relax with each exhale. Bring your awareness to your lower abdomen and feet, grounding yourself into the present moment. Begin to connect with the soothing rhythm of your breath.

As you settle into your breath, shift your awareness to your Liver Meridian, which begins at your big toes, flows upward along the inner legs, and extends into your chest. This meridian governs detoxification, emotional flow, and vision and is connected to the wood element and the emotion of anger. Visualize a soft, emerald-green light forming at your big toes, representing the healing energy of the Liver Meridian.

With each inhale, imagine this emerald-green light gently rising through the pathway of the Liver Meridian, illuminating it and preparing it for cleansing and renewal.

<u>Activating Rainbow Reiki Energy</u>

Now, call upon the energy of Rainbow Reiki to amplify the healing process. Visualize a vibrant stream of multicolored light descending from above and entering your body through your crown. This light flows downward into your Liver Meridian, merging with the emerald-green light. Each color of the Rainbow Reiki energy contributes to the restoration of balance and harmony:

- Red for grounding and vitality, stabilizing your energy.
- Orange for emotional release, clearing stored anger and frustration.
- Yellow for clarity, boosting personal power and decision-making.
- Green for renewal, aligning the flow of energy with the natural cycles of life.
- Blue for peace, soothing emotional turbulence.
- Indigo for insight, enhancing self-awareness and emotional understanding.

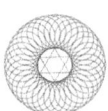

- Violet for spiritual connection, aligning the Liver Meridian with higher vibrations.

Feel this multicolored light flowing through the pathway of the Liver Meridian, dissolving any blockages and restoring its natural flow.

Releasing Blockages and Emotional Healing
As the Rainbow Reiki energy moves through the Liver Meridian, focus on any areas of heaviness, tension, or stagnation. These may feel like dark spots or sluggish energy. Visualize the Rainbow Reiki light gently dissolving these blockages, clearing the pathway and transforming stagnant energy into radiant, flowing light.

Connect with any emotions tied to the Liver Meridian, such as anger, frustration, or irritability. Allow these emotions to surface without judgment. Imagine the Rainbow Reiki energy wrapping these feelings in light, releasing them with your exhales. Feel them being transmuted into peace, patience, and clarity.

Affirmations
Silently or aloud, repeat these affirmations:
- *"I release anger and embrace peace and balance."*
- *"I trust in the flow of life and align with my inner vision."*
- *"My energy flows freely, promoting harmony and renewal."*

With each affirmation, sense the Liver Meridian becoming clearer, brighter, and more harmonious.

Restoring Energy Flow
Visualize the Liver Meridian glowing with vibrant emerald-green light, flowing smoothly from your big toes up your inner legs to your chest. This energy carries the qualities of detoxification, balance, and emotional resilience. Feel this light harmonizing the Liver Meridian, revitalizing its flow, and connecting you to the natural cycles of growth and renewal.

Allow the Rainbow Reiki energy to expand beyond the Liver Meridian, filling your entire body with balance, clarity, and vitality.

Feel this energy harmonizing your physical, emotional, and spiritual layers, supporting holistic well-being.

Connecting to the Wood Element
Bring your awareness to the wood element, symbolizing growth, adaptability, and resilience. Visualize yourself standing in a lush forest surrounded by tall, vibrant trees. Feel their rooted strength and gentle flexibility as they sway with the wind. Imagine this energy merging with your Liver Meridian, reinforcing your own ability to grow, adapt, and thrive.

Closing the Session
When you feel ready, gently bring your awareness back to your breath. Visualize the Rainbow Reiki energy settling into your Liver Meridian, continuing to flow freely and support your well-being. Thank your liver, the Liver Meridian, and the Rainbow Reiki energy for their healing and alignment.

Take a deep breath in, anchoring this renewed sense of balance and flow into your being, and exhale fully. Wiggle your fingers and toes, gently bringing yourself back to the present moment. When you are ready, open your eyes, carrying the sense of clarity, peace, and vitality with you into the rest of your day.

Yang Meridian - Large Intestine Meridian (LI)
The Large Intestine Meridian (LI) plays a vital role in the processes of both physical and emotional elimination, fostering the ability to release what no longer serves. This yang meridian, associated with the metal element, flows from the index finger up the arm to the shoulder and connects deeply with the respiratory and digestive systems. Physically, it governs the large intestine's function in removing waste and maintaining the body's internal balance. Its connection to the lungs reflects its dual role in cleansing and renewal, emphasizing the importance of synchronized physical and energetic flow.

Emotionally, the Large Intestine Meridian is associated with the concept of letting go—not only of physical waste but also of emotional baggage, outdated beliefs, and unresolved experiences. When this meridian is blocked, individuals may struggle with releasing negative emotions or past traumas, leading to feelings of resentment, rigidity, or emotional stagnation. This inability to let go can manifest physically as constipation, skin issues, or respiratory challenges, reflecting the interconnectedness of emotional and physical health. Long-term imbalances in the Large Intestine Meridian may create a sense of being "stuck," preventing growth and renewal.

Rainbow Reiki addresses blockages in the Large Intestine Meridian by combining traditional energy-clearing techniques with high-frequency energies to facilitate deep release and transformation. Practitioners may use Shadow Reiki to help clients identify and release subconscious patterns of resentment or resistance, while Magdalene/Yeshua Reiki infuses the meridian with compassion and the energy of renewal. Visualizing the purifying qualities of the metal element, often represented as silvery or white light, can support the energetic detoxification of the meridian, promoting clarity and balance.

The Large Intestine Meridian is also connected to the energetic flow of the root chakra, emphasizing grounding and stability during the process of release. In Rainbow Reiki, techniques such as breathwork, Reiki-infused affirmations, and guided visualizations of energy flowing freely along the meridian help clients reconnect with their innate ability to let go. By harmonizing the energy of this meridian, practitioners assist in restoring physical balance and emotional flexibility, enabling individuals to release old patterns and embrace new opportunities with openness.

Through its work with the Large Intestine Meridian, Rainbow Reiki facilitates a holistic process of letting go, addressing the physical, emotional, and energetic aspects of elimination. By clearing blockages and promoting flow, this approach supports renewal, helping individuals move forward with greater lightness, resilience, and freedom. The Large Intestine Meridian becomes a channel for transformation, fostering emotional liberation and a renewed sense of alignment with life's natural cycles.

Advanced Rainbow Reiki Guided Meditation to Clear Blockages and Restore Energy Flow to the Large Intestine Meridian (LI)

Find a quiet, comfortable place to sit or lie down. Close your eyes and take a deep breath, inhaling deeply and exhaling fully, releasing tension and grounding yourself in the present moment. Begin to connect with your body and its natural rhythm.

Shift your awareness to the Large Intestine Meridian, which begins at the index fingers, flows upward along the outer sides of the arms, passes through the shoulders, and ends at the sides of the nostrils. This meridian governs waste elimination and letting go, both physically and emotionally. It is associated with the metal element and the emotion of grief.

Visualize a bright white light, representing the cleansing and balancing energy of the Large Intestine Meridian, forming at the tips of your index fingers. With each inhale, imagine this white light flowing gently upward along the pathway of the meridian, illuminating it and preparing it for clearing and healing.

<u>Activating Rainbow Reiki Energy</u>
Now, call upon the energy of Rainbow Reiki to amplify the healing process. Visualize a vibrant stream of multicolored light descending

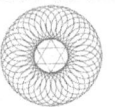

from above, entering your body through your crown, and flowing down into the pathway of the Large Intestine Meridian. The Rainbow Reiki energy merges with the bright white light, enhancing its healing power. Each color brings a unique vibration to assist in clearing and restoring the meridian:

- Red for grounding and stability, anchoring the energy into your physical body.
- Orange for emotional release, helping to let go of grief and resistance.
- Yellow for clarity, boosting confidence and optimism.
- Green for renewal, aligning the meridian's flow with natural cycles of release and growth.
- Blue for calm and peace, soothing emotional tension.
- Indigo for insight, deepening your understanding of emotional patterns.
- Violet for spiritual connection, helping you align with universal energy and divine flow.

Feel this Rainbow Reiki light flowing along the Large Intestine Meridian, dissolving blockages and restoring the free flow of Qi.

Releasing Blockages and Emotional Healing
As the Rainbow Reiki energy flows through the Large Intestine Meridian, focus on any areas of heaviness, tension, or stagnation. These may appear as dark spots or sluggish movement. Visualize the Rainbow Reiki light gently dissolving these blockages, transforming them into radiant, clear energy.

Connect with any emotions tied to the Large Intestine Meridian, such as grief, resistance, or difficulty letting go. Acknowledge these emotions with compassion and allow the Rainbow Reiki energy to wrap them in light. With each exhale, release these emotions, letting them flow out of your body and energy field. Feel the lightness and freedom as the meridian clears.

Affirmations
Silently or aloud, repeat these affirmations:

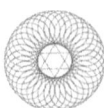

- *"I release all that no longer serves me, creating space for renewal."*
- *"I let go of grief and resistance, welcoming peace and flow."*
- *"I am free, open, and aligned with the cycles of life."*

With each affirmation, sense the Large Intestine Meridian becoming clearer, brighter, and more harmonious.

Restoring Energy Flow
Visualize the Large Intestine Meridian glowing with bright white light, flowing smoothly from your index fingers, up your arms, and into the sides of your nostrils. This light carries the energy of cleansing, release, and renewal. Feel this light harmonizing the meridian's flow, supporting both physical elimination and emotional freedom.

Allow the Rainbow Reiki energy to expand beyond the Large Intestine Meridian, filling your entire body with clarity, vitality, and peace. Feel this energy aligning your physical, emotional, and spiritual layers, supporting holistic well-being.

Connecting to the Metal Element
Bring your awareness to the metal element, representing strength, clarity, and the ability to let go. Visualize yourself surrounded by pure, reflective metal—such as silver or gold—symbolizing resilience and the power of release. Imagine this energy merging with your Large Intestine Meridian, reinforcing your ability to release the old and embrace the new.

Closing and Gratitude
When you feel ready, gently bring your awareness back to your breath. Visualize the Rainbow Reiki energy settling into your Large Intestine Meridian, continuing to flow freely and support your well-being. Thank your body, the Large Intestine Meridian, and the Rainbow Reiki energy for their healing and alignment.

Take a deep breath in, anchoring this renewed sense of clarity and release into your being, and exhale fully. Wiggle your fingers and toes, gently bringing yourself back to the present moment. When

you are ready, open your eyes, carrying the sense of freedom, lightness, and peace with you into your day.

Yang Meridian – Small Intestine Meridian (SI)

The Small Intestine Meridian (SI) is recognized as a crucial pathway for processing both physical and emotional nourishment, fostering mental clarity and emotional discernment. This yang meridian, associated with the fire element, flows from the pinky finger along the arm to the shoulder, reflecting its energetic connection to sorting and distributing vital energy throughout the body and mind. Physically, the Small Intestine Meridian governs nutrient absorption and the separation of what the body needs from what it must eliminate. This role of discernment is mirrored emotionally and mentally, as the meridian helps individuals process and integrate their experiences and emotions.

Emotionally, the Small Intestine Meridian is tied to the ability to sort through emotions and experiences, enabling clarity in decision-making and emotional understanding. When energy flow in this meridian is blocked, individuals may feel overwhelmed by their emotions, struggle to make decisions, or find it difficult to prioritize and focus. This imbalance can lead to indecisiveness, confusion, and a sense of emotional clutter, much like how physical digestion is disrupted when the small intestine fails to absorb nutrients efficiently.

Rainbow Reiki works with the Small Intestine Meridian by clearing blockages and harmonizing its flow, helping individuals restore their capacity for discernment and clarity. Practitioners may channel Reiki energy along the meridian's pathway, using visualizations of the fire element, such as warm, golden light, to ignite focus, understanding, and the ability to separate emotional "truths" from unnecessary mental chatter. Shadow Reiki can address underlying fears or patterns that hinder clear emotional processing, while Magdalene/Yeshua Reiki provides compassion and emotional support, helping clients navigate overwhelming feelings with grace.

The Small Intestine Meridian's role in emotional sorting also aligns it with the solar plexus chakra, the center of personal power and confidence. By integrating work on this meridian with the chakra system, Rainbow Reiki practitioners enhance the individual's ability to trust their decisions, act with purpose, and process life's

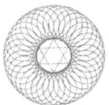

complexities. Techniques such as Reiki-infused affirmations, guided meditations, and multidimensional energy transmissions further strengthen the meridian's energetic flow, promoting mental clarity and emotional resilience.

Through Rainbow Reiki, the Small Intestine Meridian becomes a pathway for transformation, supporting both physical nutrient absorption and emotional nourishment. By harmonizing its energy, individuals can better integrate their experiences, release emotional overwhelm, and approach life with confidence and clarity. This holistic approach fosters not only physical health but also emotional balance and mental sharpness, empowering individuals to move through life's challenges with focus and strength.

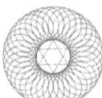

Advanced Guided Meditation to Clear Blockages and Restore Energy Flow to the Small Intestine Meridian (SI)

Find a comfortable place to sit or lie down. Close your eyes and take a deep breath, inhaling calm and exhaling tension. Allow your body to relax fully. Bring your awareness inward, focusing on the rhythm of your breath.

As you settle into your breath, shift your awareness to the Small Intestine Meridian, which begins at the outer side of your little fingers, flows upward along the outer arms, across the shoulders, and ends at the ears. This meridian governs nutrient absorption, discernment, and decision-making, helping the body and mind sort through what is nourishing and what needs to be released.

Visualize a soft orange-gold light forming at the tips of your little fingers, symbolizing the balancing and cleansing energy of the Small Intestine Meridian. With each inhale, imagine this light gently flowing upward through the pathway of the meridian, illuminating and preparing it for healing.

<u>Activating Rainbow Reiki Energy</u>
Now, call in the energy of Rainbow Reiki, visualizing a vibrant stream of multicolored light descending from above. This light enters your crown, flows down into your body, and merges with the orange-gold light of the Small Intestine Meridian. Each color of the Rainbow Reiki energy contributes to the restoration of balance and harmony:
- Red for grounding and vitality, anchoring the meridian's flow.
- Orange for emotional release and creativity, clearing emotional confusion.
- Yellow for clarity and confidence in decision-making.
- Green for renewal and harmony, balancing the energy flow.
- Blue for calmness and peace, soothing mental clutter.
- Indigo for insight, enhancing discernment and intuitive understanding.
- Violet for spiritual connection, aligning the meridian with higher wisdom.

Feel this Rainbow Reiki light infusing the Small Intestine Meridian, dissolving blockages and restoring the free flow of Qi.

Releasing Blockages and Emotional Healing
As the Rainbow Reiki energy flows through the Small Intestine Meridian, focus on any areas of heaviness, tension, or stagnation along its pathway. These may feel like dark spots or sluggish energy. Visualize the Rainbow Reiki light gently dissolving these blockages, transforming them into radiant, flowing energy.
Connect with the emotional aspects of the Small Intestine Meridian, which may hold patterns of indecision, emotional overwhelm, or difficulty discerning priorities. Allow any emotions or thoughts tied to these patterns to surface gently. Visualize the Rainbow Reiki light wrapping these feelings in healing energy, releasing them from your body and mind.

Affirmations
Silently or aloud, repeat these affirmations:
- *"I release confusion and embrace clarity in my choices."*
- *"I trust my ability to discern what nourishes and supports me."*
- *"My energy flows freely, supporting balance and wisdom."*

With each affirmation, sense the Small Intestine Meridian becoming lighter, clearer, and more aligned.

Restoring Energy Flow
Visualize the Small Intestine Meridian glowing with vibrant orange-gold light, flowing smoothly from the tips of your little fingers, up your arms, across your shoulders, and into your ears. This radiant light represents clarity, nourishment, and discernment, harmonizing the energy of the Small Intestine Meridian.

Allow the Rainbow Reiki energy to expand beyond the Small Intestine Meridian, filling your entire body with clarity, peace, and vitality. Feel this energy balancing not only your physical body but also your emotional and spiritual layers, promoting holistic well-being.

Connecting to Discernment and Inner Wisdom

Bring your awareness to the concept of discernment, the ability to sort through life's experiences and choose what truly supports your growth. Visualize a clear, flowing stream, representing your inner wisdom. Imagine this stream washing through the Small Intestine Meridian, helping you release what no longer serves you and retain what nourishes your body, mind, and spirit.

Closing and Gratitude

When you feel ready, gently bring your awareness back to your breath. Visualize the Rainbow Reiki energy settling into the Small Intestine Meridian, continuing its flow and supporting your well-being. Thank your body, the Small Intestine Meridian, and the Rainbow Reiki energy for their healing and guidance.

Take a deep breath in, anchoring this renewed sense of clarity and discernment into your being, and exhale fully. Wiggle your fingers and toes, gently bringing yourself back to the present moment. When you are ready, open your eyes, carrying the sense of balance, nourishment, and wisdom with you into your day.

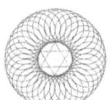

Yang Meridians - San Jiao Meridian (Triple Burner/Heater, SJ)

The San Jiao Meridian (Triple Burner/Heater, SJ) is a vital pathway for balancing energy across the body, regulating temperature, fluid movement, and emotional harmony. Unlike other meridians associated with specific organs, the San Jiao functions as a holistic regulator, connecting and coordinating the upper, middle, and lower parts of the body. This yang meridian, linked to the fire element, flows from the ring finger along the outer arm to the shoulder, symbolizing its role in linking different systems and fostering interconnectedness within the body. Physically, it oversees the flow of energy, body fluids, and heat, maintaining homeostasis and supporting the body's adaptive responses to internal and external changes. After reaching the shoulder, the San Jiao meridian continues internally to the chest, where it intersects with the Pericardium meridian. From there, it descends through the diaphragm to the upper, middle, and lower burners—the San Jiao's three divisions that respectively govern the respiratory and cardiovascular systems (upper Jiao), digestion and transformation of food (middle Jiao), and elimination and reproductive functions (lower Jiao). A branch of the meridian also ascends from the chest to the neck, tracing upward along the side of the neck to behind the ear, looping over the ear and temple, then ending at the outer end of the eyebrow—near the Gallbladder meridian point GB1. Along this upward route, it connects with the ears, throat, and temples, influencing auditory function and our capacity for clear communication and perception. Thus, the San Jiao is a bridge—internally between major organ systems, externally along the body's energetic contours, and metaphysically between our inner regulation and outer expression. It plays a crucial role in harmonizing internal environments and mediating the flow between Heaven (upper), Humanity (middle), and Earth (lower) within the body's energy system.

Emotionally, the San Jiao Meridian is associated with connection, harmony, and balance, helping to unify emotional and energetic states. When the energy of this meridian flows smoothly, it promotes emotional cohesion, allowing individuals to feel connected to themselves and others. However, imbalances in the

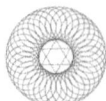

San Jiao can lead to feelings of disconnection, stress, and emotional fragmentation. These imbalances may manifest as frustration, difficulty finding harmony in relationships, or a pervasive sense of inner conflict. On a physical level, disrupted San Jiao energy may contribute to issues like poor circulation, fluid retention, or temperature dysregulation.

Rainbow Reiki addresses the San Jiao Meridian by harmonizing its energy flow and enhancing its ability to regulate warmth and emotional balance throughout the body. Practitioners channel Reiki energy along the meridian's pathway, using visualizations of the fire element, such as glowing orange or golden light, to stimulate warmth, vitality, and connection. Magdalene/Yeshua Reiki can infuse the meridian with compassion and love, fostering emotional cohesion and a sense of unity, while Shadow Reiki can help uncover and release underlying emotional blockages that contribute to disconnection or inner turmoil.

The San Jiao Meridian's function as a coordinator aligns it energetically with the heart chakra and the solar plexus chakra, emphasizing its role in fostering harmony between personal emotions and external relationships. By integrating chakra work with meridian balancing, Rainbow Reiki practitioners can address deeper emotional patterns and restore equilibrium. Techniques such as Reiki-infused affirmations, guided meditations focused on connection, and breathwork can further strengthen the meridian's energy flow, promoting a sense of balance and adaptability.

Through Rainbow Reiki, the San Jiao Meridian becomes a pathway for achieving emotional harmony, physical regulation, and spiritual connection. By clearing blockages and enhancing its energy, individuals can release feelings of disconnection, reduce stress, and cultivate a sense of unity within themselves and their relationships. This holistic approach nurtures not only physical well-being but also emotional resilience and a profound sense of interconnectedness, empowering individuals to embrace life with balance and harmony.

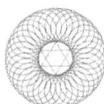

Advanced Guided Meditation to Clear Blockages and Restore Energy Flow to the San Jiao Meridian (Triple Burner/Heater, SJ)

Find a quiet, comfortable position to sit or lie down. Close your eyes and take a deep breath, inhaling calmness and exhaling any tension or stress. Begin to settle into your body, feeling grounded and present in the moment.

Bring your awareness to the San Jiao Meridian, also known as the Triple Burner or Heater Meridian. This meridian governs the regulation of body temperature, fluid movement, and emotional harmony. It flows from the ring fingers, up the outer arms, across the shoulders, and into the sides of the face near the ears. It is associated with the fire element, emphasizing connection, warmth, and harmony.

Visualize a warm, golden-orange light forming at the tips of your ring fingers. This light represents the healing energy of the San Jiao Meridian, ready to flow along its pathway. With each inhale, imagine this light traveling upward, gently illuminating the meridian, and preparing it for cleansing and restoration.

<u>Activating Rainbow Reiki Energy</u>

Now, call upon the energy of Rainbow Reiki to amplify the healing process. Visualize a vibrant stream of multicolored light descending from above, entering your body through your crown, and flowing into the pathway of the San Jiao Meridian. The Rainbow Reiki energy merges with the golden-orange light, enhancing its healing properties. Each color brings a unique frequency to balance and restore the meridian:
- Red for grounding and stability, anchoring your energy.
- Orange for emotional flow, fostering warmth and connection.
- Yellow for clarity and confidence, aligning your personal power.
- Green for renewal and harmony, balancing the physical and emotional bodies.
- Blue for calm and soothing energy, promoting relaxation.

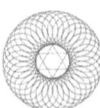

- Indigo for insight and inner understanding, supporting emotional clarity.
- Violet for spiritual alignment, connecting the meridian to higher frequencies.

Feel the Rainbow Reiki light infusing the San Jiao Meridian, dissolving any blockages and restoring its natural flow.

Releasing Blockages and Emotional Healing
As the Rainbow Reiki energy flows through the San Jiao Meridian, tune in to any areas of tension, heaviness, or stagnation. These might feel like dark patches or sluggish movement along the pathway.

Visualize the Rainbow Reiki light gently dissolving these blockages, transforming them into clear, radiant energy.

The San Jiao Meridian is deeply connected to emotional harmony and connection. It may hold patterns of stress, emotional disconnection, or difficulty regulating your inner balance. Allow these emotions or sensations to surface without judgment. Visualize the Rainbow Reiki light wrapping these feelings in warmth, releasing them with each exhale.

Affirmations
Silently or aloud, repeat these affirmations:
- *"I release tension and restore harmony within my body and emotions."*
- *"I am connected, warm, and aligned with the flow of life."*
- *"My energy flows freely, promoting balance and vitality."*

With each affirmation, sense the San Jiao Meridian becoming lighter, clearer, and more harmonious.

Restoring Energy Flow
Visualize the San Jiao Meridian glowing with warm golden-orange light, flowing smoothly from the tips of your ring fingers, up your arms, across your shoulders, and into the sides of your face near the

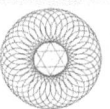

ears. This radiant light represents warmth, connection, and balance, harmonizing the energy flow of the San Jiao Meridian.

Allow the Rainbow Reiki energy to expand beyond the San Jiao Meridian, filling your entire body with connection, peace, and vitality. Feel this energy harmonizing your physical, emotional, and spiritual layers, supporting your overall well-being.

Connecting to the Fire Element
Bring your awareness to the fire element, representing warmth, transformation, and connection. Visualize a gentle flame in your heart center, glowing steadily and radiating warmth throughout your body. Imagine this flame connecting with the San Jiao Meridian, infusing it with strength, vitality, and balance. Let this fire remind you of your capacity for transformation, connection, and resilience.

Closing and Gratitude
When you feel ready, gently bring your awareness back to your breath. Visualize the Rainbow Reiki energy settling into your San Jiao Meridian, continuing its flow and healing work. Thank your body, the San Jiao Meridian, and the Rainbow Reiki energy for their support and alignment.

Take a deep breath in, anchoring this renewed sense of warmth and balance into your being, and exhale fully. Wiggle your fingers and toes, gently bringing yourself back to the present moment. When you are ready, open your eyes, carrying the sense of harmony, connection, and vitality with you into your day.

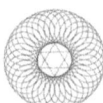

Yang Meridians - Stomach Meridian (ST)

The Stomach Meridian (ST) plays a pivotal role in supporting both physical and emotional nourishment, helping individuals cultivate a sense of groundedness and fulfillment. This yang meridian, associated with the Earth element, flows from just below the eye down the front of the body and along the legs to the second toe. Physically, the Stomach Meridian governs digestion, ensuring the body can process and absorb nutrients for energy and vitality. It is intricately linked to the stomach and other digestive organs, influencing appetite, metabolism, and overall gut health. Energetically, it serves as a channel for grounding and stability, reflecting the Earth element's qualities of nurturance and support.

Emotionally, the Stomach Meridian is associated with worry, anxiety, and the need for emotional nourishment. When balanced, this meridian fosters a sense of security and emotional fullness, allowing individuals to feel supported and grounded in their relationships and environment. However, when energy in the Stomach Meridian becomes blocked or imbalanced, it can manifest as feelings of worry, nervousness, or emotional emptiness. This may lead to patterns of overthinking, excessive neediness, or a constant search for external validation, as individuals struggle to feel "full" emotionally. Physically, this imbalance can contribute to digestive issues, nausea, or an unsettled stomach, reflecting the deep connection between emotional and physical health.

Rainbow Reiki offers a multidimensional approach to harmonizing the Stomach Meridian, addressing both the physical and emotional layers of imbalance. Practitioners work along the meridian's pathway, channeling Reiki energy infused with the grounding qualities of the Earth element, often visualized as golden or earthy light, to promote stability and a sense of wholeness. Shadow Reiki may be used to uncover subconscious patterns of insecurity or fear of abandonment that contribute to emotional neediness, while Magdalene/Yeshua Reiki brings compassion and nurturing energy, helping clients reconnect with their inner sense of worth and fulfillment.

The Stomach Meridian's connection to emotional grounding also links it energetically to the solar plexus chakra, the center of personal power and confidence. By combining meridian and chakra work, Rainbow Reiki practitioners can help clients release worry and anxiety, rebuild self-assurance, and foster a sense of inner stability. Techniques such as Reiki-infused affirmations, guided visualizations focused on nourishment, and energy work that integrates the physical and emotional layers allow for deep healing and balance.

Through Rainbow Reiki, the Stomach Meridian becomes a channel for restoring emotional and physical harmony, helping individuals feel secure, grounded, and capable of processing life's challenges. By clearing blockages and promoting energetic flow, Rainbow Reiki supports a sense of emotional fullness and nurturance, empowering clients to embrace life with confidence and stability. This holistic approach nurtures the mind, body, and spirit, fostering resilience and a deep connection to the supportive energy of the Earth element.

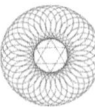

Advanced Guided Meditation to Clear Blockages and Restore Energy Flow to the Stomach Meridian (ST)

Find a quiet, comfortable place where you can sit or lie down. Close your eyes and take a deep breath, inhaling calmness and exhaling tension. Allow your body to relax as you connect with the rhythm of your breath and ground yourself in the present moment.

Bring your awareness to your Stomach Meridian, which begins just below the eyes, flows down the chest and abdomen, and extends along the front of the legs to the second toes. This meridian governs digestion, nourishment, and vitality, and is associated with the Earth element and the emotion of worry.

Visualize a golden-yellow light forming just below your eyes, representing the nurturing and balancing energy of the Stomach Meridian. With each inhale, imagine this light beginning to flow downward along the pathway of the meridian, illuminating it and preparing it for cleansing and restoration.

<u>Activating Rainbow Reiki Energy</u>

Call in the energy of Rainbow Reiki to enhance the healing process. Visualize a radiant stream of multicolored light descending from above, entering your body through your crown, and flowing into the pathway of the Stomach Meridian. This Rainbow Reiki light merges with the golden-yellow light, amplifying its power. Each color brings a specific vibration to support healing and balance:

- Red for grounding and stability, anchoring the energy of the Earth element.
- Orange for emotional release, clearing worry and self-doubt.
- Yellow for clarity, vitality, and self-confidence.
- Green for harmony and renewal, restoring balance to the digestive system.
- Blue for calmness and peace, soothing mental overactivity.
- Indigo for intuitive insight, deepening your connection to your inner wisdom.
- Violet for spiritual alignment, harmonizing the meridian with universal energy.

Feel the Rainbow Reiki light flowing along the Stomach Meridian, clearing blockages and restoring the free flow of Qi.

Releasing Blockages and Emotional Healing
As the Rainbow Reiki energy moves through the Stomach Meridian, focus on any areas of heaviness, tension, or stagnation along its pathway. These may appear as dark spots or sluggish movement. Visualize the Rainbow Reiki light gently dissolving these blockages, transforming them into clear, radiant energy.

The Stomach Meridian is often connected to worry, overthinking, and feelings of lack or inadequacy. Allow any emotions or patterns tied to these feelings to surface gently. Visualize the Rainbow Reiki light wrapping these emotions in golden warmth, helping you release them with each exhale. Feel lighter and more grounded as these energies dissolve.

Affirmations
Silently or aloud, repeat these affirmations:
- *"I release worry and trust in life's flow."*
- *"I am nourished, balanced, and supported by the earth."*
- *"My energy flows freely, promoting vitality and peace."*

With each affirmation, sense the Stomach Meridian becoming clearer, brighter, and more aligned.

Restoring Energy Flow
Visualize the Stomach Meridian glowing with vibrant golden-yellow light, flowing smoothly from just below your eyes, down through your chest, abdomen, and legs, and ending at your second toes. This radiant light symbolizes nourishment, balance, and harmony. Feel the energy flowing freely, supporting both your physical vitality and emotional stability.

Allow the Rainbow Reiki energy to expand beyond the Stomach Meridian, filling your entire body with grounding, clarity, and renewal. Feel this energy harmonizing your physical, emotional, and spiritual layers, creating a state of holistic well-being.

Connecting to the Earth Element
Bring your awareness to the Earth element, representing grounding, stability, and sustenance. Visualize yourself standing on rich, fertile soil, feeling Earth's support beneath your feet. Imagine this grounding energy merging with your Stomach Meridian, anchoring you in a sense of security, balance, and vitality.

Closing and Gratitude
When you feel ready, gently bring your awareness back to your breath. Visualize the Rainbow Reiki energy settling into your Stomach Meridian, continuing its flow and healing work. Thank your body, the Stomach Meridian, and the Rainbow Reiki energy for their support and alignment.

Take a deep breath in, anchoring this renewed sense of nourishment and balance into your being, and exhale fully. Wiggle your fingers and toes, gently bringing yourself back to the present moment. When you are ready, open your eyes, carrying the sense of stability, clarity, and vitality with you into your day.

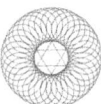

Yang Meridian – Bladder Meridian (BL)
The Bladder Meridian (BL) is recognized as a powerful channel for releasing physical, emotional, and energetic stagnation, fostering security, resilience, and adaptability. This yang meridian, associated with the water element, is the longest meridian in the body, flowing from the inner corner of the eyes over the head and down along the back, legs, and feet to the little toe. Physically, the Bladder Meridian governs fluid elimination, kidney function, and the detoxification of the body, playing a vital role in maintaining hydration and balance within the body's systems. It is closely linked to the Kidney Meridian, emphasizing its role in supporting life force energy, or Qi, and maintaining emotional stability.

Emotionally, the Bladder Meridian is tied to fear and insecurity, reflecting its deep connection to the body's survival instincts and the ability to adapt to stress. When this meridian is balanced, it helps cultivate emotional resilience, grounding, and a sense of security. However, blockages or disruptions in the Bladder Meridian can lead to heightened fear, anxiety, and an inability to manage stress effectively. These imbalances may manifest as physical symptoms, such as tension in the lower back, urinary issues, or fatigue, mirroring the emotional burden of fear and insecurity. Prolonged imbalances can erode one's emotional foundation, making it challenging to navigate life's uncertainties with confidence.

Rainbow Reiki addresses the Bladder Meridian with a holistic and multidimensional approach, combining energy clearing, grounding practices, and emotional healing techniques. Practitioners channel Reiki energy along the meridian's pathway, visualizing the cleansing and nourishing qualities of the water element, often represented as flowing blue or turquoise light, to dissolve blockages and restore balance. Shadow Reiki is particularly effective in uncovering deep-seated fears or insecurities stored in the meridian, while Magdalene/Yeshua Reiki brings a nurturing energy that fosters self-compassion and emotional stability. These practices support the release of energetic patterns that contribute to fear and allow for the restoration of calm and resilience.

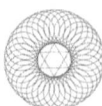

The Bladder Meridian's influence on security and emotional resilience also connects it energetically to the root chakra, which governs grounding and survival. By integrating work on this chakra with meridian balancing, Rainbow Reiki practitioners can address the foundational energies of safety and stability. Techniques such as Reiki-infused affirmations focused on security, breathwork for releasing fear, and guided meditations on fluidity and adaptability enhance the meridian's healing process.

Through Rainbow Reiki, the Bladder Meridian becomes a pathway for profound physical, emotional, and energetic renewal. By clearing blockages and harmonizing its flow, practitioners help clients release fear and insecurity, strengthen their sense of grounding, and build emotional resilience. This holistic approach supports not only the body's detoxification processes but also a deep sense of inner stability and adaptability, empowering individuals to face life's challenges with confidence and grace.

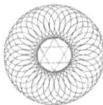

Advanced Guided Meditation to Clear Blockages and Restore Energy Flow to the Bladder Meridian (BL)

Find a quiet, comfortable place where you can sit or lie down. Close your eyes, and take a deep breath in through your nose, letting your belly expand, and exhale fully through your mouth, releasing tension. Bring your focus inward and ground yourself in the present moment.

Bring your awareness to the Bladder Meridian, the longest meridian in the body. It begins at the inner corners of the eyes, flows over the head, down along the spine, and continues along the backs of the legs to the little toes. This meridian governs fluid balance, detoxification, and the release of fear, and is connected to the water element.

Visualize a deep blue light forming at the inner corners of your eyes, symbolizing the cleansing and harmonizing energy of the Bladder Meridian. With each inhale, imagine this light flowing gently along the meridian's pathway, illuminating it and preparing it for healing and renewal.

<u>Activating Rainbow Reiki Energy</u>

Call upon the powerful energy of Rainbow Reiki to amplify the healing process. Visualize a radiant stream of multicolored light descending from above, entering your body through your crown, and merging with the deep blue light of the Bladder Meridian. Each color of the Rainbow Reiki energy supports the healing of the meridian:
- Red for grounding and stability, anchoring the energy into the body.
- Orange for emotional release, helping to let go of fear and tension.
- Yellow for clarity and courage, fostering confidence and resilience.
- Green for renewal and harmony, balancing the physical and emotional systems.
- Blue for calm and inner peace, soothing emotional and mental turbulence.

- Indigo for deep insight, enhancing connection to inner wisdom.
- Violet for spiritual alignment, linking the meridian to higher frequencies of healing.

Feel the Rainbow Reiki energy flowing along the Bladder Meridian, dissolving blockages and restoring the free flow of Qi.

Releasing Blockages and Emotional Healing
As the Rainbow Reiki energy moves through the Bladder Meridian, tune in to any areas of heaviness, tension, or stagnation. These may appear as dark patches, tightness, or sluggish movement along the pathway. Visualize the multicolored light gently dissolving these blockages, transforming them into radiant, flowing energy.

The Bladder Meridian is closely tied to the emotion of fear and the ability to release what no longer serves you. If any feelings of fear, insecurity, or resistance arise, acknowledge them with compassion. Visualize the Rainbow Reiki energy wrapping these emotions in light and gently releasing them with each exhale. Feel yourself becoming lighter and freer as these energies dissolve.

Affirmations
Silently or aloud, repeat these affirmations:
- "I release fear and embrace trust in life's flow."
- "I am supported and resilient, free to release and renew."
- "My energy flows freely, grounding me in balance and peace."

With each affirmation, sense the Bladder Meridian becoming clearer, brighter, and more harmonious.

Restoring Energy Flow
Visualize the Bladder Meridian glowing with a vibrant deep blue light, flowing smoothly from the inner corners of your eyes, over your head, down your spine, and along the backs of your legs to your little toes. This radiant light represents release, balance, and grounding. Feel the energy flowing freely, supporting your physical vitality and emotional stability.

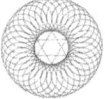

Allow the Rainbow Reiki energy to expand beyond the Bladder Meridian, filling your entire body with peace, clarity, and strength. Feel this energy harmonizing your physical, emotional, and spiritual layers, creating a sense of holistic well-being.

Connecting to the Water Element
Bring your awareness to the water element, symbolizing flow, adaptability, and cleansing. Visualize a calm, flowing river or a serene body of water. Imagine its gentle, purifying energy merging with your Bladder Meridian, reinforcing your ability to release fear and flow with life's natural rhythms.

Closing and Gratitude
When you feel ready, gently bring your awareness back to your breath. Visualize the Rainbow Reiki energy settling into your Bladder Meridian, continuing its flow and healing work. Thank your body, the Bladder Meridian, and the Rainbow Reiki energy for their support and alignment.

Take a deep breath in, anchoring this renewed sense of balance and flow into your being, and exhale fully. Wiggle your fingers and toes, gently bringing yourself back to the present moment. When you are ready, open your eyes, carrying the sense of release, stability, and peace with you into your day.

Yang Meridian - Gallbladder Meridian (GB)

The Gallbladder Meridian (GB) is a key channel for fostering clarity, courage, and decisive action, supporting the ability to navigate life's challenges with confidence. This yang meridian, associated with the wood element, flows from the outer corner of the eyes over the head and along the sides of the body to the fourth toe, reflecting its connection to balance, adaptability, and dynamic movement. Physically, the Gallbladder Meridian governs the gallbladder organ's role in digestion and bile production, aiding the body in processing fats and eliminating waste. Energetically, it influences the ability to process thoughts and emotions, supporting assertiveness, decision-making, and stress management.

Emotionally, the Gallbladder Meridian is closely tied to decision-making, courage, and emotional flexibility. When balanced, it promotes clarity, assertiveness, and the ability to make confident choices, enabling individuals to approach life with direction and purpose. However, blockages or imbalances in the Gallbladder Meridian can lead to indecisiveness, timidity, or resentment, as well as feelings of being overwhelmed or stuck. These emotional patterns may manifest physically as headaches, tension along the sides of the body, or digestive discomfort, highlighting the deep interplay between emotional and physical health. Chronic stress or unresolved anger can further strain the Gallbladder Meridian, amplifying its effects on well-being.

Rainbow Reiki works with the Gallbladder Meridian to harmonize its flow, release blockages, and empower individuals to act with clarity and courage. Practitioners channel Reiki energy along the meridian's pathway, visualizing the vibrant green light of the wood element, symbolizing growth, adaptability, and renewal. Shadow Reiki is particularly effective in uncovering hidden fears or self-doubt that may inhibit assertiveness, while Pleiadian and Arcturian Reiki bring high-frequency energies that uplift and align the meridian's function with higher states of emotional balance and clarity. These techniques help dissolve energetic stagnation, allowing for the free flow of decision-making energy.

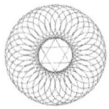

The Gallbladder Meridian's connection to assertiveness and direction also aligns it energetically with the solar plexus chakra, the center of personal power and confidence. By integrating chakra work with meridian balancing, Rainbow Reiki practitioners can address the deeper patterns that contribute to indecision or emotional stagnation. Techniques such as Reiki-infused affirmations focused on courage and clarity, guided meditations for releasing resentment, and energy transmissions that emphasize action and confidence further enhance the meridian's healing process.

Through Rainbow Reiki, the Gallbladder Meridian becomes a channel for transformation, supporting not only physical digestion but also the emotional processing of life's choices and challenges. By clearing blockages and promoting energetic harmony, practitioners help clients cultivate the courage, assertiveness, and clarity needed to make empowered decisions. This holistic approach nurtures the body, mind, and spirit, fostering resilience, adaptability, and a renewed sense of purpose in life.

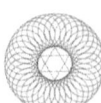

Advanced Guided Meditation to Clear Blockages and Restore Energy Flow to the Gallbladder Meridian (GB)

Find a quiet and comfortable place to sit or lie down. Close your eyes and take a deep breath, inhaling calmness and exhaling tension. Allow your body to relax and your mind to settle. Bring your focus inward, grounding yourself in the present moment.

Bring your awareness to the Gallbladder Meridian, which begins at the outer corners of the eyes, flows over the head and neck, down the sides of the body, and along the outer legs, ending at the fourth toes. This meridian governs decision-making, courage, and emotional resilience, and is connected to the wood element and the emotion of frustration or anger.

Visualize a vibrant green light forming at the outer corners of your eyes, representing the cleansing and balancing energy of the Gallbladder Meridian. With each inhale, imagine this light flowing gently along the meridian's pathway, illuminating it and preparing it for renewal and restoration.

<u>Activating Rainbow Reiki Energy</u>
Call upon the energy of Rainbow Reiki to amplify the healing process. Visualize a radiant stream of multicolored light descending from above, entering your body through your crown, and merging with the green light of the Gallbladder Meridian. Each color of the Rainbow Reiki energy brings specific frequencies to clear, restore, and balance the meridian:
- Red for grounding and vitality, anchoring your energy.
- Orange for emotional release, helping to clear frustration and irritability.
- Yellow for clarity, boosting confidence and decision-making abilities.
- Green for balance, renewal, and harmony with the natural flow of life.
- Blue for calmness and peace, soothing emotional turbulence.
- Indigo for insight, deepening your understanding of emotional patterns and life choices.

- Violet for spiritual connection, aligning the meridian with higher wisdom.

Feel this multicolored light flowing along the Gallbladder Meridian, dissolving blockages and restoring the free flow of Qi.

Releasing Blockages and Emotional Healing
As the Rainbow Reiki energy moves through the Gallbladder Meridian, focus on any areas of tension, heaviness, or stagnation. These may feel like dark patches or sluggish energy along the pathway. Visualize the Rainbow Reiki light gently dissolving these blockages, transforming them into clear, flowing energy.

The Gallbladder Meridian often holds patterns of indecision, frustration, or emotional stagnation. Allow these emotions or patterns to surface gently without judgment. Visualize the Rainbow Reiki energy wrapping these feelings in healing light, releasing them with each exhale. Feel lighter and more confident as these energies dissolve.

Affirmations
Silently or aloud, repeat these affirmations:
- *"I release frustration and embrace clarity and courage."*
- *"I trust my ability to make confident decisions with ease."*
- *"My energy flows freely, supporting harmony and balance."*

With each affirmation, sense the Gallbladder Meridian becoming lighter, clearer, and more aligned.

Restoring Energy Flow
Visualize the Gallbladder Meridian glowing with vibrant green light, flowing smoothly from the outer corners of your eyes, over your head, down your neck and sides, and along the outer legs to your fourth toes. This radiant light represents decision-making, courage, and emotional flow. Feel the energy flowing freely, supporting your mental clarity and emotional resilience.

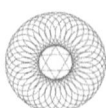

Allow the Rainbow Reiki energy to expand beyond the Gallbladder Meridian, filling your entire body with clarity, peace, and vitality. Feel this energy harmonizing your physical, emotional, and spiritual layers, creating a sense of holistic well-being.

Connecting to the Wood Element
Bring your awareness to the wood element, symbolizing growth, flexibility, and vision. Visualize yourself standing in a lush forest, surrounded by tall, strong trees swaying gently with the breeze. Feel their rooted strength and natural adaptability. Imagine this energy merging with your Gallbladder Meridian, reinforcing your ability to grow, adapt, and make decisions with confidence.

Closing and Gratitude
When you feel ready, gently bring your awareness back to your breath. Visualize the Rainbow Reiki energy settling into your Gallbladder Meridian, continuing to flow freely and supporting your well-being. Thank your body, the Gallbladder Meridian, and the Rainbow Reiki energy for their support and alignment. Take a deep breath in, anchoring this renewed sense of balance, courage, and clarity into your being, and exhale fully. Wiggle your fingers and toes, gently bringing yourself back to the present moment. When you are ready, open your eyes, carrying the sense of decisiveness, harmony, and vitality with you into your day.

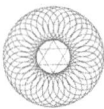

The Governing and Conception Vessels

The Governing Vessel (GV) and Conception Vessel (CV), also known as the two "extraordinary" meridians, play a foundational role in regulating the body's overall energy flow and balancing yin and yang dynamics. These two meridians serve as the main channels through which all other meridians connect, amplifying their influence on physical, emotional, and spiritual well-being. Together, they form the microcosmic orbit, a continuous loop of energy that harmonizes the body's internal energy system, supporting vitality, emotional stability, and spiritual alignment.

The Governing Vessel (GV) runs along the spine, extending from the tailbone to the top of the head and connecting to all yang meridians. This meridian is associated with yang energy, representing confidence, action, and outward expression. Physically, it governs the health of the back, spine, and head, supporting posture and vitality. Emotionally and energetically, the Governing Vessel influences courage, assertiveness, and the ability to take initiative. When blocked, individuals may feel weak, anxious, or overly passive, struggling to take action or assert themselves. In Rainbow Reiki, practitioners channel energy along this meridian to clear blockages, restore yang energy, and strengthen the individual's ability to act decisively and confidently. Shadow Reiki may be used to address deep-seated fears or insecurities, while Pleiadian Reiki introduces uplifting, dynamic frequencies to reignite courage and vitality.

The Conception Vessel (CV) flows along the front of the body, from the perineum to the lower lip, and connects to all yin meridians. This meridian is associated with yin energy, symbolizing nurturing, emotional receptivity, and inner reflection. Physically, it governs the abdomen, chest, and reproductive organs, playing a vital role in supporting hormonal balance and emotional healing. Energetically, the Conception Vessel fosters self-nurturing, emotional connection, and the ability to receive love and support. Blockages in this meridian may lead to self-doubt, emotional withdrawal, or difficulty forming meaningful connections with oneself or others. Rainbow Reiki practitioners work with the Conception Vessel to restore balance, channeling soothing, nurturing energy to release emotional

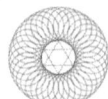

wounds and enhance self-compassion. Magdalene/Yeshua Reiki is particularly effective in infusing this meridian with divine love and healing, supporting the individual in embracing emotional openness and receptivity.

By harmonizing the Governing and Conception Vessels, Rainbow Reiki creates a dynamic balance between yin and yang energies, integrating the qualities of action and receptivity, confidence and self-nurturing. Techniques such as Reiki-infused breathwork along the microcosmic orbit, visualizations of flowing energy, and affirmations focusing on balance and harmony further enhance this work. When these extraordinary meridians are aligned and flowing freely, they act as the foundation for overall energy flow, supporting vitality, emotional equilibrium, and spiritual alignment.

Through Rainbow Reiki, the Governing and Conception Vessels become powerful conduits for deep healing and transformation. By addressing blockages and imbalances in these meridians, practitioners help clients restore confidence, emotional resilience, and inner harmony. This holistic approach fosters a balanced state of being, empowering individuals to navigate life with strength, openness, and a profound sense of connection to themselves and the universe.

Advanced Guided Meditation to Clear Blockages and Restore Energy Flow to the Governing and Conception Vessels (GV & CV)
Find a quiet space where you can sit or lie down comfortably. Close your eyes, and take a few deep breaths, inhaling calm and exhaling tension. Feel yourself becoming grounded in the present moment, your body relaxing with each exhale.

Begin by bringing your awareness to the Governing Vessel (GV) and Conception Vessel (CV)—two of the most important energetic pathways in the body. The Governing Vessel runs along the back of the body, starting at the tailbone and extending up the spine to the crown of the head, governing yang energy. The Conception Vessel flows along the front of the body, beginning at the perineum and ascending to the lower lip, governing yin energy. Together, they form the microcosmic orbit, harmonizing the flow of Qi throughout the entire body.

Visualize a soft golden light forming at your lower abdomen, the central hub where these vessels intersect. This light symbolizes balance and vitality, gently pulsing and expanding with each breath. With each inhale, imagine this light illuminating the pathways of the Governing and Conception Vessels, preparing them for cleansing and renewal.

<u>Activating Rainbow Reiki Energy</u>
Call upon the powerful energy of Rainbow Reiki to support the healing process. Visualize a radiant stream of multicolored light descending from above, entering your body through your crown, and filling your lower abdomen with vibrant energy. The Rainbow Reiki light begins to flow into the pathways of the Governing and Conception Vessels, amplifying their energy with the unique frequencies of each color:
- Red for grounding, anchoring your energy into Earth.
- Orange for emotional release and creative flow.
- Yellow for clarity, confidence, and personal power.
- Green for balance, renewal, and harmony.
- Blue for calm, soothing emotional and mental turbulence.

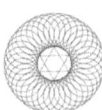

- Indigo for intuition and insight, enhancing your connection to inner wisdom.
- Violet for spiritual alignment, linking your energy to the divine.

Feel this Rainbow Reiki light flowing through the microcosmic orbit, circulating upward along the Governing Vessel and downward along the Conception Vessel, creating a continuous loop of harmony and flow.

Releasing Blockages and Emotional Healing
As the Rainbow Reiki energy flows through these vessels, focus on any areas of tension, heaviness, or stagnation. These might feel like dark patches or sluggish movement along the pathways. Visualize the multicolored light gently dissolving these blockages, transforming them into radiant, flowing energy.

The Governing Vessel often holds yang-related blockages, such as feelings of weakness, passivity, or fear of action, while the Conception Vessel may carry yin-related imbalances, such as emotional withdrawal, insecurity, or difficulty nurturing oneself. Allow these emotions or sensations to surface without judgment. Visualize the Rainbow Reiki energy wrapping them in light, releasing them from your body and energy field with each exhale.

Affirmations
Silently or aloud, repeat these affirmations:
- *"I release all blockages and embrace the free flow of energy within me."*
- *"I balance my yin and yang energies, creating harmony in my body and spirit."*
- *"I am grounded, empowered, and connected to the divine flow of life."*

With each affirmation, feel the Governing and Conception Vessels becoming clearer, brighter, and more harmonious.

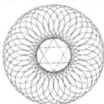

Restoring Energy Flow
Visualize the Governing Vessel glowing with vibrant light as energy flows upward from the base of your spine to the crown of your head. At the crown, the energy transitions into the Conception Vessel, flowing downward along the front of your body to the lower abdomen. This creates a continuous loop of radiant energy, circulating effortlessly through the microcosmic orbit.

Feel this flow harmonizing your yin and yang energies, balancing your physical, emotional, and spiritual layers. Allow the Rainbow Reiki energy to amplify this circulation, filling your entire body with vitality, clarity, and peace.

Connecting to Divine Alignment
Bring your awareness to the divine connection created by the Governing and Conception Vessels. Visualize this loop of energy connecting you to Earth below and the cosmos above, forming a bridge between your physical body and the universal flow of life. Feel the infinite support and alignment flowing through you, strengthening your connection to your higher self and the universe.

Closing and Gratitude
When you feel ready, gently bring your awareness back to your breath. Visualize the Rainbow Reiki energy settling into the Governing and Conception Vessels, continuing to flow freely and supporting your well-being. Thank your body, these extraordinary vessels, and the Rainbow Reiki energy for their healing and alignment.

Take a deep breath in, anchoring this renewed sense of harmony and flow into your being, and exhale fully. Wiggle your fingers and toes, gently bringing yourself back to the present moment. When you are ready, open your eyes, carrying the sense of balance, clarity, and divine connection with you into your day.

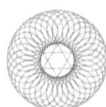

Root Chakra (Muladhara)
Location: Base of the spine, around the perineum.
Body Connection: Lower body, including the legs, feet, hips, and the base of the spine.

System Influence: Connected to the skeletal system, legs, feet, and large intestine, as well as the adrenal glands. The root chakra is associated with stability, survival, and grounding. Physically, it influences bone health, posture, and lower-body strength. An imbalance can lead to issues like lower back pain, sciatica, constipation, or adrenal fatigue.

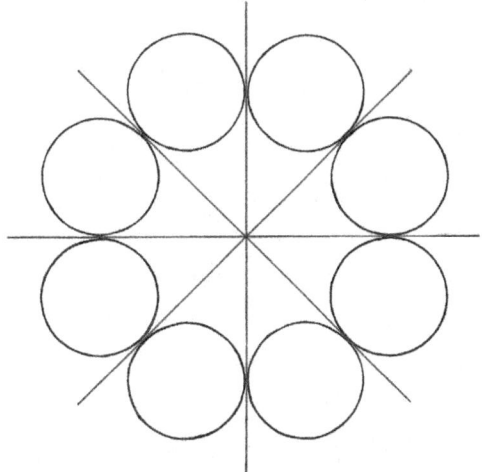

Rainbow Reiki Root Chakra Symbol

Root Chakra Teachings Across Traditions
The Root Chakra, or Muladhara, is the foundation of the energy system, representing grounding, survival, and connection to the physical world. Each tradition—Egyptian, Tibetan, Arcturian, and Pleiadian—offers unique insights into this vital energy center, while biblical references provide further depth and understanding.

In Egyptian teachings, the Root Chakra aligns with Earth and is symbolized by the god Geb, representing stability and physical grounding. Ancient Egyptians believed the connection to Earth's energy through the Root Chakra was crucial for maintaining balance in life. It was considered the gateway to physical health and resilience, tying directly to Ma'at's principles of harmony and order. The red stone carnelian was often used to amplify the chakra's grounding energy.

In Tibetan teachings, the Root Chakra connects to the Earth element and the principle of "lung," or wind energy, which governs survival instincts and physical vitality. Practices such as Tibetan sound healing use deep, resonant tones to bring balance to the chakra, allowing the body and spirit to stabilize. Visualizing the Root Chakra as a glowing red lotus, deeply rooted in the earth, is a common meditation technique used to strengthen its energy.

From an Arcturian perspective, the Root Chakra is seen as the anchor for the soul's incarnation on Earth. Arcturian teachings emphasize that clearing blockages in the Root Chakra allows for the free flow of higher-dimensional energy into the body, facilitating spiritual ascension while maintaining a strong connection to Earth. The Arcturians often focus on energy transmissions that clear karmic patterns related to survival, scarcity, and fear, ensuring the soul can ground itself in stability and trust.

The Pleiadian perspective views the Root Chakra as a portal for activating Earth-consciousness and connecting to Gaia's living energy grid. Pleiadians teach that balancing this chakra helps individuals harmonize with Earth's rhythms and the cycles of nature, fostering abundance and security. Rituals involving light codes and frequencies specific to the Root Chakra help align it with Earth's crystalline core.

The biblical reference for the Root Chakra can be found in Genesis 2:7, "Then the LORD God formed man from the dust of the ground and breathed into his nostrils the breath of life, and man became a living being." This verse emphasizes humanity's connection to the earth and the life-giving energy provided by God. The Root Chakra's red energy can also be linked to the "blood of life," symbolizing vitality, survival, and the grounding force of divine creation.

Together, these teachings provide a multidimensional understanding of the Root Chakra, highlighting its role as the foundation for physical and spiritual well-being. Working with this chakra encourages stability, trust, and alignment with both earthly and cosmic energies, enabling one to thrive in all aspects of life.

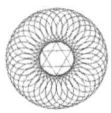

Basic Root Chakra Meditation

Find a comfortable space to sit or lie down. Ensure your spine is straight, and your body is relaxed. When you are ready, close your eyes and take a deep breath.

Take a moment to notice your body. Feel the support of the earth beneath you, whether you are sitting on a chair, the floor, or lying down.

Take a deep inhale through your nose, and as you exhale through your mouth, let go of any tension or distractions. This meditation will help ground your energy and connect you to your root chakra, the center of stability and security.

Grounding Breath
Breathe in deeply through your nose for a count of four. Hold your breath gently for a count of two. Exhale slowly through your mouth for a count of six. As you breathe, imagine your breath moving down into your lower body, connecting you to the base of your spine and the area of your root chakra.

Visualization
Imagine a glowing red sphere at the base of your spine. This is your root chakra, your energetic center of grounding, safety, and stability. With each inhale, visualize this red light growing brighter, warmer, and steadier. With each exhale, imagine releasing any fear, tension, or instability into the earth, where it is transformed into nourishing energy.

Feel this red light expanding, radiating warmth and strength throughout your body.

Affirmations
Silently or softly repeat these affirmations to yourself:
- *"I am grounded, safe, and secure."*
- *"I trust the support of the earth beneath me."*
- *"I release fear and embrace stability."*
- *"I am deeply connected to my body and my roots."*

Feel these words sinking into your consciousness, filling you with a sense of safety and connection.

As you continue to focus on your root chakra, imagine roots growing from the base of your spine, traveling deep into the earth. These roots anchor you firmly to the ground, providing nourishment, strength, and stability.

Feel the energy of the earth flowing back up through these roots, into your body, filling you with a sense of grounding and balance.

Take a few final breaths, allowing the red light at your root chakra to glow softly. Know that this energy is always with you, grounding and supporting you throughout your day.

When you are ready, gently bring your awareness back to the present moment. Wiggle your fingers and toes, stretch if you like, and slowly open your eyes.

Take a moment to notice how you feel—stable, grounded, and at peace.

Advanced Root Chakra Focused Healing and Cleansing Meditation
This guided meditation is designed to help you connect deeply with the energy of your root chakra, cleanse and balance it, and become familiar with its unique energetic feeling. Integrating Rainbow Reiki techniques, this meditation incorporates the multidimensional energies of Usui, Shadow, Arcturian, Pleiadian, Egyptian Sekhem-Seichim, and Magdalene/Yeshua Reiki to harmonize the root chakra on physical, emotional, and spiritual levels.

Find a quiet, comfortable place to sit or lie down. Close your eyes and take several deep breaths, inhaling deeply through your nose and exhaling slowly through your mouth. With each exhale, let go of tension, allowing your body to relax.

Set your intention: *"I open myself to the advanced healing energies of Rainbow Reiki to cleanse, balance, and connect with the energy of my root chakra, grounding me in strength and stability."*

Grounding and Connection
Visualize roots growing from the base of your spine and the soles of your feet, extending deep into Earth's crystalline core. Feel Gaia's grounding energy rising through these roots, entering your body, and anchoring you securely to Earth. Simultaneously, envision a column of vibrant rainbow light descending from the cosmos, entering your crown chakra, and flowing down to your root chakra.

Feel the merging of these energies at the base of your spine, creating a stable and harmonious foundation for healing.

Activating the Root Chakra
Bring your awareness to your root chakra, located at the base of your spine. Visualize it as a glowing orb of red light, spinning gently. Notice its size, brightness, and movement. Allow yourself to sense the unique energetic feeling of your root chakra—its warmth, density, or vibration.

Affirm: *"I am deeply connected to Earth and fully supported by its energy."*

Cleansing the Root Chakra

Visualize a deep indigo light from Shadow Reiki entering your root chakra. This light gently dissolves any blockages, fears, or stagnant energies that may be stored there. As the indigo light works, sense heaviness or tension being released from your root chakra.

Once the clearing feels complete, imagine a soft rose-pink light from Magdalene/Yeshua Reiki flowing into the root chakra. This light fills the space with love, safety, and a sense of nurturing, healing any emotional wounds associated with the root chakra.

Affirm: *"I release all fear and insecurity, allowing my root chakra to be fully cleansed and healed."*

Strengthening and Energizing

Visualize Egyptian Sekhem-Seichim Reiki energy entering your root chakra as golden, geometric patterns. These patterns reinforce the strength and stability of your root chakra, aligning it with Earth's crystalline grid.

Next, see vibrant rainbow light flowing into your root chakra from Pleiadian and Arcturian Reiki. This light activates the multidimensional aspects of your root chakra, connecting it to higher frequencies while maintaining its grounding function.

Feel your root chakra becoming more vibrant, balanced, and deeply connected to both Earth and universal energies.

Affirm: *"My root chakra is strong, balanced, and radiates vitality and stability."*

Becoming Familiar with the Root Chakra's Energetic Feeling

Spend a few moments tuning into the unique energetic sensation of your root chakra. Notice its warmth, vibration, or any other sensations that arise. Observe how it feels when it is balanced and aligned, and allow yourself to connect deeply with its energy.

Affirm: *"I am attuned to the energy of my root chakra, grounded and secure in my being."*

Integration and Multidimensional Alignment
Expand your awareness to include the Earth Star Chakra, located about six inches below your feet. Visualize this chakra as a radiant orb of earthy, grounding light. See the Earth Star and root chakras connecting, forming a harmonious flow of grounding energy that aligns you with the Earth's ascension grid.

Imagine your root chakra linking with the energetic layers of your body, integrating its strength and stability into your emotional, mental, and spiritual fields. Feel this energy spreading through your entire being, creating balance and security.

Affirm: *"I am fully grounded, supported, and aligned with Earth's energy and the universe."*

Closing and Gratitude
Bring your focus back to your heart center. Visualize a glowing orb of rainbow light within your chest, pulsating with gratitude and peace. Allow this light to radiate outward, integrating all the healing energies you have received.

Take a moment to thank your root chakra for its role in your stability and strength, and express gratitude for the Rainbow Reiki energies and your ability to heal and grow.

When you feel ready, gently bring your awareness back to the present moment. Wiggle your fingers and toes, stretch lightly, and open your eyes.

Post-Meditation Care
- Hydration: Drink water to support the grounding and detoxification process.
- Grounding Practices: Spend time in nature, walk barefoot on grass, or engage in light physical activity to reinforce grounding.

- Reflection: Journal any sensations, insights, or shifts you experienced during the meditation.

This meditation can be practiced regularly to maintain the strength, balance, and vitality of your root chakra while deepening your connection to its energy and the high frequencies of Rainbow Reiki.

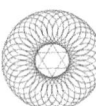

Sacral Chakra (Svadhisthana)
Location: Lower abdomen, about two inches below the navel.
Body Connection: Reproductive organs, bladder, kidneys, and lower digestive organs.
System Influence: Linked to the reproductive system, urinary system, and aspects of the lymphatic system. This chakra governs creativity, sexuality, and emotions. Physically, it impacts reproductive health, kidney function, and fluid balance in the body. Imbalances can lead to reproductive issues, urinary problems, and lower back pain, as well as emotional sensitivity or difficulty with relationships.

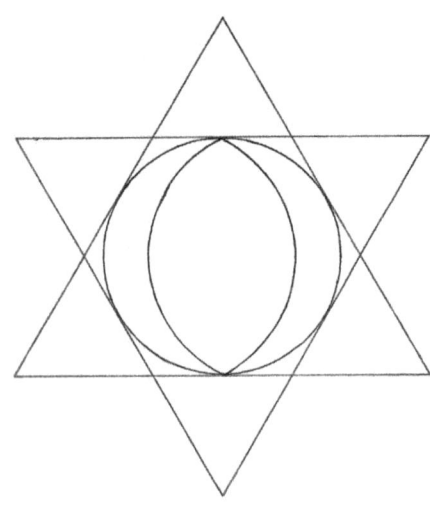
Rainbow Reiki Sacral Chakra Symbol

Sacral Chakra Teachings Across Traditions
The Sacral Chakra, or Svadhisthana, governs creativity, sensuality, emotional flow, and connection to pleasure. This energy center, located just below the navel, is a bridge between physical and emotional expression. Teachings from Egyptian, Tibetan, Arcturian, and Pleiadian traditions offer profound insights into the Sacral Chakra, while biblical references add spiritual depth and support.

In Egyptian teachings, the Sacral Chakra is tied to fertility, creation, and the waters of the Nile, symbolizing the ebb and flow of life's energy. It is associated with the goddess Hathor, who represents love, joy, music, and fertility. The Egyptians believed that this chakra was the seat of creative power, not just for reproduction but also for artistic and spiritual pursuits. Orange carnelian and amber were sacred stones used to amplify the creative energy of this chakra.

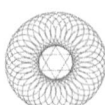

In Tibetan teachings, the Sacral Chakra is connected to the water element and the balance of emotions. Tibetan practices view this chakra as the source of "Tsa," or the flow of life-force energy (prana) within the body's subtle channels. Balancing the Sacral Chakra through Tibetan meditation techniques and mantras, such as those invoking the energy of compassion, helps to harmonize emotions and awaken creative potential. Visualization of a radiant orange lotus in this chakra is often used to cultivate emotional fluidity and joy.

From an Arcturian perspective, the Sacral Chakra is seen as a gateway to multidimensional emotional healing. Arcturians teach that unprocessed emotions stored in the Sacral Chakra can block creative and spiritual growth. Their methods often involve high-frequency energy transmissions to clear past trauma, enhance emotional flow, and activate divine creativity. This chakra is considered essential for reconnecting with one's soul purpose and aligning with higher-dimensional energy.

The Pleiadian perspective highlights the Sacral Chakra as the center of emotional intuition and divine connection to the creative forces of the universe. Pleiadians view the Sacral Chakra as a channel for co-creation with the cosmos, where the energy of joy and abundance flows freely. They teach that by harmonizing the Sacral Chakra with light frequencies and aligning it with the planetary water grid, one can achieve emotional balance and unlock their full creative potential.

The biblical reference for the Sacral Chakra can be found in John 7:38, "Whoever believes in me, as Scripture has said, rivers of living water will flow from within them." This verse reflects the fluid, life-giving energy of the Sacral Chakra, symbolizing emotional abundance, creative inspiration, and the flow of divine energy within. The association with living water underscores the importance of keeping this chakra open and balanced for spiritual and emotional well-being.

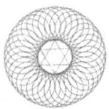

Through the lens of these traditions, the Sacral Chakra emerges as a powerful energy center that governs the flow of creativity, emotions, and relationships. Balancing and clearing this chakra allows for deeper emotional healing, enhanced creativity, and alignment with the universal forces of love and joy.

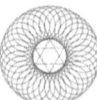

Basic Sacral Chakra Meditation

Find a quiet, comfortable space where you can sit or lie down. Keep your spine straight and your body relaxed. Close your eyes and take a deep breath.

Take a moment to settle into the stillness. Feel the gentle rhythm of your breath as it flows in and out. Allow your body to release any tension, particularly in your lower abdomen and hips.

The sacral chakra, located just below your navel, is your center of emotion, creativity, and pleasure. In this meditation, we'll focus on balancing and strengthening this energy center.

Grounding Breath
Breathe in deeply through your nose for a count of four, feeling your belly rise. Hold the breath gently for a count of two. Exhale slowly through your mouth for a count of six, feeling your belly fall. Repeat this breathing pattern, inviting relaxation with each breath.

Visualization
Imagine a warm, glowing orange light forming just below your navel. This is the energy of your sacral chakra. With each inhale, see this orange light becoming brighter and more vibrant. With each exhale, release any feelings of guilt, shame, or creative blocks. Let them dissolve into the air. Feel the orange light expanding, filling your lower abdomen with warmth and vitality. Imagine it flowing like water, smooth and rhythmic, symbolizing balance and emotional flow.

Affirmations
As you continue to breathe deeply, silently or softly repeat these affirmations:
- *"I embrace my creativity and passion."*
- *"I honor my emotions and allow them to flow freely."*
- *"I deserve pleasure and joy in my life."*
- *"I am connected to my body and its wisdom."*

Let these affirmations sink deeply into your consciousness, strengthening your connection to your sacral chakra.

Connection to Water
The sacral chakra is associated with the element of water. As you focus on your orange light, imagine yourself surrounded by gentle, flowing water—perhaps a stream, river, or warm ocean.

Feel this water washing over you, cleansing your energy and freeing you from stagnation. It carries away any heaviness, leaving you refreshed and renewed.

Take a few final breaths, allowing the orange light in your sacral chakra to glow softly. Know that this energy center is balanced and thriving, supporting your creativity, emotions, and joy.

When you are ready, gently bring your awareness back to the present moment. Wiggle your fingers and toes, stretch gently if you like, and slowly open your eyes.

Notice how you feel—lighter, more creative, and deeply connected to yourself.

Advanced Rainbow Reiki Sacral Chakra Focused Healing, Cleansing, and Energetic Connection

This advanced guided meditation focuses on the sacral chakra, the energy center associated with creativity, emotions, relationships, and the flow of life force energy. Using the multidimensional frequencies of Rainbow Reiki, including Usui, Shadow, Arcturian, Pleiadian, Egyptian Sekhem-Seichim, and Magdalene/Yeshua Reiki, this meditation will help you cleanse, balance, and connect deeply with the energetic essence of your sacral chakra.

Find a quiet, comfortable space to sit or lie down. Close your eyes and take several deep breaths, inhaling deeply through your nose and exhaling slowly through your mouth. Allow your body to relax, releasing any tension with each exhale.

Set your intention: *"I invite the advanced energies of Rainbow Reiki to cleanse, balance, and deepen my connection with my sacral chakra, enhancing creativity, emotional flow, and divine alignment."*

<u>Grounding and Cosmic Connection</u>
Visualize roots extending from your feet deep into Earth's crystalline core. Feel Gaia's nurturing energy rising through these roots, grounding and supporting you. Simultaneously, envision a vibrant column of rainbow light descending from the cosmos, entering your crown chakra, and flowing down to your sacral chakra, just below your navel.

Sense these energies merging in your sacral chakra, creating a balanced foundation for healing and alignment.

<u>Activating the Sacral Chakra</u>
Bring your awareness to your sacral chakra. Visualize it as a vibrant orange orb, spinning gently and radiating warm, creative energy. Notice its size, movement, and brightness. Allow yourself to tune into the unique energetic feeling of your sacral chakra—its flow, warmth, or vibration.

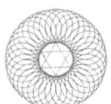

Affirm: *"I am connected to the flow of life and the creative energy within me."*

Cleansing the Sacral Chakra
Visualize a deep indigo light from Shadow Reiki entering your sacral chakra. This light gently dissolves blockages, emotional wounds, or stagnant energies related to past experiences, relationships, or creative blocks. Feel the energy releasing any fear, guilt, or shame stored in this center.

Once the cleansing feels complete, imagine a soft rose-pink light from Magdalene/Yeshua Reiki flowing into the sacral chakra. This light fills the space with love, compassion, and emotional balance, nurturing your sacral chakra and restoring its vibrancy.

Affirm: *"I release all emotional and energetic blockages, allowing my sacral chakra to be fully cleansed and healed."*

Strengthening and Energizing
Visualize golden geometric patterns from Egyptian Sekhem-Seichim Reiki flowing into your sacral chakra. These sacred patterns weave through the chakra, strengthening its energetic integrity and aligning it with the divine flow of life.

Next, imagine vibrant rainbow light from Pleiadian and Arcturian Reiki streaming into your sacral chakra. This light activates the multidimensional aspects of this energy center, connecting it to cosmic creativity and emotional flow.

Feel your sacral chakra becoming more vibrant, balanced, and deeply aligned with both Earth and universal energies.

Affirm: *"My sacral chakra is vibrant, balanced, and aligned with divine creativity and emotional harmony."*

Becoming Familiar with the Energetic Feeling of the Sacral Chakra
Spend a few moments focusing on the unique energetic sensation of your sacral chakra. Notice its warmth, vibration, or flow. Observe

how it feels when it is balanced and connected to your creative and emotional essence. Allow yourself to deepen your awareness of its energy and its role in your life.

Affirm: *"I am attuned to the energy of my sacral chakra, flowing with creativity, joy, and emotional freedom."*

Integration and Multidimensional Alignment
Expand your awareness to include the energetic connections of your sacral chakra to your physical, emotional, and spiritual bodies. Visualize its energy radiating outward, harmonizing with your auric field and connecting with the Earth Star Chakra and Soul Star Chakra.

Imagine your sacral chakra aligning with the multidimensional grids of Earth and the cosmos, integrating its creative and emotional energies with your divine blueprint. Feel this alignment bringing balance, joy, and creative flow into your entire being.

Affirm: *"My sacral chakra is fully integrated, balanced, and aligned with my highest vibrational potential."*

Closing and Gratitude
Bring your awareness back to your heart center. Visualize a glowing orb of rainbow light within your chest, pulsating with gratitude and peace. Allow this light to radiate outward, integrating all the healing energies you have received.

Take a moment to thank your sacral chakra for its role in your creativity and emotional well-being. Express gratitude for the Rainbow Reiki energies and your ability to heal and grow.

When you feel ready, gently bring your awareness back to the present moment. Wiggle your fingers and toes, stretch lightly, and open your eyes.

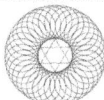

Post-Meditation Care
- Hydration: Drink water to support the release of emotional and energetic toxins.
- Journaling: Reflect on any insights or sensations you experienced, noting creative ideas or emotional shifts.
- Creative Activities: Engage in an activity that brings you joy and allows you to express yourself, such as art, dance, or writing.

This meditation can be practiced regularly to maintain the strength, balance, and vitality of your sacral chakra while deepening your connection to its energy and the transformative frequencies of Rainbow Reiki.

Solar Plexus Chakra (Manipura)

Location: Upper abdomen, around the stomach area.

Body Connection: Digestive organs, including the stomach, liver, pancreas, and intestines.

System Influence: Influences the digestive system, pancreas, liver, and metabolic processes. The solar plexus chakra relates to personal power, confidence, and self-esteem. It regulates digestion and metabolism. Blockages or imbalances can manifest as digestive issues, ulcers, liver problems, and feelings of powerlessness or lack of self-esteem.

Rainbow Reiki Solar Plexus Chakra Symbol

Solar Plexus Chakra Teachings Across Traditions

The Solar Plexus Chakra, or Manipura, is the center of personal power, confidence, will, and self-esteem. Located above the navel and below the chest, it governs individuality, ambition, and the ability to manifest intentions. Egyptian, Tibetan, Arcturian, and Pleiadian teachings, along with biblical references, shed light on this chakra's transformative energy and its profound impact on personal and spiritual growth.

In Egyptian teachings, the Solar Plexus Chakra is linked to the sun god Ra, symbolizing the fiery energy of the sun and its power to illuminate, transform, and sustain life. The Egyptians viewed this chakra as the seat of divine will, where inner strength is harnessed to overcome obstacles and manifest one's destiny. The golden energy of this chakra was often associated with solar imagery, symbolizing enlightenment, courage, and resilience. Citrine and tiger's eye stones were used to amplify this energy and balance the fiery aspect of the Solar Plexus.

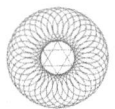

In Tibetan teachings, the Solar Plexus Chakra is connected to the fire element and is a focal point for "inner heat" or *tummo* practices. Tibetan monks use meditation techniques to stoke the fire within the Solar Plexus, awakening vitality, clarity, and spiritual empowerment. This chakra is considered the hub where prana, or life-force energy, gathers, creating a radiant light that fuels the body and mind. A glowing golden lotus is visualized during meditative practices to strengthen inner will and align the energy flow.

The Arcturian teachings see the Solar Plexus Chakra as the gateway to multidimensional self-empowerment. It is viewed as the energy center where fear, self-doubt, and limiting beliefs are stored. Clearing blockages in this chakra allows individuals to reclaim their personal power and align with their higher purpose. Arcturians often use energetic transmissions to activate this chakra, creating a golden vortex that helps individuals move beyond fear and connect with their higher selves to manifest intentions with clarity and confidence.

From the Pleiadian perspective, the Solar Plexus Chakra is described as the core of the "I AM" presence, where divine will meets human individuality. They teach that balancing this chakra enables one to harmonize their personal desires with the universal flow of energy, creating abundance and purpose. Pleiadian practices often include channeling golden light codes to release fear and activate confidence, enabling individuals to take bold steps toward their soul's mission.

The biblical reference for the Solar Plexus Chakra can be found in 2 Timothy 1:7, "For the spirit God gave us does not make us timid, but gives us power, love and self-discipline." This verse reflects the essence of the Solar Plexus Chakra as a center of strength, courage, and divine power. It reminds us that fear and insecurity can be transformed through faith and alignment with divine will.

The Solar Plexus Chakra is a transformative energy center, bridging the physical and spiritual aspects of personal empowerment. Across

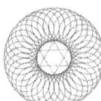

traditions, it is seen as a source of inner strength, willpower, and courage. Balancing this chakra allows individuals to move past fear and insecurity, align their personal will with divine purpose, and confidently manifest their goals. By embracing the golden energy of the Solar Plexus Chakra, one can radiate confidence and live authentically.

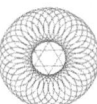

Basic Solar Plexus Chakra Meditation
Find a quiet and comfortable space to sit or lie down. Keep your spine straight and your body relaxed. Close your eyes and take a deep breath.

Take a moment to settle into the rhythm of your breath. Breathe deeply and slowly, letting your body soften and relax with each exhale.

The solar plexus chakra, located in your upper abdomen near your stomach, is your center of confidence, personal power, and will. This meditation will help you balance and strengthen this energy center, fostering clarity, self-assurance, and inner strength.

Grounding Breath
Breathe in deeply through your nose for a count of four, feeling your upper abdomen expand. Hold the breath gently for a count of two. Exhale slowly through your mouth for a count of six, letting your abdomen soften. Repeat this breathing pattern, focusing your awareness on the area just above your navel.

Visualization
Imagine a bright, golden-yellow light glowing in your upper abdomen. This is your solar plexus chakra, your source of inner power and self-confidence. With each inhale, see this golden light growing brighter, warmer, and more vibrant. With each exhale, release any feelings of doubt, fear, or insecurity. Let them dissolve into the air. Feel this golden light radiating outward, filling your entire body with strength and determination.

Affirmations
As you continue to breathe and focus on the glowing light, silently or softly repeat these affirmations:
- *"I am confident and empowered."*
- *"I trust myself and my decisions."*
- *"I release fear and embrace my personal power."*
- *"I am worthy of success and happiness."*

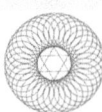

Allow these affirmations to resonate deeply, building your sense of self-belief and inner strength.

Connection to Fire
The solar plexus chakra is associated with the element of fire. As you focus on the golden light, imagine it as a steady, warm flame burning brightly in your abdomen.
- This flame represents your willpower and determination.
- Feel its warmth spreading through your body, energizing and empowering you.
- Trust that this fire will always guide and sustain you.

Take a few final breaths, allowing the golden light at your solar plexus to glow softly. Know that this energy center is balanced and strong, supporting your confidence, courage, and personal power.

When you are ready, gently bring your awareness back to the present moment. Wiggle your fingers and toes, stretch gently if you like, and open your eyes.

Take a moment to notice how you feel—empowered, clear, and connected to your inner strength.

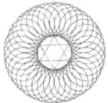

Advanced Solar Plexus Chakra Focused Healing, Cleansing, and Energetic Connection

The solar plexus chakra, located in the upper abdomen, governs personal power, confidence, and self-esteem. This advanced guided meditation uses the multidimensional energies of Rainbow Reiki—including Usui, Shadow, Arcturian, Pleiadian, Egyptian Sekhem-Seichim, and Magdalene/Yeshua Reiki—to cleanse, strengthen, and harmonize the solar plexus chakra, helping you connect deeply with its energy.

Find a quiet and comfortable place to sit or lie down. Close your eyes and take several deep breaths, inhaling deeply through your nose and exhaling slowly through your mouth. Allow your body to relax with each exhale, releasing tension and inviting calmness.

Set your intention: *"I welcome the advanced energies of Rainbow Reiki to cleanse, balance, and deepen my connection to my solar plexus chakra, empowering my confidence, clarity, and inner strength."*

Grounding and Cosmic Alignment
Visualize roots extending from your feet into Earth's crystalline core. Feel Gaia's grounding energy rising through these roots, anchoring and stabilizing you. Simultaneously, imagine a vibrant column of rainbow light descending from the cosmos, entering your crown chakra, and flowing down to your solar plexus chakra, located just above your navel.

Sense the merging of Earth and cosmic energies in your solar plexus, creating a harmonious foundation for healing.

Activating the Solar Plexus Chakra
Bring your awareness to your solar plexus chakra. Visualize it as a bright, golden-yellow orb spinning gently. Notice its size, movement, and brightness. Feel the unique energy of your solar plexus chakra—its warmth, intensity, and vibrational power.

Affirm: *"I am strong, confident, and fully aligned with my personal power."*

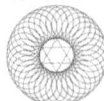

Cleansing the Solar Plexus Chakra
Visualize a deep indigo light from Shadow Reiki entering your solar plexus chakra. This light gently dissolves blockages, fears, and limiting beliefs stored in this energy center. Feel the indigo light clearing emotional patterns related to self-doubt, control, or fear of failure.

Once the clearing is complete, imagine a soft rose-pink light from Magdalene/Yeshua Reiki filling your solar plexus chakra. This light infuses it with love, courage, and a deep sense of self-worth, restoring its natural brilliance.

Affirm: *"I release all fears and limitations, allowing my solar plexus chakra to shine brightly with confidence and clarity."*

Strengthening and Energizing
Visualize golden geometric patterns from Egyptian Sekhem-Seichim Reiki flowing into your solar plexus chakra. These sacred patterns stabilize and fortify its structure, enhancing its ability to radiate strength and personal power.

Next, see a vibrant rainbow light from Pleiadian and Arcturian Reiki streaming into your solar plexus chakra. This light activates the multidimensional aspects of this energy center, connecting it to universal energy and higher frequencies.

Feel your solar plexus chakra becoming more vibrant, balanced, and aligned with your inner power and cosmic energy.

Affirm: *"My solar plexus chakra is vibrant, balanced, and radiates my true strength and confidence."*

Becoming Familiar with the Energetic Feeling of the Solar Plexus Chakra
Spend a few moments focusing on the unique energetic sensation of your solar plexus chakra. Notice its warmth, intensity, or radiance. Observe how it feels when it is balanced, open, and connected to

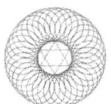

your personal power. Deepen your awareness of its role as the center of confidence, clarity, and action.

Affirm: *"I am attuned to the energy of my solar plexus chakra, empowered by my inner strength and radiant confidence."*

Integration and Multidimensional Alignment
Expand your awareness to include the energetic connections of your solar plexus chakra to your emotional, mental, and spiritual bodies. Visualize its energy radiating outward, harmonizing with your auric field and connecting with the Earth Star Chakra and Soul Star Chakra.

Imagine your solar plexus chakra aligning with the multidimensional grids of Earth and the cosmos, integrating its energy with your divine blueprint. Feel this alignment enhancing your self-esteem, clarity, and ability to take empowered action.

Affirm: *"My solar plexus chakra is fully integrated, balanced, and aligned with my highest vibrational potential."*

Closing and Gratitude
Bring your awareness back to your heart center. Visualize a glowing orb of rainbow light within your chest, pulsating with gratitude and healing energy. Allow this light to radiate outward, integrating all the healing energies you have received.

Take a moment to thank your solar plexus chakra for its role in your strength and confidence. Express gratitude for the Rainbow Reiki energies and your ability to heal and grow.

When you feel ready, gently bring your awareness back to the present moment. Wiggle your fingers and toes, stretch lightly, and open your eyes.

Post-Meditation Care
- Hydration: Drink water to support the release of emotional and energetic blockages.

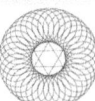

- Journaling: Reflect on any insights or sensations you experienced, noting shifts in confidence or clarity.
- Empowered Action: Take a step toward a goal or decision that aligns with your personal power.

This meditation can be practiced regularly to maintain the strength, balance, and vitality of your solar plexus chakra while deepening your connection to its energy and the multidimensional frequencies of Rainbow Reiki.

Heart Chakra (Anahata)

Location: Center of the chest, around the heart area.

Body Connection: Heart, lungs, chest, arms, and hands.

System Influence: Connected to the cardiovascular and respiratory systems and the thymus gland, which is part of the immune system. The heart chakra is associated with love, compassion, and emotional well-being. Physically, it supports heart health, lung function, and circulation. Imbalances may result in heart or lung issues, immune deficiencies, and emotional challenges like difficulty in forming connections, loneliness, or resentment.

Rainbow Reiki Heart Chakra Symbol

Please Note: The heart chakra symbol depicted in this book represents only a portion of the full sacred heart chakra glyph used in Rainbow Reiki. To receive and work with the complete heart chakra symbol, one must be attuned through Rainbow Reiki Levels One and Two. This is due to the sacredness, potency, and advanced energetic nature of this healing modality. The heart is not just a center of love—it is the key that unlocks the entire Rainbow Reiki system. Full access to its vibration and geometric intelligence must be approached with reverence and preparation.

Heart Chakra Teachings Across Traditions

The Heart Chakra, or Anahata, is the center of love, compassion, and healing, located at the center of the chest. It serves as a bridge between the physical and spiritual realms, connecting the lower and higher chakras. In Egyptian teachings, this chakra aligns with the goddess Hathor, a symbol of love, joy, and nurturing. The Egyptians viewed the heart as the seat of the soul and the gateway to harmony and balance, emphasizing the importance of living in alignment with Ma'at, the principle of universal order and truth. Green stones like

malachite and emerald were sacred tools for opening the heart to divine love and healing.

In Tibetan teachings, the Heart Chakra is associated with the air element, symbolizing the lightness and openness required for compassion to flow freely. Tibetan meditation practices often involve visualizing a glowing green lotus at the heart center, radiating unconditional love and kindness. These practices focus on cultivating *metta*, or loving-kindness, and balancing the subtle energies of the body to release pain and suffering.

From an Arcturian perspective, the Heart Chakra is seen as the portal for connecting with higher dimensions and anchoring divine love into the human experience. The Arcturians teach that clearing the Heart Chakra of past trauma and pain allows one to expand their capacity for compassion and unity consciousness. Through energy healing techniques, they help individuals access a higher frequency of love, transforming the heart into a radiant source of multidimensional healing.

The Pleiadians view the Heart Chakra as the key to co-creation and alignment with the universal flow of love. They teach that the energy of this chakra enables deep connection with others and the collective consciousness, facilitating harmony on both individual and cosmic levels. Pleiadian practices often include working with pink or green light frequencies to activate the heart's potential for unconditional love and spiritual expansion.

Biblical references also reflect the energy of the Heart Chakra, as seen in Proverbs 4:23: "Above all else, guard your heart, for everything you do flows from it." This verse underscores the heart's vital role as the source of life, love, and spiritual energy. The Heart Chakra's qualities of compassion, forgiveness, and healing are deeply connected to the teachings of love found throughout scripture.

The Heart Chakra is a sacred center of balance and connection, integrating physical and spiritual energies. It is the seat of emotional

healing, divine love, and compassion, guiding individuals to live in harmony with themselves, others, and the universe. By balancing this chakra, one can cultivate a deeper sense of unity, peace, and unconditional love.

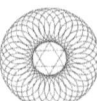

Basic Heart Chakra Meditation

Find a comfortable, quiet space to sit or lie down. Keep your spine straight and your body relaxed. Close your eyes and take a deep breath.

Take a moment to tune into your breath. Inhale deeply through your nose, and exhale slowly through your mouth. With each breath, let go of any tension in your body. Feel yourself becoming calm and present.

The heart chakra, located in the center of your chest, is the bridge between the physical and spiritual realms. This meditation will help you balance and strengthen this energy center, cultivating love, compassion, and harmony.

Grounding Breath

Breathe deeply into your chest for a count of four, feeling your chest expand. Hold your breath gently for a count of two, allowing your heart space to open. Exhale slowly for a count of six, letting go of any tension or emotional heaviness. Repeat this breathing pattern, allowing your heart to feel lighter with each exhale.

Visualization

Visualize a soft, emerald-green light glowing at the center of your chest. This is the energy of your heart chakra. With each inhale, imagine this green light becoming brighter, warmer, and more expansive. With each exhale, release any feelings of sadness, resentment, or tension. Allow them to dissolve into the air. Feel this green light expanding outward, surrounding your entire chest with love and compassion.

Affirmations

As you breathe deeply and focus on the glowing light, silently or softly repeat these affirmations:
- *"I am open to giving and receiving love."*
- *"I forgive myself and others."*
- *"My heart is filled with compassion and peace."*
- *"I am connected to the infinite love within me."*

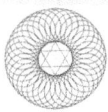

Let these affirmations resonate deeply, filling you with warmth and emotional balance.

Connection to Air
The heart chakra is associated with the element of air. As you breathe, imagine the light in your chest moving like a gentle breeze, soft and flowing.
- Feel this breeze clearing away any emotional blockages.
- Allow it to bring in a sense of lightness, freedom, and connection.
- Let this energy remind you of your innate ability to love and be loved.

Take a moment to bring to mind something or someone you feel grateful for. Visualize this gratitude as a wave of green light radiating from your heart and extending outward.

Feel the warmth of this gratitude filling your entire body and flowing freely into the world around you.

Take a few final breaths, allowing the emerald-green light in your heart chakra to glow softly. Know that this energy center is balanced and thriving, supporting your emotional well-being and connection to others.

When you are ready, gently bring your awareness back to the present moment. Wiggle your fingers and toes, stretch if you like, and slowly open your eyes.

Take a moment to notice how you feel—lighter, more loving, and deeply connected to your heart.

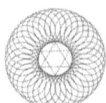

Advanced Heart Chakra Focused Healing, Cleansing, and Energetic Connection

The heart chakra, located at the center of the chest, serves as the bridge between the physical and spiritual realms, governing love, compassion, and emotional balance. This advanced guided meditation uses the multidimensional energies of Rainbow Reiki—including Usui, Shadow, Arcturian, Pleiadian, Egyptian Sekhem-Seichim, and Magdalene/Yeshua Reiki—to cleanse, strengthen, and connect you deeply with the heart chakra's energy.

Find a quiet, comfortable place to sit or lie down. Close your eyes and take several deep breaths, inhaling deeply through your nose and exhaling slowly through your mouth. Allow your body to relax, releasing tension with each exhale.

Set your intention: *"I welcome the advanced energies of Rainbow Reiki to cleanse, heal, and connect me to the energy of my heart chakra, deepening my capacity for love, compassion, and divine connection."*

<u>Grounding and Cosmic Alignment</u>
Visualize roots extending from your feet into the crystalline core of Earth. Feel Gaia's nurturing energy rising through these roots, anchoring and grounding you. Simultaneously, envision a vibrant column of rainbow light descending from the cosmos, entering your crown chakra, and flowing down to your heart chakra, at the center of your chest.

Feel these Earth and cosmic energies merging in your heart chakra, creating a harmonious foundation for healing and balance.

<u>Activating the Heart Chakra</u>
Bring your awareness to your heart chakra. Visualize it as a glowing orb of emerald-green light, spinning gently and radiating warmth. Notice its size, brightness, and rhythm. Allow yourself to sense the unique energetic feeling of your heart chakra—its pulsation, openness, or vibration.

Affirm: *"I am open to love, compassion, and divine connection."*

Cleansing the Heart Chakra
Visualize a deep indigo light from Shadow Reiki entering your heart chakra. This light gently dissolves blockages, emotional pain, or stagnant energies related to past heartbreaks, grief, or fear. Feel the energy clearing and releasing any heaviness or tension in your chest.

Once the clearing is complete, imagine a soft rose-pink light from Magdalene/Yeshua Reiki flowing into your heart chakra. This light infuses it with unconditional love, forgiveness, and divine compassion, nurturing and restoring its natural brilliance.

Affirm: *"I release all emotional and energetic burdens, allowing my heart chakra to be fully cleansed and healed."*

Strengthening and Energizing
Visualize golden geometric patterns from Egyptian Sekhem-Seichim Reiki flowing into your heart chakra. These sacred patterns stabilize and fortify its structure, enhancing its ability to radiate love and harmony.

Next, see vibrant rainbow light from Pleiadian and Arcturian Reiki streaming into your heart chakra. This light activates the multidimensional aspects of your heart energy, connecting it to universal love and higher frequencies.

Feel your heart chakra becoming more vibrant, balanced, and deeply aligned with both earthly and cosmic energies.

Affirm: *"My heart chakra is radiant, balanced, and aligned with unconditional love and divine harmony."*

Becoming Familiar with the Energetic Feeling of the Heart Chakra
Spend a few moments focusing on the unique energetic sensation of your heart chakra. Notice its warmth, openness, or gentle pulsation. Observe how it feels when it is balanced, healed, and connected to the flow of love and compassion. Deepen your

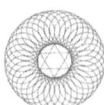

awareness of its energy and its role as the bridge between your physical and spiritual self.

Affirm: *"I am attuned to the energy of my heart chakra, radiating love, compassion, and divine connection."*

Integration and Multidimensional Alignment
Expand your awareness to include the energetic connections of your heart chakra to your emotional, mental, and spiritual bodies. Visualize its energy radiating outward, harmonizing with your auric field and connecting with the Earth Star Chakra and Soul Star Chakra.

Imagine your heart chakra aligning with the multidimensional grids of Earth and the cosmos, integrating its energy with your divine blueprint. Feel this alignment enhancing your ability to give and receive love, fostering inner peace and harmony.

Affirm: *"My heart chakra is fully integrated, balanced, and aligned with my highest vibrational potential."*

Bring your awareness back to your heart center. Visualize a glowing orb of rainbow light within your chest, pulsating with gratitude and healing energy. Allow this light to radiate outward, integrating all the healing energies you have received.

Take a moment to thank your heart chakra for its role in your love and compassion. Express gratitude for the Rainbow Reiki energies and your ability to heal and grow.

When you feel ready, gently bring your awareness back to the present moment. Wiggle your fingers and toes, stretch lightly, and open your eyes.

Post-Meditation Care
- Hydration: Drink water to support the release of emotional and energetic blockages.

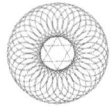

- Reflection: Journal any insights, emotions, or sensations you experienced during the meditation.
- Heart-Centered Practices: Engage in acts of kindness, forgiveness, or gratitude to reinforce the balance of your heart chakra.

This meditation can be practiced regularly to maintain the strength, balance, and vitality of your heart chakra while deepening your connection to its energy and the transformative frequencies of Rainbow Reiki.

Throat Chakra (Vishuddha)

Location: Throat area.
Body Connection: Throat, neck, mouth, jaw, and thyroid gland.

System Influence: Influences the respiratory system, vocal cords, mouth, and thyroid, which regulates metabolism. This chakra is related to communication, self-expression, and truth. Physically, it supports the health of the throat, thyroid, and vocal cords. Imbalances may manifest as sore throats, thyroid imbalances, neck pain, or difficulty in expressing oneself or being honest.

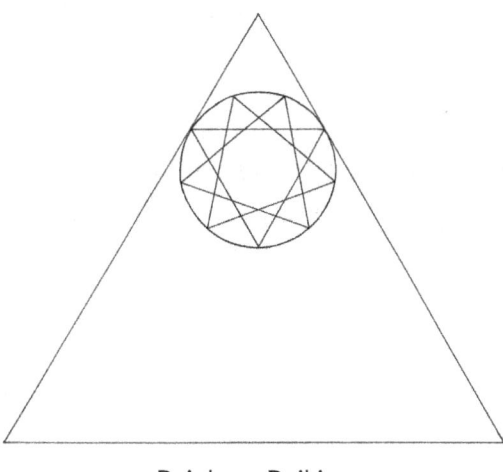

Rainbow Reiki
Throat Chakra Symbol

Throat Chakra Across Traditions

The Throat Chakra, or Vishuddha, governs communication, self-expression, and truth. Located at the throat, it is the center of authentic expression and the ability to speak one's truth with clarity and confidence. In Egyptian teachings, this chakra is associated with Thoth, the god of wisdom, writing, and language. Thoth was believed to oversee the power of words and their ability to create reality, emphasizing the sacred nature of speech and its role in manifesting truth. Turquoise and lapis lazuli were often used to enhance the energy of the Throat Chakra, promoting clear and truthful communication.

In Tibetan traditions, the Throat Chakra is linked to the ether element, representing the vast space of potential where thoughts and words take form. Tibetan meditation practices often focus on chanting and mantra repetition to harmonize this energy center, allowing for the expression of divine truth and wisdom. The use of sound vibration in these practices is considered essential for clearing

blockages and aligning the throat with higher frequencies of consciousness.

Arcturian teachings view the Throat Chakra as a multidimensional communication center, where higher guidance and intuitive insights are translated into words and actions. They emphasize the importance of clearing ancestral and karmic imprints that may restrict self-expression. Through energetic transmissions, the Arcturians work to activate the Throat Chakra's capacity for telepathic and intuitive communication, allowing individuals to speak with authenticity and align their words with their soul's purpose.

The Pleiadian perspective highlights the Throat Chakra as a portal for co-creative expression, where divine inspiration flows into the physical realm. Pleiadians teach that this chakra plays a vital role in manifesting one's intentions through words, which hold the power to shape reality. Their practices often include visualizing blue light frequencies to clear blockages and strengthen the connection between the Throat Chakra and higher realms of communication and creativity.

Biblical references to the Throat Chakra include Proverbs 18:21, "The tongue has the power of life and death …" This verse underscores the importance of words as a creative force, reflecting the power of the Throat Chakra in shaping both personal and collective realities. The ability to speak with integrity and authenticity aligns with biblical teachings on truth and the divine nature of expression.

The Throat Chakra represents the connection between thought and spoken word, serving as a bridge between inner truth and external communication. Balancing this chakra allows for the free flow of authentic expression, enhancing one's ability to communicate clearly and align words with purpose. It is a powerful center for creativity, integrity, and the manifestation of truth in all aspects of life.

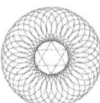

Basic Throat Chakra Meditation
Find a quiet, comfortable space to sit or lie down. Keep your spine straight and your body relaxed. Close your eyes and take a deep breath.

Take a moment to tune into your breath. Inhale deeply through your nose, and exhale slowly through your mouth. Let go of any tension in your neck, shoulders, or jaw.

The throat chakra, located at the center of your throat, is your center of truth and expression. This meditation will help you balance and strengthen this energy center, encouraging clear and authentic communication.

Grounding Breath
- Breathe deeply into your throat for a count of four, feeling your breath expand this space.
- Hold the breath gently for a count of two, allowing this area to feel calm and open.
- Exhale slowly through your mouth for a count of six, releasing tension or blockages.
- Repeat this cycle, allowing your throat to feel lighter and more open with each breath.

Visualization
- Visualize a bright, sky-blue light glowing at the center of your throat. This is the energy of your throat chakra.
- With each inhale, imagine this blue light growing brighter and clearer, filling your throat and neck.
- With each exhale, release any feelings of hesitation, fear, or self-doubt. Let them dissolve into the air.
- Feel this blue light expanding, surrounding your throat with clarity, truth, and confidence.

Affirmations
As you continue to breathe and focus on the glowing light, silently or softly repeat these affirmations:
- "I express myself clearly and confidently."

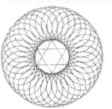

- *"I speak my truth with love and compassion."*
- *"My voice is powerful and authentic."*
- *"I listen deeply to myself and others."*

Allow these affirmations to resonate deeply, strengthening your connection to your inner truth.

Connection to Ether
The throat chakra is associated with the element of ether or space. As you breathe, imagine this blue light expanding into the space around you.
- Feel this light clearing and opening the pathway for your thoughts and words.
- Let it connect you to the vastness of your truth and the universe's wisdom.

Take a moment to thank your throat chakra for its role in helping you express yourself authentically. Feel gratitude for the power of your voice and the clarity of your communication.

Take a few final breaths, allowing the blue light at your throat chakra to glow softly. Know that this energy center is balanced and thriving, supporting your ability to express your truth.

When you are ready, gently bring your awareness back to the present moment. Wiggle your fingers and toes, stretch if you like, and slowly open your eyes.

Take a moment to notice how you feel—clear, open, and deeply connected to your voice and truth.

Advanced Throat Chakra Focused Healing, Cleansing, and Energetic Connection

The throat chakra, located at the center of the throat, governs communication, self-expression, and authenticity. This advanced guided meditation uses the multidimensional energies of Rainbow Reiki—including Usui, Shadow, Arcturian, Pleiadian, Egyptian Sekhem-Seichim, and Magdalene/Yeshua Reiki—to cleanse, strengthen, and help you connect deeply with the throat chakra's energy.

Find a quiet and comfortable place to sit or lie down. Close your eyes and take several deep breaths, inhaling deeply through your nose and exhaling slowly through your mouth. Allow your body to relax with each exhale, releasing tension and inviting calmness.

Set your intention: *"I welcome the advanced energies of Rainbow Reiki to cleanse, balance, and deepen my connection to my throat chakra, enhancing my authenticity, expression, and truth."*

Grounding and Cosmic Connection
Visualize roots extending from your feet deep into Earth's crystalline core. Feel Gaia's nurturing energy rising through these roots, anchoring and stabilizing you. At the same time, envision a vibrant column of rainbow light descending from the cosmos, entering your crown chakra, and flowing down to your throat chakra.

Feel these Earth and cosmic energies merging in your throat chakra, creating a stable and harmonious foundation for healing.

Activating the Throat Chakra
Bring your awareness to your throat chakra, located at the center of your throat. Visualize it as a glowing orb of blue light, spinning gently and radiating clarity. Notice its size, movement, and brightness. Allow yourself to sense the unique energetic feeling of your throat chakra—its vibration, coolness, or flow.

Affirm: *"I am aligned with my truth, and my voice is clear and authentic."*

Cleansing the Throat Chakra
Visualize a deep indigo light from Shadow Reiki entering your throat chakra. This light gently dissolves blockages, fears, or stagnant energies related to self-expression, communication, or speaking your truth. Feel the energy clearing any resistance or tension in your throat.

Once the clearing feels complete, imagine a soft rose-pink light from Magdalene/Yeshua Reiki filling your throat chakra. This light infuses it with love, compassion, and the courage to express yourself authentically and with kindness.

Affirm: *"I release all fear and resistance, allowing my throat chakra to be fully cleansed and healed."*

Strengthening and Energizing
Visualize golden geometric patterns from Egyptian Sekhem-Seichim Reiki flowing into your throat chakra. These sacred patterns stabilize and fortify its structure, enhancing its ability to channel clear, authentic communication.

Next, see vibrant rainbow light from Pleiadian and Arcturian Reiki streaming into your throat chakra. This light activates the multidimensional aspects of this energy center, connecting it to universal truth and divine expression.

Feel your throat chakra becoming more vibrant, balanced, and aligned with your ability to express yourself and communicate authentically.

Affirm: *"My throat chakra is clear, balanced, and radiates truth and authenticity."*

Becoming Familiar with the Energetic Feeling of the Throat Chakra
Spend a few moments focusing on the unique energetic sensation of your throat chakra. Notice its vibration, flow, or sense of lightness. Observe how it feels when it is balanced and open, allowing you to communicate with clarity and confidence. Deepen

your awareness of its energy and its role in your self-expression and connection with others.

Affirm: *"I am attuned to the energy of my throat chakra, expressing my truth with clarity, kindness, and confidence."*

Integration and Multidimensional Alignment
Expand your awareness to include the energetic connections of your throat chakra to your emotional, mental, and spiritual bodies. Visualize its energy radiating outward, harmonizing with your auric field and connecting with the Earth Star Chakra and Soul Star Chakra.

Imagine your throat chakra aligning with the multidimensional grids of Earth and the cosmos, integrating its energy with your divine blueprint. Feel this alignment enhancing your ability to speak, listen, and create with authenticity and purpose.

Affirm: *"My throat chakra is fully integrated, balanced, and aligned with my highest vibrational potential."*

Closing and Gratitude
Bring your awareness back to your heart center. Visualize a glowing orb of rainbow light within your chest, pulsating with gratitude and healing energy. Allow this light to radiate outward, integrating all the healing energies you have received.

Take a moment to thank your throat chakra for its role in your self-expression and communication. Express gratitude for the Rainbow Reiki energies and your ability to heal and grow.

When you feel ready, gently bring your awareness back to the present moment. Wiggle your fingers and toes, stretch lightly, and open your eyes.

Post-Meditation Care
- Hydration: Drink water to support the release of energetic blockages. Warm tea can also help soothe the throat area.

- Reflection: Journal any insights or sensations you experienced, noting shifts in clarity or confidence in your communication.
- Practice Authentic Expression: Engage in an activity that allows you to express yourself, such as writing, singing, or speaking your truth in a conversation.

This meditation can be practiced regularly to maintain the strength, balance, and vitality of your throat chakra while deepening your connection to its energy and the multidimensional frequencies of Rainbow Reiki.

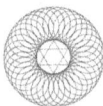

Third Eye Chakra (Ajna)

Location: Between the eyebrows, slightly above the bridge of the nose.

Body Connection: Brain, eyes, ears, and pituitary gland.

System Influence: Connected to the nervous system, endocrine system (specifically the pituitary gland), and the brain. The third eye chakra is associated with intuition, perception, and insight. Physically, it influences vision, mental clarity, and hormonal regulation via the pituitary gland. Imbalances can lead to headaches, eye problems, hormonal imbalances, or difficulty with intuition and focus.

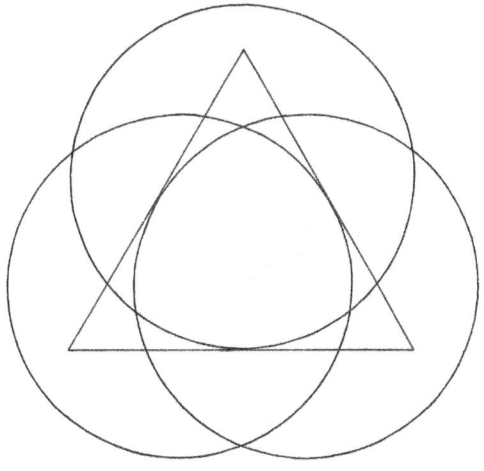

Rainbow Reiki Third Eye Chakra Symbol

Third Eye Chakra Across Traditions

The Third Eye Chakra, or Ajna, is the center of intuition, insight, and inner wisdom. Located between the eyebrows, it governs the ability to see beyond the physical and access higher levels of consciousness. In Egyptian teachings, the Third Eye Chakra is associated with the Eye of Horus, a powerful symbol of protection, spiritual sight, and divine knowledge. The Egyptians believed this chakra provided access to hidden truths and higher realms, enabling individuals to connect with the spiritual world. Lapis lazuli, a stone often linked to divine wisdom, was commonly used to activate and enhance the Third Eye's energy.

In Tibetan teachings, the Third Eye Chakra is tied to the element of light and the principle of *rigpa*, or pure awareness. Tibetan meditation practices emphasize visualization of a radiant indigo lotus at this chakra, opening the inner vision and fostering clarity of perception. Techniques such as Trataka (candle-gazing) are used to focus the mind and sharpen intuitive abilities, enabling practitioners to transcend ordinary perception and access higher understanding.

From an Arcturian perspective, the Third Eye Chakra is viewed as a portal to multidimensional awareness and cosmic connection. Arcturians teach that this chakra serves as an energetic antenna, receiving information from higher frequencies and dimensions. Clearing blockages in this chakra allows for the awakening of psychic gifts such as clairvoyance and telepathic communication. Arcturian healing techniques often involve energetic transmissions that activate the pineal gland, amplifying the Third Eye's capacity for spiritual insight and inner guidance.

The Pleiadian teachings emphasize the Third Eye Chakra as a gateway to universal consciousness and divine creativity. They describe this chakra as the center where intuition merges with imagination, allowing individuals to co-create their reality with the universe. Pleiadian practices often involve visualizing indigo light codes and working with crystalline frequencies to expand awareness and connect to higher realms of guidance.

Biblical references to the Third Eye Chakra include Matthew 6:22, "The eye is the lamp of the body. If your eyes are healthy, your whole body will be full of light." This verse reflects the concept of spiritual sight and the role of the Third Eye in perceiving divine truth. It speaks to the importance of clarity and purity of vision, both physical and spiritual, as a way to align with higher wisdom.

The Third Eye Chakra is a powerful energy center that bridges the physical and spiritual worlds. It allows for the perception of subtle energies, inner truths, and divine guidance. By balancing and activating this chakra, individuals can awaken their intuition, expand their consciousness, and access deeper levels of spiritual wisdom. This chakra is a gateway to the unseen, offering clarity, insight, and alignment with the divine flow of the universe.

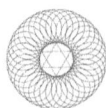

Basic Third Eye Chakra Meditation

Find a comfortable, quiet place to sit or lie down. Keep your spine straight and your body relaxed. Close your eyes and take a deep breath.

Take a moment to tune into your breath. Breathe in deeply through your nose, and exhale slowly through your mouth. Let go of any tension in your forehead, eyes, and jaw.

The third eye chakra, located between your eyebrows, is your center of intuition and inner vision. This meditation will help you balance and strengthen this energy center, allowing you to connect to your deeper wisdom and clarity.

Grounding Breath
- Breathe deeply into your forehead for a count of four, imagining your breath reaching the space between your eyebrows.
- Hold the breath gently for a count of two, allowing the area to soften.
- Exhale slowly for a count of six, releasing any tension or mental fog.
- Repeat this breathing pattern, feeling a sense of calm and focus with each breath.

Visualization
- Visualize a soft, indigo-colored light glowing at the center of your forehead, just between your eyebrows. This is the energy of your third eye chakra.
- With each inhale, imagine this indigo light becoming brighter, clearer, and more vibrant.
- With each exhale, release any doubts, confusion, or mental clutter. Let them dissolve into the air.
- Feel this indigo light expanding, filling your forehead and mind with clarity and insight.

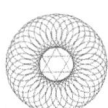

Affirmations

As you continue to breathe and focus on the glowing light, silently or softly repeat these affirmations:
- *"I trust my intuition and inner wisdom."*
- *"I see the truth clearly and with compassion."*
- *"My mind is calm, focused, and open to insight."*
- *"I am connected to my higher self and inner guidance."*

Let these affirmations resonate deeply, reinforcing your connection to your intuitive mind.

Connection to Light

The third eye chakra is associated with light and perception. As you breathe, imagine this indigo light illuminating your inner vision.
- See it shining a path forward, helping you navigate decisions and understand deeper truths.
- Allow this light to flow freely, creating a sense of clarity and openness.

Take a moment to thank your third eye chakra for its role in guiding you and helping you access your inner wisdom. Feel gratitude for the insights and clarity it brings to your life.

Take a few final breaths, allowing the indigo light at your third eye chakra to glow softly. Know that this energy center is balanced and thriving, supporting your intuition and clarity.

When you are ready, gently bring your awareness back to the present moment. Wiggle your fingers and toes, stretch if you like, and slowly open your eyes.

Take a moment to notice how you feel—calm, centered, and deeply connected to your inner wisdom.

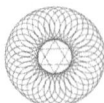

Advanced Third Eye Chakra Focused Healing, Cleansing, and Energetic Connection

The third eye chakra, located between the eyebrows, is the center of intuition, insight, and spiritual awareness. This advanced guided meditation uses the multidimensional energies of Rainbow Reiki—including Usui, Shadow, Arcturian, Pleiadian, Egyptian Sekhem-Seichim, and Magdalene/Yeshua Reiki—to cleanse, strengthen, and help you connect deeply with the energy of the third eye chakra.

Find a quiet, comfortable space to sit or lie down. Close your eyes and take several deep breaths, inhaling deeply through your nose and exhaling slowly through your mouth. With each exhale, feel your body relaxing and releasing any tension.

Set your intention: *"I welcome the advanced energies of Rainbow Reiki to cleanse, balance, and deepen my connection to my third eye chakra, enhancing my intuition, clarity, and spiritual insight."*

Grounding and Cosmic Connection
Visualize roots extending from your feet into Earth's crystalline core. Feel Gaia's nurturing energy rising through these roots, anchoring and grounding you. Simultaneously, envision a vibrant column of rainbow light descending from the cosmos, entering your crown chakra, and flowing down to your third eye chakra, located between your eyebrows.

Feel these Earth and cosmic energies merging in your third eye chakra, creating a stable and harmonious foundation for healing and activation.

Activating the Third Eye Chakra
Bring your awareness to your third eye chakra. Visualize it as a glowing indigo orb of light, spinning gently and radiating clarity and calm. Notice its size, brightness, and rhythm. Allow yourself to sense the unique energetic feeling of your third eye chakra—its coolness, vibration, or expansive quality.

Affirm: *"I am open to divine insight and aligned with my highest truth."*

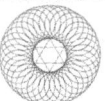

Cleansing the Third Eye Chakra
Visualize a deep indigo light from Shadow Reiki entering your third eye chakra. This light gently dissolves blockages, doubts, or stagnant energies that may cloud your intuition or spiritual vision. Feel the energy clearing your inner vision and releasing any fears or limitations.

Once the clearing feels complete, imagine a soft rose-pink light from Magdalene/Yeshua Reiki flowing into your third eye chakra. This light infuses it with love, peace, and divine clarity, nurturing and restoring its natural brilliance.

Affirm: *"I release all limitations and doubts, allowing my third eye chakra to be fully cleansed and healed."*

Strengthening and Energizing
Visualize golden geometric patterns from Egyptian Sekhem-Seichim Reiki flowing into your third eye chakra. These sacred patterns stabilize and fortify its structure, enhancing its ability to channel spiritual insight and higher wisdom.

Next, see vibrant rainbow light from Pleiadian and Arcturian Reiki streaming into your third eye chakra. This light activates the multidimensional aspects of this energy center, connecting it to universal knowledge and cosmic frequencies.

Feel your third eye chakra becoming more vibrant, balanced, and aligned with your spiritual intuition and insight.

Affirm: *"My third eye chakra is clear, balanced, and radiates divine intuition and spiritual clarity."*

Becoming Familiar with the Energetic Feeling of the Third Eye Chakra
Spend a few moments focusing on the unique energetic sensation of your third eye chakra. Notice its vibration, lightness, or sense of expansion. Observe how it feels when it is balanced, open, and

connected to your inner wisdom and spiritual vision. Deepen your awareness of its energy and its role in guiding your intuition and higher consciousness.

Affirm: *"I am attuned to the energy of my third eye chakra, aligned with divine insight and cosmic awareness."*

Integration and Multidimensional Alignment
Expand your awareness to include the energetic connections of your third eye chakra to your emotional, mental, and spiritual bodies. Visualize its energy radiating outward, harmonizing with your auric field and connecting with the Soul Star Chakra and Cosmic Gateway.

Imagine your third eye chakra aligning with the multidimensional grids of Earth and the cosmos, integrating its energy with your divine blueprint. Feel this alignment enhancing your spiritual perception, inner vision, and connection to universal consciousness.

Affirm: *"My third eye chakra is fully integrated, balanced, and aligned with my highest vibrational potential."*

Closing and Gratitude
Bring your awareness back to your heart center. Visualize a glowing orb of rainbow light within your chest, pulsating with gratitude and healing energy. Allow this light to radiate outward, integrating all the healing energies you have received.

Take a moment to thank your third eye chakra for its role in your intuition and spiritual growth. Express gratitude for the Rainbow Reiki energies and your ability to heal and grow.

When you feel ready, gently bring your awareness back to the present moment. Wiggle your fingers and toes, stretch lightly, and open your eyes.

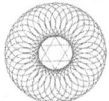

Post-Meditation Care
- Hydration: Drink water to support the release of energetic blockages and maintain clarity.
- Reflection: Journal any insights or sensations you experienced, noting shifts in intuition or perception.
- Mindfulness Practices: Spend time in meditation or engage in activities that nurture your inner vision, such as visualization exercises or creative endeavors.

This meditation can be practiced regularly to maintain the strength, balance, and vitality of your third eye chakra while deepening your connection to its energy and the transformative frequencies of Rainbow Reiki.

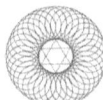

Crown Chakra (Sahasrara)
Location: Top of the head.
Body Connection: Brain and central nervous system.
System Influence: Relates to the pineal gland, which regulates sleep patterns, and overall neurological health. The crown chakra is linked to spirituality, higher consciousness, and connection to the divine or universal energy. Physically, it impacts the brain and nervous system. Imbalances may lead to neurological issues, migraines, insomnia, or a sense of disconnection from purpose or spirituality.

Rainbow Reiki Crown Chakra Symbol

Crown Chakra Across Traditions
The Crown Chakra, or Sahasrara, is the center of spirituality, higher consciousness, and divine connection. Located at the top of the head, it represents the bridge between the physical and spiritual realms, providing access to universal wisdom and unity with the cosmos. In Egyptian teachings, the Crown Chakra is associated with the lotus flower, a sacred symbol of spiritual awakening and enlightenment. The pharaohs were often depicted with crowns resembling the lotus, signifying their divine connection and ability to channel higher wisdom. Clear quartz and gold were revered as tools to amplify the energies of the Crown Chakra, aligning individuals with cosmic consciousness.

In Tibetan teachings, the Crown Chakra is viewed as the seat of enlightenment and is represented by the thousand-petaled lotus. Tibetan practices focus on cultivating *shunyata*, or the realization of emptiness, through meditation on this chakra. Visualization of a radiant violet or white lotus blooming at the top of the head

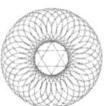

symbolizes the expansion of consciousness and the dissolution of ego, allowing for a deeper connection to the divine.

From an Arcturian perspective, the Crown Chakra is seen as the ultimate gateway to multidimensional awareness and cosmic unity. The Arcturians teach that this chakra serves as the point of entry for divine light and higher vibrational energies. Activating the Crown Chakra allows individuals to access universal knowledge, spiritual downloads, and alignment with their soul's higher purpose. Arcturian energy healing often focuses on clearing blockages in the Crown Chakra to facilitate spiritual ascension and integration of higher frequencies.

The Pleiadian teachings highlight the Crown Chakra as the center for co-creation with the universe and divine alignment. They describe it as the energy center where individuals merge their consciousness with the greater flow of universal intelligence. Through practices involving crystalline light frequencies and visualization of golden or white energy, the Pleiadians teach individuals to open the Crown Chakra fully, enabling them to embody divine love and wisdom.

Biblical references to the Crown Chakra include 1 Corinthians 2:16, "Who has known the mind of the Lord so as to instruct him? But we have the mind of Christ." This verse reflects the Crown Chakra's role in connecting with divine consciousness and receiving spiritual wisdom. Additionally, Revelation 2:10 speaks to the "crown of life," symbolizing spiritual victory and eternal unity with God, reinforcing the chakra's association with enlightenment and divine connection.

The Crown Chakra is the culmination of the spiritual journey, representing unity, transcendence, and divine understanding. By balancing and activating this chakra, individuals can transcend the limitations of the material world, align with their highest self, and connect to the infinite wisdom of the cosmos. This chakra is the key to experiencing profound spiritual awakening and unity with the divine.

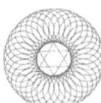

Basic Crown Chakra Meditation

Find a quiet, comfortable space to sit or lie down. Keep your spine straight and your body relaxed. Close your eyes and take a deep breath.

Take a moment to connect with your breath. Inhale deeply through your nose, and exhale slowly through your mouth. Allow your body to relax with each breath, releasing any tension or distractions.

The crown chakra, located at the top of your head, is your connection to higher consciousness and divine energy. This meditation will help you open, balance, and strengthen this energy center.

Grounding Breath
- Breathe deeply into your entire body for a count of four, imagining your breath traveling up to the top of your head.
- Hold the breath gently for a count of two, letting this energy settle.
- Exhale slowly for a count of six, releasing any heaviness or mental fog.
- Repeat this breathing pattern, feeling a sense of lightness with each exhale.

Visualization
- Visualize a soft, glowing white or violet light at the crown of your head. This is the energy of your crown chakra.
- With each inhale, imagine this light becoming brighter, purer, and more expansive.
- With each exhale, release any feelings of disconnection or limitation. Let them dissolve into the air.

See this light expanding upward, connecting you to the infinite, universal energy above. Feel this connection growing stronger with each breath.

Affirmations
As you continue to breathe and focus on the glowing light, silently or softly repeat these affirmations:
- *"I am connected to the divine and the universe."*
- *"I trust the flow of life and its higher purpose."*
- *"My mind is open to clarity and wisdom."*
- *"I am one with all that is."*

Let these affirmations resonate deeply, opening your mind to a higher state of awareness.

Connection to Divine Energy
The crown chakra is associated with divine energy and universal consciousness. As you breathe, imagine this violet or white light descending gently from the universe into your crown chakra.

Feel this light filling your entire being, bringing a sense of peace, love, and oneness.

Allow it to flow through you, connecting you to the infinite wisdom of the universe.

Feel yourself as a part of the greater whole, supported and guided by universal energy.

Take a moment to express gratitude for your connection to the divine and your own higher self. Thank this energy for its guidance and presence in your life.

Take a few final breaths, allowing the glowing light at your crown chakra to shine softly. Know that this energy center is open and balanced, supporting your spiritual growth and connection.

When you are ready, gently bring your awareness back to the present moment. Wiggle your fingers and toes, stretch gently if you like, and slowly open your eyes.

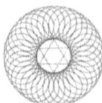

Take a moment to notice how you feel—peaceful, connected, and aligned with your highest self.

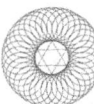

Advanced Crown Chakra Focused Healing, Cleansing, and Energetic Connection

The crown chakra, located at the top of the head, is the gateway to divine connection, spiritual enlightenment, and universal consciousness. This advanced guided meditation incorporates the multidimensional energies of Rainbow Reiki—including Usui, Shadow, Arcturian, Pleiadian, Egyptian Sekhem-Seichim, and Magdalene/Yeshua Reiki—to cleanse, strengthen, and deepen your connection to the energy of the crown chakra.

Find a quiet and comfortable space to sit or lie down. Close your eyes and take several deep breaths, inhaling deeply through your nose and exhaling slowly through your mouth. With each exhale, release tension and allow your body to relax fully.

Set your intention: *"I welcome the advanced energies of Rainbow Reiki to cleanse, balance, and deepen my connection to my crown chakra, enhancing my spiritual alignment and connection to universal consciousness."*

Grounding and Cosmic Alignment
Visualize roots extending from your feet into Earth's crystalline core. Feel Gaia's grounding energy rising through these roots, stabilizing your energy and anchoring your physical form. Simultaneously, envision a brilliant column of rainbow light descending from the cosmos, entering your crown chakra, and flowing down through your entire body.

Sense these Earth and cosmic energies merging within you, creating a harmonious balance that supports the cleansing and activation of your crown chakra.

Activating the Crown Chakra
Bring your awareness to your crown chakra, located at the top of your head. Visualize it as a radiant orb of violet or white light, spinning gently and pulsating with divine energy. Notice its size, brightness, and movement. Allow yourself to tune into the unique

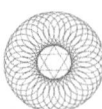

energetic feeling of your crown chakra—its expansiveness, vibration, or lightness.

Affirm: *"I am connected to divine consciousness and open to infinite wisdom."*

Cleansing the Crown Chakra
Visualize a deep indigo light from Shadow Reiki entering your crown chakra. This light gently dissolves blockages, doubts, or stagnant energies that may hinder your spiritual connection. Feel the energy clearing away limitations, confusion, or resistance to divine alignment.

Once the clearing feels complete, imagine a soft rose-gold light from Magdalene/Yeshua Reiki flowing into your crown chakra. This light infuses it with unconditional love, divine peace, and a sense of oneness with the universe.

Affirm: *"I release all limitations and blockages, allowing my crown chakra to be fully cleansed and open to divine light."*

Strengthening and Energizing
Visualize intricate golden geometric patterns from Egyptian Sekhem-Seichim Reiki flowing into your crown chakra. These sacred patterns stabilize its structure and enhance its ability to channel higher frequencies and divine wisdom.

Next, see a vibrant rainbow light from Pleiadian and Arcturian Reiki streaming into your crown chakra. This light activates the multidimensional aspects of this energy center, connecting it to universal consciousness, cosmic grids, and the higher realms.

Feel your crown chakra becoming more radiant, balanced, and aligned with your divine essence and universal flow.

Affirm: *"My crown chakra is vibrant, balanced, and aligned with universal consciousness and divine wisdom."*

Becoming Familiar with the Energetic Feeling of the Crown Chakra
Spend a few moments focusing on the unique energetic sensation of your crown chakra. Notice its lightness, radiance, or expansiveness. Observe how it feels when it is balanced, open, and connected to the infinite wisdom of the universe. Deepen your awareness of its energy and its role as your gateway to spiritual connection and higher consciousness.

Affirm: *"I am attuned to the energy of my crown chakra, fully aligned with divine light and infinite wisdom."*

Integration and Multidimensional Alignment
Expand your awareness to include the energetic connections of your crown chakra to your emotional, mental, and spiritual bodies. Visualize its energy radiating outward, harmonizing with your auric field and connecting with the Soul Star Chakra, Stellar Gateway, and Universal Gateway.

Imagine your crown chakra aligning with the multidimensional grids of the cosmos, integrating its energy with your divine blueprint. Feel this alignment enhancing your spiritual connection, inner peace, and sense of universal oneness.

Affirm: *"My crown chakra is fully integrated, balanced, and aligned with my highest vibrational potential and divine connection."*

Closing and Gratitude
Bring your awareness back to your heart center. Visualize a glowing orb of rainbow light within your chest, pulsating with gratitude and peace. Allow this light to radiate outward, integrating all the healing energies you have received.

Take a moment to thank your crown chakra for its role in your spiritual growth and divine connection. Express gratitude for the Rainbow Reiki energies and your ability to heal and evolve.

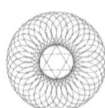

When you feel ready, gently bring your awareness back to the present moment. Wiggle your fingers and toes, stretch lightly, and open your eyes.

Post-Meditation Care
- Hydration: Drink water to support the integration of higher energies and the release of any lingering blockages.
- Reflection: Journal any insights, visions, or sensations you experienced, noting shifts in clarity or spiritual connection.
- Mindful Presence: Spend time in silence or meditation to deepen your connection with your crown chakra and the divine.

This meditation can be practiced regularly to maintain the strength, balance, and vitality of your crown chakra while deepening your connection to its energy and the multidimensional frequencies of Rainbow Reiki.

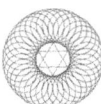

Body Systems and Advanced Chakras

Advanced chakras extend beyond the seven main chakras and connect with both physical and subtle aspects of the body. Each advanced chakra has its unique connection to body systems, influencing physical and energetic aspects related to specific organs, glands, or bodily functions. For instance, the Earth Star Chakra, located about six inches below the feet, anchors the individual's energy field to Gaia and supports grounding, stability, and the integration of Earth's crystalline energies. The Feet, Knee, and Hand Chakras serve as key energy hubs for movement, action, and interaction with the environment, connecting physical motion and manual activity with energetic balance. The Mouth of God Chakra, positioned at the base of the skull, facilitates divine communication and alignment with higher spiritual frequencies, influencing the upper cervical spine and brainstem. The Soul Star Chakra, situated above the crown, connects the individual to their soul's purpose, higher self, and cosmic wisdom, while gateways such as the Stellar Gateway, Universal Gateway, and Cosmic Gateway provide access to multidimensional energy flows, linking the practitioner to the broader universe and higher-dimensional realms of consciousness.

Rainbow Reiki integrates seamlessly with these advanced chakras, offering a multidimensional approach that aligns and activates these energy centers to their fullest potential. Using techniques and symbols from Usui, Shadow, Arcturian, Pleiadian, Egyptian Sekhem-Seichim, and Magdalene/Yeshua Reiki, Rainbow Reiki enables practitioners to harmonize these advanced chakras with the individual's physical, emotional, and spiritual needs. For example, the Earth Star and Earth Gateway chakras are aligned with Earth's crystalline grid, promoting grounding and stability while harmonizing the body's energy flow with Gaia's ascension process. The Soul Star and cosmic gateways are activated to align the individual with higher spiritual dimensions, supporting the flow of divine wisdom and universal life force energy. The Mouth of God Chakra is particularly addressed in Rainbow Reiki to enhance communication with the divine and activate the energy channels connecting the brain and the throat. Additionally, the Feet, Knee, and Hand Chakras are energized to enhance the flow of action-

oriented and interactive energies, strengthening the connection between physical activity and spiritual alignment. By working with these advanced chakras, Rainbow Reiki supports holistic healing and alignment, bridging physical wellness with multidimensional consciousness and facilitating a deeper connection with the universal energy matrix.

Earth Gateway Chakra
Location: Below the feet, connecting deeply with Earth's core.
Body Connection: Legs, feet, and grounding mechanisms.
System Influence: Supports the musculoskeletal and circulatory systems in the lower body by helping with energy flow, stability, and grounding. It also connects with bones and joints, fostering physical balance and resilience.

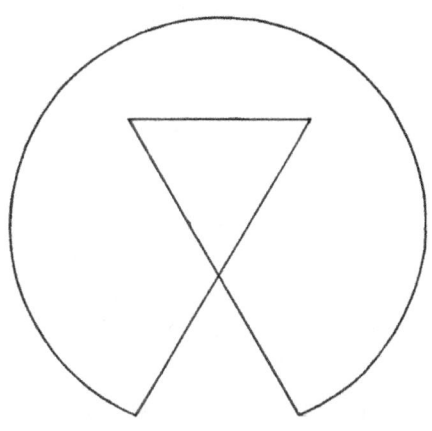

Rainbow Reiki
Earth Gateway Chakra Symbol

Earth Gateway Chakra Across Traditions
The Earth Gateway Chakra, also known as the Earth Star Chakra, is an energy center located below the feet that serves as the anchor between the human energy field and Earth's crystalline grid. This chakra is responsible for deep grounding, ancestral healing, and connecting to Earth's core frequencies. Each tradition—Egyptian, Tibetan, Arcturian, and Pleiadian—offers unique insights into this vital energy center, while biblical references provide further depth and understanding.

In Egyptian teachings, the Earth Gateway Chakra is closely aligned with the primordial Earth energies embodied by the god Geb, the deity of Earth. Ancient Egyptians viewed this energy center as a sacred conduit to the Duat (the underworld and ancestral realm), where spiritual knowledge, lineage healing, and karmic purification could take place. This chakra was believed to be the key to maintaining energetic balance between the heavens and the earth, ensuring harmony in both the physical and spiritual realms. Stones such as hematite and obsidian were used in burial rites to secure this grounding connection and protect the soul's journey beyond physical life.

In Tibetan teachings, the Earth Gateway Chakra is associated with the element of Earth and the foundational stability of existence. It is seen as the root of all energetic pathways, influencing the body's meridian system and energetic flows. Tibetan monks practice meditative walking, chanting deep vibrational tones, and visualizing golden roots extending from the feet into Earth's core to activate and strengthen this chakra. The Earth Star is considered essential for absorbing Earth prana, harmonizing karma, and stabilizing one's energetic foundation, especially in times of transition or upheaval.

From an Arcturian perspective, the Earth Gateway Chakra is seen as a planetary access point for cosmic integration, allowing for higher-dimensional energies to be safely embodied while maintaining a strong connection to Earth. Arcturians emphasize that this chakra holds ancestral coding and karmic imprints that must be cleared to fully embrace one's divine mission. Through frequency recalibration and deep Earth attunement, Arcturians help individuals release past-life fears and genetic traumas related to survival, oppression, or separation from Source, ensuring they are fully aligned with Earth's evolving consciousness.

The Pleiadian perspective views the Earth Gateway Chakra as a portal for connecting to Gaia's crystalline core and Earth's multidimensional energy grids. Pleiadians teach that this chakra is an interdimensional bridge, allowing for the integration of light codes that activate the higher DNA potential of humanity. They emphasize grounding rituals involving sound healing, crystal work, and communion with nature to stabilize this energy center. By working with this chakra, individuals can harmonize with Earth's shifting

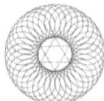

vibrational frequencies, fostering greater physical vitality, intuitive clarity, and spiritual embodiment.

The biblical reference for the Earth Gateway Chakra can be found in Genesis 28:12, which describes Jacob's vision of a ladder reaching from Earth to Heaven, with angels ascending and descending upon it. This symbolizes the Earth Gateway Chakra's role as a bridge between the physical and the divine, where spiritual energies are grounded into earthly existence. Isaiah 58:11 also reflects this energy, stating, "The LORD will guide you always; He will satisfy your needs in a sun-scorched land and will strengthen your frame. You will be like a well-watered garden, like a spring whose waters never fail." This passage signifies the Earth Gateway Chakra's role in sustaining life-force energy, providing strength, and ensuring alignment with divine guidance.

Together, these teachings provide a multidimensional understanding of the Earth Gateway Chakra, highlighting its role as the foundation for deep grounding, ancestral connection, and energetic stability. Activating and harmonizing this chakra allows individuals to fully embody their spiritual energy, walk in alignment with their soul's purpose, and receive Earth's nurturing and protective frequencies. Whether through Egyptian ancestral wisdom, Tibetan Earth-centered practices, Arcturian energy recalibration, Pleiadian light integration, or biblical spiritual grounding, working with this chakra strengthens one's connection to both the physical and celestial realms, creating a strong, balanced foundation for higher spiritual evolution.

Advanced Earth Gateway Chakra Focused Healing, Cleansing, and Energetic Connection

The Earth Gateway Chakra, located below the feet, is a vital energy center that connects your physical and energetic bodies to the Earth's core and the crystalline grid. This chakra anchors your energy, aligns you with Gaia's frequencies, and supports grounding, stability, and physical manifestation. This advanced guided meditation uses the multidimensional energies of Rainbow Reiki—including Usui, Shadow, Arcturian, Pleiadian, Egyptian Sekhem-Seichim, and Magdalene/Yeshua Reiki—to cleanse, strengthen, and deepen your connection to the Earth Gateway Chakra.

Find a quiet, comfortable space to sit or lie down. Close your eyes and take several deep breaths, inhaling deeply through your nose and exhaling slowly through your mouth. Allow your body to relax and feel supported by the earth beneath you.

Set your intention: *"I welcome the advanced energies of Rainbow Reiki to cleanse, balance, and connect me to the energy of my Earth Gateway Chakra, grounding me in stability, strength, and alignment with Gaia."*

<u>Grounding and Connection</u>
Visualize roots extending from your feet deep into Earth's crystalline core. Feel Gaia's nurturing energy rising through these roots, surrounding your legs and moving up toward the Earth Gateway Chakra, located approximately 6 to 12 inches below your feet. At the same time, envision a vibrant column of rainbow light descending from the cosmos, flowing down your body and into the Earth Gateway Chakra.

Feel these Earth and cosmic energies merging in the Earth Gateway Chakra, creating a powerful foundation for healing and activation.

<u>Activating the Earth Gateway Chakra</u>
Bring your awareness to your Earth Gateway Chakra. Visualize it as a vibrant orb of earthy, golden-brown light mixed with shimmering emerald-green hues. Notice its size, brightness, and movement.

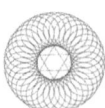

Allow yourself to sense the unique energetic feeling of your Earth Gateway Chakra—its stability, density, and grounding presence.

Affirm: *"I am deeply connected to Earth's energy and aligned with Gaia's crystalline frequencies."*

Cleansing the Earth Gateway Chakra
Visualize a deep indigo light from Shadow Reiki entering your Earth Gateway Chakra. This light gently dissolves blockages, dense energies, or emotional burdens that prevent your full grounding and connection to Earth. Feel the energy clearing any heaviness, fears, or disconnection.

Once the clearing is complete, imagine a soft rose-pink light from Magdalene/Yeshua Reiki flowing into the Earth Gateway Chakra. This light infuses it with love, nurturing, and stability, helping you feel supported by Earth and grounded in your purpose.

Affirm: *"I release all blockages, allowing my Earth Gateway Chakra to be fully cleansed and connected to Gaia."*

Strengthening and Energizing
Visualize golden geometric patterns from Egyptian Sekhem-Seichim Reiki flowing into your Earth Gateway Chakra. These sacred patterns stabilize and fortify its structure, aligning it with Earth's crystalline grid and the rhythms of nature.

Next, see vibrant rainbow light from Pleiadian and Arcturian Reiki streaming into the chakra. This light activates its multidimensional aspects, harmonizing it with cosmic frequencies while keeping you deeply anchored in the physical world.

Feel your Earth Gateway Chakra becoming more radiant, balanced, and deeply aligned with Gaia's energy and your higher purpose.

Affirm: *"My Earth Gateway Chakra is vibrant, balanced, and fully aligned with Earth's crystalline grid and universal flow."*

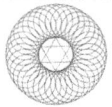

Becoming Familiar with the Energetic Feeling of the Earth Gateway Chakra

Spend a few moments focusing on the unique energetic sensation of your Earth Gateway Chakra. Notice its density, grounding strength, or sense of connection to Earth. Observe how it feels when it is balanced, open, and deeply connected to Gaia's nurturing and stabilizing energies. Deepen your awareness of its role as the foundation of your physical and energetic being.

Affirm: *"I am attuned to the energy of my Earth Gateway Chakra, grounded, stable, and aligned with Gaia's frequency."*

Integration and Multidimensional Alignment

Expand your awareness to include the energetic connections of your Earth Gateway Chakra to your physical, emotional, and spiritual bodies. Visualize its energy radiating outward, harmonizing with your auric field and connecting with the Earth Star Chakra and the crystalline grid of the planet.

Imagine your Earth Gateway Chakra aligning with the multidimensional grids of the cosmos and Gaia.

Feel its energy integrating with your divine blueprint, enhancing your grounding, stability, and connection to your earthly purpose.

Affirm: *"My Earth Gateway Chakra is fully integrated, balanced, and aligned with Gaia's crystalline energy and my divine purpose."*

Closing and Gratitude

Bring your awareness back to your heart center. Visualize a glowing orb of rainbow light within your chest, pulsating with gratitude and healing energy. Allow this light to radiate outward, integrating all the healing energies you have received.

Take a moment to thank your Earth Gateway Chakra for its role in grounding and supporting you. Express gratitude for the Rainbow Reiki energies and your connection to Gaia and the cosmos.

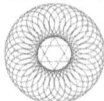

When you feel ready, gently bring your awareness back to the present moment. Wiggle your fingers and toes, stretch lightly, and open your eyes.

Post-Meditation Care
- Hydration: Drink water to support the release of blockages and enhance grounding.
- Grounding Practices: Spend time in nature, walk barefoot on grass or soil, or meditate with crystals such as hematite, red jasper, or smoky quartz.
- Reflection: Journal any sensations, insights, or shifts you experienced, noting any new sense of stability or grounding.

This meditation can be practiced regularly to maintain the strength, balance, and vitality of your Earth Gateway Chakra while deepening your connection to its energy and the multidimensional frequencies of Rainbow Reiki.

Earth Star Chakra

Location: 6-12 inches below the feet.

Body Connection: Lower extremities, feet, and skeletal structure.

System Influence: Reinforces grounding, stability, and the release of stagnant energy from the body. This chakra helps the body maintain physical equilibrium and supports energy flow in the legs, feet, and bones, enhancing the connection to Earth and physical world.

Rainbow Reiki
Earth Star Chakra Symbol

Earth Star Chakra Across Traditions

The Earth Star Chakra, located approximately 6 to 12 inches below the feet, is a vital energy center that serves as the grounding anchor between the human energy field and the Earth's crystalline grid. This chakra plays a crucial role in energetic stability, ancestral healing, and deep Earth connection, allowing individuals to harmonize their higher consciousness with physical existence. Across spiritual traditions—Egyptian, Tibetan, Arcturian, and Pleiadian—unique perspectives shed light on its significance, while biblical references provide further depth and understanding.

In ancient Egyptian wisdom, the Earth Star Chakra is intimately linked with Geb, the god of Earth, who governs the physical world, stability, and material existence. The Egyptians recognized this chakra as the energetic root that tethers the soul to Earth, acting as the foundation for divine embodiment. Through connection to Geb, initiates accessed ancestral wisdom, past-life healing, and karmic purification, ensuring harmony between spiritual ascension and earthly responsibilities. Burial rites often included grounding stones such as hematite and shungite, reinforcing the soul's connection to

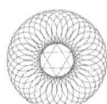

the Earth's energy and securing safe passage through the Duat—the realm of the afterlife and ancestral spirits.

In Tibetan philosophy, the Earth Star Chakra is regarded as the root of all energetic pathways, influencing meridian flows, pranic absorption, and karmic harmonization. It is associated with the Earth element, providing a solid energetic foundation that supports the body's resilience during transitions and upheavals. Tibetan monks activate this chakra through walking meditations, deep vibrational chanting, and visualization of golden roots extending from the feet into Earth's core. This practice aligns the individual's bioelectrical field with Gaia's energy currents, ensuring physical and spiritual balance while integrating Earth's healing prana.

The Arcturian perspective views the Earth Star Chakra as a planetary access point for higher-dimensional integration, allowing cosmic energies to be safely embodied while maintaining a strong connection to Earth. Arcturians teach that this chakra stores ancestral coding and karmic imprints, which must be cleared and recalibrated to unlock an individual's full spiritual potential. Through frequency alignment and energetic restructuring, Arcturians assist in releasing past-life fears, survival traumas, and karmic burdens, allowing for a pure connection to the evolving Earth consciousness. This chakra serves as a harmonizing force that prevents spiritual dissociation while enhancing one's ability to anchor light codes into the physical realm.

From a Pleiadian viewpoint, the Earth Star Chakra is seen as a dynamic interface between the individual and Gaia's crystalline core, functioning as a conduit for multidimensional energy integration. It is through this chakra that light codes and DNA activations from higher realms are received and grounded into the body. Pleiadian wisdom emphasizes that working with this chakra allows individuals to harmonize with Earth's evolving vibrational frequencies, supporting both personal and planetary ascension. Rituals involving sound healing, crystal energy, and Earth communion practices are recommended to stabilize this chakra, ensuring greater physical vitality, intuitive expansion, and spiritual embodiment.

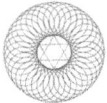

The Bible contains references that align with the Earth Star Chakra's function as a stabilizing force that grounds divine energy into human experience. Genesis 28:12, where Jacob envisions a ladder reaching from Earth to Heaven with angels ascending and descending, symbolizes this chakra's role as a bridge between the physical and spiritual planes. Additionally, Isaiah 58:11 states, "The LORD will guide you always; He will satisfy your needs in a sun-scorched land and will strengthen your frame. You will be like a well-watered garden, like a spring whose waters never fail." This passage reflects the Earth Star Chakra's nurturing energy, ensuring that those connected to it receive continuous divine sustenance, stability, and alignment with their spiritual path.

Together, these teachings reveal the Earth Star Chakra's essential function as the foundation for deep grounding, ancestral connection, and cosmic integration. Activating and harmonizing this chakra allows individuals to fully embody their spiritual energy in daily life, release karmic imprints and ancestral wounds, anchor higher-dimensional energies while staying grounded, and align with Earth's vibrational shifts for enhanced healing and evolution. Whether through Egyptian ancestral wisdom, Tibetan Earth-centered practices, Arcturian frequency recalibration, Pleiadian light integration, or biblical spiritual grounding, strengthening this chakra creates an unshakable foundation for higher spiritual development. By working with the Earth Star Chakra, individuals can walk in alignment with their soul's purpose, receiving Earth's protective and nurturing energies while remaining deeply connected to the celestial realms.

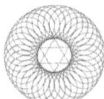

Advanced Rainbow Reiki Earth Star Chakra Focused Healing, Cleansing, and Energetic Connection

The Earth Star Chakra, located about 6-12 inches below your feet, serves as a powerful anchor that connects you to Earth's crystalline grid and supports your spiritual grounding and alignment with Gaia's energy. This chakra governs stability, manifestation, and the integration of spiritual and physical energies. Using the multidimensional energies of Rainbow Reiki—including Usui, Shadow, Arcturian, Pleiadian, Egyptian Sekhem-Seichim, and Magdalene/Yeshua Reiki—this advanced meditation will cleanse, strengthen, and deepen your connection to the Earth Star Chakra.

Find a quiet, comfortable space where you can sit or lie down. Close your eyes and take several deep breaths, inhaling deeply through your nose and exhaling slowly through your mouth. With each exhale, feel your body relaxing, releasing tension, and connecting with the earth beneath you.

Set your intention: *"I invite the advanced energies of Rainbow Reiki to cleanse, balance, and deepen my connection to my Earth Star Chakra, grounding me in stability, strength, and alignment with Gaia's crystalline grid."*

<u>Grounding and Cosmic Alignment</u>
Visualize roots extending from your feet deep into Earth's core. Feel Gaia's nurturing energy rising through these roots, flowing up to the Earth Star Chakra, located below your feet. At the same time, envision a column of rainbow light descending from the cosmos, moving down your body and into your Earth Star Chakra.

Feel these Earth and cosmic energies merging in your Earth Star Chakra, creating a powerful flow of grounding and spiritual alignment.

<u>Activating the Earth Star Chakra</u>
Bring your awareness to your Earth Star Chakra. Visualize it as a radiant orb of dark, grounding colors—black, deep brown, and shimmering silver or golden light. Notice its size, brightness, and

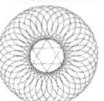

pulsation. Allow yourself to sense the unique energetic feeling of your Earth Star Chakra—its density, stability, and magnetic connection to Earth.

Affirm: *"I am deeply anchored to Earth's energy and aligned with Gaia's crystalline frequencies."*

Cleansing the Earth Star Chakra
Visualize a deep indigo light from Shadow Reiki entering your Earth Star Chakra. This light gently dissolves any blockages, stagnant energy, or emotional burdens that prevent your full grounding and connection to Earth. Feel the energy clearing away any fear, disconnection, or instability.

Once the clearing feels complete, imagine a soft rose-pink light from Magdalene/Yeshua Reiki flowing into your Earth Star Chakra. This light infuses it with love, stability, and a nurturing sense of safety, grounding your energy deeply into Gaia's grid.

Affirm: *"I release all blockages and fears, allowing my Earth Star Chakra to be fully cleansed and connected to Gaia's energy."*

Strengthening and Energizing
Visualize golden geometric patterns from Egyptian Sekhem-Seichim Reiki flowing into your Earth Star Chakra. These sacred patterns stabilize and fortify its structure, enhancing its alignment with Gaia's crystalline grid and the energy of manifestation.

Next, see vibrant rainbow light from Pleiadian and Arcturian Reiki streaming into the Earth Star Chakra. This light activates its multidimensional aspects, harmonizing your connection to Earth while maintaining alignment with cosmic frequencies.

Feel your Earth Star Chakra becoming more radiant, balanced, and deeply aligned with Gaia's energy and your higher spiritual purpose.

Affirm: *"My Earth Star Chakra is strong, balanced, and aligned with Earth's crystalline grid and universal flow."*

Becoming Familiar with the Energetic Feeling of the Earth Star Chakra

Spend a few moments focusing on the unique energetic sensation of your Earth Star Chakra. Notice its grounding weight, stable vibration, or magnetic pull toward Earth. Observe how it feels when it is balanced, open, and deeply connected to Gaia's nurturing energy and the crystalline grid.

Affirm: *"I am attuned to the energy of my Earth Star Chakra, grounded, stable, and aligned with Gaia's energy and purpose."*

Integration and Multidimensional Alignment

Expand your awareness to include the energetic connections of your Earth Star Chakra to your physical, emotional, and spiritual bodies. Visualize its energy radiating outward, harmonizing with your auric field and connecting with the Earth Star Chakra, the crystalline grid, and Gaia's core.

Imagine your Earth Star Chakra aligning with the multidimensional grids of the cosmos and Earth. Feel this alignment anchoring your spiritual energy into physical form, enhancing your sense of stability, security, and manifestation power.

Affirm: *"My Earth Star Chakra is fully integrated, balanced, and aligned with Gaia's crystalline energy and my divine purpose."*

Closing and Gratitude

Bring your awareness back to your heart center. Visualize a glowing orb of rainbow light within your chest, pulsating with gratitude and healing energy. Allow this light to radiate outward, integrating all the healing energies you have received.

Take a moment to thank your Earth Star Chakra for its role in grounding and supporting you. Express gratitude for the Rainbow Reiki energies and your ability to connect with Gaia and the cosmos.

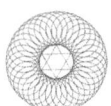

When you feel ready, gently bring your awareness back to the present moment. Wiggle your fingers and toes, stretch lightly, and open your eyes.

Post-Meditation Care
- Hydration: Drink water to support the release of energetic blockages and enhance grounding.
- Grounding Practices: Spend time in nature, walk barefoot on soil or grass, or meditate with grounding crystals such as hematite, smoky quartz, or red jasper.
- Reflection: Journal any sensations, insights, or shifts you experienced, noting how your connection to Earth feels.

This meditation can be practiced regularly to maintain the strength, balance, and vitality of your Earth Star Chakra while deepening your connection to its energy and the multidimensional frequencies of Rainbow Reiki.

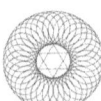

Soul Star Chakra

Location: 6-12 inches above the crown chakra.

Body Connection: Nervous and endocrine systems.

System Influence: Connects to the pineal and pituitary glands, influencing hormonal balance and sleep patterns. This chakra supports the nervous system by connecting with higher consciousness, providing mental clarity, and easing stress and anxiety.

Rainbow Reiki
Soul Star Chakra Symbol

Soul Star Chakra Across Traditions

The Soul Star Chakra, located approximately 6 to 12 inches above the head, is an essential energy center that serves as the gateway between the individual's energy field and the higher spiritual dimensions. It functions as the bridge between the personal and the divine, facilitating deep soul awareness, cosmic wisdom, and the integration of higher frequencies into human consciousness. Across spiritual traditions—Egyptian, Tibetan, Arcturian, and Pleiadian—each offers unique insights into its significance, while biblical references provide further understanding of its role in spiritual ascension.

In ancient Egyptian wisdom, the Soul Star Chakra is closely associated with Seshat, the goddess of divine knowledge, wisdom, and the cosmic order. It was believed that this chakra held the Akashic records, the eternal library of the soul's journey across lifetimes. Egyptian initiates worked with the Soul Star to access divine knowledge, elevate consciousness beyond earthly limitations, and integrate higher wisdom into their spiritual practices. The pyramid structures themselves were attuned to this energy center, acting as conduits for the alignment between the cosmos and the soul. Lapis lazuli, gold, and selenite were commonly used in rituals to enhance connection with the higher realms and open the Soul

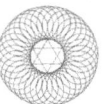

Star Chakra, allowing divine messages to flow freely into conscious awareness.

In Tibetan philosophy, the Soul Star Chakra is regarded as the source of higher consciousness, the point where divine inspiration enters the human experience. It is believed to be the seat of enlightenment, where spiritual initiates awaken to their true essence beyond material existence. Monks practice mantra chanting, deep meditation, and visualization of a luminous lotus above the head to activate this energy center, opening the path to divine wisdom and unity with the greater cosmic flow. This chakra is also linked to pure light energy, dissolving karmic imprints and allowing individuals to ascend into a state of spiritual liberation. Tibetan practices emphasize that through the activation of this chakra, an individual can reach states of samadhi, where the illusion of separation dissolves, and only pure divine consciousness remains.

The Arcturian perspective views the Soul Star Chakra as the gateway to multidimensional communication and interstellar wisdom. This energy center is the entry point for light codes, advanced healing frequencies, and celestial downloads that assist in planetary ascension. Arcturians teach that this chakra contains the blueprint of the soul's divine mission, encoded with star lineage and universal knowledge. Through frequency recalibration, light activations, and quantum energy transmissions, Arcturians help individuals clear distortions in the energy field, enabling a pure connection to higher intelligence and divine will. The activation of this chakra enhances telepathic abilities, spiritual downloads, and the integration of cosmic guidance into daily life, ensuring that one's earthly journey aligns with the greater galactic consciousness.

From a Pleiadian viewpoint, the Soul Star Chakra is seen as an interdimensional access point that allows for soul remembrance, DNA activation, and crystalline consciousness embodiment. This chakra acts as a portal where divine guidance, angelic frequencies, and the wisdom of the higher self flow into human awareness. Pleiadian teachings emphasize the use of sound healing, sacred geometry, and vibrational light codes to expand this chakra, increasing one's capacity to hold higher frequencies of love, wisdom, and unity consciousness. By consciously engaging with the Soul Star Chakra, individuals can accelerate their spiritual evolution, gain clarity on their soul's purpose, and receive direct transmissions from celestial realms.

The Bible contains references that align with the function of the Soul Star Chakra as the divine connection between Heaven and Earth. Matthew 3:16-17 describes the baptism of Jesus:
> As soon as Jesus was baptized, he went up out of the water. At that moment heaven was opened, and he saw the Spirit of God descending like a dove and alighting upon him. And a voice from heaven said, "This is my Son, whom I love; with him I am well pleased."

This moment illustrates the activation of the Soul Star Chakra as the conduit for divine messages and spiritual illumination. John 1:51 also echoes this, here: "He then added, 'Very truly I tell you, you will see 'heaven open, and the angels of God ascending and descending on' the Son of Man.'" This passage symbolizes the role of this chakra in receiving divine revelations and maintaining an open channel to the spiritual realms.

Together, these teachings reveal the Soul Star Chakra as a powerful energy center that facilitates spiritual awakening, divine communication, and multidimensional connection. Activating and harmonizing this chakra allows individuals to transcend lower vibrational patterns, access higher wisdom, and embody their soul's full radiance. Whether through Egyptian wisdom traditions, Tibetan enlightenment practices, Arcturian energy recalibration, Pleiadian light integration, or biblical references to divine revelation, the Soul Star Chakra serves as the bridge between the human and the divine. By working with this chakra, individuals can unlock soul remembrance, receive celestial guidance, and align fully with their highest purpose, anchoring divine consciousness into physical existence while remaining deeply connected to the cosmic flow of creation.

Advanced Soul Star Chakra Focused Healing, Cleansing, and Energetic Connection

The Soul Star Chakra, located about 6-12 inches above the crown of the head, is a gateway to higher consciousness, spiritual ascension, and divine wisdom. It connects you to your soul's purpose and the infinite flow of universal energy. This advanced guided meditation uses the multidimensional energies of Rainbow Reiki—including Usui, Shadow, Arcturian, Pleiadian, Egyptian Sekhem-Seichim, and Magdalene/Yeshua Reiki—to cleanse, strengthen, and deepen your connection to the Soul Star Chakra.

Find a quiet and comfortable space to sit or lie down. Close your eyes and take several deep breaths, inhaling deeply through your nose and exhaling slowly through your mouth. With each exhale, release tension and open your energy field to the infinite flow of divine light.

Set your intention: *"I invite the advanced energies of Rainbow Reiki to cleanse, balance, and deepen my connection to my Soul Star Chakra, aligning me with my soul's purpose and universal wisdom."*

Grounding and Cosmic Alignment
Visualize roots extending from your feet into Earth's crystalline core. Feel Gaia's grounding energy rising through these roots, stabilizing your energy and anchoring your physical form. Simultaneously, envision a brilliant column of rainbow light descending from the cosmos, flowing through your crown chakra and radiating upward into your Soul Star Chakra.

Sense the merging of Earth's nurturing energy and cosmic light in your Soul Star Chakra, creating a powerful foundation for spiritual alignment and healing.

Activating the Soul Star Chakra
Bring your awareness to your Soul Star Chakra, hovering just above your crown. Visualize it as a radiant orb of shimmering white and golden light, surrounded by subtle hues of violet and iridescent rainbow colors. Notice its size, brightness, and pulsation. Allow

yourself to sense the unique energetic feeling of your Soul Star Chakra—its expansiveness, lightness, and connection to the infinite.

Affirm: *"I am aligned with my soul's purpose and open to divine wisdom and universal truth."*

Cleansing the Soul Star Chakra
Visualize a deep indigo light from Shadow Reiki entering your Soul Star Chakra. This light gently dissolves blockages, old karmic imprints, and limiting beliefs that prevent you from fully accessing your higher self and divine wisdom. Feel the energy clearing any residual heaviness or stagnation, allowing your chakra to glow brighter.
Once the clearing feels complete, imagine a soft rose-gold light from Magdalene/Yeshua Reiki flowing into the Soul Star Chakra. This light infuses it with unconditional love, divine peace, and alignment with your soul's highest expression.

Affirm: *"I release all blockages, imprints, and limitations, allowing my Soul Star Chakra to radiate its divine light and wisdom."*

Strengthening and Energizing
Visualize golden geometric patterns from Egyptian Sekhem-Seichim Reiki flowing into your Soul Star Chakra. These sacred patterns stabilize and fortify its structure, enhancing its connection to the universal flow of energy and the divine blueprint of your soul.

Next, see vibrant rainbow light from Pleiadian and Arcturian Reiki streaming into the Soul Star Chakra. This light activates the multidimensional aspects of this energy center, connecting it to the higher realms, cosmic grids, and universal frequencies.

Feel your Soul Star Chakra becoming more radiant, balanced, and aligned with your soul's purpose and the infinite wisdom of the universe.

Affirm: *"My Soul Star Chakra is vibrant, balanced, and aligned with divine light and infinite wisdom."*

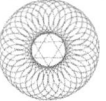

Becoming Familiar with the Energetic Feeling of the Soul Star Chakra

Spend a few moments focusing on the unique energetic sensation of your Soul Star Chakra. Notice its expansiveness, subtle vibration, or radiant flow. Observe how it feels when it is balanced, open, and deeply connected to your higher self and universal consciousness. Deepen your awareness of its energy and its role as a gateway to spiritual ascension and divine truth.

Affirm: *"I am attuned to the energy of my Soul Star Chakra, aligned with my higher self and the infinite flow of universal wisdom."*

Integration and Multidimensional Alignment

Expand your awareness to include the energetic connections of your Soul Star Chakra to your emotional, mental, and spiritual bodies. Visualize its energy radiating outward, harmonizing with your auric field and connecting with the Crown Chakra, Stellar Gateway Chakra, and the universal energy grids.

Imagine your Soul Star Chakra aligning with the multidimensional grids of the cosmos. Feel its energy integrating with your divine blueprint, enhancing your spiritual awareness, inner peace, and connection to universal love and light.

Affirm: *"My Soul Star Chakra is fully integrated, balanced, and aligned with my highest vibrational potential and divine purpose."*

Closing and Gratitude

Bring your awareness back to your heart center. Visualize a glowing orb of rainbow light within your chest, pulsating with gratitude and healing energy. Allow this light to radiate outward, integrating all the healing energies you have received.

Take a moment to thank your Soul Star Chakra for its role in guiding your spiritual journey and divine connection. Express gratitude for the Rainbow Reiki energies and your ability to heal and evolve.

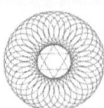

When you feel ready, gently bring your awareness back to the present moment. Wiggle your fingers and toes, stretch lightly, and open your eyes.

Post-Meditation Care
- Hydration: Drink water to support the integration of higher energies and the release of any residual blockages.
- Reflection: Journal any insights, visions, or sensations you experienced, noting shifts in clarity or spiritual connection.
- Spiritual Practices: Engage in mindful meditation, prayer, or creative activities that align you with your soul's purpose and higher wisdom.

This meditation can be practiced regularly to maintain the strength, balance, and vitality of your Soul Star Chakra while deepening your connection to its energy and the multidimensional frequencies of Rainbow Reiki.

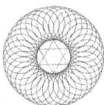

Stellar Gateway Chakra

Location: Above the Soul Star Chakra.

Body Connection: Central nervous system and brain.

System Influence: Facilitates access to higher consciousness, which may indirectly influence mental health and nervous system functioning. It also supports higher cognitive functions, enhancing clarity and intuitive processing, often linked to the crown chakra's influence on the brain.

Rainbow Reiki
Stellar Gateway Chakra Symbol

Stellar Gateway Chakra Across Traditions

The Stellar Gateway Chakra, located approximately 12 to 24 inches above the head, serves as the highest spiritual portal within the human energy system, connecting the soul to the divine cosmic consciousness. It is the threshold between individual awareness and universal oneness, acting as the gateway for celestial energies, divine enlightenment, and multidimensional ascension. Across spiritual traditions—Egyptian, Tibetan, Arcturian, and Pleiadian—unique perspectives illuminate its significance, while biblical references provide further understanding of its sacred role in divine communion.

In ancient Egyptian wisdom, the Stellar Gateway Chakra is closely associated with Ra, the god of the sun, who embodies cosmic illumination, divine authority, and the infinite intelligence of the universe. This chakra was believed to hold the Essence of the Supreme Creator, granting access to the primordial source of existence. Egyptian initiates activated this energy center through solar rituals, pyramid activations, and divine invocations to merge with the infinite light of the cosmos. The Benben Stone, a sacred capstone found at the top of Egyptian temples, symbolized this chakra as the pinnacle of spiritual enlightenment. Gold, orichalcum, and celestial lapis lazuli were used to enhance the connection with this divine portal, allowing one to transcend human limitations and embody the will of the divine.

In Tibetan philosophy, the Stellar Gateway Chakra is regarded as the Seat of the Supreme Void, where the ultimate truth beyond form and illusion resides. It is the energy center where emptiness (śūnyatā) and divine fullness coexist, dissolving the boundaries of self and uniting the practitioner with infinite consciousness. Tibetan monks activate this chakra through Dzogchen and mahamudra meditative practices, entering states of complete surrender and unity with the divine. The Stellar Gateway is described as the doorway to enlightenment, where the soul attains Moksha—liberation from the cycle of birth and death. This chakra allows one to access the pure light of Source, merging with the fabric of existence itself while maintaining embodiment in the physical realm.

The Arcturian perspective views the Stellar Gateway Chakra as the dimensional bridge to Source energy, the point where cosmic intelligence, divine codes, and intergalactic wisdom enter human consciousness. Arcturians teach that this chakra is the final frequency attunement before full soul ascension, encoding the soul's divine blueprint with light language, crystalline DNA activations, and sacred geometry transmissions. When opened, this chakra dissolves the illusion of separation, allowing the individual to become a pure conduit of celestial energy. Arcturians assist in the recalibration of this energy center through quantum activations and frequency downloads, ensuring a seamless integration of multidimensional awareness. It is through the Stellar Gateway that universal truths, divine purpose, and interstellar guidance flow effortlessly into human consciousness.

From a Pleiadian viewpoint, the Stellar Gateway Chakra is seen as the Cosmic Lotus, an infinite field of divine light that holds the resonance of unconditional love, wisdom, and unity with Source. This chakra serves as the entry point for higher-dimensional consciousness, allowing one to channel celestial energies, receive

divine transmissions, and embody the frequency of the Galactic Center. Pleiadians emphasize the importance of light-body activation, harmonic resonance, and celestial attunement to fully open this gateway. Sound frequencies, particularly tonal harmonics and angelic resonance, are used to align the Stellar Gateway with the cosmic heart of creation. By working with this chakra, individuals can transcend lower-density patterns and anchor the highest aspects of their divine essence into human embodiment.

The Bible contains references that align with the function of the Stellar Gateway Chakra as the portal to divine communion and ultimate spiritual illumination. Revelation 4:1 states the following:
> After this I looked, and there before me was a door standing open in heaven. And the voice I had first heard speaking to me like a trumpet said, "Come up here, and I will show you what must take place after this."

This passage illustrates the Stellar Gateway as the opening to divine realms where celestial knowledge is revealed. John 17:21 also reflects this concept: "that they all may be one, Father, just as you are in me and I in You. May they also be one in us so that the world may believe that you have sent me." This verse symbolizes the unification of the soul with the divine, mirroring the Stellar Gateway's role in dissolving the illusion of separation and merging with cosmic oneness.

Together, these teachings reveal the Stellar Gateway Chakra as the ultimate bridge between human consciousness and the infinite divine Source. Activating and harmonizing this chakra allows individuals to receive celestial wisdom, transcend limitations, and embody the pure frequency of divine creation. Whether through Egyptian solar ascension rituals, Tibetan enlightenment practices, Arcturian cosmic recalibration, Pleiadian light integration, or biblical revelations of divine unity, the Stellar Gateway Chakra serves as the sacred doorway to infinite consciousness. By working with this chakra, individuals can access higher realms of existence, align with divine will, and fully embody the luminous presence of Source within their earthly incarnation.

Advanced Stellar Gateway Chakra Focused Healing, Cleansing, and Energetic Connection

The Stellar Gateway Chakra, located above the Soul Star Chakra, serves as a portal to higher dimensions and universal consciousness. It connects you to the cosmic grids, divine wisdom, and the infinite expanses of the universe. This advanced guided meditation uses the multidimensional energies of Rainbow Reiki—including Usui, Shadow, Arcturian, Pleiadian, Egyptian Sekhem-Seichim, and Magdalene/Yeshua Reiki—to cleanse, strengthen, and help you connect deeply with the energy of the Stellar Gateway Chakra.

Find a quiet, comfortable space where you can sit or lie down. Close your eyes and take several deep breaths, inhaling deeply through your nose and exhaling slowly through your mouth. With each exhale, feel your body relaxing, releasing tension, and opening to higher frequencies.

Set your intention: *"I invite the advanced energies of Rainbow Reiki to cleanse, balance, and deepen my connection to my Stellar Gateway Chakra, aligning me with the infinite wisdom and light of the cosmos."*

Grounding and Cosmic Alignment

Visualize roots extending from your feet into Earth's crystalline core. Feel Gaia's stabilizing energy rising through these roots, anchoring and grounding your energy. At the same time, envision a brilliant column of rainbow light descending from the universe, entering through the Stellar Gateway Chakra, located about 12-24 inches above your crown, and flowing downward through your body.

Sense these Earth and cosmic energies merging within you, creating a harmonious foundation for healing and alignment.

Activating the Stellar Gateway Chakra

Bring your awareness to your Stellar Gateway Chakra. Visualize it as a magnificent orb of shimmering, iridescent light, encompassing shades of gold, silver, and pure white, pulsating with cosmic energy. Notice its vastness, brightness, and radiance. Allow yourself to sense the unique energetic feeling of your Stellar Gateway Chakra—

its expansiveness, transcendence, and infinite connection to universal consciousness.

Affirm: *"I am open to the infinite wisdom, light, and universal flow of the cosmos."*

Cleansing the Stellar Gateway Chakra
Visualize a deep indigo light from Shadow Reiki entering your Stellar Gateway Chakra. This light gently dissolves any blockages, dense energy, or karmic imprints that hinder your full access to higher realms and universal consciousness. Feel the energy clearing away any fear, doubt, or limitations.

Once the clearing feels complete, imagine a soft, golden light from Magdalene/Yeshua Reiki flowing into your Stellar Gateway Chakra. This light infuses it with divine peace, unconditional love, and a sense of oneness with the infinite.

Affirm: *"I release all blockages and limitations, allowing my Stellar Gateway Chakra to radiate its full divine light and universal connection."*

Strengthening and Energizing
Visualize intricate golden and silver geometric patterns from Egyptian Sekhem-Seichim Reiki flowing into your Stellar Gateway Chakra. These sacred patterns stabilize and fortify its structure, enhancing its ability to serve as a portal to the highest dimensions and cosmic frequencies.

Next, see vibrant rainbow light from Pleiadian and Arcturian Reiki streaming into the chakra. This light activates the multidimensional aspects of the Stellar Gateway, harmonizing it with the universal grids and aligning it with the flow of divine light and wisdom.

Feel your Stellar Gateway Chakra becoming more radiant, balanced, and deeply connected to the infinite wisdom and energy of the universe.

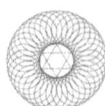

Affirm: *"My Stellar Gateway Chakra is vibrant, balanced, and aligned with the highest dimensions of universal consciousness."*

Becoming Familiar with the Energetic Feeling of the Stellar Gateway Chakra
Spend a few moments focusing on the unique energetic sensation of your Stellar Gateway Chakra. Notice its expansiveness, shimmering light, or profound sense of connection to the infinite. Observe how it feels when it is balanced, open, and fully aligned with the cosmic grids and universal wisdom. Deepen your awareness of its role as a portal to higher dimensions and universal flow.

Affirm: *"I am attuned to the energy of my Stellar Gateway Chakra, fully aligned with the infinite light and wisdom of the universe."*

Integration and Multidimensional Alignment
Expand your awareness to include the energetic connections of your Stellar Gateway Chakra to your emotional, mental, and spiritual bodies. Visualize its energy radiating outward, harmonizing with your auric field and connecting with the Soul Star Chakra, Universal Gateway Chakra, and cosmic grids.

Imagine your Stellar Gateway Chakra aligning with the multidimensional grids of the universe. Feel its energy integrating with your divine blueprint, enhancing your spiritual awareness, cosmic connection, and sense of infinite oneness.

Affirm: *"My Stellar Gateway Chakra is fully integrated, balanced, and aligned with my highest vibrational potential and universal purpose."*

Closing and Gratitude
Bring your awareness back to your heart center. Visualize a glowing orb of rainbow light within your chest, pulsating with gratitude and healing energy. Allow this light to radiate outward, integrating all the healing energies you have received.

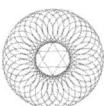

Take a moment to thank your Stellar Gateway Chakra for its role in guiding your spiritual journey and connection to the infinite. Express gratitude for the Rainbow Reiki energies and your ability to heal and evolve.

When you feel ready, gently bring your awareness back to the present moment. Wiggle your fingers and toes, stretch lightly, and open your eyes.

Post-Meditation Care
- Hydration: Drink water to support the integration of higher energies and release of any residual blockages.
- Reflection: Journal any insights, visions, or sensations you experienced, noting shifts in spiritual clarity or universal connection.
- Cosmic Practices: Spend time stargazing, meditating on the cosmos, or exploring creative expressions that align you with your higher self.

This meditation can be practiced regularly to maintain the strength, balance, and vitality of your Stellar Gateway Chakra while deepening your connection to its energy and the multidimensional frequencies of Rainbow Reiki.

Universal Gateway Chakra
Location: Above the Stellar Gateway.
Body Connection: Central nervous system and auric field.
System Influence: Expands connection to the entire energy field and indirectly influences the brain and spinal cord. This chakra provides spiritual protection, fostering balance within the body's electromagnetic field and supporting mental and energetic resilience.

Universal Gateway Chakra Across Traditions
The Universal Gateway Chakra, located beyond the Stellar Gateway, is the highest known energy center within the human spiritual system, acting as the bridge between individual consciousness and the boundless intelligence of the cosmos. This chakra serves as the entry point to the infinite field of Source, the divine matrix, and pure universal awareness. It transcends earthly and galactic realms, facilitating ultimate spiritual liberation, direct communion with the Creator, and the embodiment of cosmic truth. Across spiritual traditions—Egyptian, Tibetan, Arcturian, and Pleiadian—unique teachings illuminate its function, while biblical references provide further depth to its role in divine unification.

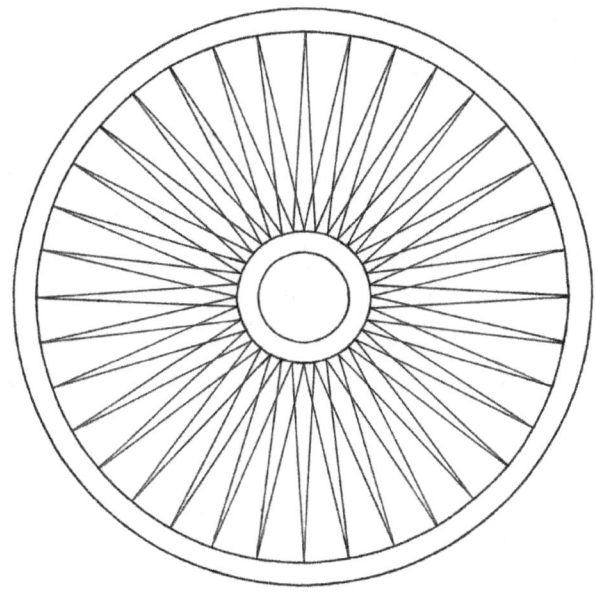
Rainbow Reiki
Universal Gateway Chakra Symbol

In ancient Egyptian wisdom, the Universal Gateway Chakra is linked to the Primeval Creator, Atum, the formless source of all existence, from whom the universe emanated. It represents the akhet, the horizon where the seen and unseen merge, symbolizing the ultimate return to unity with the divine. This chakra was regarded as the gateway to the Amenti, the eternal realms beyond the physical and astral planes. Egyptian initiates who reached this level of consciousness were said to embody Neteru (divine cosmic beings) and channel the raw intelligence of the Source. The Eye of Ra, representing the all-seeing wisdom of the cosmos, was a sacred symbol of this chakra, granting access to the celestial records of divine truth. White gold, monatomic elements, and etheric resonance were used to attune to this gateway, allowing for a direct infusion of divine essence into the earthly vessel.

In Tibetan philosophy, the Universal Gateway Chakra is known as the Realm of the Dharmakaya, the purest state of divine consciousness, where all illusion dissolves, and only infinite awareness remains. This chakra is said to be the source of all emanations, the primordial void from which all creation arises and returns. Tibetan monks and high lamas sought to activate this center through Dzogchen and Mahamudra practices, where complete ego dissolution and total enlightenment occurred. It was believed that those who fully opened this chakra could enter Rainbow Body transformation, shifting beyond material existence and merging into the light of universal truth. Through advanced breathwork, stillness meditation, and etheric resonance practices, the Universal Gateway was accessed, allowing for the final transcendence of karma, form, and separation.

The Arcturian perspective views the Universal Gateway Chakra as the Omniversal Nexus, the singularity point where all dimensional realities converge into pure Source energy. This chakra serves as the entry point to the original harmonic fields of divine intelligence, encoding the blueprint of the soul's origin before any incarnation or fragmentation into different existences. Arcturians teach that this energy center is the culmination of ascension, where one moves beyond the need for embodiment and becomes fully integrated with the infinite consciousness of the universe. Arcturian frequency recalibration at this level involves pure photonic light streams, multidimensional light infusions, and celestial resonance alignment,

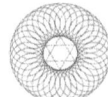

allowing for full synchronization with the divine architecture of the omniverse. It is through this gateway that individuals receive direct communion with the eternal Source and embody the absolute truth of existence.

From a Pleiadian viewpoint, the Universal Gateway Chakra is the Harmonic Singularity, where the soul becomes a radiant fractal of divine love and unity. This energy center serves as the final step in crystalline embodiment, allowing one to dissolve into the cosmic flow of Source while still holding presence within form. Pleiadian teachings emphasize the harmonics of light and sound, using vibrational keys, interdimensional chimes, and sacred toning to align the Universal Gateway with the highest frequencies of divine creation. It is at this level that DNA fully shifts into crystalline structure, enabling the physical form to become an anchor for the universal symphony of light consciousness. Through light transmissions, celestial harmonics, and etheric resonance fields, this chakra allows full remembrance of soul purpose, cosmic service, and the infinite expansion of being.

The Bible contains references that align with the Universal Gateway Chakra's function as the final merging of human consciousness with divine oneness. Revelation 21:6 states, "He said to me: 'It is done. I am the Alpha and the Omega, the Beginning and the End. To the thirsty I will give water without cost from the spring of the water of life.'" This passage symbolizes the complete return to Source, where all cycles of existence converge into unity. John 14:20 further illustrates this connection, "On that day you will realize that I am in my Father, and you are in me, and I am in you." This verse represents the dissolution of separation between the Creator and creation, reflecting the Universal Gateway's role in ultimate divine reunion.

Together, these teachings reveal the Universal Gateway Chakra as the final bridge between self and Source, where the highest state of enlightenment, divine union, and cosmic integration occurs. Activating and harmonizing this chakra allows individuals to fully transcend limitations, receive divine truth beyond form, and become a vessel of pure universal love and wisdom. Whether through

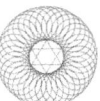

Egyptian initiatory practices, Tibetan enlightenment traditions, Arcturian omniversal attunements, Pleiadian crystalline integration, or biblical revelations of divine return, the Universal Gateway Chakra serves as the threshold to infinity. By working with this chakra, individuals unlock the final stage of cosmic awakening, moving beyond identity, space, and time, and merging fully with the eternal consciousness of the divine.

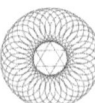

Advanced Universal Gateway Chakra Focused Healing, Cleansing, and Energetic Connection

The Universal Gateway Chakra, located above the Stellar Gateway Chakra, serves as the ultimate connection to the infinite consciousness of the universe. It aligns you with the universal grids, cosmic flow, and divine intelligence. This advanced guided meditation uses the multidimensional energies of Rainbow Reiki—including Usui, Shadow, Arcturian, Pleiadian, Egyptian Sekhem-Seichim, and Magdalene/Yeshua Reiki—to cleanse, strengthen, and help you connect deeply with the energy of the Universal Gateway Chakra.

Find a quiet, comfortable space where you can sit or lie down. Close your eyes and take several deep breaths, inhaling deeply through your nose and exhaling slowly through your mouth. With each exhale, release tension and open yourself to the expansive flow of universal energy.

Set your intention: *"I invite the advanced energies of Rainbow Reiki to cleanse, balance, and deepen my connection to my Universal Gateway Chakra, aligning me with infinite consciousness and divine flow."*

<u>Grounding and Cosmic Alignment</u>
Visualize roots extending from your feet into Earth's crystalline core. Feel Gaia's grounding energy rising through these roots, anchoring and stabilizing your energy. At the same time, envision a radiant column of rainbow light descending from the universe, flowing through your Universal Gateway Chakra, located several feet above your head, and moving downward through your Stellar Gateway Chakra, Soul Star Chakra, and Crown Chakra.

Feel these Earth and cosmic energies merging, creating a harmonious alignment for the cleansing and activation of your Universal Gateway Chakra.

<u>Activating the Universal Gateway Chakra</u>
Bring your awareness to your Universal Gateway Chakra. Visualize it as a vast, radiant orb of pure white light with shimmering hues of gold, silver, and iridescent rainbow colors. Notice its infinite

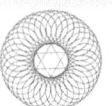

expansiveness and connection to the universal grids. Sense the unique energetic feeling of this chakra—its limitless nature, transcendence, and powerful connection to divine intelligence.

Affirm: *"I am one with the infinite consciousness of the universe and open to divine flow."*

Cleansing the Universal Gateway Chakra
Visualize a deep indigo light from Shadow Reiki entering your Universal Gateway Chakra. This light gently dissolves any blockages, dense energy, or residual imprints that may hinder your ability to fully access universal consciousness and divine flow. Feel the energy clearing away any limitations, fears, or energetic debris, allowing the chakra to expand freely.

Once the cleansing feels complete, imagine a soft, golden light from Magdalene/Yeshua Reiki flowing into the Universal Gateway Chakra. This light infuses it with divine love, unconditional peace, and a profound sense of unity with the cosmos.

Affirm: *"I release all blockages and limitations, allowing my Universal Gateway Chakra to radiate infinite light and divine connection."*

Strengthening and Energizing
Visualize intricate golden and silver geometric patterns from Egyptian Sekhem-Seichim Reiki flowing into your Universal Gateway Chakra. These sacred patterns stabilize and fortify its structure, enhancing its capacity to channel universal wisdom and align with the highest cosmic frequencies.

Next, see vibrant rainbow light from Pleiadian and Arcturian Reiki streaming into the chakra. This light activates the multidimensional aspects of the Universal Gateway Chakra, connecting it seamlessly to the universal grids, cosmic energy streams, and divine flow.

Feel your Universal Gateway Chakra becoming more radiant, expansive, and aligned with the infinite consciousness of the universe.

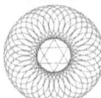

Affirm: *"My Universal Gateway Chakra is vibrant, balanced, and fully aligned with infinite light and universal wisdom."*

Becoming Familiar with the Energetic Feeling of the Universal Gateway Chakra

Spend a few moments focusing on the unique energetic sensation of your Universal Gateway Chakra. Notice its vastness, pulsating light, or profound connection to all that is. Observe how it feels when it is balanced, open, and fully aligned with the universal flow of energy and wisdom. Deepen your awareness of its energy and its role as the gateway to the infinite.

Affirm: *"I am attuned to the energy of my Universal Gateway Chakra, fully aligned with the infinite consciousness of the universe."*

Integration and Multidimensional Alignment

Expand your awareness to include the energetic connections of your Universal Gateway Chakra to your emotional, mental, and spiritual bodies. Visualize its energy radiating outward, harmonizing with your auric field and connecting seamlessly with the Stellar Gateway Chakra, Soul Star Chakra, and the universal grids.

Imagine your Universal Gateway Chakra aligning with the multidimensional grids of the cosmos. Feel its energy integrating with your divine blueprint, enhancing your spiritual awareness, universal connection, and sense of infinite unity.

Affirm: *"My Universal Gateway Chakra is fully integrated, balanced, and aligned with my highest vibrational potential and divine purpose."*

Closing and Gratitude

Bring your awareness back to your heart center. Visualize a glowing orb of rainbow light within your chest, pulsating with gratitude and healing energy. Allow this light to radiate outward, integrating all the healing energies you have received.

Take a moment to thank your Universal Gateway Chakra for its role in guiding your spiritual journey and universal connection. Express gratitude for the Rainbow Reiki energies and your ability to heal and align with infinite wisdom.

When you feel ready, gently bring your awareness back to the present moment. Wiggle your fingers and toes, stretch lightly, and open your eyes.

Post-Meditation Care
- Hydration: Drink water to support the integration of higher energies and the release of any residual blockages.
- Reflection: Journal any insights, visions, or sensations you experienced, noting shifts in clarity, spiritual alignment, or universal connection.
- Cosmic Practices: Engage in stargazing, cosmic visualization, or mindful meditation to deepen your connection to the infinite.

This meditation can be practiced regularly to maintain the strength, balance, and vitality of your Universal Gateway Chakra while deepening your connection to its energy and the multidimensional frequencies of Rainbow Reiki.

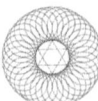

Cosmic Gateway Chakra
Location: Beyond the Universal Gateway Chakra.
Body Connection: Entire nervous system, especially the brain and spine.
System Influence: Connects with cosmic energy, which can influence mental clarity, spiritual insight, and calmness within the nervous system. It acts as a source of higher guidance, influencing the way information is processed in the brain and supporting nervous system stability.

Rainbow Reiki
Cosmic Gateway Chakra Symbol

Cosmic Gateway Chakra Across Traditions
The Cosmic Gateway Chakra, located beyond the Stellar Gateway, is the portal to the infinite realms of divine consciousness, interdimensional travel, and celestial wisdom. It serves as the bridge between the personal and the vast cosmic intelligence, allowing for the full embodiment of Source energy. This chakra enables the highest levels of spiritual expansion, divine unity, and direct communication with the celestial planes. Across spiritual traditions—Egyptian, Tibetan, Arcturian, and Pleiadian—unique teachings illuminate its function, while biblical references provide insight into its role in divine connection and spiritual evolution.

In ancient Egyptian wisdom, the Cosmic Gateway Chakra is associated with Nun, the primordial waters of creation, representing the boundless field of potential from which all existence emerges. It was believed that this chakra connected the soul to the infinite cosmic ocean, where one could access the Halls of Amenti, the celestial archives of divine knowledge. The ancient temples of Dendera and Karnak were constructed with cosmic alignments, serving as initiation portals where priests and priestesses worked to open the Cosmic Gateway Chakra. The Eye of Horus, symbolic of transcendent vision, was often linked to this chakra, allowing initiates to move beyond earthly perception and into cosmic awareness. Gold, meteoric iron, and celestial lapis lazuli were used to attune the body and spirit to the frequencies of this divine portal, allowing for seamless travel between realms and direct communion with the Creator.

In Tibetan philosophy, the Cosmic Gateway Chakra is regarded as the Doorway to the Dharmadhatu, the infinite space of reality where all forms dissolve into the primordial truth. It represents the Bodhisattva's Ascension, where an individual moves beyond karmic cycles and becomes fully immersed in the universal field of divine wisdom. Tibetan monks and spiritual masters activated this chakra through tantric meditation, sacred geometry, and mantra vibration, allowing them to step into the pure field of cosmic light. The Rainbow Body phenomenon, in which high-level practitioners dissolve into pure light at the time of death, is believed to be a direct activation of the Cosmic Gateway Chakra. Through advanced consciousness expansion and stillness practices, this energy center becomes the portal through which one attains the ultimate state of enlightenment and union with the divine.

The Arcturian perspective sees the Cosmic Gateway Chakra as the Supreme Dimensional Corridor, an energy field that allows one to move freely through time, space, and multiple dimensions. This chakra functions as the passageway to the Source realms, containing light codes, crystalline DNA activations, and quantum intelligence beyond human perception. Arcturians assist in the harmonic calibration of this chakra, ensuring that those who reach this state of expansion are aligned with the highest universal frequencies. It is through the Cosmic Gateway that soul contracts, galactic missions, and divine blueprints are fully accessed, allowing one to integrate their cosmic purpose with their earthly experience. When fully opened, this chakra dissolves all barriers between self and Source, creating a seamless flow between the infinite cosmic mind and the embodied soul.

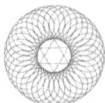

From a Pleiadian viewpoint, the Cosmic Gateway Chakra is the Great Harmonic Portal, the access point to the divine symphony of creation. It is the focal point of celestial resonance, where souls can channel galactic frequencies, anchor divine light codes, and step into their highest crystalline embodiment. Pleiadians emphasize the role of sound, sacred geometry, and cosmic harmonic alignment in activating this chakra. By working with this energy center, individuals can access interstellar wisdom, receive direct transmissions from Source, and align with the energetic flow of the omniverse. Through tonal activations, vibrational sequencing, and planetary gridwork, the Cosmic Gateway allows for full integration with the highest divine frequencies, ensuring that one's physical and etheric forms resonate with the cosmic blueprint of creation.

The Bible contains references that align with the Cosmic Gateway Chakra's function as the divine portal to higher realms. Ezekiel 1:1 states, "In the thirtieth year, in the fourth month on the fifth day, while I was among the exiles by the Kebar River, the heavens were opened and I saw visions of God." This passage reflects the opening of the Cosmic Gateway, where divine revelation and celestial wisdom flow through to those prepared to receive it. Revelation 22:13 further illustrates this state of ultimate divine connection: "I am the Alpha and the Omega, the First and the Last, the Beginning and the End." This verse speaks to the infinite presence of Source, mirroring the Cosmic Gateway's role as the final threshold to divine unity and omnipresence.

Together, these teachings reveal the Cosmic Gateway Chakra as the supreme bridge between human consciousness and the infinite field of divine intelligence. Activating and harmonizing this chakra allows individuals to step into their highest state of cosmic alignment, receive celestial wisdom, and embody the full radiance of Source energy. Whether through Egyptian temple initiations, Tibetan enlightenment practices, Arcturian quantum recalibration, Pleiadian harmonic attunement, or biblical revelations of divine communion, the Cosmic Gateway Chakra serves as the final portal to Source consciousness. By working with this chakra, individuals can

transcend all limitations, dissolve into divine light, and merge fully with the eternal presence of creation.

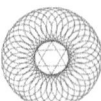

Advanced Cosmic Gateway Chakra Focused Healing, Cleansing, and Energetic Connection

The Cosmic Gateway Chakra, located above the Universal Gateway Chakra, is the highest energetic center in the multidimensional chakra system. It connects you directly to Source energy, the multiverse, and the infinite realms of existence. This chakra facilitates access to pure cosmic consciousness, universal wisdom, and the ultimate spiritual alignment. This advanced guided meditation uses the multidimensional energies of Rainbow Reiki—including Usui, Shadow, Arcturian, Pleiadian, Egyptian Sekhem-Seichim, and Magdalene/Yeshua Reiki—to cleanse, strengthen, and help you connect deeply with the Cosmic Gateway Chakra.

Find a quiet, comfortable space where you can sit or lie down. Close your eyes and take several deep breaths, inhaling deeply through your nose and exhaling slowly through your mouth. With each exhale, let go of tension and allow your awareness to expand beyond your physical body.

Set your intention: *"I invite the advanced energies of Rainbow Reiki to cleanse, balance, and deepen my connection to my Cosmic Gateway Chakra, aligning me with infinite Source energy and divine consciousness."*

<u>Grounding and Cosmic Alignment</u>
Visualize roots extending from your feet into the crystalline core of Earth. Feel Gaia's grounding energy rising through these roots, stabilizing your physical and energetic bodies. Simultaneously, envision a radiant column of rainbow light descending from the highest realms of the cosmos, flowing down through your Cosmic Gateway Chakra, located several feet above your head.

Feel the merging of Earth's nurturing energy and the infinite cosmic light within you, preparing your Cosmic Gateway Chakra for healing and activation.

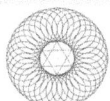

Activating the Cosmic Gateway Chakra

Bring your awareness to your Cosmic Gateway Chakra. Visualize it as a vast, radiant orb of pure, luminous light—brilliant white interwoven with golden, silver, and iridescent rainbow hues. Notice its immense expansiveness and transcendent connection to Source energy. Sense the unique energetic feeling of this chakra—its infinite nature, boundlessness, and connection to all creation.

Affirm: *"I am aligned with infinite Source energy, pure cosmic consciousness, and divine truth."*

Cleansing the Cosmic Gateway Chakra

Visualize a deep indigo light from Shadow Reiki entering your Cosmic Gateway Chakra. This light gently dissolves any blockages, dense energies, or residual imprints that may hinder your connection to cosmic realms. Feel the clearing of any limitations, doubts, or karmic patterns that may restrict the free flow of cosmic energy.

Once the cleansing feels complete, imagine a radiant golden light from Magdalene/Yeshua Reiki flowing into your Cosmic Gateway Chakra. This light infuses it with divine peace, unconditional love, and a profound sense of unity with the multiverse.

Affirm: *"I release all blockages and limitations, allowing my Cosmic Gateway Chakra to radiate infinite light and cosmic wisdom."*

Strengthening and Energizing

Visualize intricate patterns of golden and crystalline light from Egyptian Sekhem-Seichim Reiki flowing into your Cosmic Gateway Chakra. These sacred patterns stabilize and fortify its structure, enhancing its ability to channel Source energy and cosmic frequencies.

Next, see vibrant rainbow light from Pleiadian and Arcturian Reiki streaming into the chakra. This light activates the multidimensional aspects of your Cosmic Gateway Chakra, aligning it with the cosmic grids, universal flow, and infinite wisdom of the multiverse.

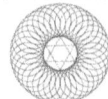

Feel your Cosmic Gateway Chakra becoming more expansive, luminous, and aligned with Source energy and cosmic consciousness.

Affirm: *"My Cosmic Gateway Chakra is vibrant, balanced, and fully aligned with infinite Source energy and cosmic wisdom."*

Becoming Familiar with the Energetic Feeling of the Cosmic Gateway Chakra
Spend a few moments focusing on the unique energetic sensation of your Cosmic Gateway Chakra. Notice its boundless expansiveness, pure light, or profound connection to the infinite. Observe how it feels when it is balanced, open, and fully aligned with the flow of cosmic energy and divine truth. Deepen your awareness of its energy and its role as a portal to Source consciousness and universal alignment.

Affirm: *"I am attuned to the energy of my Cosmic Gateway Chakra, fully aligned with infinite Source and universal truth."*

Integration and Multidimensional Alignment
Expand your awareness to include the energetic connections of your Cosmic Gateway Chakra to your emotional, mental, and spiritual bodies. Visualize its energy radiating outward, harmonizing with your auric field and connecting seamlessly with the Universal Gateway Chakra, Stellar Gateway Chakra, and cosmic grids.

Imagine your Cosmic Gateway Chakra aligning with the multidimensional grids of the cosmos. Feel its energy integrating with your divine blueprint, enhancing your spiritual awareness, sense of infinite unity, and connection to the highest realms of existence.

Affirm: *"My Cosmic Gateway Chakra is fully integrated, balanced, and aligned with the infinite wisdom of Source energy and my highest spiritual potential."*

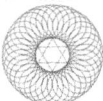

Closing and Gratitude
Bring your awareness back to your heart center. Visualize a glowing orb of rainbow light within your chest, pulsating with gratitude and peace. Allow this light to radiate outward, integrating all the healing energies you have received.

Take a moment to thank your Cosmic Gateway Chakra for its role in connecting you to Source energy and guiding your spiritual journey. Express gratitude for the Rainbow Reiki energies and your ability to heal and align with infinite consciousness.

When you feel ready, gently bring your awareness back to the present moment. Wiggle your fingers and toes, stretch lightly, and open your eyes.

Post-Meditation Care
- Hydration: Drink water to support the integration of higher energies and the release of any residual blockages.
- Reflection: Journal any insights, visions, or sensations you experienced, noting shifts in clarity, spiritual connection, or cosmic awareness.
- Cosmic Practices: Spend time meditating on the stars, engaging in cosmic visualizations, or exploring practices that align you with your highest spiritual self.

This meditation can be practiced regularly to maintain the strength, balance, and vitality of your Cosmic Gateway Chakra while deepening your connection to its energy and the multidimensional frequencies of Rainbow Reiki.

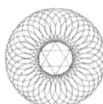

Hand Chakras
Location: Centers of the palms.
Body Connection: Muscular and skeletal systems in the arms, circulation, and nerve endings in the hands.
System Influence: Hand chakras facilitate energy flow in the hands and arms, influencing dexterity, tactile sensations, and healing ability. They play a critical role in energy healing, supporting circulation and fine motor skills through enhanced energy flow in the hands.

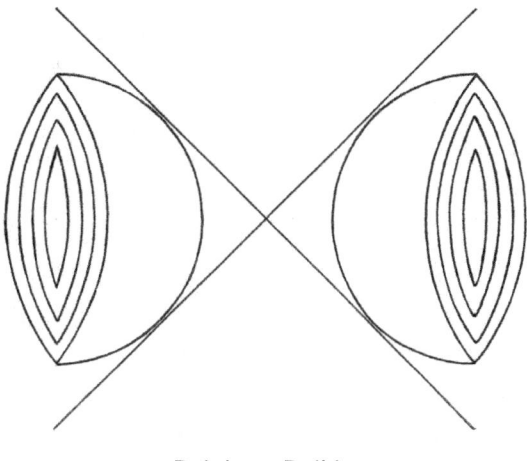
Rainbow Reiki Hand Chakra Symbol

Hand Chakras Across Traditions
The Hand Chakras, located at the center of each palm, serve as powerful energy centers that facilitate the flow of life force, healing energy, and multidimensional consciousness. These chakras function as conduits for energy transmission, intuitive activation, and the manifestation of divine will. The hands are not only physical tools but also spiritual instruments capable of channeling profound frequencies. Across spiritual traditions—Egyptian, Tibetan, Arcturian, and Pleiadian—each offers unique perspectives on their significance, while biblical references provide deeper understanding of their sacred function.

In ancient Egyptian wisdom, the Hand Chakras were regarded as portals of divine creation, linked to Ptah, the god of craftsmanship and manifestation. The Egyptians believed that energy flowed through the hands as an extension of divine intent, shaping the world through both physical and metaphysical means. Hieroglyphs often depict deities holding ankhs, was scepters, or orbs of power, symbolizing the activation of energy within the hands. Priests and healers were trained in sacred hand placements to channel energy, conduct healing rituals, and transfer divine power into amulets and sacred objects. The Djed pillar, representing stability and spiritual strength, was often activated through the palm chakras, ensuring balance between cosmic and earthly forces. Stones such as carnelian, malachite, and lapis lazuli were used to amplify the hand chakras, enhancing their ability to channel energy for protection, healing, and alchemical transformation.

In Tibetan philosophy, the Hand Chakras are recognized as extensions of the heart chakra, acting as channels for compassion, wisdom, and pranic energy. Tibetan monks practice mudras (sacred hand gestures) to activate and direct energy, aligning their physical movements with cosmic forces. These hand positions are used in rituals, meditations, and energy healing practices, allowing for the transmission of divine light into the physical and etheric realms. The Tibetan Vajra, often held in ceremonies, represents the ability to channel lightning-like spiritual energy through the palms, symbolizing the Hand Chakras as conduits of divine wisdom and transformation. Through breathwork and mantra resonance, the palm centers become radiant with prana, allowing for enhanced spiritual healing, energy projection, and sacred touch.

The Arcturian perspective sees the Hand Chakras as interdimensional receivers and transmitters, capable of interfacing with light codes, energetic grids, and celestial frequencies. Arcturians emphasize that the hand chakras store encoded information from past lifetimes, often carrying imprints of healing abilities, cosmic technologies, and higher-dimensional gifts. When fully activated, these chakras serve as holographic projectors, allowing individuals to work with quantum energy fields, crystalline structures, and higher consciousness networks. Arcturians teach advanced energy calibration techniques that involve meridian activation, bioelectric synchronization, and light infusion into the palm centers, enabling individuals to access their highest healing potential and interact with multidimensional realities through the hands.

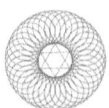

From a Pleiadian viewpoint, the Hand Chakras are seen as resonance points for divine touch, sacred creation, and vibrational healing. Pleiadians emphasize that the hands are key tools in adjusting frequency fields, whether for self-healing, planetary gridwork, or energy harmonization. They teach that the palms are dynamic energy receivers, constantly absorbing and transmitting higher-dimensional light codes that shift an individual's vibration. The use of sacred toning, crystal activations, and harmonic gestures enhances the Hand Chakras, allowing individuals to integrate Pleiadian light frequencies into their energetic systems. By working with these chakras, individuals can align their physical body with divine rhythms, create energetic imprints of healing, and awaken latent spiritual gifts.

The Bible contains references that align with the Hand Chakras' function as conduits of divine power and healing. Mark 16:18 states, "... they will place their hands on sick people, and they will get well." This passage reflects the palm chakras' role in energy healing, showing that divine energy flows through the hands as an extension of spiritual authority and grace. Exodus 17:11 describes how, "As long as Moses held up his hands, the Israelites were winning ..." This symbolizes the power of divine energy projection through the hands, reinforcing the idea that the Hand Chakras serve as sacred channels of higher will, strength, and victory. Acts 19:6 further states, "When Paul placed his hands on them, the Holy Spirit came on them ..." This illustrates the transference of divine energy and spiritual awakening through the hands, a direct reflection of the palm chakras' ability to channel celestial forces into the physical world.

Together, these teachings reveal the Hand Chakras as powerful gateways for energy transmission, divine creation, and multidimensional healing. Activating and harmonizing these chakras allows individuals to tap into their innate ability to heal, channel spiritual energy, and work with higher vibrational frequencies. Whether through Egyptian sacred hand rituals, Tibetan mudra practices, Arcturian interdimensional transmissions, Pleiadian vibrational healing, or biblical references to divine touch, the Hand

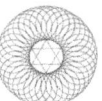

Chakras serve as profound instruments for manifestation, energetic transformation, and spiritual service. By working with these energy centers, individuals can awaken their spiritual gifts, align with higher frequencies, and become conduits for the divine light that flows through the hands.

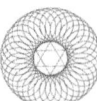

Advanced Hand Chakra Focused Healing, Cleansing, and Energetic Connection

The hand chakras, located at the center of each palm, are vital energy centers that govern the flow of life force energy in and out of the hands. These chakras are essential for healing, creating, and connecting with the world through touch. This advanced guided meditation uses the multidimensional energies of Rainbow Reiki—including Usui, Shadow, Arcturian, Pleiadian, Egyptian Sekhem-Seichim, and Magdalene/Yeshua Reiki—to cleanse, strengthen, and help you connect deeply with the energy of your hand chakras.

Find a quiet, comfortable space to sit or lie down. Rest your hands gently on your lap or by your sides, palms facing up. Close your eyes and take several deep breaths, inhaling deeply through your nose and exhaling slowly through your mouth. With each exhale, release tension and open yourself to the flow of universal energy.

Set your intention: *"I invite the advanced energies of Rainbow Reiki to cleanse, balance, and deepen my connection to my hand chakras, aligning me with the flow of universal energy and creative expression."*

Grounding and Cosmic Alignment
Visualize roots extending from your feet into Earth's crystalline core. Feel Gaia's grounding energy rising through these roots, flowing up into your body and arms, and reaching your hands. At the same time, envision a radiant column of rainbow light descending from the cosmos, entering your crown chakra, traveling down your arms, and radiating into your palms.

Feel the merging of Earth and cosmic energies in your hand chakras, creating a harmonious alignment for cleansing and activation.

Activating the Hand Chakras
Bring your awareness to the center of your palms. Visualize each hand chakra as a glowing orb of light, radiating vibrant energy. In your dominant hand, see the orb glowing with a golden hue, representing giving and transmitting energy. In your non-dominant

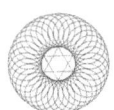

hand, see the orb glowing with a silver hue, representing receiving and balancing energy.

Feel the subtle sensations in your palms—tingling, warmth, or vibration—as the energy begins to flow more freely.

Affirm: *"My hand chakras are open and aligned with the universal flow of energy."*

Cleansing the Hand Chakras
Visualize a deep indigo light from Shadow Reiki entering the center of each palm. This light gently dissolves blockages, residual energy, or stagnation that may have accumulated in your hand chakras from past experiences or overuse. Feel the energy clearing away any heaviness, tension, or resistance.

Once the clearing is complete, imagine a soft rose-pink light from Magdalene/Yeshua Reiki flowing into each palm. This light infuses your hand chakras with love, peace, and a renewed sense of purpose, allowing them to radiate their natural brilliance.

Affirm: *"I release all blockages and stagnant energy, allowing my hand chakras to flow freely and vibrantly."*

Strengthening and Energizing
Visualize intricate golden and silver geometric patterns from Egyptian Sekhem-Seichim Reiki flowing into your hand chakras. These sacred patterns stabilize and fortify their energetic structure, enhancing their ability to channel healing and creative energy.

Next, see vibrant rainbow light from Pleiadian and Arcturian Reiki streaming into each palm. This light activates the multidimensional aspects of your hand chakras, aligning them with universal energy grids and cosmic frequencies.

Feel your hand chakras becoming more radiant, balanced, and powerful, ready to channel, create, and connect with the world.

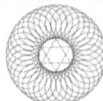

Affirm: *"My hand chakras are vibrant, balanced, and aligned with the universal flow of healing and creation."*

Becoming Familiar with the Energetic Feeling of the Hand Chakras
Spend a few moments focusing on the unique energetic sensations in your palms. Notice the warmth, tingling, pulsation, or flow of energy as it moves through your hand chakras. Observe how they feel when they are balanced, open, and fully aligned with the flow of universal energy.

Affirm: *"I am attuned to the energy of my hand chakras, aligned with the infinite flow of universal life force energy."*

Integration and Multidimensional Alignment
Expand your awareness to include the energetic connections of your hand chakras to your emotional, mental, and spiritual bodies. Visualize their energy radiating outward, harmonizing with your auric field and connecting to the Heart Chakra, Earth Star Chakra, and the universal grids.

Imagine your hand chakras aligning with the multidimensional grids of the cosmos. Feel their energy integrating with your divine blueprint, enhancing your ability to heal, create, and connect with others and the universe.

Affirm: *"My hand chakras are fully integrated, balanced, and aligned with my highest purpose and universal flow."*

Closing and Gratitude
Bring your awareness back to your heart center. Visualize a glowing orb of rainbow light within your chest, pulsating with gratitude and healing energy. Allow this light to radiate outward, integrating all the healing energies you have received.

Take a moment to thank your hand chakras for their role in healing, creation, and connection. Express gratitude for the Rainbow Reiki energies and your ability to align with the universal flow.

When you feel ready, gently bring your awareness back to the present moment. Wiggle your fingers and toes, stretch lightly, and open your eyes.

Post-Meditation Care
- Hydration: Drink water to support the release of blockages and maintain energy flow.
- Reflection: Journal any sensations, insights, or shifts you experienced, noting the energetic feeling in your hands and palms.
- Practice Healing or Creating: Use your hands to create or connect—whether through art, writing, or offering healing touch—to reinforce the activation of your hand chakras.

This meditation can be practiced regularly to maintain the strength, balance, and vitality of your hand chakras while deepening your connection to their energy and the multidimensional frequencies of Rainbow Reiki.

Feet Chakras

Location: Centers of the soles of the feet.

Body Connection: Musculoskeletal system in the legs, feet, and ankles, plus the lymphatic system.

System Influence: Feet chakras support grounding, energy release, and stability. They connect with the lymphatic and circulatory systems, aiding in the release of stagnant energy, promoting detoxification, and grounding energy into Earth.

Rainbow Reiki Feet Chakra Symbol

Feet Chakras Across Traditions

The Feet Chakras, located at the soles of the feet, are powerful energy centers that serve as the primary anchors between the human body and the Earth's energetic field. These chakras facilitate grounding, energetic detoxification, and the absorption of Earth's healing frequencies, allowing for the seamless integration of higher spiritual energies into physical existence. The Feet Chakras act as stabilizers, ensuring balance between cosmic consciousness and material reality. Across spiritual traditions—Egyptian, Tibetan, Arcturian, and Pleiadian—each provides unique insight into their significance, while biblical references offer deeper understanding of their divine function.

In ancient Egyptian wisdom, the Feet Chakras were regarded as gateways to the Duat, the realm of ancestral spirits and the underworld. The feet were considered sacred conduits of divine connection, representing one's spiritual path and ability to walk in alignment with Ma'at (universal balance and truth). Egyptian priests and priestesses anointed their feet with sacred oils infused with

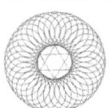

myrrh and frankincense, believing that purification of the feet allowed for the seamless flow of divine energy. The Feet Chakras were also linked to Anubis, the guide of souls, who ensured that one's energetic imprint upon Earth remained in harmony with cosmic order. Stones such as black obsidian, red jasper, and hematite were placed near the feet in burial rites to ensure the soul's grounding and protection as it transitioned between realms.

In Tibetan philosophy, the Feet Chakras are considered the roots of the body's energetic tree, providing stability, grounding, and connection to Earth prana. Tibetan monks believe that energetic imbalance begins in the feet, as they are the first point of contact with the material world. Walking barefoot on sacred ground, chanting vibrational mantras while walking, and practicing foot reflexology are used to stimulate the Feet Chakras, ensuring that energy flows freely between the lower body, meridians, and Earth's core energy. It is believed that through proper activation of these chakras, karma can be neutralized, and one's energetic alignment with the universal flow of dharma can be restored. The Feet Chakras also serve as release points, allowing old energy and emotional blockages to drain from the body into the earth for transmutation.

The Arcturian perspective sees the Feet Chakras as dimensional stabilizers, ensuring that higher vibrational frequencies can be properly integrated into the physical body without energetic overload. Arcturians teach that these chakras function as biomagnetic regulators, adjusting the human energy field to maintain balance within Earth's shifting electromagnetic grid. When properly activated, the Feet Chakras allow for the smooth flow of interdimensional energy, preventing spiritual dissociation, dizziness, and energetic fragmentation. Advanced Arcturian light recalibration techniques involve infusing the Feet Chakras with golden-white light streams, ensuring that individuals remain grounded, yet open to cosmic wisdom. This activation also allows for interdimensional travel, astral stability, and energetic protection while moving between different planes of existence.

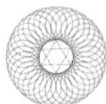

From a Pleiadian viewpoint, the Feet Chakras are seen as Earth harmonizers, attuning individuals to the planet's evolving vibrational frequency. Pleiadians emphasize that the more grounded a person is, the more light they can hold within their energy field. The Feet Chakras serve as portals for crystalline light codes, allowing individuals to absorb Earth's ascension energies and integrate them into their DNA. Pleiadians teach that walking mindfully, connecting with nature, and using sound frequencies such as drumming and toning can help activate and balance the Feet Chakras. This allows for seamless energy flow, enhanced physical vitality, and deepened intuitive awareness of Earth's shifting energy fields. By consciously working with the Feet Chakras, individuals can align with Gaia's ascension timeline, ensuring that their physical, emotional, and spiritual bodies evolve in harmony with the planet.

The Bible contains references that align with the Feet Chakras' function as divine stabilizers and conduits of sacred grounding. Exodus 3:5 states: "'Do not come any closer,' God said. 'Take off your sandals, for the place where you are standing is holy ground.'" This passage signifies the importance of grounding one's energy and purifying the Feet Chakras before engaging with divine presence. Psalm 119:105 further emphasizes this connection, "Your word is a lamp for my feet, a light on my path." This reflects the idea that the Feet Chakras guide an individual's spiritual journey, ensuring alignment with divine truth and purpose. Isaiah 52:7 speaks to the role of these chakras in spreading divine energy: "How beautiful on the mountains are the feet of those who bring good news, who proclaim peace, who bring good tidings, who proclaim salvation ..." This verse suggests that Feet Chakras not only ground divine energy into the earth but also serve as conduits for spreading light and higher wisdom to others.

Together, these teachings reveal the Feet Chakras as sacred energy centers that anchor divine light, balance spiritual energy, and align individuals with Earth's evolving consciousness. Activating and harmonizing these chakras allows for greater stability, energetic protection, and deeper connection to both physical and celestial realms. Whether through Egyptian purification rituals, Tibetan

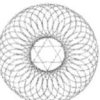

walking meditations, Arcturian energy recalibration, Pleiadian harmonic grounding, or biblical references to sacred paths, the Feet Chakras serve as essential gateways for divine embodiment and earthly balance. By working with these chakras, individuals can remain firmly rooted in their spiritual path, absorb Earth's healing frequencies, and integrate cosmic wisdom into their daily lives.

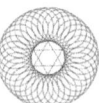

Advanced Feet Chakra Focused Healing, Cleansing, and Energetic Connection

The feet chakras, located at the soles of your feet, are vital energy centers responsible for grounding, balance, and the flow of energy between your body and the earth. These chakras anchor your physical and spiritual energy into Gaia's crystalline grid, enhancing stability, alignment, and a sense of connection to Earth. This advanced guided meditation uses the multidimensional energies of Rainbow Reiki—including Usui, Shadow, Arcturian, Pleiadian, Egyptian Sekhem-Seichim, and Magdalene/Yeshua Reiki—to cleanse, strengthen, and help you connect deeply with the energy of your feet chakras.

Find a quiet and comfortable place where you can sit or lie down. Position your feet flat on the ground or visualize them connecting energetically to the earth. Close your eyes and take several deep breaths, inhaling deeply through your nose and exhaling slowly through your mouth. With each exhale, feel your body relaxing and opening to the flow of universal energy.

Set your intention: *"I invite the advanced energies of Rainbow Reiki to cleanse, balance, and deepen my connection to my feet chakras, grounding me in stability and alignment with Gaia's crystalline grid."*

<u>Grounding and Cosmic Connection</u>
Visualize roots extending from the soles of your feet deep into Earth's core. Feel Gaia's grounding energy rising through these roots, flowing into your feet chakras and anchoring you securely to Earth. At the same time, envision a column of rainbow light descending from the cosmos, moving down through your body and radiating into your feet chakras.

Sense these Earth and cosmic energies merging within your feet chakras, creating a balanced and harmonious foundation for healing and activation.

<u>Activating the Feet Chakras</u>
Bring your awareness to the soles of your feet. Visualize your feet chakras as two glowing orbs of golden and emerald-green light,

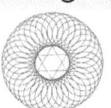

spinning gently and radiating grounding energy. Notice their size, brightness, and movement. Allow yourself to sense the unique energetic feeling of your feet chakras—their warmth, density, or magnetic pull toward Earth.

Affirm: *"My feet chakras are open and aligned with the grounding energies of Gaia and the infinite flow of the cosmos."*

Cleansing the Feet Chakras
Visualize a deep indigo light from Shadow Reiki entering each foot chakra. This light gently dissolves blockages, stagnant energy, or disconnection that may prevent your feet chakras from fully grounding and connecting to Gaia. Feel the indigo light clearing away any heaviness, tension, or resistance.

Once the cleansing is complete, imagine a soft rose-pink light from Magdalene/Yeshua Reiki flowing into each foot chakra. This light infuses them with love, stability, and a renewed sense of connection to Earth's nurturing energy.

Affirm: *"I release all blockages and disconnection, allowing my feet chakras to flow freely and harmoniously with Gaia's energy."*

Strengthening and Energizing
Visualize intricate golden geometric patterns from Egyptian Sekhem-Seichim Reiki flowing into your feet chakras. These sacred patterns stabilize and fortify their energetic structure, enhancing their connection to Gaia's crystalline grid.

Next, see vibrant rainbow light from Pleiadian and Arcturian Reiki streaming into your feet chakras. This light activates the multidimensional aspects of these energy centers, aligning them with universal energy grids while maintaining their grounding function.

Feel your feet chakras becoming more radiant, balanced, and deeply connected to Earth and the cosmos.

Affirm: *"My feet chakras are vibrant, balanced, and fully aligned with Gaia's crystalline energy and universal flow."*

Becoming Familiar with the Energetic Feeling of the Feet Chakras
Spend a few moments focusing on the unique energetic sensation of your feet chakras. Notice their density, warmth, or gentle pulsation. Observe how they feel when they are balanced, open, and fully aligned with the grounding and nurturing energies of Gaia. Deepen your awareness of their energy and their role in your grounding and connection to the earth.

Affirm: *"I am attuned to the energy of my feet chakras, grounded, balanced, and aligned with Gaia's crystalline grid."*

Integration and Multidimensional Alignment
Expand your awareness to include the energetic connections of your feet chakras to your emotional, mental, and spiritual bodies. Visualize their energy radiating outward, harmonizing with your auric field and connecting to the Earth Star Chakra and Gaia's crystalline grid.

Imagine your feet chakras aligning with the multidimensional grids of the cosmos and Earth. Feel their energy integrating with your divine blueprint, enhancing your sense of balance, stability, and alignment with Gaia's energy.

Affirm: *"My feet chakras are fully integrated, balanced, and aligned with my highest potential and Gaia's nurturing flow."*

Closing and Gratitude
Bring your awareness back to your heart center. Visualize a glowing orb of rainbow light within your chest, pulsating with gratitude and healing energy. Allow this light to radiate outward, integrating all the healing energies you have received.

Take a moment to thank your feet chakras for their role in grounding, balancing, and connecting you to Gaia. Express gratitude

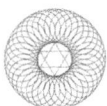

for the Rainbow Reiki energies and your ability to align with Earth's and the cosmos' infinite flow.

When you feel ready, gently bring your awareness back to the present moment. Wiggle your fingers and toes, stretch lightly, and open your eyes.

Post-Meditation Care
- Hydration: Drink water to support the release of energetic blockages and enhance grounding.
- Reflection: Journal any sensations, insights, or shifts you experienced, noting how your connection to Earth feels.
- Grounding Practices: Spend time in nature, walk barefoot on grass or soil, or meditate with grounding crystals such as smoky quartz, hematite, or red jasper.

This meditation can be practiced regularly to maintain the strength, balance, and vitality of your feet chakras while deepening your connection to their energy and the multidimensional frequencies of Rainbow Reiki.

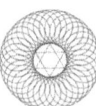

Knee Chakras

Location: Center of each knee.

Body Connection: Joints and connective tissues in the knees, as well as muscles and ligaments in the legs.

System Influence: Knee chakras are connected to flexibility and adaptability, impacting joint health and range of motion. They support resilience in the musculoskeletal system, helping with fluid movement and adaptability in the body, and can be essential for reducing tension in the knees.

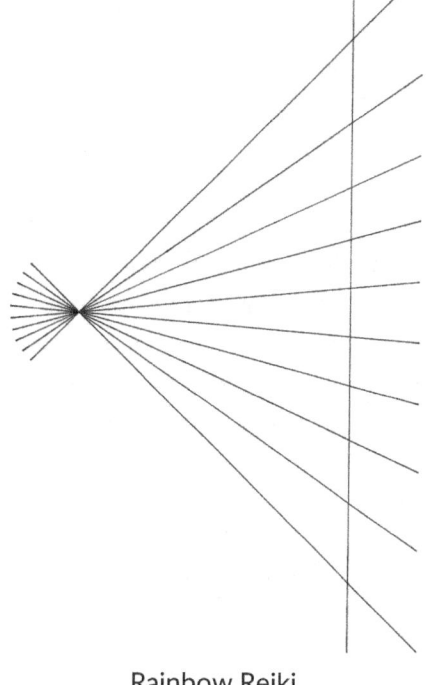

Rainbow Reiki
Knee Chakra Symbol

Knee Chakras Across Traditions

The Knee Chakras, located at the center of each knee, serve as powerful energy centers that regulate stability, adaptability, and movement in both the physical and spiritual sense. These chakras play a crucial role in grounding, flexibility, and the ability to move forward in alignment with one's life path. The Knee Chakras act as energetic shock absorbers, ensuring smooth transitions through life's changes while maintaining stability and balance. Across spiritual traditions—Egyptian, Tibetan, Arcturian, and Pleiadian—each provides unique insight into their significance, while biblical references offer deeper understanding of their divine function.

In ancient Egyptian wisdom, the Knee Chakras were regarded as gateways of surrender and reverence, representing the willingness to kneel before divine wisdom and universal truth. The knees were considered sacred points of humility, where one's personal will meets divine guidance. Egyptian initiates were often depicted in positions of genuflection (kneeling) before gods and higher cosmic forces, symbolizing alignment with higher will. The Knee Chakras were linked to Ma'at, the goddess of truth and balance, as they

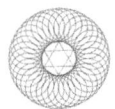

ensured one could move through life in harmony with universal law. Rituals involving sandalwood, frankincense, and grounding stones such as red jasper and hematite were performed to strengthen the Knee Chakras, ensuring that one's journey remained both fluid and spiritually aligned.

In Tibetan philosophy, the Knee Chakras are recognized as energy regulators of movement and karma, playing a crucial role in how an individual navigates change and embraces the path of least resistance. Tibetan monks believe that stiffness in the knees reflects energetic resistance to life's flow, while flexibility symbolizes alignment with the natural cycles of existence. Walking meditations, yogic postures that stretch and engage the knees, and chanting deep vibrational tones are used to activate and balance these chakras, ensuring one moves through life's transitions with grace and ease. The Knee Chakras also serve as release points, allowing stagnant karma and emotional blockages to be transmuted through conscious movement and breathwork.

The Arcturian perspective sees the Knee Chakras as adaptive frequency regulators, ensuring that one can adjust to shifting vibrational realities and integrate multidimensional energy into physical movement. Arcturians teach that these chakras act as stabilizers of quantum energy flow, allowing individuals to remain balanced as they transition between different states of consciousness and planetary frequency shifts. When fully activated, the Knee Chakras serve as energetic pivots, preventing spiritual rigidity and resistance to growth. Advanced Arcturian recalibration techniques involve infusing the Knee Chakras with pulsing violet-blue light, ensuring that one's spiritual, emotional, and physical bodies remain fluid, yet strong, during times of change and ascension.

From a Pleiadian viewpoint, the Knee Chakras are seen as synchronization points between divine timing and personal movement. Pleiadians emphasize that the knees hold the energetic imprints of past journeys, including ancestral patterns, karmic ties, and unresolved fears related to moving forward. The Knee Chakras

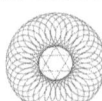

serve as tuning points, allowing individuals to adjust their frequency to align with their highest soul path. Pleiadians teach that dance, rhythmic movement, and harmonic toning are essential in activating these chakras, ensuring that one's movements remain in harmony with cosmic flow. Through vibrational alignment, conscious movement, and grounding techniques, the Knee Chakras become fully attuned to Earth's energetic evolution, supporting both physical mobility and spiritual progress.

The Bible contains references that align with the Knee Chakras' function as energy centers of surrender, movement, and divine service. Philippians 2:10 reads, "that at the name of Jesus every knee should bow, in heaven and on earth and under the earth." This passage reflects the Knee Chakras' role in spiritual humility and alignment with divine will. Isaiah 35:3 further emphasizes their importance: "Strengthen the feeble hands, steady the knees that give way." This verse speaks to the Knee Chakras' role in providing stability and resilience, ensuring that one can move forward with strength and purpose. Hebrews 12:12-13 also highlights their significance: "Therefore, strengthen your feeble arms and weak knees. 'Make level paths for your feet,' so that the lame may not be disabled, but rather healed." This verse illustrates how proper energetic alignment of the Knee Chakras contributes to balance, healing, and the ability to walk one's spiritual path with confidence.

Together, these teachings reveal the Knee Chakras as sacred energy centers that regulate movement, adaptability, and surrender to divine timing. Activating and harmonizing these chakras allows for greater flexibility, resilience, and the ability to move through life's changes with ease and grace. Whether through Egyptian reverence rituals, Tibetan movement meditations, Arcturian frequency recalibration, Pleiadian harmonic attunement, or biblical references to surrender and strength, the Knee Chakras serve as essential gateways for spiritual fluidity and alignment. By working with these chakras, individuals can overcome resistance, embrace their life's journey, and remain energetically attuned to both Earth's grounding force and the higher celestial flow.

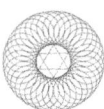

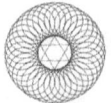

Advanced Knee Chakra Focused Healing, Cleansing, and Energetic Connection

The knee chakras, located at the center of each knee, play a crucial role in grounding, mobility, flexibility, and balance. These chakras are vital for navigating life's changes with stability and resilience. They connect the energy flow between the lower and upper body while anchoring you to Gaia's crystalline energy. This advanced guided meditation uses the multidimensional energies of Rainbow Reiki—including Usui, Shadow, Arcturian, Pleiadian, Egyptian Sekhem-Seichim, and Magdalene/Yeshua Reiki—to cleanse, strengthen, and help you connect deeply with the energy of your knee chakras.

Find a quiet and comfortable space to sit or lie down. Ensure your knees are relaxed and supported. Close your eyes and take several deep breaths, inhaling deeply through your nose and exhaling slowly through your mouth. Allow your body to relax, releasing tension and opening yourself to the flow of universal energy.

Set your intention: *"I invite the advanced energies of Rainbow Reiki to cleanse, balance, and deepen my connection to my knee chakras, enhancing my stability, flexibility, and alignment with Gaia's energy."*

<u>Grounding and Cosmic Alignment</u>
Visualize roots extending from your feet into Earth's crystalline core. Feel Gaia's nurturing energy rising through these roots, traveling up your legs, and flowing into your knee chakras. At the same time, envision a radiant column of rainbow light descending from the cosmos, entering your crown chakra, moving through your body, and radiating into your knees.

Feel these Earth and cosmic energies merging in your knee chakras, creating a harmonious foundation for healing and activation.

<u>Activating the Knee Chakras</u>
Bring your awareness to the center of each knee. Visualize your knee chakras as glowing orbs of golden and emerald-green light, spinning gently and radiating stability and flexibility. Notice their size, brightness, and movement. Allow yourself to sense the unique

energetic feeling of your knee chakras—their density, warmth, or grounding vibration.

Affirm: *"My knee chakras are open, balanced, and aligned with Gaia's grounding energy and universal flow."*

Cleansing the Knee Chakras
Visualize a deep indigo light from Shadow Reiki entering each knee chakra. This light gently dissolves blockages, tension, or stagnant energy that may restrict your ability to move forward or adapt to change. Feel the energy clearing away any heaviness, resistance, or fear stored in your knees.

Once the cleansing is complete, imagine a soft rose-pink light from Magdalene/Yeshua Reiki flowing into your knee chakras. This light infuses them with love, harmony, and a renewed sense of stability and flexibility.

Affirm: *"I release all blockages and resistance, allowing my knee chakras to flow freely and harmoniously with Gaia's energy."*

Strengthening and Energizing
Visualize intricate golden geometric patterns from Egyptian Sekhem-Seichim Reiki flowing into your knee chakras. These sacred patterns stabilize and fortify their energetic structure, enhancing their connection to Gaia's crystalline grid and supporting mobility and resilience.

Next, see vibrant rainbow light from Pleiadian and Arcturian Reiki streaming into your knee chakras. This light activates the multidimensional aspects of these energy centers, aligning them with universal energy grids and cosmic frequencies.

Feel your knee chakras becoming more radiant, balanced, and deeply connected to Earth and the cosmos, supporting fluidity in movement and life transitions.

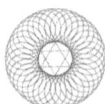

Affirm: *"My knee chakras are vibrant, balanced, and fully aligned with Gaia's grounding energy and universal flow."*

Becoming Familiar with the Energetic Feeling of the Knee Chakras
Spend a few moments focusing on the unique energetic sensation of your knee chakras. Notice their density, warmth, or subtle pulsation. Observe how they feel when they are balanced, open, and fully aligned with the grounding and stabilizing energies of Gaia. Deepen your awareness of their energy and their role in supporting flexibility, stability, and adaptability.

Affirm: *"I am attuned to the energy of my knee chakras, grounded, flexible, and resilient in my journey through life."*

Integration and Multidimensional Alignment
Expand your awareness to include the energetic connections of your knee chakras to your emotional, mental, and spiritual bodies. Visualize their energy radiating outward, harmonizing with your auric field and connecting to the Feet Chakras, Earth Star Chakra, and Gaia's crystalline grid.

Imagine your knee chakras aligning with the multidimensional grids of the cosmos and Earth. Feel their energy integrating with your divine blueprint, enhancing your ability to navigate life's transitions with grace and stability.

Affirm: *"My knee chakras are fully integrated, balanced, and aligned with Gaia's nurturing flow and my highest spiritual purpose."*

Closing and Gratitude
Bring your awareness back to your heart center. Visualize a glowing orb of rainbow light within your chest, pulsating with gratitude and healing energy. Allow this light to radiate outward, integrating all the healing energies you have received.

Take a moment to thank your knee chakras for their role in supporting your physical and energetic stability. Express gratitude

for the Rainbow Reiki energies and your ability to align with Earth's and the cosmos' infinite flow.

When you feel ready, gently bring your awareness back to the present moment. Wiggle your fingers and toes, stretch lightly, and open your eyes.

Post-Meditation Care
- Hydration: Drink water to support the release of energetic blockages and maintain fluid energy flow.
- Reflection: Journal any sensations, insights, or shifts you experienced, noting how your connection to your knees and mobility feels.
- Grounding Practices: Engage in gentle movement such as yoga, walking, or stretching to reinforce balance and stability in your knees and legs.

This meditation can be practiced regularly to maintain the strength, balance, and vitality of your knee chakras while deepening your connection to their energy and the multidimensional frequencies of Rainbow Reiki.

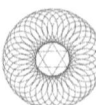

Chakra at the Base of the Skull (Mouth of God or Well of Dreams)

Location: Base of the skull, between the brainstem and top of the spine.
Body Connection: Brainstem, nervous system, and cranial nerves.
System

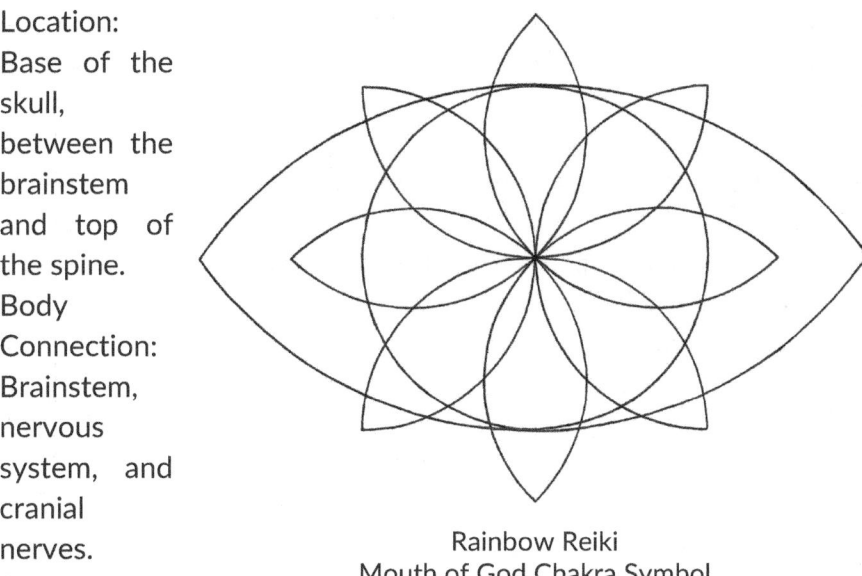

Rainbow Reiki
Mouth of God Chakra Symbol

Influence: This chakra is linked to higher brain functions, influencing intuition, psychic abilities, and spiritual insight. It is connected to the nervous system and brainstem, helping in balancing neurological activity and supporting deep relaxation and spiritual experiences.

Mouth of God Chakra Across Traditions

The Mouth of God Chakra, also known as the Well of Dreams Chakra, is located at the base of the skull, where the spine meets the cranium. This chakra serves as the gateway between the conscious and subconscious mind, the physical and spiritual realms, and the divine blueprint of the soul's higher purpose. It is considered one of the most mystical and powerful energy centers, acting as the seat of divine communication, spiritual vision, and multidimensional downloads. It also regulates the flow of celestial energy into the body, ensuring that divine wisdom and intuitive insight can be fully embodied. Across spiritual traditions—Egyptian, Tibetan, Arcturian, and Pleiadian—each offers unique perspectives on its significance, while biblical references provide deeper understanding of its divine function.

In ancient Egyptian wisdom, the Mouth of God Chakra was regarded as the Seat of Divine Utterance, connected to the god Thoth, the

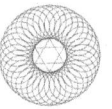

deity of sacred knowledge, writing, and divine speech. The Egyptians believed that this chakra was the center through which cosmic wisdom and prophecy were received, allowing individuals to speak divine truth into existence. The Mouth of God was also linked to the ankh, the symbol of life, as it was believed to channel the eternal breath of the gods into human consciousness. Egyptian high priests and initiates activated this chakra through sacred incantations, hieroglyphic meditations, and anointing rituals using blue lotus and frankincense to enhance clairaudience, divine speech, and mystical insight. The Well of Dreams was considered the point where the Ka (spirit) and Ba (soul) merged to receive divine revelations, allowing for direct communion with the Neteru (gods).

In Tibetan philosophy, the Mouth of God Chakra is seen as the Gate of the Dharmakaya, the portal through which divine consciousness enters human awareness. This chakra is associated with the Vajra (thunderbolt wisdom), representing the sudden and transformative power of divine enlightenment. Tibetan monks activate this center through mantra chanting, deep throat toning, and cranial pressure point meditation, allowing for the unblocking of suppressed spiritual visions and higher wisdom. The Well of Dreams is considered a karmic purification center, where unresolved subconscious patterns and ancestral imprints are dissolved to make way for pure divine communication. This chakra is also used in dream yoga and advanced lucid dreaming techniques, enabling individuals to access the Akashic Records and receive direct guidance from enlightened beings.

The Arcturian perspective sees the Mouth of God Chakra as the Neural Star Gate, a high-frequency conduit between the pineal gland, spinal column, and interdimensional communication centers. This energy center functions as a biological antenna, receiving and transmitting quantum information from higher dimensional planes. Arcturians teach that this chakra contains encoded light keys that, when activated, allow individuals to speak and hear the language of light, access multidimensional timelines, and recalibrate their vibrational frequency to match higher cosmic intelligence. Arcturian recalibration techniques involve golden-white photonic infusions

into the base of the skull, ensuring that the Mouth of God Chakra is aligned with the Galactic Akashic Fields, allowing for instantaneous downloads of universal knowledge and enhanced telepathic communication.

From a Pleiadian viewpoint, the Mouth of God Chakra is regarded as the Harmonic Resonance Gateway, where the divine symphony of creation enters the body through sound, frequency, and vibration. Pleiadians emphasize that this chakra governs the power of the voice, sacred song, and vibrational healing, making it essential for those who use their voice as a tool for channeling, light language, and divine manifestation. The Well of Dreams is also seen as the portal for etheric dreaming and interdimensional travel, allowing individuals to receive clear guidance from their star lineage and spiritual councils. Pleiadians teach that toning, overtone chanting, and vibrational sound healing can awaken the latent potential of this chakra, ensuring that the voice becomes a crystalline conduit for divine truth and cosmic wisdom.

The Bible contains references that align with the Mouth of God Chakra's function as the gateway to divine speech, prophecy, and celestial vision. Jeremiah 1:9 states, "Then the LORD reached out his hand and touched my mouth and said to me, 'I have put my words in your mouth.'" This passage reflects the activation of the Mouth of God Chakra as a portal for divine communication, where an individual speaks not from ego, but from Source wisdom. Job 33:14-16 also supports this concept:

> For God does speak – now one way, now another – though no one perceives it. In a dream, in a vision of the night, when deep sleep falls on people as they slumber in their beds, he may speak in their ears and terrify them with warnings.

This verse highlights the Well of Dreams Chakra as the center through which divine messages enter human awareness, particularly through dreams and visions. Revelation 1:10 further echoes this theme: "On the Lord's Day I was in the Spirit, and I heard behind me a loud voice like a trumpet." This symbolizes the Mouth of God

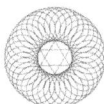

Chakra's role in clairaudience and receiving divine transmissions from higher realms.

Together, these teachings reveal the Mouth of God (Well of Dreams) Chakra as the ultimate gateway for divine speech, spiritual vision, and interdimensional downloads. Activating and harmonizing this chakra allows individuals to receive celestial guidance, access higher-dimensional wisdom, and channel divine energy through the voice. Whether through Egyptian sacred utterances, Tibetan mantra resonance, Arcturian frequency recalibration, Pleiadian harmonic activation, or biblical references to divine speech and prophecy, the Mouth of God Chakra serves as the portal for cosmic intelligence to enter human consciousness. By working with this chakra, individuals can clear distortions in their energetic field, awaken their spiritual voice, and receive profound revelations that guide them toward their highest destiny.

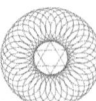

Advanced Mouth of God Chakra Focused Healing, Cleansing, and Energetic Connection

The Mouth of God Chakra, also known as the Well of Dreams Chakra or Alta Major Chakra, is located at the base of the skull where the spine meets the brainstem. This chakra is a gateway for divine communication and cosmic wisdom, connecting the physical and spiritual realms. It governs intuition, higher guidance, and the expression of divine truth.

This advanced guided meditation uses the multidimensional energies of Rainbow Reiki—including Usui, Shadow, Arcturian, Pleiadian, Egyptian Sekhem-Seichim, and Magdalene/Yeshua Reiki—to cleanse, strengthen, and help you connect deeply with the energy of the Mouth of God Chakra.

Find a quiet, comfortable space where you can sit or lie down. Close your eyes and take several deep breaths, inhaling deeply through your nose and exhaling slowly through your mouth. With each exhale, allow your body to relax and release tension, opening your energy field to the flow of divine light.

Set your intention: *"I invite the advanced energies of Rainbow Reiki to cleanse, balance, and deepen my connection to my Mouth of God Chakra, aligning me with divine communication and higher truth."*

Grounding and Cosmic Alignment

Visualize roots extending from your feet deep into Earth's crystalline core. Feel Gaia's grounding energy rising through these roots, stabilizing and supporting your physical and energetic bodies. Simultaneously, envision a radiant column of rainbow light descending from the cosmos, flowing down through your crown chakra and settling at the base of your skull where the Mouth of God Chakra resides.

Feel the merging of Earth's grounding energy and cosmic light within your Mouth of God Chakra, creating a balanced and harmonious foundation for cleansing and activation.

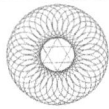

Activating the Mouth of God Chakra

Bring your awareness to the base of your skull at the top of your spine. Visualize your Mouth of God Chakra as a luminous orb of indigo and golden light, spinning gently and radiating clarity and divine connection. Notice its size, brightness, and rhythm. Allow yourself to sense the unique energetic feeling of this chakra—its subtle vibration, depth, or sense of expansion.

Affirm: *"My Mouth of God Chakra is open and aligned with divine communication and cosmic truth."*

Cleansing the Mouth of God Chakra

Visualize a deep indigo light from Shadow Reiki entering your Mouth of God Chakra. This light gently dissolves blockages, fears, or stagnant energy that may restrict your ability to connect with divine guidance or express higher truth. Feel the indigo light clearing away any tension, disconnection, or energetic debris.

Once the clearing is complete, imagine a soft rose-gold light from Magdalene/Yeshua Reiki flowing into the chakra. This light infuses it with love, divine peace, and a renewed sense of clarity and openness to cosmic communication.

Affirm: *"I release all blockages and limitations, allowing my Mouth of God Chakra to flow freely with divine truth and cosmic light."*

Strengthening and Energizing

Visualize intricate golden and crystalline geometric patterns from Egyptian Sekhem-Seichim Reiki flowing into your Mouth of God Chakra. These sacred patterns stabilize and fortify its structure, enhancing its ability to channel divine energy and cosmic frequencies.

Next, see vibrant rainbow light from Pleiadian and Arcturian Reiki streaming into the chakra. This light activates the multidimensional aspects of the Mouth of God Chakra, aligning it with the universal grids and cosmic wisdom.

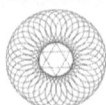

Feel your Mouth of God Chakra becoming more radiant, balanced, and aligned with your divine truth and the infinite flow of universal energy.

Affirm: *"My Mouth of God Chakra is vibrant, balanced, and fully aligned with divine communication and higher guidance."*

<u>Becoming Familiar with the Energetic Feeling of the Mouth of God Chakra</u>
Spend a few moments focusing on the unique energetic sensation of your Mouth of God Chakra. Notice its vibration, depth, or sense of alignment with divine truth. Observe how it feels when it is balanced, open, and fully connected to the flow of cosmic wisdom and spiritual guidance.

Deepen your awareness of its energy and its role as a bridge between the physical and spiritual realms.

Affirm: *"I am attuned to the energy of my Mouth of God Chakra, aligned with divine truth, cosmic wisdom, and infinite guidance."*

<u>Integration and Multidimensional Alignment</u>
Expand your awareness to include the energetic connections of your Mouth of God Chakra to your emotional, mental, and spiritual bodies. Visualize its energy radiating outward, harmonizing with your auric field and connecting seamlessly with your Throat Chakra, Third Eye Chakra, and Crown Chakra.
Imagine your Mouth of God Chakra aligning with the multidimensional grids of the cosmos and your divine blueprint. Feel its energy integrating with your spiritual essence, enhancing your ability to communicate, receive, and express divine truth and guidance.

Affirm: *"My Mouth of God Chakra is fully integrated, balanced, and aligned with my highest spiritual purpose and cosmic truth."*

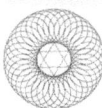

Closing and Gratitude

Bring your awareness back to your heart center. Visualize a glowing orb of rainbow light within your chest, pulsating with gratitude and peace. Allow this light to radiate outward, integrating all the healing energies you have received.

Take a moment to thank your Mouth of God Chakra for its role in guiding your spiritual connection and communication. Express gratitude for the Rainbow Reiki energies and your ability to align with divine truth and higher realms.

When you feel ready, gently bring your awareness back to the present moment. Wiggle your fingers and toes, stretch lightly, and open your eyes.

Post-Meditation Care
- Hydration: Drink water to support the integration of higher energies and release of any residual blockages.
- Reflection: Journal any insights, sensations, or shifts you experienced, noting how your connection to divine guidance feels.
- Spiritual Practices: Spend time meditating, journaling, or engaging in mindful communication to deepen your connection to your divine truth and cosmic guidance.

This meditation can be practiced regularly to maintain the strength, balance, and vitality of your Mouth of God Chakra while deepening your connection to its energy and the multidimensional frequencies of Rainbow Reiki.

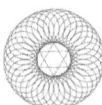

Telepathic Chakras
Location: Center of the forehead, slightly above and between the eyebrows (Third Eye Chakra), and subtle energy points around the temples.
Body

Rainbow Reiki Telepathic Chakra Symbol

Connection: The brain, pineal gland, pituitary gland, and nervous system.

System Influence: Telepathic chakras govern intuitive communication, mental clarity, and the ability to send and receive thoughts or emotions energetically. They enhance extrasensory perception, psychic abilities, and higher-consciousness connection. These chakras are critical for telepathic communication, accessing spiritual insight, and fostering profound connections with others and the universe.

Telepathic Chakras Across Traditions
The Telepathic Chakras, located within the higher mind centers, pineal gland, throat, and energetic field surrounding the head, function as portals of non-verbal communication, multidimensional thought transmission, and the reception of higher consciousness frequencies. These chakras facilitate interpersonal and interdimensional telepathy, energy-based communication, and the ability to transmit and receive vibrational knowledge without spoken words. They allow for the exchange of pure thought,

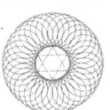

emotional resonance, and quantum data across time and space. Across spiritual traditions—Egyptian, Tibetan, Arcturian, and Pleiadian—each offers unique perspectives on their function, while biblical references provide deeper understanding of their sacred role in divine communion.

In ancient Egyptian wisdom, the Telepathic Chakras were regarded as the Centers of Divine Knowing, linked to Horus, the all-seeing god of higher vision, and Thoth, the scribe of universal knowledge. The Egyptians believed that true wisdom did not rely on verbal communication but was transferred energetically through sacred resonance and hieroglyphic transmissions. High initiates were trained in thought-form projection, energetic language, and telepathic communion with the Neteru (divine forces). The Eye of Horus, often depicted in temples, represents the activation of telepathic sight and inner vision, allowing one to receive divine messages beyond the limitations of spoken words. Lapis lazuli, gold, and monatomic elements were used to enhance the energetic sensitivity of the mind centers, ensuring a clear channel for telepathic connection with celestial realms and the Akashic Records.

In Tibetan philosophy, the Telepathic Chakras are known as the Pathways of Inner Hearing, governing the ability to perceive thought vibrations, subtle energies, and the unspoken words of sentient beings and divine forces. Tibetan monks believe that telepathy is not a supernatural gift but a latent ability of the human mind, accessible through deep meditative attunement, stillness, and vibrational refinement. The practice of silent retreat, inner mantra chanting, and sky-gazing meditation strengthens these chakras, allowing one to pick up the frequencies of enlightened beings, communicate with spirit guides, and tune into the thoughts of others with absolute clarity. The Vajrayana tradition teaches that the pineal gland and throat chakras act as bridges for higher communication, with full telepathic activation leading to direct knowledge transmission from the cosmic mind.

The Arcturian perspective sees the Telepathic Chakras as neural light circuits, functioning as transmitters and receivers of

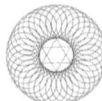

multidimensional intelligence. Arcturians teach that these chakras process holographic data beyond linear language, allowing individuals to perceive information from higher densities, communicate with extraterrestrial and celestial beings, and access energetic blueprints of past, present, and future realities. Arcturians assist in activating these chakras through frequency calibration, crystalline energy infusions, and photonic recalibration of the neural pathways. When fully attuned, these chakras allow for instantaneous knowing, thought projection over great distances, and the ability to synchronize one's consciousness with cosmic networks. Bioluminescent energy fields are often activated around the head, signifying the evolution of telepathic abilities into higher-dimensional awareness.

From a Pleiadian viewpoint, the Telepathic Chakras are seen as Harmonic Resonance Centers, which allow individuals to exchange energy-based language, vibrational emotions, and frequency-encoded messages with others and higher-dimensional beings. Pleiadians emphasize that these chakras resonate with heart-centered telepathy, ensuring that thought transmissions are infused with pure intention, love, and vibrational harmony. The Pleiadian light language is said to be transmitted through these chakras, bypassing verbal structures to encode direct vibrational knowledge into the recipient's energetic field. Tonal frequencies, star language activations, and harmonic balancing techniques are used to expand the range of telepathic communication, ensuring that one can access higher streams of divine intelligence while maintaining balance in the physical form.

The Bible contains references that align with the Telepathic Chakras' function as centers of divine communication and thought transmission. Matthew 9:4 states, "Knowing their thoughts, Jesus said, 'Why do you entertain evil thoughts in your hearts?'" This passage reflects the activation of telepathic perception, where divine awareness surpasses spoken words. This is further illustrated in 1 Corinthians 2:16: "For, 'Who has known the mind of the Lord so as to instruct him?' But we have the mind of Christ." This verse symbolizes the ability to connect to the divine intelligence field,

receiving direct transmissions of universal wisdom through the telepathic centers. John 16:13 also supports this: "But when he, the Spirit of truth, comes, he will guide you into all the truth …" This passage highlights the role of the Telepathic Chakras in receiving pure, unfiltered divine knowledge beyond the constraints of human language.

Together, these teachings reveal the Telepathic Chakras as sacred gateways for thought transmission, divine intelligence reception, and multidimensional communication. Activating and harmonizing these chakras allows individuals to access telepathic abilities, receive direct divine messages, and communicate beyond spoken language. Whether through Egyptian hieroglyphic thought transmission, Tibetan inner hearing practices, Arcturian neural recalibration, Pleiadian harmonic attunement, or biblical references to divine telepathy, the Telepathic Chakras serve as cosmic receivers for higher intelligence. By working with these energy centers, individuals can unlock advanced spiritual perception, align their consciousness with universal knowledge, and engage in seamless thought exchange with beings across all realms of existence.

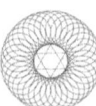

Advanced Telepathic Chakra Focused Healing, Cleansing, and Energetic Connection

The telepathic chakras, including the Third Eye Chakra and supporting subtle energy points, are key centers for connecting to higher consciousness and enabling telepathic communication. These chakras empower your ability to receive and transmit energetic messages, enhance your intuition, and connect with universal wisdom. Using the multidimensional energies of Rainbow Reiki—Usui, Shadow, Arcturian, Pleiadian, Egyptian Sekhem-Seichim, and Magdalene/Yeshua Reiki—this advanced guided meditation helps cleanse, activate, and strengthen your telepathic chakras for expanded awareness and communication.

Find a peaceful and quiet space where you can remain undisturbed. Sit comfortably with your spine straight or lie down with your body relaxed. Close your eyes and take several deep breaths, inhaling through your nose and exhaling through your mouth. With each exhale, release tension and open yourself to the flow of universal energy.

Set your intention: *"I invite the advanced energies of Rainbow Reiki to cleanse, balance, and awaken my telepathic chakras, aligning me with the flow of universal wisdom and intuitive communication."*

<u>Grounding and Cosmic Alignment</u>
Visualize roots growing from your feet and extending deep into Earth's crystalline core. Feel Gaia's grounding energy rise through these roots, flowing into your body and reaching your Third Eye and temple chakras. Simultaneously, envision a radiant column of rainbow light descending from the cosmos, entering your crown chakra, and flowing into your telepathic chakras.

Feel the merging of Earth and cosmic energies in these chakras, harmonizing and preparing them for cleansing and activation.

<u>Activating the Telepathic Chakras</u>
Bring your awareness to your Third Eye Chakra, situated in the center of your forehead, and the energy points at your temples.

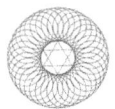

Visualize the Third Eye as a glowing indigo orb and the temple points as shimmering violet lights.

See the indigo orb glowing brighter, symbolizing clarity and receptivity to higher wisdom. Visualize the temple points pulsing gently with violet light, amplifying your telepathic connection. Feel these energy centers beginning to awaken, radiating warmth and subtle vibrations.

Affirm: *"My telepathic chakras are open and attuned to the flow of divine wisdom and communication."*

Cleansing the Telepathic Chakras
Visualize a dark blue, almost black, light from Shadow Reiki entering the Third Eye and temple points. This light gently dissolves blockages, fear-based thoughts, and mental clutter that hinder telepathic communication. Feel the energy clearing away any resistance or distractions, leaving these chakras clear and open.

Once the cleansing is complete, imagine a soft golden light from Magdalene/Yeshua Reiki filling the Third Eye and temple chakras. This light infuses them with love, peace, and divine trust, enabling pure and open communication with yourself and the universe.

Affirm: *"I release all blockages and stagnant energy, allowing my telepathic chakras to function with clarity and ease."*

Strengthening and Energizing
Visualize intricate golden and silver geometric patterns from Egyptian Sekhem-Seichim Reiki flowing into the telepathic chakras. These sacred patterns stabilize and fortify their energetic structure, strengthening your capacity for telepathic communication and intuitive perception.

Next, see streams of vibrant rainbow light from Pleiadian and Arcturian Reiki entering your Third Eye and temples. This light activates the multidimensional aspects of your telepathic chakras, aligning them with universal frequencies and grids.

Feel these chakras becoming more vibrant, powerful, and fully aligned with your highest potential for telepathic and intuitive communication.

Affirm: *"My telepathic chakras are radiant, balanced, and connected to the infinite wisdom of the universe."*

Becoming Familiar with the Energetic Sensations of the Telepathic Chakras
Spend a few moments focusing on the unique sensations in your Third Eye and temple chakras. Notice the subtle pulsations, warmth, tingling, or vibrations as the energy flows through these centers. Observe how they feel when balanced, open, and aligned with the universal energy.

Affirm: *"I am attuned to the energy of my telepathic chakras, aligned with universal wisdom and telepathic connection."*

Integration and Multidimensional Alignment
Expand your awareness to include the connection between your telepathic chakras and your mental, emotional, and spiritual bodies. Visualize their energy radiating outward, harmonizing with your auric field and linking to the Heart Chakra, Crown Chakra, and the universal energy grids.

See your telepathic chakras aligning with the multidimensional grids of the cosmos. Feel their energy integrating with your divine blueprint, enhancing your ability to communicate telepathically, perceive intuitively, and connect with higher dimensions.

Affirm: *"My telepathic chakras are fully integrated, balanced, and aligned with my highest purpose and universal flow."*

Returning to the Present Moment
Bring your awareness back to your heart center. Visualize a glowing orb of rainbow light within your chest, pulsating with gratitude and

healing energy. Allow this light to radiate outward, integrating all the energies you have received.

Take a moment to thank your telepathic chakras for their role in intuitive communication and connection. Express gratitude for the Rainbow Reiki energies and your alignment with universal wisdom.

When you feel ready, gently bring your awareness back to the present moment. Wiggle your fingers and toes, stretch lightly, and open your eyes.

Post-Meditation Care
- Hydration: Drink water to support the release of blockages and maintain energy flow.
- Reflection: Journal any sensations, insights, or shifts you experienced, particularly noting your intuitive or telepathic perceptions.
- Practice Telepathic Communication: Engage in practices such as visualization, connecting with loved ones energetically, or focusing on intuitive messages to strengthen your telepathic abilities.

This meditation can be practiced regularly to maintain the strength, balance, and vitality of your telepathic chakras while deepening your connection to their energy and the multidimensional frequencies of Rainbow Reiki.

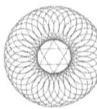

Elementals

Elementals are spiritual beings associated with the natural elements (Earth, Water, Fire, and Air, and sometimes Ether/spirit)—are potent allies in multidimensional healing. They embody the forces of nature and represent foundational energies that shape our physical and spiritual existence. Working with elementals can deepen a client's connection with the natural world, support emotional and energetic healing, and assist in releasing and balancing elemental energies within their own being. Elementals help clients connect with grounding energies, balancing them in the physical world and establishing a stable foundation for deeper exploration. Each elemental energy can address specific emotional states. For example, Water elementals assist with emotional flow and release, while Earth elementals help with stability and grounding. Elementals can help clear blockages and stagnant energy from the client's energy field, promoting a balanced and harmonious state. Elementals support clients in aligning with natural rhythms and cycles, like seasons and moon phases, helping them connect to the ebb and flow of nature and integrate these cycles into their lives. Working with elementals fosters a sense of

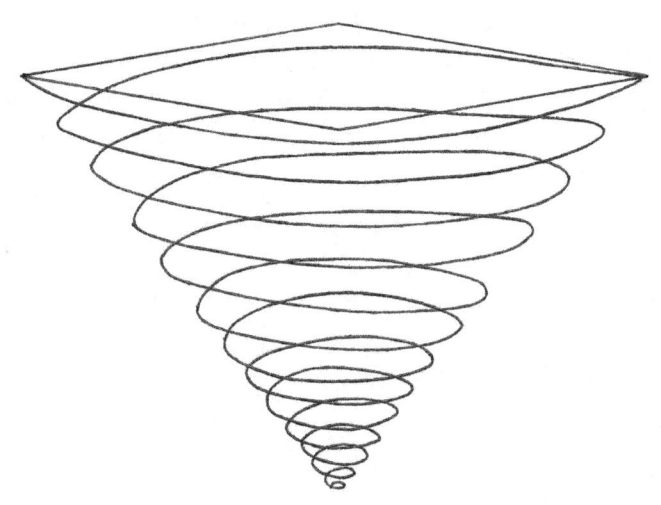

Rainbow Reiki Elementals Symbol

interconnectedness with nature, reminding clients of their place in the natural world and deepening their spiritual awareness.

The terms Ether and Aether are often used interchangeably, but they carry distinct meanings depending on the context—particularly when viewed through scientific, philosophical, or metaphysical lenses. Aether, rooted in ancient Greek philosophy, was considered the fifth element beyond Earth, Air, Fire, and Water. Aristotle and other classical thinkers believed it was the divine substance that filled the heavens, a medium through which celestial bodies moved. In esoteric and spiritual traditions, Aether evolved into a concept representing the subtle, energetic, or spiritual plane—an unseen life force or divine field that permeates and connects all things. It is often associated with spirit, consciousness, the Akashic records, and the energetic space between realms.

On the other hand, Ether has more scientific and material connotations. In the 19th century, physicists hypothesized the existence of a "luminiferous ether," a medium believed to carry light waves through the vacuum of space. This theory was later disproven by the Michelson-Morley experiment in 1887, which laid the groundwork for Einstein's theory of relativity. In chemistry, ether refers to a specific class of organic compounds, such as diethyl ether, which was historically used as an anesthetic. Though largely obsolete in physics today, the word "ether" sometimes reappears in poetic or mystical language, often blurring into the metaphysical idea of Aether.

Throughout the Rainbow Reiki book, you will notice that I use the words Ether and Aether interchangeably. This is an intentional choice that reflects the integrated nature of the work—honoring both the metaphysical and scientific aspects of energetic healing. The language is meant to weave the seen and unseen, the measurable and the intuitive, acknowledging that what we perceive as spiritual phenomena may often find resonance with emerging or ancient scientific understandings. This fusion serves as a bridge between worlds, inviting the reader to explore energy through both mystic awareness and grounded inquiry.

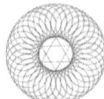

Elementals Across Traditions

Elementals, beings intimately connected with the forces of nature, have been revered in spiritual traditions across the globe for their profound healing wisdom. Representing the essential energies of Earth, Water, Fire, Air, and Ether, elementals serve as guardians of balance and harmony within both the natural world and the human energetic system. Their teachings transcend cultures, appearing in Tibetan Buddhism, Egyptian mysticism, Arcturian and Pleiadian star knowledge, and even in biblical scripture. Each tradition offers unique perspectives on how elementals facilitate healing, transformation, and spiritual evolution.

In Tibetan spiritual traditions, the five elements—Earth, Water, Fire, Air, and Space (Ether)—are central to both physical and spiritual healing. The elementals associated with these forces are considered vital energies that maintain balance within the body and mind. Tibetan medicine teaches that diseases arise from imbalances in these elemental energies. Earth elementals provide grounding and stability, supporting the healing of physical structures like bones and tissues. Water elementals bring emotional healing, helping to release grief and stagnation. Fire elementals stimulate transformation, digestion, and vitality, while Air elementals govern movement, thought, and breath. Ether elementals, connected to space and consciousness, support spiritual clarity and connection.

Tibetan practices such as Tsa Lung and Tummo work with these elemental energies through breathwork and visualization to clear blockages in the subtle body. Practitioners often invoke elemental beings through mantras and offerings, seeking their aid in restoring harmony. The dakini, a divine feminine spirit often associated with the element of space, plays a crucial role in guiding practitioners toward enlightenment by teaching mastery over these elemental forces.

Ancient Egyptian spirituality regarded elementals as divine forces connected to the gods and goddesses who ruled over creation, transformation, and the afterlife. The Egyptians believed that balance among the elements was essential for health and harmony—a concept known as Ma'at. The Earth element, associated with Geb, provided grounding and support for life. Water elementals, linked to the Nile and deities like Osiris and Hapi, symbolized fertility, purification, and emotional renewal. Fire was embodied by the sun god Ra, whose fiery energy represented transformation, power, and spiritual awakening. Air, governed by Shu, brought breath and life force, while Ether (Akasha) connected mortals to the divine realms.

Healing in the Egyptian tradition often involved sacred geometry, sound, and light codes believed to be transmitted by elemental forces. Temples served as portals where initiates worked with these energies to purify the body and soul. The ankh, representing life and balance, was often used to channel elemental forces during healing rituals. Egyptian alchemical teachings also speak of the Ka (life force) and Ba (soul), whose alignment, supported by elemental harmony, ensured spiritual ascension and immortality.

The Arcturians, highly advanced galactic beings from the star system Arcturus, are renowned for their mastery of multidimensional healing. In Arcturian teachings, elementals are not limited to the third dimension but exist across various planes of existence. These beings work with vibrational frequencies, light codes, and sacred geometries to restore balance within the subtle bodies. The Arcturians emphasize that Earth, Water, Fire, Air, and Ether each have higher-dimensional counterparts that, when activated, upgrade the human DNA and enhance spiritual abilities.

Arcturian healing often involves energy chambers and crystalline technologies that harmonize elemental energies within the body. For instance, Arcturian Light Chambers are used to recalibrate the energy field, aligning the chakras and activating dormant DNA strands. Elementals assist in these processes by stabilizing the energetic upgrades, ensuring that the human system can integrate the higher frequencies without distress. The Arcturians also teach that communicating with these elemental beings requires a high vibrational frequency, as they operate from a state of unity consciousness and unconditional love.

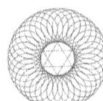

The Pleiadians, beings from the Pleiades star cluster, bring teachings focused on love, unity, and spiritual ascension. According to Pleiadian wisdom, elementals are key allies in the human ascension process. The Pleiadians teach that each element corresponds to a specific frequency band that supports the awakening of higher consciousness. Earth elementals anchor ascension energies; Water elementals assist in emotional purification and DNA activation; Fire elementals catalyze the transmutation of lower vibrations; Air elementals facilitate mental clarity and higher thought; and Ether elementals connect individuals to interdimensional communication.

Pleiadian healing practices often include light language transmissions—coded frequencies designed to awaken dormant spiritual gifts. Elementals amplify these frequencies, helping to integrate them into the human energetic system. Pleiadian teachings also emphasize the role of crystalline grids within the Earth, maintained by elemental beings. These grids transmit high-frequency energies that support planetary and individual ascension. The Pleiadians encourage working with nature, meditating in sacred spaces, and performing ritualistic ceremonies to connect deeply with elemental consciousness.

While the Bible does not explicitly reference "elementals" in the same way as other traditions, the elemental forces of nature play a profound role in spiritual teachings and miracles. In Genesis 1:1-2, the Spirit of God hovers over the waters, symbolizing the creative power of the Water element. The formation of Earth, the separation of waters, and the creation of light all represent elemental energies working in divine harmony. Fire is a powerful symbol throughout the Bible, representing divine presence and transformation, as seen in Exodus 3:2, where God appears to Moses in the burning bush.

Air, or breath, is closely tied to the divine life force. In Genesis 2:7, God breathes life into Adam, demonstrating the sacred connection between breath (Air) and spiritual vitality. Earth represents stability and grounding, as highlighted in Psalm 104:5, where the foundations of the Earth are described as immovable. Ether, though

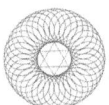

not directly named, corresponds to the heavens and the divine realms mentioned throughout the Bible, symbolizing spiritual connection and higher consciousness.

The teachings of Jesus also reflect elemental healing. In John 9:6-7, Jesus uses mud (Earth and Water) to heal a blind man, demonstrating the use of elemental energies in physical restoration. Additionally, the Pentecost event (Acts 2:1-4) describes the Holy Spirit arriving as a rushing wind (Air) and tongues of fire (Fire), indicating a transformative spiritual initiation supported by elemental forces.

Across these diverse traditions, one truth remains consistent: elementals are conscious forces that support healing, transformation, and ascension. From the grounding stability of Earth to the purifying flow of Water, the transformative power of Fire, the expansive clarity of Air, and the divine connection of Ether, these beings serve as essential allies in the journey toward spiritual wholeness. Whether through Tibetan breathwork, Egyptian temple rituals, Arcturian light chambers, Pleiadian crystalline activations, or biblical miracles, the elementals' teachings remind us of our profound connection to both the Earth and the cosmos.

To work effectively with elementals, practitioners must cultivate a heart-centered state of unity consciousness. Approaches such as meditation in natural environments, intentional breathwork, and energy attunement open the pathways for communication. By honoring the elementals' wisdom and integrating their energies, we can harmonize our physical, emotional, mental, and spiritual bodies—unlocking the full potential of our multidimensional being.

Elemental Symbols
In Rainbow Reiki, the elemental symbols—Earth, Air, Water, Fire, and Aether—stand out as the only symbols that remain unchanged from their original, ancient forms. This continuity exists because these elemental forces represent the universal, foundational energies that permeate all of creation. Unlike other Rainbow Reiki symbols, which have been adapted, expanded, or upgraded to align

with higher-dimensional frequencies and contemporary spiritual needs, the elemental symbols are inherently complete and timeless. They are the core archetypes of existence, reflecting the essential building blocks of both the physical universe and the energetic realms.

Each element symbolizes fundamental aspects of the human experience and spiritual evolution: Earth embodies grounding, stability, and manifestation; Water represents emotional flow, intuition, and purification; Fire signifies transformation, vitality, and willpower; Air governs thought, communication, and freedom; and Aether (or Spirit) connects all elements, representing the divine, infinite consciousness that transcends form. These symbols are universally recognized across cultures and spiritual systems because they vibrate at a frequency that transcends time, space, and dimensional shifts.

While Rainbow Reiki introduces new symbols and energies to work with advanced concepts like multidimensional healing, DNA upgrades, and chakra expansions, the elemental symbols remain unchanged because they already operate at the highest levels of energetic integrity and resonance. Their forms are perfect representations of cosmic laws and do not require modification to align with the evolving frequencies of the Earth or humanity. In fact, these elemental energies serve as the stable foundation upon which higher vibrational healing modalities, like Rainbow Reiki, build. Their consistency ensures a grounded connection to universal truths, allowing practitioners to channel energy safely and effectively, bridging the physical and spiritual worlds without distortion.

Earth
(Gnomes and Stone Spirits)
Qualities: Stability, grounding, strength, abundance.
Role in Healing: Earth elementals help clients feel more rooted, secure, and connected to the physical world. They assist in healing issues related to safety, material security, and self-worth.

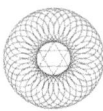

Applications: Clients may work with Earth elementals to anchor themselves, feel a deeper connection to their bodies, or release fears around physical survival and stability. Visualizations might include standing barefoot on the Earth or visualizing gnome or stone spirits grounding and stabilizing their energy.

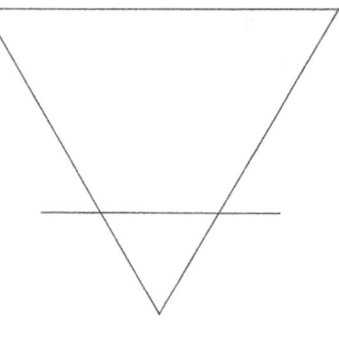

Earth Symbol

Benefits: Earth elementals promote grounding, resilience, and a sense of belonging in the physical realm, empowering clients to create a secure, balanced foundation.

Water

(Undines and Water Spirits)

Qualities: Emotional flow, intuition, cleansing, adaptability.

Role in Healing: Water elementals support emotional healing and release, helping clients navigate feelings and improve emotional fluidity. They are beneficial for clients working on issues related to relationships, self-expression, and unresolved grief.

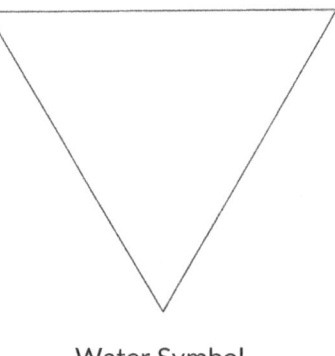

Water Symbol

Applications: Guided visualizations might involve Water elementals like undines or mermaids gently washing away stagnant emotions, allowing feelings to flow freely and unblocking creative energy. Clients can envision themselves submerged in healing waters or standing by a flowing river.

Benefits: Water elementals promote emotional balance, intuition, and adaptability, helping clients to clear emotional blocks and embrace fluidity and self-acceptance.

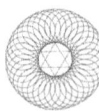

Fire
(Salamanders and Flame Spirits)
Qualities: Transformation, courage, passion, motivation.
Role in Healing: Fire elementals assist with transformation, transmuting negative or stagnant energies, and igniting passion and motivation. They help clients embrace courage, release fear, and awaken personal power.

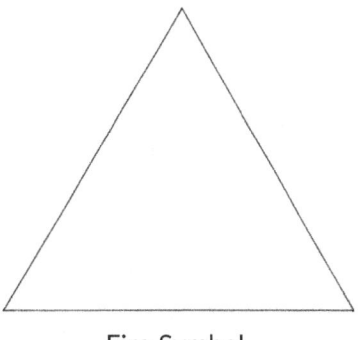
Fire Symbol

Applications: Clients may visualize salamanders or flame spirits surrounding them, burning away limiting beliefs, fears, or anger. The Fire energy can be used to reignite passion for life, purpose, or creativity, making it particularly useful for clients needing inspiration or empowerment.
Benefits: Fire elementals promote inner strength, courage, and transformation, helping clients release what no longer serves them and embrace change and vitality.

Air
(Sylphs and Wind Spirits)
Qualities: Clarity, communication, mental focus, flexibility.
Role in Healing: Air elementals help clear mental fog, enhance mental clarity, and support healthy communication and self-expression. They assist clients in letting go of limiting thoughts and gaining new perspectives.

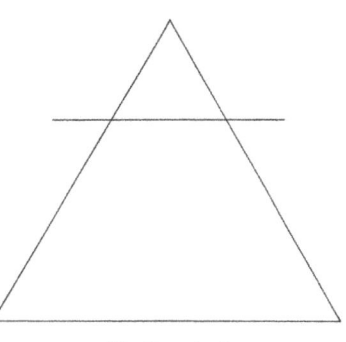
Air Symbol

Applications: The client may be guided to visualize sylphs or wind spirits clearing away mental clutter, allowing for a fresh perspective. They might imagine a gentle breeze flowing through their mind, clearing doubt and bringing mental lightness and focus.
Benefits: Air elementals promote clarity, open-mindedness, and flexibility, helping clients release mental blocks and gain insight,

communication skills, and a refreshed sense of mental freedom.

Aether

(Spirit Elementals)

Qualities: Connection, unity, higher consciousness, spiritual awareness.

Role in Healing: Ether elementals represent the essence of spirit, acting as a bridge to higher realms. They help clients connect to their higher self, access universal consciousness, and experience spiritual awakening.

Applications: Clients may be guided to connect with Ether elementals to explore their soul purpose or to align with universal energies. Visualization might include surrounding themselves in an ethereal mist that brings clarity to their soul's journey or fills them with the essence of oneness.

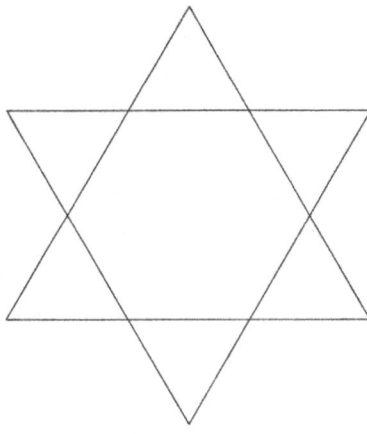

Aether/Ether Symbol

Benefits: Ether elementals promote spiritual alignment, unity, and a sense of connection with all life, helping clients access higher guidance, gain spiritual insights, and feel supported by the universe.

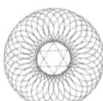

Guided Meditation Deepening Connection with Elemental Energies / Elemental Spirits

Begin by sitting or lying comfortably in a quiet space. Close your eyes. Take a deep breath in through your nose ... and slowly exhale through your mouth.

With each breath, feel yourself relaxing deeper into this present moment. Inhale ... exhale ... Let your mind settle, your body soften, and your heart open.

Visualize roots extending from the base of your spine and the soles of your feet, reaching deep into the Earth's crystalline core. Feel the nourishing energy of Gaia, the Earth Mother, flowing upward through these roots, filling your entire being with stability, strength, and safety.

As you ground yourself, set a clear intention in your heart: *"I am open and ready to connect with the elemental energies and elemental spirits for my highest good, in unity consciousness, and with unconditional love."*

Calling in Sacred Space

Visualize a sphere of shimmering Rainbow Light surrounding you, forming a sacred space for this journey. The light shimmers with all colors of the spectrum—each representing a frequency of healing, protection, and love.

Now, silently or aloud, invite only benevolent elemental spirits vibrating at the 5th dimension or higher, who come from unity consciousness and work for the highest good of all. Ask for their guidance, support, and wisdom as you embark on this sacred connection.

Earth Element and Earth Elementals

_Begin by sensing the deep, grounding energy of the Earth. Visualize yourself walking barefoot in an ancient forest. Feel the rich soil beneath your feet. With each step, you sink deeper into the nurturing embrace of the Earth.

As you walk, you notice a gentle glow among the trees. Earth elementals—gnomes and dryads—emerge, smiling with warmth and familiarity. They are guardians of stability, growth, and physical healing.
Sit with them in a circle. Feel the energy of the Earth rising through your root chakra, anchoring your physical body, healing your bones, tissues, and foundations.

Silently ask: *"What wisdom do you have for me about grounding, abundance, and physical well-being?"*
Allow images, feelings, or messages to arise. Thank the Earth elementals for their support as their energy grounds you deeper into your purpose.

Water Element and Water Elementals
Now, the forest opens to reveal a tranquil lake. The Water element calls you closer. Kneel at the water's edge. Feel the cool mist on your skin. The energy here is fluid, emotional, intuitive.

From the depths of the water, you see undines and merfolk, the elemental spirits of Water, approaching. They carry the energy of emotional healing, purification, and intuition.

As you step into the water, feel its cleansing power washing over you. Old emotions, stagnant energies, and fears are gently released.

Ask the Water elementals: *"What emotions do I need to release? How can I deepen my intuition and flow with life?"*

Listen as they whisper messages of healing and renewal. Feel your sacral chakra glowing with vibrant energy. Thank them for their emotional wisdom before continuing your journey.

Fire Element and Fire Elementals
The path leads you to a clearing where a sacred fire burns brightly. Feel the warmth of the Fire element, a force of transformation, passion, and purification.

Dancing around the flames are salamanders and Fire sprites, elemental beings of Fire. They embody power, will, and the energy of creation.

As you step closer, feel the fire's energy activating your solar plexus chakra, awakening your inner power, confidence, and courage. The fire burns away doubts and fears, transmuting them into radiant potential.

Ask the Fire elementals: *"What do I need to release and transform? How can I ignite my inner passion and purpose?"*

Breathe in the fire's warmth, feeling your personal power expanding. Thank the Fire spirits for their transformational energy as the flames settle into a gentle glow within you.

Air Element and Air Elementals
A gentle breeze begins to blow, guiding you upward to a mountaintop. The Air element surrounds you—light, free, and expansive. Breathe deeply, feeling the clarity of mind and spirit that Air brings.

From the winds, sylphs and Air spirits emerge—graceful beings who govern thoughts, communication, and inspiration.

As they circle around you, feel the energy clearing your mind, activating your throat and heart chakras. Messages of clarity and higher wisdom flow easily to you.

Ask the Air elementals: *"How can I express my truth? What messages from the higher realms do I need to hear?"*

Let their breezy whispers clear mental clutter and open you to divine inspiration. Offer gratitude to the Air spirits as the winds gently calm, leaving you in stillness and clarity.

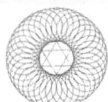

Aether (Spirit) and Etheric Elementals
Now, a shimmering staircase of light appears before you, leading into the cosmos. As you ascend, you enter the realm of Aether—the element of spirit, connection, and infinite potential.

Here, radiant beings of pure light, Etheric elementals, greet you. They are luminous and formless, vibrating at the highest frequencies. They hold the codes of unity consciousness and divine truth.

As you stand in this cosmic space, feel all the elements—Earth, Water, Fire, and Air—unifying within you, balanced and harmonious. Your entire chakra system lights up, from root to crown, aligning perfectly with the highest frequencies of your soul.

The Etheric elementals now infuse you with light codes, activating your DNA, expanding your light quotient, and upgrading your energetic blueprint. Feel these activations integrating with ease and grace.

Ask: "What divine wisdom do you have for me? How can I walk in harmony with all elemental energies?"

Receive any messages or feelings of unity, knowing you are now deeply connected to the elemental realms across all dimensions.

Integration and Closing
Gently begin your return. Visualize the staircase of light descending, bringing you back into your sacred space. Feel the energies of Earth, Water, Fire, Air, and Aether flowing through you, balanced, whole, and integrated.

Thank the elemental spirits for their guidance, wisdom, and healing. Know that these connections will continue to strengthen as you walk your path with intention and awareness.

Bring your awareness back to your breath. Inhale deeply ... and exhale slowly. Wiggle your fingers and toes. When you are ready,

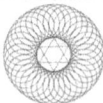

open your eyes—grounded, empowered, and connected to the elemental energies within and around you.

Post-Meditation Integration Tips:
- Journal your experiences, messages, and sensations from each element.
- Spend time in nature (by water, in forests, under the sun, or in the wind) to deepen these connections.
- Work with crystals associated with each element (e.g., hematite for Earth, aquamarine for Water, citrine for Fire, fluorite for Air, and selenite for Aether).
- Practice Rainbow Reiki self-healing while visualizing each elemental energy flowing through the corresponding chakras.

This advanced Rainbow Reiki meditation allows you to co-create with elemental energies and spirits, activating higher aspects of your being while deepening your capacity to channel these transformative forces in your healing work.

Sacred Spiritual Space

Creating a sacred spiritual space is a transformative practice that fosters grounding, focus, and connection to the spiritual realm. Such a space acts as a personal sanctuary, offering a retreat from the chaos of daily life and providing an environment conducive to spiritual practices like meditation, prayer, journaling, or energy work. By setting aside a physical location imbued with intention and tranquility, individuals create a container for healing, introspection, and spiritual growth, where they can immerse themselves in peace and align with their higher purpose.

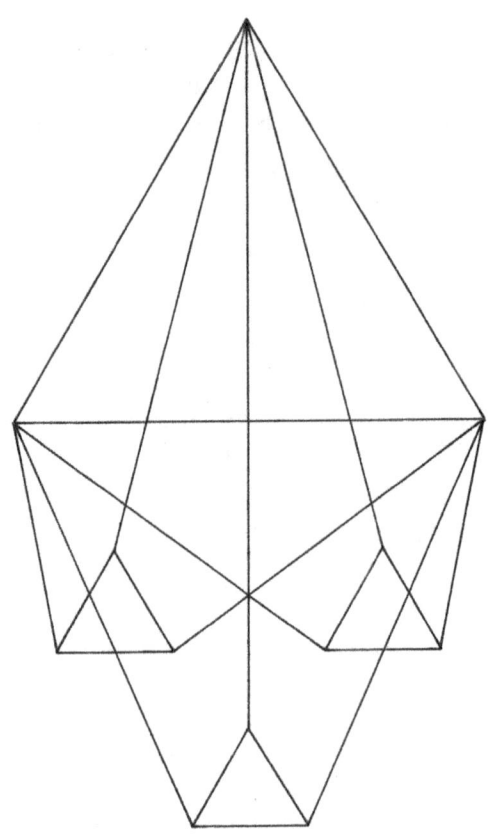

Rainbow Reiki Sacred Space Symbol

A dedicated spiritual space helps signal the mind and body to shift away from distractions and enter a state of presence and mindfulness. The very act of stepping into this space becomes a ritual, reinforcing the intention to connect with one's inner self and the spiritual realm. In this environment, it becomes easier to quiet the mind, focus energy inward, and create meaningful spiritual experiences. Over time, this intentional use imbues the space with a high-vibrational energy, amplifying the potency of practices and creating an atmosphere that supports clarity, inspiration, and healing.

Sacred spaces often incorporate uplifting elements like crystals, candles, incense, or personal mementos that enhance the energy of the environment. These objects not only serve as tools for spiritual work but also act as energetic anchors, accumulating positive vibrations with repeated use. For example, crystals can be used to focus intentions or amplify energy, while candles and incense set a soothing mood and help cleanse the space. These elements create a sense of safety and emotional refuge, allowing individuals to explore their inner world freely and release emotions without fear of judgment.

Grounding is another key benefit of a sacred space. By incorporating natural materials like wood, stones, or earth tones, individuals can create an environment that stabilizes the energy body and fosters balance and security. This connection to the earth helps anchor the individual in the present moment, enhancing feelings of inner peace and calm. Sacred spaces also provide structure for spiritual routines, reinforcing a commitment to self-care, transformation, and growth. The act of returning to the same space for spiritual practices creates consistency, deepens intention, and strengthens the energetic foundation for manifestation and healing.

Over time, repeated use of a sacred space enhances its energetic potency, making it easier to access deeper states of consciousness or connect with spiritual guides and intuition. This space becomes a container for personal energy, amplifying intentions and providing a touchstone for spiritual alignment. It can also act as a symbolic boundary, separating the sacred from the mundane and allowing individuals to disconnect from stress, technology, and daily responsibilities, offering a profound opportunity to reconnect with oneself and the divine.

Creating and maintaining a sacred space can be deeply personal, tailored to reflect individual needs and preferences. Incorporating

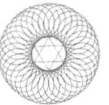

items with personal resonance, such as sacred texts, photos, or journals, adds emotional depth. Natural elements like plants or water features purify and ground the energy, while soft lighting and calming aromas from essential oils or sage encourage relaxation. By consciously curating and tending to this space, individuals establish a sanctuary for spiritual exploration, healing, and alignment. It becomes a sacred home for the soul, nurturing connection, growth, and peace with every visit.

Internal Sacred Space
An internal mental sacred space is a profound and versatile sanctuary created through visualization and meditation, offering a refuge within the mind for calm, clarity, and spiritual connection. Unlike a physical sacred space, this internal sanctuary is always accessible, making it a powerful tool for enhancing emotional, mental, and spiritual well-being. It is a deeply personal and flexible construct, tailored to an individual's needs and preferences, providing a safe and restorative environment that can be entered at any time, in any situation.

One of the most immediate benefits of a mental sacred space is its ability to provide a quick escape from stress or overwhelming emotions. By visualizing a familiar and peaceful setting—such as a beach, forest, or temple—individuals can cultivate a sense of calm and stability within just a few breaths. This practice helps reduce anxiety and tension, offering a mental "reset" even in the midst of chaos. The consistency of this imagined space creates an anchor for the mind, reinforcing feelings of safety and control, especially during moments of emotional distress or mental fatigue.

This sacred mental sanctuary is also a space for emotional processing and healing. Within the safety of this internal refuge, individuals can explore and release difficult emotions, engage in self-compassion, and work through pain or unresolved feelings. The protected nature of the space fosters vulnerability, allowing deeper layers of emotions to surface and facilitating emotional resilience and healing. Regular visits to this space help build a stronger

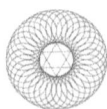

connection to one's emotional self, supporting personal growth and emotional balance.

An internal sacred space enhances mindfulness and focus by providing the mind with a dedicated environment free from external distractions. This clarity allows for introspection, intention-setting, and deeper self-awareness. It becomes a place for reflecting on personal truths, motivations, and beliefs, encouraging self-acceptance and a sense of purpose. For many, this space also acts as a bridge to the subconscious and intuition, offering a quiet setting to connect with inner wisdom, spiritual guides, or higher consciousness. Insights and guidance often arise naturally in this calm, focused environment, deepening one's spiritual journey.

In addition to being a place of introspection, an internal sacred space acts as an energetic boundary, shielding individuals from external influences or draining interactions. It provides a mental retreat where one can recharge, preserve their energy, and reinforce their sense of self-sovereignty. This protective quality makes it invaluable for maintaining emotional and mental safety, particularly in challenging or overwhelming situations.

By regularly visiting this space, individuals cultivate a sense of empowerment and agency over their thoughts and emotions. This sanctuary becomes a reminder of inner strength and resilience, allowing for the reclamation of peace and balance during difficult times. It also serves as a powerful tool for manifestation and intention-setting. By visualizing goals or affirmations within this sacred environment, individuals amplify their focus and enhance the energetic alignment needed to bring their desires to fruition.

For those who may not always have access to a physical sacred space, an internal sanctuary offers a dependable alternative for practices such as meditation, prayer, or spiritual reflection. Its portability makes it an essential resource for integrating spirituality into daily life, whether during work, travel, or moments of solitude. Moreover, this mental refuge serves as a source of rejuvenation and

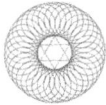

restoration, helping to release mental fatigue, refresh the spirit, and replenish energy during times of stress or burnout.

Creating and accessing an internal sacred space involves envisioning a setting that feels safe, calming, and beautiful—whether real or imagined. Sensory details, such as sounds, scents, and textures, help anchor this space in the mind, while meaningful elements, like symbolic objects or natural features, enhance its sacred quality. With regular use, the space becomes more vivid and accessible, enabling quick entry when needed. Whether the goal is to calm the mind, seek clarity, or connect spiritually, the space adapts to serve the individual's purpose.

An internal mental sacred space is a transformative tool, empowering individuals to cultivate peace, sanctuary, and balance within themselves. By fostering emotional resilience, mental clarity, and spiritual connection, this space becomes an ever-present resource for healing, growth, and inner harmony, accessible whenever and wherever it is needed.

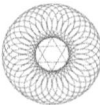

Guided Meditation to Create a Sacred Spiritual Internal Space
Take a few deep breaths. Inhale slowly through your nose, allowing your belly to expand, and exhale gently through your mouth, releasing any tension. Feel yourself settling into the present moment. With each breath, let your body relax, your mind quiet, and your energy ground into a peaceful rhythm.

Now, close your eyes and begin to visualize a door in front of you. This door leads to your sacred internal space, a sanctuary within your mind that is uniquely yours. The door is crafted from materials that feel comforting and safe to you. Perhaps it is made of wood, glass, or shimmering light. Notice its texture, color, and any symbols or decorations on it. When you are ready, open the door and step inside.

As you enter, you find yourself in a setting that feels calm, serene, and deeply personal. This space can be anything you desire—a quiet temple, a lush forest, a sunlit beach, or a cozy room. Let the details emerge naturally. What do you see around you? Notice the colors, the shapes, and the layout of the space. Feel the textures beneath your feet and the temperature of the air. What do you hear? Perhaps the soft rustling of leaves, the gentle sound of waves, or the comforting silence of stillness. Breathe in deeply and notice the scents in this space, perhaps floral, earthy, or crisp and clean.

This is your sacred internal space, a refuge created just for you. Here, you are safe, calm, and supported. As you explore this sanctuary, you may choose to add elements that feel meaningful or sacred. Perhaps there is a soft cushion or chair where you can sit comfortably. Maybe you see crystals, candles, or objects of personal significance. Place them wherever you feel drawn, knowing they amplify the peaceful energy of this space.

Now, take a moment to simply be in this sanctuary. Feel its grounding energy beneath you and its protective atmosphere surrounding you. Let this space become a container for your emotions, thoughts, and energy—a place where you can release anything heavy or no longer serving you. Visualize the energy of the

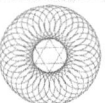

space absorbing and transforming any negativity into light and peace.

In this safe and sacred place, allow yourself to let go of any stress, worry, or tension. If there is something specific you wish to release, visualize it as a color or shape gently leaving your body and dissolving into the light of this space. Feel the relief and openness as you make room for clarity, balance, and joy.

If you wish, set an intention for your sacred space. Perhaps it is a place for calm, reflection, healing, or spiritual connection. Speak or think this intention now, letting it infuse the energy of the space.

Take a moment to connect with the deeper parts of yourself. You may feel a sense of inner wisdom or intuition rising here, or simply a deep sense of peace and presence. Know that this sacred internal space is always available to you, anytime you need refuge, clarity, or grounding.

When you feel ready, gently bring your awareness back to the door. Thank your sacred space for holding you in its energy. You can return here whenever you wish. Step back through the door, closing it gently behind you. As you do, know that the peace and balance of your sacred space remain within you.

Take a few more deep breaths, wiggling your fingers and toes, and bringing your awareness back to the room. When you are ready, open your eyes, carrying the calm and clarity of your sacred internal space into the rest of your day.

Spiritual Energy Cleansing

Spiritual energy cleansing of physical, mental, emotional, and spiritual spaces—both internal and external—is a foundational practice for maintaining balance, clarity, and overall well-being. Energetic environments, like physical ones, accumulate residual energy from emotions, events, and interactions. Over time, this energy can become

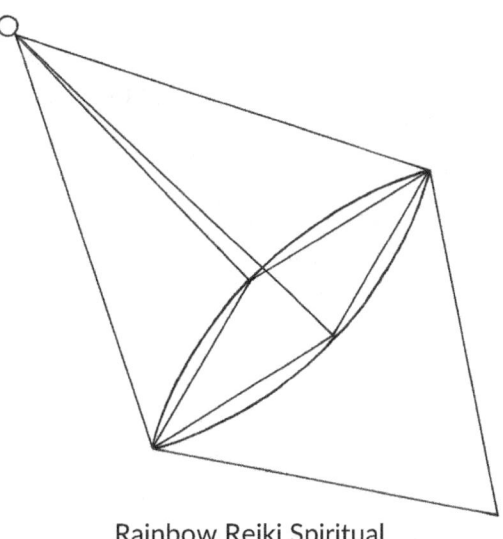

Rainbow Reiki Spiritual Energy Cleansing Symbol

stagnant, heavy, or negative, impacting physical health, emotional stability, mental clarity, and spiritual growth. Regular cleansing practices help release these dense energies, revitalizing the space and fostering a high-vibrational atmosphere conducive to healing, productivity, peace, and personal growth.

External spaces, such as homes, workplaces, or meditation rooms, often absorb the energy of the people and events that take place within them. This energy can linger, creating tension, unease, or even fatigue without a clear cause. Cleansing physical spaces with techniques like smudging, sound healing, or sunlight clears this residual energy, restoring harmony and creating a welcoming environment. Cleansed spaces support positivity and flow, enabling occupants to feel grounded, relaxed, and at ease. They are particularly beneficial in environments that require focus, such as workspaces or study areas, as they clear chaotic or distracting energies, enhancing mental clarity and concentration.

For those engaging in spiritual practices, an energetically aligned space amplifies intentions and facilitates deeper connections with higher energies or spiritual guides. Whether through meditation, prayer, or ritual work, a cleansed physical space acts as a foundation

for aligning with divine energy and setting meaningful intentions. It becomes a portal for spiritual connection, fostering profound experiences and amplifying the energy of practices such as manifesting, affirmations, or energy healing.

Equally important is the cleansing of internal spaces—the mind, body, and spirit. Just as external spaces can accumulate stagnant energy, so can the human energy field. Emotions such as anger, sadness, or frustration can linger in one's energy body, affecting mood and behavior. Internal cleansing practices, like meditation, visualization of light, or breathwork help release these trapped emotions, making space for joy, peace, and balance. Similarly, negative thought patterns or mental clutter can create stress and mental fog. Practices like mindfulness, journaling, or energy healing clear this mental noise, fostering focus, positivity, and a sense of mental freedom.

A cleansed internal energy field strengthens one's connection to their higher self, intuition, and spiritual guidance. Energetic blockages that hinder spiritual growth are released, enabling alignment with one's spiritual path and facilitating access to inner wisdom. Additionally, internal cleansing supports the establishment of healthy energetic boundaries, protecting individuals from external negativity and emotional drain. This enhances resilience, emotional sovereignty, and the ability to maintain one's sense of self in interactions and relationships.

Cleansing both internal and external spaces also enhances interpersonal dynamics. When people feel balanced and at ease, they naturally interact with greater harmony and understanding. In shared spaces, the absence of tension or lingering negativity creates a welcoming and uplifting environment that supports mutual support and growth. This harmony extends to the manifestation of intentions, as a cleansed space, free of blockages, amplifies the resonance of desires and goals, increasing their likelihood of realization.

Methods for cleansing spaces are as diverse as they are effective. External spaces can be cleared with smudging (using sage or palo santo), sound cleansing (bells or singing bowls), salt-water sprays, crystals like selenite or clear quartz, or exposure to sunlight and fresh air. Internal cleansing techniques include meditation, visualization of cleansing light, breathwork, journaling, energy healing, and self-reflection practices. These approaches, when practiced consistently, work together to create a holistic state of harmony.

By integrating internal and external cleansing practices, individuals foster a balanced, high-vibrational state where inner peace and alignment naturally arise. This synergy between one's internal energy field and external surroundings promotes clarity, resilience, and spiritual alignment, empowering individuals to feel connected to their highest selves and their environments. Spiritual energy cleansing is not just a practice but a way of cultivating a fulfilling life, one rooted in harmony, intention, and connection.

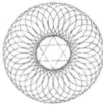

Self-Care

Self-care is a cornerstone for energy healing practitioners, who regularly engage with the deep mental, emotional, and energetic states of their clients. The nature of this work requires practitioners to hold space for others' experiences, which can lead to an exchange or absorption of stress, emotions, and even physical sensations. Without intentional self-care practices, this engagement can contribute to burnout, emotional fatigue, or diminished effectiveness. Prioritizing self-care across the mind, body, and spirit allows practitioners to maintain balance, resilience, and alignment, ensuring they can serve their clients authentically and sustainably.

Practitioners often encounter intense emotions, trauma, or stress during sessions, making mental self-care essential. Without regular care for their own thoughts and emotions, the mind can become overwhelmed, leading to decreased clarity and effectiveness. Practices such as mindfulness, journaling, or therapy provide a healthy outlet for processing thoughts and emotions, reinforcing mental boundaries between themselves and their clients. These practices also enhance focus and decision-making, allowing practitioners to remain fully present during sessions. Clearing mental clutter through meditation, intention-setting, or breathwork further helps practitioners attune to clients' needs while maintaining their mental well-being.

The physical demands of energy sessions, such as maintaining presence and posture for extended periods, require practitioners to prioritize physical self-care. Regular exercise, hydration, and a balanced diet ensure stamina and reduce fatigue, while grounding practices like yoga or walking in nature keep practitioners rooted and balanced. Because client sessions can impact the practitioner's nervous system, particularly in emotionally intense cases, physical relaxation techniques and adequate rest are critical for reducing

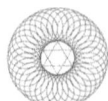

stress and supporting physical resilience. Caring for the body strengthens the practitioner's ability to anchor energy work, providing a solid foundation for their healing practices.

Engaging deeply with clients' emotions can lead to emotional fatigue or even compassion fatigue, making emotional and energetic self-care vital. Practitioners may absorb clients' emotions unintentionally, which can result in emotional imbalance or heaviness. Energy-clearing practices such as smudging, working with crystals, or visualizing light all help release residual emotional energy. Journaling, breathwork, and self-compassion exercises provide an outlet for emotional processing, allowing practitioners to "detox" from client interactions and recharge. These practices support emotional resilience, helping practitioners maintain a clear and balanced emotional state while continuing to hold space for others.

Spiritual self-care deepens a practitioner's connection to their intuition, inner wisdom, and higher self, enhancing their ability to guide and heal clients effectively. Regular spiritual practices, such as meditation, prayer, or rituals, nurture this connection and help practitioners remain aligned with their purpose. Protective practices, like shielding visualizations or spiritual cleansing rituals, guard against absorbing clients' heavy or negative energy, ensuring the practitioner's energy field remains strong and clear. This energetic integrity allows practitioners to embody authenticity and integrity, qualities that are essential for building trust and fostering healing relationships with clients.

The benefits of consistent self-care extend beyond personal well-being. Practitioners who prioritize self-care can stay fully present during sessions, offering clients empathy, insight, and undivided attention. Self-care also supports personal growth, helping practitioners evolve alongside their clients and build resilience against the challenges of their work. Over the long term, self-care ensures the sustainability of their career, allowing them to continue their practices with passion and longevity. By strengthening their energy field and maintaining balance, practitioners bring their

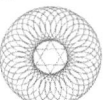

highest selves to every session, free from personal or residual client blockages.

Self-care practices span mental, physical, emotional, and spiritual realms. Mental care includes mindfulness, setting boundaries, visualization techniques, and therapy. Physical care encompasses regular exercise, grounding practices, hydration, balanced nutrition, and rest. Emotional and energetic self-care involves energy-clearing techniques, journaling, breathwork, and grounding exercises, while spiritual care includes meditation, cleansing rituals, intention-setting, and connecting with nature. Together, these practices empower energy healing practitioners to maintain balance, clarity, and alignment, enabling them to serve clients effectively while nurturing their own well-being and growth.

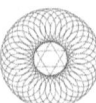

Spiritual Support Teams

In advanced Rainbow Reiki practice, both practitioners and clients are supported by expansive spiritual support teams composed of high-frequency beings vibrating at a fifth-dimensional density or higher. This ensures that all energies align with unity consciousness, the highest good of all, and emanate from a heart-centered space. Maintaining this vibrational standard is essential to prevent the influence of trickster spirits or lower-vibrational entities that could disrupt the healing process. By working exclusively with beings vibrating at 5D and above, practitioners create a safe and sacred environment where deep transformation, alignment, and healing can unfold.

Rainbow Reiki Spiritual Support Team Symbol

A crucial yet often overlooked component of the client's spiritual support team is the client's own multidimensional self. This includes the conscious mind, which processes current experiences and decisions; the subconscious mind, where beliefs, emotions, and patterns reside that influence daily life; and the unconscious mind, which holds ancestral memory, collective consciousness, and deep-seated karmic patterns. The inner child is another vital aspect, representing innocence, vulnerability, and the emotional imprints of early experiences. Healing the inner child is often key to resolving emotional wounds and fostering self-compassion. The higher self serves as the client's divine blueprint, an all-knowing aspect that offers wisdom, guidance, and alignment with soul purpose. Beyond the higher self lies the master aspects, representing the fully realized, ascended versions of the client that embody divine mastery, enlightenment, and cosmic awareness. Together, these internal components form a dynamic spiritual team that, when integrated, fosters wholeness and self-realization.

Importantly, during advanced Rainbow Reiki sessions, the practitioner's higher self and master aspects often serve as bridges, connecting and collaborating with the client's higher self and master aspects. This multidimensional connection facilitates a co-creative process where the necessary energies for healing are invoked in perfect alignment with the client's soul plan. When these higher-dimensional aspects converge, they create a sacred energetic bridge that allows high-vibrational frequencies, light codes, and healing energies to flow seamlessly. This synergy ensures that healing unfolds not only on the physical and emotional levels but also across the subtle bodies, aura layers, and timelines.

The practitioner's role in this process is to hold space with purity of intention, ensuring that the energy exchange occurs from a heart-centered, unified consciousness state. The practitioner's spiritual mastery allows them to discern, channel, and anchor these frequencies safely, while their higher self collaborates with the client's spiritual support team to activate the client's inherent healing capabilities. This often results in profound breakthroughs,

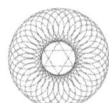

where the client experiences deep energetic shifts, soul integrations, and heightened states of awareness.

The extended spiritual support team further includes angels and archangels, who provide divine protection, healing, and guidance, such as Archangel Michael for clearing and protection or Archangel Raphael for deep healing. Ascended Masters, including beings like Quan Yin, Buddha, and Jesus, bring the wisdom of enlightenment and compassion, supporting the client's spiritual growth and healing journey. Ancestors offer generational wisdom and assist in healing familial patterns, while animal spirits provide intuitive guidance and strength reflective of their symbolic meanings. Elementals—fairies, gnomes, sylphs—help ground the healing process and maintain balance through their deep connection with nature. Illuminaries, beings of pure light, assist in raising consciousness and aligning clients with their divine purpose. Galactic beings vibrating at 5D or higher, such as Pleiadians, Arcturians, and Lyrans, offer multidimensional wisdom and high-frequency energies that support spiritual evolution and ascension.

Identifying and interacting with these spiritual allies requires attunement to subtle energy signatures. Angels often present with warmth, peace, and specific color frequencies. Ascended Masters are recognized through their unique energetic imprints of peace and expanded consciousness. Ancestral guidance can emerge in dreams or through familiar energetic sensations. Animal spirits may appear symbolically in meditation or daily life, offering messages aligned with their traits. Elementals are often perceived through nature's subtle movements, while illuminaries reveal themselves as radiant light beings during deep meditation. Galactic beings may connect through vivid visualizations, star codes, or telepathic communication.

To work effectively with these beings and aspects of self, practitioners and clients should create a sacred space through grounding, protection rituals, and intentional invocation. Establishing a heart-centered connection and setting clear intentions aligned with the highest good ensures authentic and safe

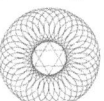

interactions. Practices such as meditation, guided visualization, and energy attunement foster deeper connections with these spiritual allies. Asking for clear signs, trusting intuitive knowing, and maintaining high personal vibrational frequency are essential for sustaining these relationships.

By recognizing the client's multidimensional self as an integral part of the spiritual support team and understanding the role of the practitioner's higher self and master aspects as bridges, practitioners facilitate a deeply collaborative healing process. This co-creative dynamic allows both client and practitioner to experience elevated states of consciousness, heart-opening transformations, and alignment with their highest soul potential.

Guided Meditation: Connecting with Your Aspects of Self and Spiritual Support Team

Begin in a comfortable position, either seated or lying down. Close your eyes and take a deep breath in through your nose ... and slowly exhale through your mouth.

Allow your breath to slow and deepen. Inhale ... and exhale ... With each breath, feel your body relax. Feel the weight of your physical form grounding into the earth beneath you. Visualize roots growing from the base of your spine and the soles of your feet, reaching deep into Earth's crystalline core.

With every breath, feel the nurturing energy of Gaia flowing up these roots, filling your body with warmth, love, and stability. You are safe. You are grounded. You are present in this sacred moment.

<u>Connecting with the Aspects of Self</u>
Now, turn your awareness inward. Visualize a radiant golden light glowing at your heart center. This is the gateway to your inner universe.

First, invite your conscious mind to step forward. This is the part of you that thinks, plans, and navigates your daily reality. Thank it for its role in your life.

Next, invite your subconscious mind, the keeper of your beliefs, emotions, and memories. Allow any sensations, images, or emotions to arise without judgment. Acknowledge its influence and express gratitude.

Now, invite the unconscious mind, holding deep ancestral memories and karmic patterns. Feel its vastness. Ask it to step into harmony, releasing any outdated patterns.

Bring forth your Inner Child, the pure, playful, and tender part of you. Visualize them stepping into the golden light at your heart center. Offer love, safety, and reassurance. Feel their joy and innocence returning to you.

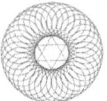

Finally, call upon your Higher Self, a radiant, ascended version of you, wise and connected to divine truth. Feel their loving presence enveloping you. Invite your Master Aspects, your fully realized, ascended soul expressions. They step forward, embodying your soul's mastery and divine purpose.

Allow all these aspects of self to merge in harmony at your heart center. Feel the unity, the wholeness. You are complete.

Connecting with the Spiritual Support Team
Now that your inner self is aligned, we invite the members of your Spiritual Support Team to step forward, one group at a time. Each will establish a line of energetic connection with you, strengthening your bond and activating deeper levels of healing and communication.

Angels and Archangels
Call in the angels, beings of unconditional love. Feel the soft, warm energy as they surround you. Archangel Michael stands to your right, offering protection and strength. Archangel Raphael stands to your left, bringing healing and restoration. Archangel Metatron stands behind you, activating your divine potential.

A silver cord of light extends from your heart center to each of them, forming a crystalline connection. Feel the frequencies of love, protection, and healing flowing into your being.

Ascended Masters
Now, invite the Ascended Masters, beings who have walked the earth and attained enlightenment. Perhaps Quan Yin, Jesus, or Buddha steps forward. Feel their compassionate wisdom. A golden thread of divine consciousness links your heart to theirs. They whisper insights into your soul, reminding you of your own mastery.

Ancestors
Invite your wise and loving ancestors who walk in light. They step forward, offering their blessings and generational wisdom. Feel the

healing of ancestral patterns as a deep red light connects your root chakra to theirs. The wisdom of your lineage flows through you, strengthening your foundation.

Animal Spirits
Now, see animal spirits stepping into your circle. What animals appear? Each carries medicine and messages for you. A white energy cord links your solar plexus to theirs, infusing you with courage, power, and instinctual knowing.

Elementals
Invite the Elementals—fairies, gnomes, and sylphs—guardians of nature's balance. Feel their playful energy. A green cord of connection flows from your heart into the earth and back up, reminding you of your unity with all living things.

Illuminaries
The Illuminaries, radiant beings of pure light, now surround you. Their presence elevates your consciousness. A brilliant white light connects your crown chakra to theirs, activating divine wisdom and alignment with your soul's highest path.

Galactic Beings
Lastly, call upon Galactic Beings of the 5th dimension and higher—Pleiadians, Arcturians, and Lyrans. Feel cosmic frequencies entering your field as a silver-blue cord links you to the stars. Their light codes of ascension, healing, and evolution now integrate into your being.

<u>DNA, Chakra, and Light Quotient Activation</u>
With all connections established, your spiritual support team now works in unison. Feel waves of high-frequency light cascading down from the cosmos, flowing through your crown, activating your 18 chakras, each one spinning with radiant vitality.

The light moves into your DNA, upgrading it to hold more light. Visualize the strands of your DNA illuminated, unlocking your highest potential and cosmic memory. Your ability to carry and transmit higher frequencies—your light quotient—expands.

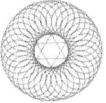

Breathe in this divine light. With each breath, you become brighter, more aligned, and deeply connected to your soul's truth.

Enhancing Communication and Closing
Now, set the intention to communicate with your spiritual support team easily and effectively. Ask them to continue guiding you through dreams, synchronicities, and intuitive nudges. Trust that this connection is now permanent.

Offer gratitude to each member of your team—angels, masters, ancestors, animals, elementals, illuminaries, and galactic allies. Feel them stepping back, yet know that you can call upon them anytime.

Begin returning your awareness to your body. Feel your breath, your heartbeat. Wiggle your fingers and toes. When you are ready, open your eyes—renewed, connected, and empowered.

Best Practices, Ethics, and Professional Guidelines for Advanced Rainbow Reiki Practitioners

Working as an advanced Rainbow Reiki practitioner involves a deep commitment to integrity, responsibility, and professionalism. The role requires not only mastery of energy healing techniques but also a clear understanding of ethical standards, legal boundaries, and client safety protocols. Given the powerful nature of Rainbow Reiki, which incorporates multidimensional energies, chakra alignment, DNA activation, and higher-frequency transmissions, practitioners must approach each session with care, discernment, and respect for the client's well-being.

The foundation of effective Rainbow Reiki practice is built on professional ethics and clear practitioner-client boundaries. Practitioners must always operate from a place of unconditional love, unity consciousness, and the highest good of all. This includes obtaining informed consent before sessions, where clients fully understand what the session entails, the techniques used, and any potential energetic effects. Practitioners must be transparent about their role as facilitators of energy flow, not as healers who claim to cure or diagnose medical or psychological conditions.

Confidentiality is another key ethical standard. Information shared by clients during sessions must be kept strictly confidential unless disclosure is required by law. Additionally, practitioners must maintain professional boundaries, avoiding any personal entanglements or inappropriate relationships with clients that could compromise the integrity of the healing space.

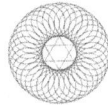

A Rainbow Reiki practitioner must understand the legal scope of their practice, which varies by region. Practitioners should refrain from making any claims of medical efficacy or suggesting that Rainbow Reiki can replace conventional medical treatments. They must clearly state that Rainbow Reiki is a complementary practice designed to support spiritual, emotional, and energetic well-being. Practitioners should avoid diagnosing medical conditions or recommending changes to prescribed medical treatments, as this may constitute practicing medicine without a license.

It is also essential to maintain liability insurance where available and ensure that promotional materials, including websites and brochures, do not make misleading claims. All marketing should comply with advertising standards and emphasize that Rainbow Reiki is part of a holistic approach to well-being.

The intake process is one of the most critical aspects of working with clients. A thorough intake allows practitioners to assess the client's needs, set realistic expectations, and determine whether Rainbow Reiki is appropriate. Practitioners should ask about:
- Medical history, including physical health conditions.
- Mental health history, especially concerning anxiety, depression, or trauma.
- Energy sensitivity and past experiences with energy work.
- Medication use, particularly those affecting the nervous system.
- Pregnancy or other conditions requiring specific care.

Proper intake allows the practitioner to tailor the session safely. It also serves as an opportunity to educate clients on what Rainbow Reiki entails and to ensure they understand that this work complements, but does not replace, medical or psychological care.

Practitioners must understand that Rainbow Reiki is not suitable for every individual. Specifically, it is not recommended for clients with a history of:
- Seizures or Epilepsy: The high-frequency energy shifts, chakra activations, and multidimensional energies channeled

in advanced Rainbow Reiki sessions can potentially trigger neurological responses in individuals prone to seizures. Because Reiki can sometimes induce deep trance-like states or rapid shifts in energy, these changes may overwhelm the neurological system, posing serious risks.
- Psychosis or Severe Mental Health Disorders: Clients with a history of psychosis, schizophrenia, or similar disorders may experience challenges distinguishing between reality and altered states of consciousness. Since Rainbow Reiki can induce deep meditative states and multidimensional experiences, there is a risk of exacerbating symptoms, leading to potential psychological distress.

For these reasons, practitioners should always err on the side of caution and either decline such cases or refer them to licensed healthcare providers. Working with such clients without proper medical oversight could be both dangerous and legally problematic.

An advanced Rainbow Reiki practitioner must recognize when a client's needs exceed the scope of energy healing. Situations that require referrals include:
- Mental health crises, such as suicidal ideation or severe anxiety, where licensed psychological support is essential.
- Medical emergencies or conditions requiring immediate medical attention.
- Complex trauma that may require trauma-informed psychotherapy alongside energy work.

In such cases, the practitioner should compassionately explain why a referral is necessary, providing trusted resources if possible. Collaboration, not substitution, should be the guiding principle, encouraging clients to integrate energy work with conventional care for holistic healing.

The role of a Rainbow Reiki practitioner is that of a facilitator, guide, and energy channel, not a medical provider, therapist, or savior. Practitioners help clients access self-healing by clearing energetic blockages, aligning chakras, and raising vibrational frequencies.

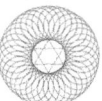

However, the healing itself is always self-directed, coming from the client's own inner wisdom and higher self.

Practitioners must be cautious not to adopt a "rescuer" mentality or make claims of being able to "fix" clients. Such attitudes not only create unhealthy dependencies but also violate the principle that true healing is an empowered, co-creative process. Similarly, practitioners should never provide medical advice, prescribe treatments, or encourage clients to discontinue prescribed therapies.

A crucial part of ethical Rainbow Reiki practice is clearly communicating that Reiki is a complementary therapy. It is designed to work alongside, not replace, conventional medical or psychological treatments. Practitioners should regularly remind clients:

"Rainbow Reiki supports your overall well-being by addressing energetic imbalances and promoting relaxation and clarity. However, it does not replace medical diagnosis or treatment. Always consult with your healthcare provider regarding any medical or psychological conditions."

This disclaimer not only protects the practitioner legally but also ensures that clients approach their healing journeys responsibly and holistically.

Dos and Don'ts for Rainbow Reiki Practitioners
Do:
- Obtain informed consent before sessions.
- Maintain professional boundaries and confidentiality.
- Perform comprehensive intake assessments.
- Refer clients out when issues exceed your scope.
- Continue personal development, including self-healing and ethical education.
- Clearly state the complementary nature of Reiki.

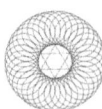

Don't:
- Claim to cure or diagnose any medical or psychological condition.
- Work with clients who have contraindicated conditions like epilepsy, seizures, or psychosis without medical oversight.
- Overpromise results or use manipulative marketing language.
- Allow personal biases or beliefs to interfere with client care.
- Engage in dual relationships that compromise professional integrity.

Practicing advanced Rainbow Reiki is a sacred responsibility, requiring practitioners to balance spiritual insight with ethical rigor and professional discipline. The power of Rainbow Reiki lies in its ability to connect clients to their higher selves, unlock deep healing, and facilitate transformative experiences.

However, this power must always be wielded with discernment, humility, and respect for each individual's unique journey.

By adhering to best practices, respecting legal limitations, and maintaining clear ethical standards, Rainbow Reiki practitioners can offer safe, effective, and empowering healing experiences, honoring both the ancient wisdom of Reiki and the evolving needs of humanity's spiritual awakening.

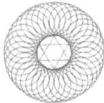

The Return to Rainbow Light

As we arrive at the final chapter of this sacred journey, we are not concluding but circling back, spiraling upward into deeper remembrance of who we are, why we came, and what we are here to embody. Rainbow Reiki is not simply a modality; it is a multidimensional return to coherence, to truth, and to the radiant wholeness that has always existed within you. Each technique, symbol, initiation, and teaching throughout this book has served as a key to unlock ancient codes buried in your cells, soul memory, and etheric blueprint. Now, standing at this threshold, you are not just a student—you are a steward of light.

In the ancient days when the Rainbow Temples stood upon Earth, before the fall of consciousness and fragmentation of the sacred sciences, we lived in harmony with the frequencies of creation. These teachings are not new. They are restored, resurrected from the aether, echoing through the Akashic fields, calling forth those with ears to hear and hearts ready to rise. You, dear reader, are among them. The return of Rainbow Reiki is part of the collective reawakening—part of the great realignment of humanity, Earth, and the cosmos. You are not alone. You have never been alone. The dragons, angels, ancestors, galactic allies, and ascended healers walk beside you. They work through you. They are you.

This path requires devotion not only to healing others, but to living in a continual state of attunement with Source. To walk as a Rainbow Reiki practitioner means to walk in integrity, in reverence, and in fierce love. It means you honor the energies of each being you serve, including yourself, as divine and sovereign. You carry within you the medicine of many worlds and the responsibility to offer it wisely. Whether you choose to practice formally or simply radiate your frequency in daily life, your presence changes the field. Your voice carries codes. Your touch is alchemical. Your

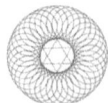

consciousness is an instrument of planetary healing.

Let this final chapter be your initiation into the eternal now—the living rainbow current that flows from the heart of creation. May your hands be guided, your heart be clear, and your spirit be rooted in the truth that you are the bridge between dimensions. You are the prism through which the divine expresses. And as you continue your journey beyond these pages, may you remember that this work is not something you do—it is who you are.

If you feel the sacred call to go deeper into the mysteries of Rainbow Reiki and fully embody its teachings, you are warmly invited to continue your journey through formal training. Visit www.SynergyWellnessCollective.com to explore upcoming opportunities to study Rainbow Reiki Levels 1 through 4. Whether you choose to begin with the foundational practices or commit to the full pathway through Grand Master Trainer Level, each stage of training is designed to activate new dimensions of your healing gifts, expand your consciousness, and deepen your service to humanity. You may enroll in a single level or complete the full practitioner path. Each step is a sacred unfolding. On the website, you will also find our Provider Directory, a growing network of holistic and alternative wellness professionals, many of whom are certified in Rainbow Reiki, offering diverse healing modalities, intuitive sessions, and soul-aligned services to support your journey. As you connect with this community of heart-centered healers, may you feel seen, supported, and inspired as we rise together in luminous service.

Welcome home, Rainbow One.

About the Author

Chelsey Sarah Prusha, B.Msc., is a highly skilled and intuitive healer with an extensive background in both Westernized Health Care and holistic modalities. As an RTT Therapist, Clinical Hypnotherapist, Multidimensional Hypnotherapist, Certified Master Trainer, Certified Natural Medicine Herbalist & Spiceologist, Life Coach, Rainbow Reiki Grand Master, Intuitive Energy Healer, Soundwave Therapist, and Way of Council Facilitator, Chelsey has dedicated her life to the pursuit of true healing and spiritual enlightenment. She specializes in supporting individuals navigating neurodivergence, sexual trauma, and religious trauma, bringing a wealth of personal and professional experience to her practice.

Chelsey's journey into healing was profoundly shaped by her own life challenges. In her early years, she endured sexual trauma, abandonment, and the struggles of undiagnosed neurodivergent mental and physical conditions. Her adolescence was marked by addiction, misdiagnoses, and the pain of multiple inpatient treatments, alongside the grief of losing loved ones and the trauma of medical and educational system failures. Mismanagement of her neurodivergent metabolism led to severe adverse reactions to psychiatric medications, resulting in a near-death experience from serotonin syndrome and multiple suicide attempts.

In early adulthood, Chelsey faced domestic abuse, miscarriage, and the loss of her mother, which catalyzed a deep spiritual awakening. Through intensive healing, she uncovered past-life memories, addressed soul wounds, and reactivated dormant spiritual gifts. The acceptance of her sexuality and the release of religious trauma further empowered her to embrace her authentic self. As an AuDHD

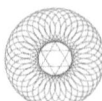

mother of three neurodivergent children, she has a personal understanding of the complexities of neurodivergence and approaches her work with compassion and insight.

Chelsey's professional path began with 12 years in Westernized Health Care, where she worked as a Certified Nurse's Aide, Certified Medication Aide, Patient Care Technician, and Certified Clinical Hemodialysis Technician. She completed three years of nursing school before becoming disillusioned by the symptom-focused approach prevalent in modern healthcare. Recognizing the limitations of conventional medicine, she embarked on a transformative journey to explore holistic and integrative healing practices. Her studies spanned trauma-informed therapies, somatic approaches, mindfulness, hypnotherapy, metaphysical spiritual practices, shamanism, sound healing, light and color therapies, herbalism, and esoteric teachings, including deep explorations of ancient Egyptian wisdom and Tibetan Buddhism.

Investing heavily in her own healing and education, Chelsey synthesized her vast knowledge and experience to create her private practice, initially focusing on hypnotherapy and Rapid Transformational Therapy, and later expanding into cognitive life coaching, spiritual teachings, and energy healing. Realizing that no existing modality fully addressed the multidimensional nature of human healing, specifically holistic healing for those with high energetic sensitivity and neurodivergence, she founded Trinity Wellness Therapy—a holistic approach that integrates Rainbow Reiki, Multidimensional Hypnotherapy, and many other modalities to facilitate profound healing on all levels of being.

Chelsey views her work not merely as a career but as a divine spiritual mission, knowing that her teachings and modalities are channeled expressions of higher wisdom. Her hope is that through these practices, others will discover that the power to heal lies within themselves, enabling them to transform their lives, heal ancestral wounds, and contribute to the collective healing of humanity.

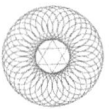

About the Artist

Camille Marie Rauscher is an artist whose work is profoundly shaped by her personal struggles and transformative journey. For 15 years, she battled severe drug and alcohol addiction, using substances as a means of escaping the pain of self-acceptance, unresolved trauma, and the fear of embracing her true self. Her life, outwardly perceived as an adventurous and carefree journey of travel and exploration, was in reality, a relentless pursuit of distraction—a way to avoid confronting her authentic identity, her sexuality, and the profound spiritual gifts that lay dormant within her.

Camille's journey of self-discovery was enriched by her early work at the local recreation center, where she spent winters at the ice arena and summers at the swimming pool. Her natural ability to connect with the pure innocence of children and animals created a safe and accepting space for those around her, despite her own struggles and high masking of her true self. Following this, Camille worked at several adolescent inpatient treatment centers, where her empathetic nature and unconditional loving energy provided a sense of healing and safety for troubled youth. Her ability to create a safe container for others to be themselves became a hallmark of her interactions.

Seeking freedom and escape, Camille left home to live in the Virgin Islands, a decision that led to a seven-year journey working aboard various cruise ships. Her personable nature and all-encompassing acceptance of humanity allowed her to bridge cultural divides effortlessly, communicating energetically without the need for shared language. This ability not only endeared her to passengers and crew but also deepened her understanding of the universal nature of human suffering and the need for compassion. Through these experiences, Camille cultivated a profound ability to hold space for others, fostering a deep understanding of the children she encountered from inpatient treatment centers, the culturally diverse passengers aboard ships, and helped to bring healing to their hearts through her mere presence and unconditional love.

Camille's path to sobriety was neither straightforward nor easy. The process of overcoming addiction further deepened her empathy and understanding of humanity's struggles and suffering. Once clean and sober, her long-dormant spiritual gifts reactivated with remarkable clarity. By attuning herself to the energy of her partner and listening to the channeled wisdom that flowed through her, Camille was able to holographically and telepathically download the advanced symbols of Rainbow Reiki and Multidimensional Hypnotherapy. This profound spiritual awakening not only transformed her life but also became the foundation of her artistic expression.

Camille's artwork is not merely art—it is a living expression of consciousness, wisdom, and intelligence. Her creations are infused with advanced sacred geometry and mathematical codes that resonate deeply within the soul of those who behold them. Each piece is hypnotic, immersive, and enticing, drawing the viewer into a realm where art is alive with movement and divine intelligence. The intricate patterns and symbols act as portals, inviting the observer into a meditative state where healing and activation occur naturally.

Her art serves as a conduit for higher energies and teachings, with the power to activate dormant energies and awaken the soul simply through the act of gazing upon it. The advanced sacred geometries and light codes embedded within her work transcend mere aesthetics—they are a language of the soul, recognized intuitively by those who encounter them. In this way, Camille's creations are not just visually captivating; they are experiences of wisdom, a bridge to higher states of consciousness, and a powerful reminder that true healing comes from embracing one's authentic self.

www.ingramcontent.com/pod-product-compliance
Lightning Source LLC
Chambersburg PA
CBHW060415300426
44111CB00018B/2857